Death, Dismemberment, and Memory

Diálogos
A series of course-adoption books on Latin America:

Series advisory editor: Lyman L. Johnson,
University of North Carolina-Charlotte

Body
Politics

Death, Dismemberment, and Memory

in Latin
America

**Edited by
Lyman L. Johnson**

University of New Mexico Press
Albuquerque

©2004 by the University of New Mexico Press
All rights reserved. Published 2004
Printed in the United States of America

10 09 08 07 06 05 04   1 2 3 4 5 6 7

Library of Congress Cataloging-in-Publication Data

Death, dismemberment, and memory : body politics in Latin America /
Lyman L. Johnson, editor.— 1st ed.
      p. cm.— (Diálogos)
Includes bibliographical references and index.
ISBN 0-8263-3200-5 (cloth : alk. paper)—
ISBN 0-8263-3201-3 (pbk. : alk. paper)
   1. Latin America—Politics and government. 2. Political culture—Latin
America. 3. Body, Human—Symbolic aspects—Latin America. 4. Body,
Human—Political aspects—Latin America. 5. Symbolism in politics—
Latin America. 6. Memory—Political aspects—Latin America.
7. Heroes—Latin America. 8. Nationalism—Latin America.
I. Johnson, Lyman L. II. Title. III. Diálogos (Albuquerque, N.M.)

F1410.D33 2004
320.98—dc22

                                            2004017308

Design and composition: Maya Allen-Gallegos
Typeset in Janson 10.5/13
Display type set in Humanist 521 BT

For Sue

Contents

Illustrations

Preface

Lyman L. Johnson

Books about history have their own histories. From the beginning my interest in this topic and my desire to produce this book developed unpredictably. As readers and writers of history we know the typical cases best. Historians commonly embrace their topics in response to the controversies of the moment or in response to the discovery of new evidence that might alter long-held assumptions about historical processes or events. In some cases historians realize that new methods or new perspectives introduced in other disciplines or newly applied to their own fields hold the potential for illuminating the past in novel ways. In this case, my path to this book began casually. A series of small, unanticipated steps drew me toward a new field of history and a new way of examining the politics of Latin America.

Over a cup of coffee with a colleague, Joanne Maguire Robinson, in the Religious Studies Department, I was introduced to the literature on the early cult of Christian saints. Her intelligent and funny summary of the literature revealed a world where bodies and body parts were suffused with complex meanings. These grisly artifacts were devices for the instruction of the faithful and evidence of exemplary lives eagerly surrendered to martyrdom. Once "discovered," often in very unlikely places, bones and other artifacts were distributed by a burgeoning market in relics, or, sometimes, by theft or even military action. The literature on this topic portrays the religious passions and euphoria that accompanied these miraculous discoveries of bones and other sacred relics and the disputes and conflicts that decided their placement in appropriate locations. Once introduced to the literature I pushed ahead.

The human remains of saints were understood by early Christian communities to be potential intermediaries that could facilitate access to God for the devout. As pointed out by Peter Brown, saints were believed to be present both in Heaven and at their tombs. The inscription on the tomb of St. Martin at Tours makes this continued action in the world clear: "[H]e is fully here, present and made plain in miracles of every kind."[1] The usefulness of the bodies of saints as intermediaries and as sources of miracles was enhanced, if not created, by a literary genre, the *passio*, that detailed the lives, especially the sufferings, of the saints. These vehicles were a common feature at the great festivals of the saints where they were read to the illiterate masses gathered for the event. These stories made real the suffering and example of martyrs, operating as instructional tools in the propagation of appropriate values and actions for believers. I was struck by the calculated selection and telling of these tales and the oftentimes unpredictable ways in which these remembered lives were accessed and then embraced or rejected by the humble folk who heard them through the *passio* or through less formal retellings.

As I began to read the books suggested by my colleague, I found it difficult to appreciate either the representational vocabulary of martyrdom and redemption or the uses of relics in the promotion of pilgrimages and religious festivals. Like other modern tourists I had seen the bones of saints displayed in the reliquaries of the great cathedrals and convents of Europe. But as a secular citizen of the modern world, I typically saw these relics as alternately odd or humorous. I had rolled my eyes and moved on, never making the effort to understand how women and men could be moved by these pathetic remains, or how these bones provoked action in the world and guided human experience.

My daughter, Eliza Ablovatski, a historian of Central Europe, had been a student at Columbia University when Katherine Verdery gave the 1997 W. Averell Harriman Lecture titled "Postsocialist Necrophilia, Or the Political Lives of Dead Bodies." Expanded and published in 1999, Verdery's discussion of the exhumations and reburials of scores of bodies in Eastern Europe following the fall of the Soviet Union made clear the usefulness of this topic to any effort to understand nationalism and nation building. Verdery's book made clear that these special bodies (really the constellation of human remains, places, and events associated with the remembered life) often manifested an enduring power to mobilize passions and symbolize collective ideals. I was convinced that these themes needed to be studied as a part of Latin American political history, but I had no plans to pursue the topic.

On vacation in Santa Fe, New Mexico, six months later, I entered this project almost by accident. While sitting in the plaza, I finished the book I had brought along and needed to find something to read. I walked down San Francisco Street to Allá, one of my favorite bookstores, and worked my way back and forth through the shelves of Spanish-language books. I picked up *Los Hallazgos de Ichcateopan* by Alejandra Moreno Toscano. This was one title among the hundreds devoted to Mexican history at Allá. I cannot remember why I picked it up. The book appeared unexceptional; there was nothing to suggest the unlikely events chronicled by the author. After reading a few pages I was hooked. As a historian of Argentina I knew nothing of the events described in the book, the purported discovery in 1949 of the bones of the last Aztec emperor, Cuauhtémoc.

This discovery had set off a firestorm of controversy in Mexico. Academic commissions dismissed the discovery as an intellectual fraud at worst, or alternatively, as a naive scheme set in motion by local boosters. Mexican intellectuals of all stripes, left and right, weighed in. Newspapers, magazines, and books argued the fine points of archaeological method and historical sources. More important, however, nearly everyone seemed ready to dismiss opposing views as ideologically tainted. Why all this passion? Why were the bones of this tragic figure executed more than four hundred years earlier so obviously of political significance to Mexicans in 1949?

Nearly every Latin American historian explores the symbolic forms through which Latin American heroes are remembered in a survey lecture or two. I remember well the comedic details of "Santa Anna's Leg" related by a professor in my first course in Latin American history, but our exploration of the topic in that class never got past the megalomania of the Mexican caudillo. Was it possible to treat this topic with the seriousness that had allowed scholars to illuminate the cult of Christian saints? I set out to answer these questions but realized that neither the controversy nor the political passions were uniquely Mexican.

Latin America has a confused, and often confusing, political iconography. The labels of hero and villain have seldom proved enduring. Modern Latin American cityscapes reflect this. The statues of once mortal enemies often sit near each other, sharing the indignities imposed by pigeons and graffiti artists. To a North American the number of monuments dedicated to history's losers in Latin America is often surprising. The cities and towns of the United

States, and Canada as well, have more predictable inventories of remembered heroes. With the very important exception of the American South where Robert E. Lee or Stonewall Jackson are likely to be prominently remembered in public spaces, Washington, Lincoln, F.D.R., and now Kennedy and Martin Luther King serve as nearly universal representations of what is urged on citizens as a single, uncontested, history of the United States. From this invented perspective, the United States is a nation constructed unambiguously by history's winners.

Latin American nations remember their pasts in more complex ways. In Buenos Aires, for example, the statue of Manuel Dorrego, a Federalist who briefly served as governor of the Province of Buenos Aires, sits only three blocks from Calle Lavalle, the street named after General Juan Lavalle, the Unitarian who ordered Dorrego's execution. Ultimately what these heroes had in common was a violent death at the hands of enemies, not contributions to a shared national political tradition. In the tumultuous political history of Latin America, collective memory is plastic and political judgments are revocable. The past has been worked over in the backwash of nearly every revolution or period of substantial reform as new leaders searched for usable symbols to service their own ambitions or undermine those of their enemies.

Can we identify shared biographical characteristics that predict which men and women from the past will be selected to serve the need of future generations for heroes? What are the essential elements discovered in these politically useful biographies? I am struck by the region's strong inclination to focus on political martyrs, men and women who, like Cuauhtémoc, suffered defeat, even torture and execution. Nearly everywhere in Latin America the bones, bodies, and monuments associated with the past's martyrs are enduring props of political culture utilized to mobilize factions, parties, or, sometimes, mobs. This predilection suggests that the literature on the early cult of Christian saints might provide a vocabulary and interpretive framework for exploring these enthusiasms. Why is it common both in traditional Christian iconography and in Latin American political discourse that the defeated, the tortured, the assassinated, and the executed have exercised such an enduring hold on popular imagination? These questions led to this book.

Because I was committed to another project when I began to explore the discovery of Cuauhtémoc's bones, I looked for collaborators to help me develop these issues historically across the sweep of Latin American history. It was my good fortune to find a wonderful group of historians who quickly agreed to cooperate in this project. I am grateful for this opportunity to work with them. The results of our explorations into this sometimes macabre topic are collected in this volume. Together these essays explore many of the most interesting and unusual cases of Latin American political martyrs and the ways these lives and deaths have been used as symbols of political identity and as vehicles of cultural discourse. The collection is not comprehensive. This is, we believe, a beginning.

So there you have it, a conversation over coffee, a suggestion from my daughter, and a trip to a bookstore led me to this book. It has been my experience that intellectual give and take, even its most playful manifestations, can take us in unanticipated directions. My own research on Cuauhtémoc's remains as well as my efforts to understand the regional significance of the topic were deeply influenced by the work of the other authors who contributed to this collection. I have learned a great deal from them. It is my hope that this work of scholarship will illuminate Latin American political culture in new ways and encourage additional research. I believe that with these essays we have at least begun to produce a nomenclature and a method to make sense of the political uses of bodies and body parts, the melancholy evocation of martyrdom as nation building.

Putting this project together was a great pleasure. I want to thank my collaborators for their contributions and suggestions. I also want to thank Joanne Maguire Robinson for the reading list, Eliza Ablovatski for her ideas and encouragement, and Jim Dunlap and Barbara Sommer for the serendipity of their wonderful bookstore. My wife, Sue, has read and corrected all my contributions to this collection. For this and much more, thanks.

Notes

1. Peter Brown, *The Cult of the Saints: Its Rise and Function in Latin Christianity* (Chicago: University of Chicago Press, 1981), 3–4.

[T]he location of Cuauhtémoc's tomb is not known. The mystery of his burial place is our obsession. To discover it would mean nothing less than to return to our origins, to reunite ourselves with our ancestry, to break out of our solitude. It would be resurrection.

—Octavio Paz, *The Labyrinth of Solitude*

Chapter One

Why Dead Bodies Talk: An Introduction

Lyman L. Johnson

Since ancient times, human societies have devised ways to identify and publicly remember their heroes. These forms of remembrance are everywhere around us in the names of cities, parks, and streets, in public statuary, in political speeches and patriotic holidays, and in the printed images on currency and stamps.[1] In Latin America, as in Europe and the United States, the names and images of dead heroes have been long-used as texts to instruct living citizens in the behaviors and values (bravery, sacrifice, and honor among others) that are useful to the nation. These forms of remembrance have proliferated in the modern era with the appearance of new media. The nineteenth century's use of place names, statues, and paintings to achieve these patriotic ends have been supplemented in the twentieth century by films, television shows, and, more recently, Web sites.

Because of the importance of these images and the political messages they transmit, governments exercise great care to conserve and protect the reputations of heroes regarded as essential to the development and defense of the nation. As a result, school curricula, textbooks, speeches delivered on patriotic holidays, and other forms of public memory are routinely scrutinized by bureaucrats and politicians to defend the official versions of these remembered lives from criticism or dismissal. Despite these efforts, official versions of heroic biographies are often contested by professional historians or by mainstream opposition groups and even by revolutionaries. It is also common to find alternative, often subversive, versions of these famous lives recounted in folk songs or oral traditions that are passed from generation to generation among common people. In these cases, men and women portrayed as bandits or rebels by official sources are remembered as defenders of the poor and oppressed. In other cases, regions, classes, or ethnic groups dispute figures from the past. More recently, commercialized forms of political memory, like T-shirts and tote bags emblazoned with names and images of heroes, have proliferated on an industrial scale as well.[2]

In Buenos Aires today, for example, T-shirts decorated with the face of Ernesto "Che" Guevara, one of the twentieth century's most implacable foes of capitalism, are sold in almost all the city's most exclusive shopping areas. What do affluent young women and men intend when they purchase one of these shirts? What does Che mean to them? It seems unlikely that these are potential revolutionaries committed to the overthrow of capitalism. Are they reinventing the Marxist rebel of the 1960s as a symbol of generational conflict? Or, is their Che merely a celebrity, like Madonna or Bono? Certainly this commercialized Che is different from both the living man and the official cult that has immortalized him in Cuba where he was Fidel Castro's chief lieutenant during the Cuban Revolution. As this case makes clear, heroic figures can have different meanings at different times and in different settings. Images printed on T-shirts by profit-seeking merchants speak a different language and address a different constituency than statues erected at government expense. In turn these forms of remembrance are distinct from popular forms of remembering heroes such as roadside shrines, folk songs, and oral traditions. All these forms of symbolic political speech are too important to ignore if we are interested in the ways that nations understand the past and prepare for the future.

This book is a contribution to an important, but often neglected, corner of this large topic, the political meanings associated with the bodies, or body parts, of martyred heroes in Latin America. The processes through which these bodies are selected as political vessels, the forms in which they are venerated and memorialized, and the ways in which these bodies are invested with meaning are all worthy of our attention. Since colonial times both governments and their political enemies in Latin America have struggled to control or direct the powerful symbolism associated with the bodies of the revered dead. Early examples discussed in this book include Cuauhtémoc, the Aztec ruler executed by Spanish conquistador Hernán Cortés in 1524, and Túpac Amaru, a rebel Inca ruler executed by a Spanish viceroy in Peru in 1572. In both cases the bodies were denied to followers by authorities but were reclaimed symbolically by later generations who found enduring meaning in the sufferings of these martyrs.

In two recent cases "lost" bodies were recovered and reburied so as to reconnect martyrs and their adherents. The body of Evita Perón, wife of the president of Argentina and popular voice of the nation's masses in the 1940s and 50s, for example, was kidnapped by the military after the overthrow of her husband in 1955 and buried under a false name in Italy. The body of Che Guevara, Castro's chief lieutenant in the Cuban Revolution, was first displayed in triumph by the Bolivian military that had executed him and then buried anonymously to hinder veneration by those who shared his convictions. In these cases the political forces that had opposed Evita and Che in life recognized the political potency of their dead bodies and made every effort to deny these powerful symbols to their enemies. In the end, both bodies were recovered and reburied in what partisans believed were appropriate ways, Evita in Buenos Aires and Che in Cuba.

This form of body politics has intensified in twentieth-century Latin America with the development of modern mass media. Movies and television, even radio broadcasts and theatrical presentations, allow the living to put words into the mouths of the long dead, appropriating the past to serve the needs of the present. The easy verisimilitude of the mass media can often produce powerful reactions, but public response is difficult to anticipate and the intentions of those who produced or sponsored these presentations are often thwarted. In the 1990s there were three versions of the life of Evita Perón competing for public attention, the Andrew Lloyd Webber musical, the Hollywood movie featuring Madonna, and an Argentine musical *Eva*. None of these three very different political reconstitutions of Evita's life proved capable of denting the enduring mythology embraced by the Argentine working class. It is clear that these new ways of portraying the lives of martyred heroes multiply the usefulness of body politics, although sometimes reducing the actual importance of the bodies themselves. Governments and political parties, as well as protest groups of various kinds, can now project their preferred images of martyred heroes over greater distances and to broader audiences.[3] But these innovations have not completely eclipsed earlier forms of remembrance in Latin America.

The name and image of Emiliano Zapata, the Mexican revolutionary assassinated in 1919, has long been a venerated symbol in Mexico. In his native region, he is remembered in stories and folk songs. The towns and villages of this region compete for control of his legacy, each erecting monuments or creating museums in the hope of deriving political or commercial benefits. The national government also claims Zapata as a progenitor, periodically evoking his legacy and image. More recently, the Zapatistas, a largely indigenous protest movement in Chiapas, Mexico, has claimed to be the appropriate heir to the revolutionary legacy of Emiliano Zapata. The movement rejects the NAFTA treaty implemented in 1994 and protests the economic policies of the national government. Among the group's most potent political tools is the worldwide web where Zapata's image is highlighted.[4]

The human remains of these heroes, and the locations associated with their sacrifices and martyrdoms, retain powerful emotional content that can be used to mobilize mass action on behalf of a nation, an ethnic group, or a class. Although the passions evoked by these forms of veneration and remembrance have been remarked upon by both Latin Americans and outsiders for decades, few commentators have examined this topic seriously. Many have seen this concern with the dead bodies of heroes and other political figures as the dark underbelly of politics, the place where the crass ambitions of populist politicians and the ill-informed enthusiasms of the masses intersected.[5] The leg of Antonio López de Santa Anna is the most commonly discussed example in this repertory. Jürgen Buchenau explores this case in detail in his essay on Alvaro Obregón in this collection. Santa Anna lost his leg to a canon ball in 1838 as he defended Mexico from French attack. In a macabre twist Santa Anna lost this leg a second time when his prosthesis was captured by the United States army in 1847 at the battle of Cerro Gordo. The artificial leg is now displayed by the Illinois National Guard at Camp Lincoln (see Illustration 1.1).[6] In 1838 the loss of Santa Anna's leg had elevated the reputation of this controversial figure because the sacrifice was associated with the successful defense of national honor. In 1847 the loss of his prosthesis in a disastrous war was portrayed as farce by the

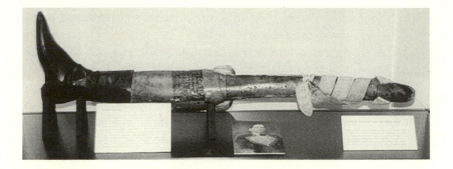

1.1 *The artificial leg of General Antonio López de Santa Anna captured by the U.S. Army at Battle of Cerro Gordo (Photo: printed with permission of Illinois State Military Museum, Department of Military Affairs, Springfield, Illinois).*

American army and by Mexican rivals, deflating this image. As this case suggests, the careers of bodies and body parts can experience unpredictable trajectories, like the careers of living politicians.

The authors of the essays collected in this book believe that these highly political dead bodies, their symbolic uses, and the conflicts that have surged around them have the potential to illuminate Latin American political culture in very useful ways. However, the Latin American experience should be examined and evaluated within a global context. Examples of the symbolic connections that tie political institutions or political movements to the remains of dead heroes can be traced across the globe and through political and religious history to ancient times.[7] In the Western tradition we can identify innumerable examples where the physical remains of famous or powerful men and women have been used as vehicles for mobilizing populations or as tools for identifying and achieving collective ends. As noted in the Preface, the exemplary deaths of saints were used with great success to inculcate Christian virtues and to demonstrate to the faithful the power of God acting in the world.[8] In secular history the heroic deaths of kings or of modern political and military leaders have been used in varied settings to illustrate and transmit the ideal of sacrifice on behalf of a nation, a government, or a party as well as to mobilize resistance to foreign threats or domestic insurgencies. The dead bodies and burial places of both saints and patriotic martyrs have proved useful, linking remembered acts of sacrifice and treasured virtues to specific places and times and attaching illustrative human narratives to abstract beliefs and ideals.[9]

Believers or, in modern times, patriotic citizens as well as participants in political movements have often accessed the values, virtues, and experiences of saints or secular heroes by drawing near their human remains or by viewing representations, such as statues or paintings, that evoke acts of heroism or sacrifice. The tombs of martyred heroes or, sometimes, locations associated with the most celebrated acts of these heroes frequently serve as preferred venues of patriotic remembrance and commitment. What is it that sanctifies these places? Surely, it is the idea that these lives were given willingly on behalf of a set of beliefs, a people, or a nation. The self-conscious sacrifice of the hero, the quality of the death, bonds the hero to future generations. The identification and remembrance of martyrs is, therefore, a form of intergenerational communication or communion and pilgrimage to locations sanctified by these exemplary deaths is a nearly universal form of remembrance that can have either a secular or a sacred character.

Like the pilgrimages of Christians to the Holy Land a thousand years ago, visits to Gettysburg or the Normandy beaches, or to Ground Zero in New York City, facilitate connections with the venerated dead. The small sacrifice of the pilgrim who disrupts her or his daily life to travel to a sacred place, a place associated with a hero's martyrdom, imitates the larger and more consequential sacrifice of the dead hero or heroes. We need to recall that these forms of memory are seldom spontaneous or original. Instead, they derive from scripts (the biographies and iconographies of the celebrated dead) plagiarized or adapted from earlier generations or other places. In modern times, the heavy hand of governments and political parties are evident everywhere these connections are made. In Argentina the names of those who lost their lives fighting the British in the Malvinas Islands in 1982 are memorialized by the government near the location in Buenos Aires that celebrates the defeat of a British invasion in 1807. The intent is to transform a recent defeat into a chapter in an ongoing struggle.

The commonness of these forms of political reverence across historical time and geographic space provides the appropriate context as we begin to explore the political uses of dead bodies in Latin American history. It is perhaps fitting that the remains of Christopher Columbus, the man whose 1492 voyage initiated Latin America's complex political trajectory, have been disputed by the Dominican Republic and Spain for decades. Columbus is now a highly contentious figure in Western Hemisphere history, a man more likely to be dismissed as the cruel exploiter of indigenous peoples than celebrated as the founder of new societies or as an explorer. Yet his bones remain useful symbolically and commercially. Seville, Spain, and Santo Domingo, Dominican Republic, have both welcomed generations of tourists to competing "genuine" burial locations. Recently Spanish scientists took DNA samples from the Columbus crypt in the Cathedral of Seville as well as from the undisputed remains of other Columbus family members buried in Spain to determine authenticity, hoping that a scientific match would validate or invalidate their nation's claims. Yet, given the passions of this contest, it seems unlikely that this or any other technology can settle a conflict sustained in two nations by a combination of national pride and tourist-industry bottom line.

While this dispute has continued for most of the twentieth century, the politics have changed. In recent decades Spain has been transformed by democracy and by membership in the European Union. As the nation has prospered, neither Columbus's connection to the Spanish people nor Spain's history as a colonial power seems as important as in the past. Columbus's legacy, summarized as conquest and empire by his detractors and as the heroic opening of a New World by his supporters, is no longer a flash point for political mobilization or protest in Spain. Although the five hundredth anniversary of Columbus's first voyage in 1992 provoked protests in the Dominican Republic and elsewhere in the Americas, there is still a powerful local political constituency that defends the Dominican Republic's claim to his remains. For these modern Dominicans the burial of Columbus in Santo Domingo ratifies the nation's claim to be the point of origin for Latin American history and culture, the place where indigenous and European worlds first intersected. But Columbus is not portrayed as the first Dominican, the progenitor of the nation. Unlike the cases to be discussed later, Columbus cannot be narrowly tied to the history of a single people or single nation; he was an Italian who served the kings of first Portugal and then Spain and then made his fame in the Americas; the roots that connect him to either Spain or the Dominican Republic are not deep. In the modern era it is the nation-state with its anxieties about identity and citizenship that typically serves as the arena where political meanings are assigned to the martyred dead. Columbus is, therefore, too large a presence to be forgotten but too marginal to any one national history to be as potent or as meaningful as the cases examined in this volume.

While Latin American uses of these highly charged political connections between the living and the dead have evolved within the broad boundaries of Western tradition and experience, we can also identify a set of distinctive regional characteristics that are rooted in Latin America's history and culture.[10] The region's "body politics" rely on a symbolic language uniquely informed by the enduring importance of Catholic Christianity, by the region's experience of conquest and colonization, and by the complexity of cultural practices derived from the mixture of indigenous, African, and European origins. Underdevelopment and the persistence of economic and social injustice are also central to the region's history. As a result, dead bodies in Latin America are as likely to speak the language of social protest or to urge resistance to foreign exploiters as to celebrate national greatness.

The individual cases explored in these essays are all connected, sometimes in unpredictable ways, to this matrix of Latin American cultural practices and historical experiences. From Túpac Amaru I, the indigenous rebel executed by Spanish colonial authorities in 1572, to Che Guevara, a twentieth-century revolutionary executed without trial by an agent of the Bolivian government in 1967, Latin Americans have often discovered political meanings and expressed political aspirations through the historical filter of heroic lives and deaths. The essays collected in this volume offer an introduction to this topic rather than a comprehensive analysis. Although many interesting and important examples of the phenomenon have been left out for reasons of focus and length, these essays, taken collectively, provide, we believe, an illuminating and representative discussion of body politics across the region.

In the history of Latin America very few men and even fewer women have exhibited in life the qualities that attract enduring veneration and reverence in death.[11] It is obvious that the bodies of the majority of those who created new nations, gained great political power or wealth, or won battles against foreign or domestic enemies are not invested with political meaning by succeeding generations. The men and women whom Latin Americans remember in these secular body cults were important and visible members of their societies during their lives, but they were not necessarily the most important or the most visible. Very few of Latin America's powerful, rich, or heroic are remembered or continue to stir political passions or influence events long after their deaths. Mere fame, mere success, cannot be translated into immortality in a predictable way. Public places across Latin America are filled with the statues of the now forgotten. Why do the bodies of so many of the powerful lie mute while a small number continue to speak?

Our task would be easier if a single template could be placed across the region's history to predict or explain this remarkable subset of humankind. While the bodies of most heroes decay in peace and obscurity, the bodies of others are fought over, kidnapped, cut to pieces, hidden, discovered, or, in a small number of cases, celebrated. Although some broad similarities can be identified in this tiny subset of history's great and famous, the lives and deaths of the men and women in this subpopulation of the dead are too different, one from the other, to be forced into a narrowly conceived pattern. Some were born to wealthy and powerful families; others grew up in obscurity. Cuauhtémoc, now a national icon embraced by Mexico's governing elite, was a member of the Aztec aristocracy, and Túpac Amaru II, now nearly universally embraced by the Left in Latin America, claimed a similar descent from the Inca royal line. The lives and deaths of indigenous leaders, it seems, can be successfully invoked to enhance the institutionalized power of established governments and to mobilize armed resistance to the existing order. We find representatives of both the humble and the advantaged remembered among the twentieth-century's revolutionary martyrs. Two of the most important Mexican revolutionaries, Alvaro Obregón and Emiliano Zapata, grew up in obscurity and received little formal education. The Cuban Revolution's Ernesto "Che" Guevara, by contrast, grew up in relative comfort and was trained as a medical doctor. Neither class privilege nor poverty and deprivation appear to either promote or restrict access to these forms of immortality.

Although the circumstances of the hero's death are often remembered and represented in iconographic ways, as was true in the cult of Christian saints, the deaths of these men and women were as different as their origins. Juan Manuel de Rosas, the son of a wealthy Argentine landowner, died peacefully in exile. Getúlio Vargas, a wealthy landowner known in Brazil as the father of the poor, took his own life, and Evita Perón, an actress who became the charismatic leader of Argentina's poor, died of cancer.

If the trajectories of these political bodies are so different, how should we proceed in identifying some general characteristics that will illuminate this potent intersection of human remains and political memory in Latin America? The scholarly literature devoted to mythic heroes offers a place to begin our analysis.[12] Contributors to this literature noticed general patterns in the lives of mythic heroes; the circumstances of their births, the heroic deeds and tests that distinguished their lives, as well as their forms of death were often remarkably similar in character and sequence. These patterns held true across cultural boundaries and across time periods from ancient India to imperial Rome. The heroic lives and political bodies examined in this volume, although distinguished by origins, actions, and forms of death, suggest that some broad similarities can be discovered, although exceptions abound. Establishing patterns, no matter how imperfect, offers the best opportunity to understand why and how these political dead bodies speak to the living.

It appears that great success in life may limit the usefulness of a martyred hero to succeeding generations. The remains of two of the most important figures of Latin America's nineteenth century, Benito Juárez of Mexico and Domingo Sarmiento of Argentina, do not play prominent roles in the political lives of their respective societies today. Both men are remembered in place names, statues, and on the stamps and currency of their respective nations. Their biographies remain familiar to school children, but there are no body cults. Could it be that failures and trials, not great successes, predict the likelihood that a political body will prove useful to future generations? Many of those whose lives and deaths are examined in this collection of essays could be characterized as failures in life; they were defeated politically or militarily, died at the hands of their enemies, or suffered imprisonment and exile. Yet we know that most of Latin America's "failures" are ignored as well. Neither great success nor tragic failure alone can explain how an individual life comes to be seen as embodying the aspirations of an ethnicity, an ideological movement, or a nation.

In some cases, historical figures endure because their characters have proved useful to both their political friends and enemies. Facundo Quiroga is one such figure. In the 1820s and 1830s Argentina was torn by civil wars and regional conflicts. With no strong central government, power was disputed among charismatic leaders of informal military forces made up of gauchos and rural outlaws. Known by his first name, Facundo was among the most notorious and feared men of his era. Despite his fame, or infamy, Facundo is remembered today because of a very critical book written by his enemy, Domingo Sarmiento, an opposition intellectual who was later elected president of Argentina. Forced to flee Argentina to escape Facundo's wrath, Sarmiento summarized this bloody period by emphasizing the arbitrary cruelty and brutality of Facundo. Yet, it is clear that Sarmiento was also fascinated by the physical courage and raw masculine force of Facundo's personality. In his book he invoked the dead Facundo, "I now conjure you up, so that, by shaking the blood-stained dust that covers your ashes, you will arise to explain to us the secret life and internal convulsions that claw at the entrails of a noble people!"[13] While portraying Facundo as murderous, Sarmiento found his spontaneity, intuition, and natural brutishness essential to his own purposes. Argentina's progress, he asserted, must be rooted in self-discipline, education, and the imitation of European culture, the self-conscious rejection of Facundo's legacy.

The rural poor of Facundo's native region remember him in songs and stories as a hero, not as the cruel brute characterized by Sarmiento. However, these popular characterizations of Facundo commonly invoke the same events, actions, and values excoriated by Sarmiento and other Argentine partisans of democracy and progress. This popular Facundo is cruel, crafty, and headstrong, ignoring, for example, repeated warnings of a planned assassination as he traveled without escort until ambushed and killed. Folklore versions of his death emphasize Facundo's fatalism and courage when confronting death, asking his killers only for a chance to confess.[14] Facundo's fierce masculinity is celebrated in the often repeated story that he was buried standing up in the Recoleta cemetery in Buenos Aires (see Illustration 1.2), refusing to bend his knee to his enemies in death as in life.[15] In the case of Facundo (as with Túpac Amaru II, Zapata, Evita, and Che, among those discussed in this collection) a single set of remembered attributes and anecdotes continue to be harvested and broadcast by both modern political heirs and their rivals. It is the attachment of these historical figures to enduring and unresolved conflicts over identity, social justice, and cultural constructions that give their bodies such potency as vehicles of political discourse.

Nevertheless, there are few guarantees that those initially venerated in death will endure as political symbols. The history of Latin American churns with invasions, rebellions, revolutions, and mass movements of various kinds. With each surge and retreat of these

I.2   *The tomb of Facundo Quiroga in the Recoleta cemetery in Buenos Aires, Argentina (Photo: Daryle Williams).*

forces powerful men and women rise and fall in public estimation. As a result, individual reputation and political memory often have a temporary character in Latin America. It would be difficult to imagine events that might lead the United States to dislodge George Washington, Abraham Lincoln, or even Franklin Delano Roosevelt from its pantheon of national heroes. Yet, as Jeffrey Shumway points out, Juan Manuel de Rosas, a contemporary and ally of Facundo, has been recently resurrected by the nation's then-president Carlos Menem as a symbol of reconciliation, despite being viewed by most educated Argentines for more than one hundred years as the symbol of antidemocratic excess and brutal political repression. Túpac Amaru II, who was viewed as a symbol of destructive violence and ethnic hatred by many of his contemporaries and by most propertied

Peruvians after independence, now has broad appeal in a nation disheartened by decades of corruption, economic failures, and military excesses. These cases and others suggest that the powerful political tides that have swept Latin America since independence have created an environment where death sometimes stalls, rather than ends, the trajectory of a political life. Facing altered circumstances, Latin American nations have often reexamined their inventories of historical figures, discarding current idols and embracing those previously despised. Body cults persist only where they remain useful. The most enduring have a plastic quality that allows them to be bent to new uses.

In Mexico it is Cuauhtémoc, the last *tlatoani* (ruler) of the Aztecs, defeated militarily, captured, tortured, and cruelly executed, who is today celebrated as one of the most important symbols of the nation. Hernán Cortés, the conqueror of the Aztec Empire and certainly one of the great men of his era, is now forgotten or, alternatively, despised by Mexicans. In Peru Spanish authorities executed two men named Túpac Amaru in the colonial period. The first was the last ruler of a much-reduced Inca state that survived the initial wave of conquest. He was captured and beheaded in 1572 in Cuzco, the ancient capital of the Inca Empire. The second and more famous Túpac Amaru, commonly referred to as Túpac Amaru II, led a mass rebellion two centuries later. After his capture he was cruelly executed in Cuzco like his predecessor. Defeated and humiliated in life, today both men are remembered as symbols of resistance in Peru and more generally everywhere in the Western Hemisphere where indigenous peoples continue to suffer injustice. The remains of Francisco Pizarro, the Spanish conqueror of the Inca Empire, are no more than a macabre tourist attraction in Lima displayed in a glass casket in the cathedral. In Mexico the achievement of independence is remembered in an impressive monument in Mexico City (see Illustration 1.3) where the remains of Padre Miguel Hidalgo and Padre José María Morelos are interred.[16] Both men failed to defeat Spain and both were executed by firing squad. Agustín de Iturbide, the man who actually achieved Mexico's independence from Spain, by contrast, has been held at arm's length since the 1820s by patriotic Mexicans.

The variability of these postmortem careers is worth our attention. If Juan Manuel de Rosas, Argentina's most brutal politician of the nineteenth century, can be reinvented as a symbol of patriotic resistance to foreign oppression, then similar reputational transformations are likely to be found elsewhere in Latin America. Two Mexican

1.3   *Monument of Independence in Mexico City, where the remains of the patriots Miguel Hidalgo, José María Morelos, and other participants in the struggle with Spain are displayed (Photo: Susan Johnson).*

revolutionaries who were assassinated by their enemies, Emiliano Zapata and Alvaro Obregón, illustrate the pattern. Zapata, the agrarian revolutionary assassinated in 1919, has been sanctified, even commercialized, as symbol of a political incorruptibility in Mexico, sweeping aside his more influential contemporaries. Obregón survived the revolution to be twice elected president of Mexico. Today he is remembered more narrowly for his machismo and political and military successes, while the defeated Zapata has become a symbol of self-sacrifice for the Mexican people. Finally, Getúlio Vargas of Brazil and Juan and Evita Perón of Argentina were controversial and divisive political actors, seen as heroic defenders of the masses as well as corrupt and self-interested villains during their lives. Each of them left behind deeply fractured political movements and muddled objectives. Nevertheless, decades after their deaths each continues to influence the politics of his or her nation. In all these cases historical

memories were culled and images of sacrifice and heroic action periodically were harvested by new generations of politicians to mobilize
protests or electoral campaigns.

It is clear that agents of governments have played a central role in
the creation and manipulation of these powerful symbols. Adrian
Hastings has suggested that this is because "nations as they grew more
self-conscious, or come under threat, produced nationalisms."[17] The
feelings of shared identity and origin associated with this process
require the discovery or invention of common antecedents. Heroes,
especially martyrs, are the standard coin of these new realms. Bodies
and body parts, the forms of body language prevalent in Latin
America, have proved very useful in promoting a sense of shared experience. Governments use their resources to build and maintain tombs,
shrines, and monuments. They organize and promote vigils, marches,
and other rituals that build emotional connections between living citizens and the useful dead. States commission speeches, memorial
services, portraits. They also subsidize allies in the press and sympathetic intellectuals who write biographies that enhance and celebrate
the lives of preferred martyrs. But these efforts, no matter the scale,
are not always successful.

The efforts of the most powerful groups in Latin American societies to select heroes and invent rituals to further their own selfish
purposes are often defeated by the refusal of the masses to embrace
these preferred historical figures or to endorse "official" biographies.
One of the most important contributors to the discussion of mythic
figures, Alan Dundes, stated, "The fact that a hero's biography con-
forms to the Indo-European hero pattern does not necessarily mean
that the hero never existed. It suggests rather that the folk [common
people] repeatedly insist upon making their versions of the lives of
heroes follow the lines of a specific series of incidents."[18] The Latin
American "folk" have often rejected the preferred heroes of the elite
and embraced or invented their own. Donna Guy focuses on this
point in her examination of the very different postmortem careers
experienced by Juan and Evita Perón. Samuel Brunk and Jürgen
Buchenau also note the limited ability of successive Mexican leaders
to impose "appropriate" memorials and monuments for Zapata and
Obregón on the Mexican people.

It is clear, therefore, that the state or powerful political movements
are never the sole custodians of these heroic lives (and the bodies,
body parts, and burial locations that signify them). The past is not

inherited unambiguously by the powerful. What Dundes called the "folk," the rural and urban masses of Latin America, for example, often establish their own claims on martyrs and other heroes, producing in effect their own versions of these lives, versions that emphasize qualities and actions subversive to elite political needs. Nevertheless, it would be a mistake to ignore the ability of the modern state to establish official cults around preferred heroes or to impose the dominant narrative of an individual hero's life. Among those discussed in this book, Cuauhtémoc, Rosas, Zapata, Obregón, Vargas, and Guevara have all proven useful symbols to the purposes of governments and have been promoted on an industrial scale.

Monuments, streets, and public buildings have been named for these men by the state and the anniversaries of their deaths commemorated with rituals and ceremonies. In each case, the state has interested itself in the details of the burials and in maintaining the integrity of these bodies. But these actions as well as the expenditures that made them possible did not guarantee either the popularity of official observances or the acceptance of official interpretations of the lives and deaths. Spontaneous forms of remembrance that have proliferated where Che Guevara died in Bolivia, for example, are very different in both content and meaning from the official cult propagated by the Cuban government. The connections between these very political dead bodies and national memory are, in the end, determined in unpredictable ways by the intersection of heroes and peoples.

Each of the lives examined here has served as a useful metaphor for the larger experience of a nation or a people, but there has been great variability in the endurance of the individual cults. In general, the connection between the people and one of these heroes was forged in life. In every case examined in this collection there was a deep emotional connection between the political leader and followers during life. But in some cases, like the Peróns of Argentina, Vargas of Brazil, Zapata of Mexico, and Guevara of Cuba, these were contentious and divisive figures whose actions generated both deep affection and violent hatred. In each of these cases some of the trajectories of the postmortem cults resulted from the success or failure of the figure's adherents and partisans after death. It seems unlikely, for example, that the Cuban cult of Che will survive the Castro regime without dramatic reformulation, although the Bolivian cult filled with popular religious content that has evolved where Che died probably will. Similarly the popular memories of Juan Perón of Argentina and

Getúlio Vargas of Brazil have ebbed and flowed in response to the rhythms of national politics in these two nations.

The changed fortunes of a nation, an ethnic group, or a class can force the reevaluation of deceased heroes, taking once discarded figures like Cuauhtémoc or Túpac Amaru II and turning them into popular symbols. These redemptive possibilities are only available to the already famous dead, however. Those ignored in life will not be celebrated in death. All the individuals discussed here were consequential political actors who held the public's attention for lengthy periods. In the cases of Rosas, Vargas, the Peróns, and Guevara, visibility and influence was played out over decades. But that was not always the case. For example, with independence from Spain achieved in the nineteenth century the peoples of Peru and Mexico inventoried their histories to find suitable heroes who could illustrate the essential characters of these new and fragile nations, lives that might anticipate the struggle to overturn Spanish colonial rule. As a result, Túpac Amaru II in Peru and Cuauhtémoc in Mexico were eventually reworked as national, not narrowly ethnic, symbols. Although both indigenous heroes held the political stage for months, not years, their actions were easily freighted by subsequent generations with new meanings. What has been successfully asserted in both cases is the potent modern notion that death is preferable to foreign oppression. In every case examined here, however, celebrity was the essential precondition to veneration.

As Donna Guy points out in her essay, there is an important connection between the ways that Argentines today remember and celebrate (or remember and condemn) the lives and deaths of Juan and Evita Perón and the ways that Argentines have remembered and continue to remember and celebrate the lives and deaths of rock stars, murder victims, and even criminals.[19] There are important similarities in the ways that rituals, memories, and symbols are invented and used in both politics and pop culture. The roots of both can be traced to a shared cultural descent from the cult of saints that evolved in early Christianity.[20] That is, forms of remembering the "revered dead" tend to follow inherited scripts; they are derivative and generally predictable. But these two related forms of memory are also different. In all the cases examined here, the individual life and death is infused with unambiguous political content, unlike related cults associated with murder victims or rock stars killed in car wrecks.[21] Nevertheless, these scripts, the anticipated forms that ideal lives should take, are deeply rooted in traditional Catholic narratives as performed in festivals or as integrated in sermons and religious instruction. The ubiquity and potency of these narratives provide real leverage for popular refashioning of official cults supported by governments. As Daryle Williams and Barbara Weinstein point out in their essay on Getúlio Vargas, neither the Brazilian government nor the Vargas family was able to impose a sanitized and uncomplicated version of Vargas's life. In life and death, Vargas's legacy remained messy.

Once we closely interrogate the connections between these symbolic lives and the imagined nations they are attached to, the underlying metaphor that informs all these stories reveals itself fully. Although each of these remembered heroes experienced periods of triumph, military victories, public acclaim, or political power, each is remembered more for the humiliations, defeats, and political trials he or she endured. The Aztec tlatoani Cuauhtémoc, both the sixteenth-century Inca ruler Túpac Amaru and his eighteenth-century descendent of the same name, and the three greatest heroes of Mexico's independence struggle were all executed. Revolutionaries Emiliano Zapata, Alvaro Obregón, and Che Guevara were assassinated. Getúlio Vargas committed suicide. Although Juan and Evita Perón and Juan Manuel de Rosas died of natural causes, Rosas and Juan Perón both experienced defeat and exile. Evita was first humiliated by the Argentine elite and then suffered the terrible effects of uterine cancer. Suffering and sacrifice are essential components of these idealized lives. In fact, it is often suffering that invests the bodies of dead heroes with meaning.

Indeed, the nations of Latin America typically turn to dead heroes in times of crisis, the very endurance of the hero serving as a model for peoples tested by political or economic threats. As Argentina sank into crisis in 2001 with banks closed and presidents expelled from office for their failures, the walls in Buenos Aires were covered with hand-painted graffiti, "Evita vive" (Evita lives). This was not a manifestation of the official cult of the Peronist Party; it was instead the "folk" finding their own strength in the suffering of Evita and expressing their own anger in imitation of Evita's angry voice. With Peru roiled by corruption and political incompetence revolutionary movements in the 1970s and 1980s took the name of Túpac Amaru II, the defeated leader forced to watch the brutal execution of his family before enduring his own terrible death. His anguish seemed to anticipate their own and his courage was taken as an admonition to rise. That is, the useful life, the still political body, is often distinguished by patience and courage in the face of calamity, by the endurance of terrible pain like that of Cuauhtémoc who was staked out by Cortés, his feet coated with oil, and burned. The vast majority of Latin American presidents, who serve their terms, do their duty, and then leave the national political stage, need not apply for membership in this small club.

This concern with and attention to suffering and sacrifice has an iconographic character as well. The major statue devoted to Cuauhtémoc in Mexico City displays the humiliation of his capture and the terrible torments of his torture on two brass panels attached to the pedestal. The execution of the first Túpac Amaru had already become a motif in Andean folk art before the second Túpac Amaru initiated his rebellion in 1780. As Ward Stavig points out, the beheading of Túpac Amaru I engendered a belief that a new Inca would grow from the head, foreshadowing the recreation of an idealized indigenous world. Mexicans were more fascinated than repelled by the gory images of the dead Emiliano Zapata with his terrible wounds. Evita Perón who died of cancer in 1952 is often remembered and portrayed in the grip of this debilitating disease, weak and emaciated, rather than as the beautiful and highly sexual young woman who dominated the Argentine political stage in the 1940s. Suffering and sacrifice, not mere success, seem the common experience remembered by the most influential and enduring of these body cults. Could it be that the limited traction of the official effort to celebrate the body of Rosas returned to Argentina or the declining influence of official cults attached to bodies of Juan Perón, Getúlio Vargas, and Alvaro Obregón is explained by the poor fit of the biographies and iconographic expectations derived from the cult of saints? Had they suffered enough?

In most cases there is focused interest in the hero's death.[22] It might be argued, in fact, that it was the quality of the death that forged the enduring connection between the hero and the people. What were the qualities of the "good" death? It would seem that those who died at the hands of their enemies later enjoyed the most potent connections with their political followers and heirs.[23] The executed or assassinated, Cuauhtémoc, Hidalgo, and Che, for example, demonstrated in their deaths human and patriotic qualities that can be harvested routinely when needed. They demonstrated quiet courage while in the hands of implacable and cruel enemies.[24] Even

Vargas and Evita, the first a suicide and the second a victim of cancer, nevertheless, died in ways that suggest sacrifice and selflessness. The didactic utility of these idealized deaths is demonstrated in painting, statuary, and, in the modern era, photographic images. Almost always the hero seems to embrace these terrible torments or even death itself and the representations of these trials often imitate the iconography of Christ crucified. This death, the image suggests, gives life to a people and a nation.

As the authors of these essays make clear, there is often a ghoulish aspect to representations of the bodies, body parts, or death sites of these martyrs. The illustrations help make this point. The bones of Cuauhtémoc displayed in a crystal casket designed by Mexico's most famous artist, Diego Rivera, provide one clear example. The body of Evita Perón was plasticized for display, although it is now hidden from view in a family mausoleum. Zapata's killers displayed his body, like a hunter's trophy, to convince his followers and partisans that his revolution had ended while not anticipating the complex ways these witnesses would understand the meaning of the display. The government of Mexico later chose to display the severed arm of Obregón and to mark the exact spot where Obregón was repeatedly shot by his assassin, suggesting that the gruesome nature of his sacrifices would assure immortality. Even where efforts were made to hide a hero's body or destroy it in order to obliterate its political power (the cases of Túpac Amaru II and Che Guevara come to mind as examples) faithful followers were able to articulate powerful movements focused on the discovery of the body or its corporal reconstruction. These representational conventions, it seems to me, are clearly derived from the earlier cult of saints where the torments were lovingly portrayed in the *passio*, the story of the martyrdom read to the illiterate masses at festivals. The images concocted in Latin America to retell the lives of political martyrs often imitate the narrative development of these early Christian models. The people endure through the sacrifices of their heroes.

This connects logically with the importance of the remains themselves to the success of these cults of political memory. The followers and adherents of these figures pursue proximity with the bodies or body parts. In many cases, Cuauhtémoc, Rosas, Evita, and Che, for example, the remains of defeated heroes had been lost or buried in exile so that memory became attached to the hope for repatriation or discovery. In other cases the remains had been dispersed, like those of Túpac Amaru I and Hidalgo. In these cases finding and restoring these remains were explained rhetorically as efforts to repair the nation. Very often political movements actually borrow the language of Christ's resurrection to give meaning to this process. Installing the remains of the hero in their appropriate place, among the faithful, is represented as recovery and completion. As discussed by Christon Archer, Mexico City's streets were filled by crowds when the remains of Hidalgo and Morelos were returned to serve as memorials to independence in the 1820s. This emotional content of these recoveries, the remains of long-lost heroes, has often been interpreted as a miracle. The disputed bones of Cuauhtémoc rest in a church. In Bolivia both the location of Che's execution and the location where he was first buried now have the appearance of popular religious shrines, complete with testimonies of miracles and cures.

This powerful sentiment that martyrs and deceased heroes should be buried in appropriate places, commonly the arenas of their celebrated actions and sacrifices, is often marshaled by governments or political movements to mobilize the masses during periods of uncertainty or crisis. Following the death of Juan Perón in 1974, his widow, María Estela (aka Isabelita), became president, accelerating Argentina's decent into violence and economic misery. Isabelita's government arranged to bring the body of Evita back to Argentina, attracting vast crowds and briefly distracting public attention from the swelling chaos. However, this outpouring of emotion resulted from popular memory of Evita as an advocate of social justice and could not be converted into reliable support for the government, which lost power to a military coup that same year. Evita's body had spoken to the Argentine people with predictable effect, but this government was too disconnected from her image to capture the benefits. The decision to return the remains of Juan Manuel de Rosas in 1989 occurred in another period of economic and political crisis. The government of Carlos Menem sought to imitate the spontaneous mobilization that followed Evita's return, but the clumsy attempts of Menem to control and manipulate the events drained it of passion.[25]

The return of Rosas did set in motion a series of corporeal repatriations and reburials in Argentina that sent the remains of many of nineteenth-century political leaders back to their birthplaces. It soon became clear that the desire of politicians to resolve disputes about the appropriate resting places for the remains of the nation's heroes by imposing a single rule—dead heroes should be buried where they were born—would be resisted by popular opinion. The nation's most important hero of the independence era, the "Liberator" José de San Martín, died in exile in France in 1850. His remains had been returned to Argentina in 1878 and reburied in the Cathedral of Buenos Aires where they have been guarded continuously by soldiers of the regiment he had created to defeat Spanish armies in Argentina and Chile. Among the ironies of this reburial in the cathedral is the fact that San Martín, no supporter of the Catholic Church in his life, prohibited "any form of funeral service" in his will.[26]

Following the return of Rosas's remains, politicians from San Martín's native province of Corrientes pushed for his repatriation, even though he had spent only three years in his birthplace. The effort failed because both popular opinion and the national political leadership asserted that the memory of San Martín belonged to the nation and therefore belonged in the national capital. San Martín would stay in the cathedral, located across the plaza from the presidential palace, a handy symbol to be evoked on patriotic holidays.[27] The often restless postmortem careers of these martyred heroes attests to their abiding political utility and to the contested nature of historical memory. The appropriate locations for remains are often disputed, but popular opinion, more than the actions of national political authorities, has proven predictably influential.[28]

Because of the special qualities of these deaths, the remains require an appropriate setting. The place must also be connected to the life of the hero in a convincing way. The place must be marked by suitable markers or transformed to fit this requirement by the actions of the faithful. Evita's body experienced a restless trajectory, from a trade union building in Buenos Aires, to secret burial in Italy, to Juan Perón's home in exile in Madrid, to her family's tomb in Buenos Aires, with many strange stops along the way. Denied an impressive final resting place by her enemies, her family tomb has been transformed by the devotion of her many followers who decorate it every day with flowers.[29] Che Guevara was born and raised in Argentina, gained fame in Cuba as Fidel Castro's lieutenant, and died in Bolivia in a failed revolution. Where should he be buried? Did his death have greater meaning in Cuba where he succeeded, or in Bolivia where he failed? This concern to locate remains in the appropriate place explains the restless political lives of some dead bodies. Hidalgo, Rosas, Evita, Zapata, and Che were all buried, exhumed, and then reburied.

Not only is the appropriate physical setting for the burial crucial, but the remains themselves must be vetted and authenticated as well. Typically the enduring power of these remembered lives and deaths required the physical presence of the remains. There are some exceptions. The body of Túpac Amaru II was torn apart in 1781, his head, arms, and legs displayed in the villages that had supported his rebellion and the rest of his body burned, for example. His cult does not depend on the physical presence of his remains. More commonly, however, the human remains serve as conductors transmitting the ideals of the past to the nation today. In the essays that follow both the concern for discovering and authenticating remains and the struggle to locate appropriate locations for veneration are explored for each of these representative cases. In the case of Cuauhtémoc the controversy over the legitimacy of the remains exhumed in 1949 endures today, giving the patriotic cult that surrounds this Aztec hero an unfinished and incomplete character. Can his memory be recovered and adequately celebrated without the remains?

These, then, are stories that evoke and illuminate the presence of the past in Latin America's present. These exemplary lives, as they are remembered, dissected, and reconstructed, help Latin Americans make sense of the present and prepare for the future. The bodies and burial sites help give meaning to these lives. In some cases the deaths of these heroes and the treatment of their bodies produce a second, more powerful, symbolic narrative to supplement that of the life itself. In many ways, Túpac Amaru I (d. 1572) and Túpac Amaru II (d. 1781) as well as Cuauhtémoc (d. 1525) and Che Guevara (d. 1967) are all more influential today than during their lives. In each of these cases the form of death, its cruelty or injustice, and the treatment of the body, its dismemberment or mistreatment, dominate the popular narratives that are popularly embraced.

These forms of memory cannot push aside the other useful ways in which we access nation building and nationalism in Latin America. Nor should we attempt to infuse this form of symbolic language with meanings it cannot bear. But the importance of body language to politics in Latin America is clear. By treating it seriously we illuminate not only the intentions of the powerful, government officials and party leaders but also important forms of popular political expression. At the center of this dialog is the refusal of common people to surrender their understandings of identity, citizenship, and justice to political institutions. Disputes over bodies are disputes about power,

power over the past and power in the present. These disputed meanings force new life into long-dead bodies.

Notes

1. See this asserted in Rafael Samuel, "Continuous National History," in *Patriotism: The Making of British National Identity*, ed. Rafael Samuel (London: Routledge, 1987), 10.
2. On the modern world's mania for memory, see David Lowenthal, *The Heritage Crusade and the Spoils of History* (New York: Cambridge University Press, 1998).
3. See, for example, the following Web site devoted to Túpac Amaru, *www.sinectis.com.ar/mcagliani/Túpac.htm*, and a site devoted to his indigenous ally in Alto Peru, Túpac Catari, *www.llacta.org/organiz/ecuarunari/ecuarunari.htm*.
4. See, for example, *http://www.zapatistas.org/*.
5. A classic of this genre is Lesley Byrd Simpson's discussion of "Santa Anna's Leg" in *Many Mexicos*, 4th rev. ed. (Berkeley: University of California Press, 1967), 242–48.
6. See *http://www.news-gazette.com/story.cfm?number=2464*.
7. See Katherine Verdery, *The Political Lives of Dead Bodies: Reburial and Postsocialist Change* (New York: Columbia University Press, 1998); and for a related discussion, see Ann Anagnost, "The Politicized Body," in *Body, Subject and Power in China*, ed. Angela Zito and Tani E. Barlow (Chicago: University of Chicago Press, 1994), 131–56.
8. Among the numerous works devoted to this topic, I recommend Peter Brown, *The Cult of the Saints* (Chicago: University of Chicago Press, 1981).
9. Another useful way into this topic is through the literature devoted to mythic heroes. See, for example, Robert A. Segal, ed., *In Quest of the Hero* (Princeton, NJ: Princeton University Press, 1990).
10. Rebecca Earle, "'Padres de la Patria' and the Ancestral Past: Commemorations of Independence in Nineteenth-Century Spanish America," *Journal of Latin American Studies* 34 (2002): 775–805.
11. Verdery, *Political Lives of Dead Bodies*, 41, notes that "nearly all the ancestors recognized in national ideologies are male." The Latin American phenomenon is not unusual.
12. A good place to start is with *In Quest of the Hero*, a compilation of influential studies by Otto Rank, Lord Ragland, and Alan Dundes compiled and introduced by Robert A. Segal.

13. Quoted in Nicolas Shumway, *The Invention of Argentina* (Berkeley: University of California Press, 1991), 133.

14. This section relies on Ariel de la Fuente's very fine, *Children of Facundo: Caudillo and Gaucho Insurgency during the Argentine State-Formation Process* (Durham, NC: Duke University Press, 2000), 125–42.

15. Many Argentines believe that Evita, like Facundo, was buried standing up, still challenging her enemies in death.

16. The mausoleum also contains the remains of other heroes of the independence movement: Vicente Guerrero, Guadalupe Victoria, Leona Vicario, Andés Quintano Roo, Ignacio María Allende y Unzaga, Juan Aldama, José Mariano Jimenéz, Mariano Matamoros y Orive, and Nicolás Bravo.

17. Adrian Hastings, *The Construction of Nationhood: Ethnicity, Religion and Nationalism* (Cambridge: Cambridge University Press, 1997), 11.

18. Segal, *In Quest of the Hero*, xxix.

19. In addition to Donna Guy's essay, see Rosana Guber, "Las manos de la memoria," in *Desarrollo Económico* 36, no. 141 (1996): 423–41, for a close look at the violation of Juan Perón's tomb and the theft of his hands.

20. I recommend Agostino Paravicini-Bagliani, *The Pope's Body*, trans. David S. Peterson (Chicago and London: University of Chicago Press, 2000).

21. This follows obviously the experience of early Christian saints. See Peter Brown, *Authority and the Sacred: Aspects of the Christianization of the Roman World* (Cambridge and New York: Cambridge University Press, 1995).

22. This theme is usefully explored by James M. Boyden, "The Worst Death Becomes a Good Death: The Passion of Don Rodrigo Calderón," in *The Place of the Dead*, ed. Bruce Gordon and Peter Marshall (Cambridge: Cambridge University Press, 2000), 240–65.

23. This topic is worth pursuing in related areas. See Lisa Silverman, *Tortured Subjects: Pain, Truth, and the Body in Early Modern France* (Chicago: University of Chicago Press, 2001), see especially the chapter "'The Executioner of his Own Life': Lay Piety and the Valorization of Pain," 111–32.

24. See Marco Antonio León León, " Justicia, ceremonia, y sacrificio: Una aproximación a las ejecuciones públicas en el Chaile colonial," *Notas Historicas y Geograficas* 11 (2000): 89–122, for an interesting article on public executions. As he points out the intentions of the

authorities who order executions are also broadly didactic. They seek
to instruct, or intimidate, the community so that the actions of the
condemned would not be repeated. The more terrible the form of
execution, the quartering of Túpac Amaru II, for example, the clearer
the fears of the authorizing authorities. The cases examined here
make clear that these closely scripted actions also provided an alternative narrative of courage and patriotism that subverted these
official "texts."

25. It is worth noting that President Carlos Saul Menem named a son
Facundo and affected the long sideburns associated with the caudillo
Facundo Quiroga.

26. José de San Martín had been reburied once in France, where he had
lived in exile, before the repatriation of his remains to Buenos Aires.
See Ricardo Rojas, *El Santo de la Espada* (Buenos Aires: Editorial
Losada, 1940), especially 498–513.

27. These events had been anticipated by the return of the remains of
Argentina's early modernizer Bernardino Rivadavia who had also
died in exile. Tulio Halperín Donghi reprints the celebratory speech
of Bartolomé Mitre on the occasion of his reburial in *Proyecto y
Construcción de una Nación* (Caracas: Biblioteca Ayacucho, 1980),
185–89.

28. See the wonderful discussion in Tomás Eloy Martinez, *El sueño
Argentino* (Buenos Aires: Planeta, 1999), especially the essay
"Necrofilias Argentinas,"133–36.

29. The question of who controls the remains and memory of the illustrious dead is explored for the Christian experience in Patrick J.
Geary, *Phantoms of Remembrance: Memory and Oblivion at the End of
the First Millennium* (Princeton, NJ: Princeton University Press,
1994).

Chapter Two

Túpac Amaru, the Body Politic, and the Embodiment of Hope:

Inca Heritage and Social Justice in the Andes

Ward Stavig

On September 24, 1572, Túpac Amaru, the last in the line of the Incas who had risen in rebellion against their Spanish conquerors in 1536, was led into the Plaza de Armas of Cuzco surrounded by Spanish troops and some four hundred Cañari Indians. This was no honor guard (see Illustration 2.1). Those gathered in the Cuzco plaza were there to witness the execution of this young Inca. "The multitude of Indians, who completely filled the square, saw that lamentable spectacle [and knew] that their lord and Inca was to die there, they deafened the skies, making them reverberate with their cries and wailing. His relatives, who were near him, celebrated that sad tragedy with tears and sobbing."[1]

Then the Inca's executioner, a Cañari Indian whose people had been conquered by the Inca and who had been selected by the Spanish for the "honor," stepped forward and "taking the hair [of the Inca] in his left hand, severed the head with a cutlass at one blow, and held it high for all to see. As the head was severed the bells of the cathedral began to toll, and were followed by those of all the monasteries and parish churches in the city. The execution caused the greatest sorrow and brought tears to the eyes of all."[2]

After the execution government officials ordered the head to be placed on a pole and raised up in the center of Cuzco for all to see

2.1 *Guamán Poma drawing depicting the capture of the first Túpac Amaru* *(Source: Felipe Guamán Poma de Ayala*, Nueva Corónica y Buen Gobierno *[Paris: Institut d'Ethnologie, 1936]).*

that the Inca, and all he represented to his people, was truly dead. Implicit in this "message" was the understanding that other rebels could expect the same. The reaction of the indigenous people to the death of their Inca, however, was not what the Spanish had foreseen. Something had gone wrong with their plan, and they soon became very concerned. Multitudes of indigenous people gathered around the severed head to "mourn and worship their Inca." Soon even the hard-bitten Viceroy Toledo, the Spanish official who had pushed for the capture of the Inca and then ordered the execution, concurred that Túpac Amaru's "head could not be allowed to remain on the pike for more than two days, since no punishment could have sufficed to [prevent] the adoration they made towards it."[3] The head was removed from public display and unceremoniously buried with the body somewhere on a hill above Cuzco.

While Andean historians and Peruvians are familiar with the story of the death of the teenage Túpac Amaru after his surrender to Viceroy Toledo in 1572, when most people hear the name Túpac Amaru they do not have this Inca in mind. Instead, they are usually thinking of the eighteenth-century Andean rebel leader, also known as Túpac Amaru, who rose up against Spanish rule, proclaimed himself Inca, and led a largely indigenous army that challenged Spanish rule and shook Andean society to its core in the 1780s as he and his followers sought a more just social order.

Although the eighteenth-century Túpac Amaru is now the most famous, the first Túpac Amaru's flesh and blood existence, and royal heritage, made it possible for the second Túpac Amaru to be "reborn" and for the memory of the Inca to be kept alive. Thus, in many ways, the first Túpac Amaru gave "birth" to the second, and the second, in turn, became the physical manifestation and then symbol of hope for generations of Andean peoples.

In the Andes the lives and cultural memories of the two Túpac Amarus are fused into a single historical memory. The collective story of the two Túpac Amarus, both captured and then beheaded by Spanish authorities in the central plaza of Cuzco some two hundred and ten years apart, has helped to forge an enduring, yet evolving, vision of long-lasting cultural and political importance. Memories of the Inca, Inca rule, and the society they created resonated with Andean peoples in the colonial era, and they continue to resonate down to the present. Thus, the lives of the two Túpac Amarus took on exceptional meaning—real and symbolic—not only for the world in which they lived, but for places, times, and peoples for whom their existence is almost in the realm of myth. Their fused memory became a wellspring of longed-for redemption and justice. However, it was not just their lives that provided inspiration. Even their deaths assumed extraordinary meaning as the public memory of their executions was transformed by followers into a source of hope. This is all the more remarkable in that both were defeated and executed, their efforts bringing neither freedom nor triumph to their people during their lifetimes, but what they died trying to achieve, and what their bodies represented, has greatly affected the Andean "body politic."

The first Túpac Amaru assumed the "Inca" throne in the mid sixteenth century because he was the son of Manco Inca. Manco was the younger brother of Huascar and Atahualpa, the two brothers who had

been engaged in a civil war for control of the Inca Empire—
Tawantinsuyu—when Pizarro and the Spanish came to the Andes. All
three brothers were the children of Huayna Capac, the last great Inca
ruler before the arrival of Europeans. The eighteenth-century Túpac
Amaru also became Inca in part by birth, but his route to being "recognized" as the Inca was more circuitous and certainly not obvious.
He was a *kuraka* (curaca), or ethnic leader, in the rural Cuzco province
of Canas y Canchis (also known as Tinta). He inherited his position
as kuraka or ethnic leader due to the fact that he was the great-great-
great-grandchild of the first Túpac Amaru, making him of royal lineage, but he was born into a world in which no Inca had ruled for
almost two centuries. However, with the weight of this history on his
shoulders and with conditions for his people worsening, this eighteenth-century Túpac Amaru proclaimed himself to be the Inca, the
rightful leader and defender of his people, and he set out to end the
abuses and affronts suffered under the Spanish yoke.

From November 1780 to May 1781 the second Túpac Amaru (see
Illustration 2.2) led a rebellion that spread like wildfire over much
of the southern Andes and threatened Spanish dominion in the
Andes in a way it had not been threatened since the first years after
the fall of Cuzco to the Spanish in 1532. The level of carnage of the
1780 rebellion was tremendous. This was no minor frontier rebellion, no village revolt. It clearly dwarfed, in scale and destructive-
ness, the rebellions of the Lakota and other indigenous peoples in
the North American (U.S.) West. Some Andean scholars believe that
at least one hundred thousand, if not more, perished in the couple
of years the rebellion lasted. In traditional Andean terms this was a
near *pachacuti*, a cataclysm or reversal of the world order. It was similar to previous *pachacuties* that had destroyed and created the Andean
world in the historical past as well as the always present mythical past.
The Andean world that the colonial indigenous observer and com-
mentator Guamán Poma had said was "a world turned upside down,"
when he wrote in the late sixteenth and early seventeenth centuries,
seemed to be on the verge of having its "proper" order restored by
this rebellion.

How had such a profound social and political movement arisen
more than two hundred years after Viceroy Toledo's decapitation of
the first Túpac Amaru, the last leader of the postconquest Inca

Inca Rulers at the Time of the Conquest and During Colonial Resistance

Sixteenth Century

Huayna Capac. Last ruler of a united Inca Empire. Died before the arrival of the Spanish.

Huascar. Son of Huayna Capac. Killed on orders of his brother, Atahualpa, during the civil war between them for control of Tawantinsuyu.

Atahualpa. Son of Huayna Capac. Controlled much of Tawantisuyu when the Spanish arrived. Executed by the Spanish in 1533.

Manco. Son of Huayna Capac. Led a rebellion against the Spanish in Cuzco and then established a new Inca stronghold in Vilcabamba. Was killed by Spaniards in 1544.

Sayri-Túpac. Young son of Manco. Regents ruled for him. He then agreed to live in Spanish society outside of Vilcabamba. Died in 1560.

Titu Cusi Yupanqui. Son of Manco. Was crowned in Vilcabamba in 1560. Carried out negotiations with the Spanish. Died in 1571.

Túpac Amaru. Son of Manco. Assumed throne of the Vilcabamba Incas upon death of Titu Cusi Yupanqui in 1571. Was captured by Spanish in 1572 and executed in Cuzco that year.

Eighteenth Century

Juan Santos Atahualpa. Eighteenth-century indigenous leader who claimed descent from Inca Atahualpa and led an insurrection from 1742–52.

Túpac Amaru (José Gabriel Condorcanqui). Kuraka in the province of Canas y Canchis (Cuzco) who was a direct descendant of the first Túpac Amaru. Declared himself Inca and led the great rebellion of 1780. Was executed by the Spanish in Cuzco in 1781.

2.2 *Túpac Amaru, the eighteenth-century Inca who led a rebellion against the Spanish in the 1780s. He relied on his Inca heritage to rally followers (Source: Mariella Corvetto).*

resistance that emerged in the 1530s shortly after what many Spanish had assumed to be their triumph. The rebellion originally had been initiated by Manco Inca, the first Túpac Amaru's father. Its defeat was meant to not only put an end, once and for all, to the rebellion, but it was also meant to permanently behead the Inca imperial legacy and thereby prevent native resistance by ending hope of unity for those who still might feel allegiance to the Inca or who might turn to the Inca as a rallying force in the future. Thus, the public, almost ritual, severing of the first Túpac Amaru's head was supposed to have prevented the very type of indigenous upheaval that occurred two centuries later when the next Túpac Amaru rose up and led a primarily indigenous force against Spanish authority.

The strength of the eighteenth-century rebellion and the level of participation are all the more impressive when one considers that in the 1780s, just as in the 1570s, indigenous unity could not be taken for granted. Andean peoples had never marched to the beat of a single drummer. These divisions were readily apparent on the day the first Túpac Amaru was executed. Viceroy Toledo had the proceedings guarded not only by Spaniards but also by the Cañari, an ethnic group conquered by the Inca after a fierce war just a decade or so prior to the arrival of Pizarro. The Cañari had quickly become allies of the Spanish in the hope of freeing themselves from the Inca yoke. While those sympathetic to the Inca were said to have been consumed with sorrow and tears, such was not the case with the Cañari or other indigenous onlookers who had chaffed under the Inca yoke. They were triumphant in their revenge. However, for those who called the Inca their ruler not because of force or defeat, the Inca and the empire were not joyously or readily dismissed.

In 1572 the Spanish convinced the doomed the Inca to publicly accept the Christian God, confess, and denounce his own religion before his execution. "Lords, you are here from all the four *suyos* [the Inca Empire had four (*tawa*) division or suyos, hence Tawantinsuyo]. Be it known to you that I am a Christian, they have baptised me and I wish to die under the law of God. And I have to die. All that I and my ancestors the Incas have told you up to now—that you should worship the sun Punchao and the huacas, idols, stones, rivers, mountains, and *vilcas*—is completely false."4

By the combined acts of conversion, spiritual denial, and bloodletting, the Spanish had hoped to put the last nail in the coffin of Inca rule and legitimacy. The intent was to end forever the threat created by an Inca who might rally his people, and their gods, to keep alive dreams of Inca survival and restoration, just as Manco Inca had done when he fled and established a new body politic in Vilcabamba.

The impact of Túpac Amaru's confession, followed by the bloody execution, was not what the Spanish had thought was in the cards. The Inca's denial of his Andean faith did not sway those who mourned the Inca. Either they did not believe what he had said due to the circumstances, or his denial alone was not enough to shake their allegiance. Perhaps this was because they had already internalized sentiments, like those expressed by Túpac Amaru's father, Manco Inca, that placed in doubt such public compliance with colonial demands. Manco had been placed on the throne by the Spanish to be a puppet ruler, but this had not been Manco's understanding. He sought to exercise traditional authority. Seeing that he was not really in power and having been forced to endure humiliations such as being held in chains, having been urinated upon, and having the women of his house raped, Manco rose against the Spaniards and laid siege to Cuzco. When the revolt did not bring immediate victory he sought refuge in the strong defense of the nearby city of Ollantaytambo and then moved on to Vilcabamba where he established a government in exile. He led the Inca resistance from Vilcabamba until he was killed by a Spaniard who he had allowed to stay in his camp seeking refuge from Spanish authorities. According to his son Titu Cusi, who assumed the Inca royal fringe after his brother Sayri-Túpac died, Manco had advised his people on how they should remember the Inca as well as how they should deal with the Spanish.

> Reflect on how long my grandparents and great-grandparents and I myself have looked after you and protected you, cared for you and governed . . . making provisions that you had plenty, so that it behooves all of you not to forget us, not in your lifetimes, nor the time of your descendants. . . .
>
> What you can do is give them the outward appearance of complying with their [Spanish] demands. And give them a little tribute, whatever you can spare from your lands, because these people are so savage and so different from us that if you don't give it to them they will take it from you by force. . . .
>
> They did with me as you have seen . . . taking from us our property, our wives, our sons, our daughters, our fields, our food, and many other things that we used to have in this land. . . .
>
> I know that someday, by force or deceit, they will make you worship what they worship, and when that happens, when you can resist no longer, do it in front of them, but on the other hand do not forget our ceremonies. And if they tell you to break your shrines, and force you to do so, reveal just what you have to, and keep hidden the rest.[5]

Was it the heeding of advise like that given by Manco, or deeply felt antagonisms against the colonial order and abuses, that eventually led to the events of 1781 in which another Spanish official, José

Antonio de Areche, oversaw the beheading of another Túpac Amaru in the central plaza of Cuzco? How had this second Inca arisen? How, after more than two hundred years of apparent quiet and Spanish rule that had followed Toledo's execution of the first Túpac Amaru, had the leadership of an Inca resonated with such a large segment of the indigenous population, particularly in regions close to Cuzco? In the most basic sense—the biological—the eighteenth-century Túpac Amaru was descended from the line of Huayna Capac, Manco Inca, and the first Túpac Amaru. Viceroy Toledo had presided over the execution of the Inca, but he had not destroyed the lineage. This new Inca had inherited royal blood from Juana Pinco Huaco, the daughter of Juana Quispe Sisa and Túpac Amaru. Juana had married Felipe Condorcanqui who was the kuraka of the communities of Pampamarca, Sorimana, and Tungasuca in the province of Canas y Canchis (also known as Tinta). The rebel leader José Gabriel Condorcanqui Túpac Amaru was the descendant (great-great-grand-child) of this pair. He eventually pressed for and was named kuraka of the same communities as his ancestor.

Perhaps more important to the movement led by the second Túpac Amaru, during the course of the colonial period *naturales* (a common colonial term for indigenous people) labored under the increasingly heavy demands and oppression of the Spanish, and the reign of the Inca came to be looked upon by more and more sectors of indigenous society with increasing sympathy and nostalgia. Negative memories of the Inca conquest faded and the reign of the Inca began to be seen as a period of benevolent and just rule. The tremendous loss of life due to plagues, the usurping of indigenous lands, the oppressive forced-labor obligations including the dreaded *mita* for the mines of Potosí, the disruptions of life, the demanding of tribute not just in labor as in the Inca times but in actual goods or money, not to mention other colonial projects in which naturales were compelled to work, made Spanish colonial rule ever-more burdensome. In these circumstances many Andean people began to long for the rule of the Inca. At the same time, however, the Inca and Inca rule, even Inca society, came to be viewed as more of a composite entity—individual, state, and society came to be viewed more and more as one and the same.

One of the first chroniclers to put these sentiments into writing was Garcilaso de la Vega, the son of an Inca princess and a Spanish conqueror. While Garcilaso lived his adult life in Spain, his formative years were spent in the company of his mother and other indigenous relatives. They had managed to escape the wrath of Atahualpa who had sought to destroy the line of his rival and brother, Huascar, and Garcilaso's mother was related to Huascar. As a boy, Garcilaso loved to hear stories of the Inca. He recalled that when the family got together

> conversation was always of the origin of the Inca kings, their greatness, the grandeur of their empire, their deeds and conquests, their government in peace and war, and the laws they ordained so greatly to the advantage of their vassals. . . .
>
> From the greatness and prosperity of the past they turned to the present, mourning their dead kings, their lost empire, and their fallen state, etc. These and similar topics were broached by the Incas and Pallas (female royalty) on their visits, and on recalling their departed happiness, they always ended these conversations with tears and mourning saying: "Our rule is turned to bondage."[6]

The arguments made by Garcilaso about Tawantinsuyu were steeped in European and Christian forms to appeal to Spanish readers, but the intent was to glorify the Inca past and to appeal for better treatment in the present. He noted, "We do not read in all the histories of Asia, Africa, or Europe that ever those kings were so gracious to their subjects as these [Incas]."[7] In the midst of this early Spanish colonial world, Garcilaso drew attention to the ordered and benign control of lands and people under the Inca by way of contrast.

> In the matter of working and cultivating the fields they also established good order and harmony. First they worked the fields of the sun, then those of the widows and orphans and all those disabled by old age or illness: all such were regarded as poor people, and therefore the Inca ordered that their lands should be cultivated for them. . . .
>
> The Inca decreed that the fields of their vassals should have precedence before their own, for they said that the prosperity of his subjects was the source of good service to the king; that if they were poor and needy they could not serve well in war and peace.
>
> The last fields to be cultivated were those of the king. They worked them in common; all the Indians went to the

fields of the king and the sun, generally with great good cheer and rejoicing, dressed in the vestments and finery that they kept for their principal festivals, adorned with gold and silver ornaments and wearing large feathered headdresses. When they plowed the land (and this was the labor that gave them the greatest pleasure), they sang many songs that they composed in praise of their Inca; thus they converted their work into merrymaking and rejoicing, because it was in the service of their God and of their kings.[8]

In the eighteenth century many of the literate indigenous elite were familiar with the work of Garcilaso. The vision he portrayed of a more harmonious world under the Inca stirred pride in many of them. Before his premature death, Alberto Flores Galindo, one of the leading Peruvian scholars of the late twentieth century, especially of Andean utopian thought, argued that the *Royal Commentaries* of Garcilaso were seen by Túpac Amaru and others in the eighteenth century as a denunciation of the colonial order, of the work of Viceroy Toledo (resettlement of people into villages, imposition of state tribute, the mita), and as a "veiled suggestion that a just and equitable empire ought to be reconstructed."

> Garcilaso turned the Inca era, Tawantinsuyo, into a golden age . . . [Garcilaso] believed that the past could fill a moralizing functioning by offering models for the present: his historical conception was infected by utopia in the strictest European sense of the word. . . . The eighteenth century indigenous elite [like Túpac Amaru], which had easy access to Spanish language and to the printed word, understood this inner message of the book; they, in turn, transported it orally to other social sectors. We know "a work by Garcilaso" accompanied Túpac Amaru in his travels.[9]

Garcilaso was not alone in his complaints about the nature of Spanish governance and the desire to do something about it. The indigenous chronicler Felipe Guamán Poma de Ayala was also greatly distressed by the colonial world he observed. In the early seventeenth century he sent a letter some thousand pages in length to the Spanish king that described the disorder, bad government, sexual abuse, beatings, forced labor, in short, most of the horrors of the dark side of the colonial regime. By bringing these abuses to the attention of the king, Guamán Poma hoped to spur reform, but he also planted troubling questions for the crown. His work went far beyond simple pleas for reform and condemnation of colonial outrages. Guamán Poma argued that the Spaniards were really outsiders in the Andean realm and as such they needed to obey the laws of the land as they had been promulgated by the Incas. He made it clear that the Spanish must not take the Indians' land and that "they reverse themselves and give back the said fields and yards and pasture lands sold in the name of his Majesty because, according to [Christian] conscience, they cannot take them away from the natives, the legitimate proprietors of the aforementioned lands." The chronicler also wrote that because of their actions the Christians "are all condemning yourselves to hell . . . as long as you do not make restitution and pay what you owe, you will be condemned to the inferno."¹⁰ Guamán Poma even went so far as to suggest that the Spanish monarch had no real authority in the New World. For Guamán Poma authority rested with the legitimate indigenous authorities, the Inca, the Inca state structure, and other ethnic leaders and kurakas. "All the world is God's, and thus Castile belongs to the Spaniards and the Indies to the Indians. . . . And thus there must be obedience to the chief lords and magistrates, the legitimate proprietors of the lands, whether they be male or female."¹¹

Guamán Poma's letter to the king did not have an immediate impact; indeed it had no impact at all until early in the twentieth century when the lost and unknown manuscript—dead to the world—was found on the shelves of a Danish library. In the last few decades new translations and scholarship have given "rebirth" to this work that condemned Spanish abuses and extolled, for the most part, the virtuous nature of indigenous society under Inca rule. While Guamán Poma's work obviously did not influence people in the colonial era, there is evidence that the thoughts and attitudes he held—looking to the Inca period as a time of better government—were becoming increasingly common in the Andes during his lifetime and influenced his writings. It may well have been these attitudes that led this knowledgeable indigenous chronicler, who almost surely knew that Atahualpa had been garroted, to state that Pizarro had ordered his beheading (see Illustration 2.3) and to create one of his powerful drawings that portrayed Atahualpa about to suffer decapitation, like the first Túpac Amaru.

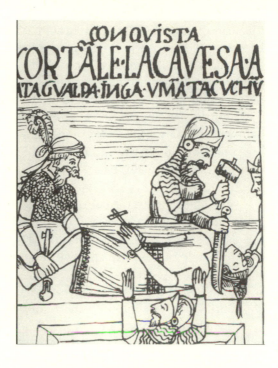

2.3 *Guamán Poma drawing showing Atahualpa being beheaded instead of
being garroted (Source: Felipe Guamán Poma de Ayala*, Nueva
Corónica y Buen Gobierno *[Paris: Institut d'Ethnologie, 1936]).*

After the execution of the first Túpac Amaru a legend grew in
which the head of the Inca, far from rotting on the post on which it
had been placed, had become each day more resplendent and gained
more worshipers until it had to be removed by colonial authorities.[12]
Did Guamán Poma represent the death of Atahualpa as decapitation—as in the later execution of Túpac Amaru—as a way to connect
this image of "rebirth" or "resurrection" to Atahualpa, and by implication to Inca rule in general? It is quite possible that Guamán Poma
was putting into words and pictures "provincial and local version of
Peruvian history" as they developed and were passed down through
the first generations of colonial rule.[13] This indigenous muckraker
may have been making a conscious decision to render the story of
Atahualpa, as it had been popularized in his lifetime, in order to
strengthen the growing mystique of the Inca Empire and further dele-
gitimize Spanish rule. Flores Galindo argued that by the time of

Guamán Poma the Christian notion of resurrection had already become linked to Andean beliefs in their gods, in the return of the Inca, and the need for a more orderly rule. In this cosmovision, according to Flores Galindo, the term "Inca" came to signify the idea or principle of organizer or one who puts things in order, and Tawantinsuyu and the Incas became a utopian time "without hunger, without exploitation, and where Andean people [*hombres*] returned to govern." Thus, the term Inca expanded beyond a specific individual, or even a people, to also be a vision of a better world order.

> The idea of the return of the Inca did not appear in a spon-taneous manner in the Andean culture. It was not a mechan-ical response to colonial domination. In the memory . . . the Andean past was reconstructed and it was converted into an alternative to the present. . . . [This included the notion that] Christ after the crucifixion . . . was resuscitated on the third day to rise into heaven. Bodies could regain (*recobrar*) life. Death was not an irreversible fact. The promise of res-urrection did exist.[14]

It is in this setting—the syncretic combination of Andean gods and ancestor worship with Christian resurrection—that the concept of *Inkarrí* was born. According to the Inkarrí belief, the Inca could be reborn from his buried head. The Inca would grow new arms, legs, and a body, and when this was accomplished a new age would be born. In this mythical understanding the Inca and the Inca Empire also became intertwined, even inseparable. Thus, when a whole and vital Inca was reborn who would turn the world right side up again—the Inca restored, the Spanish defeated or driven out, and order, har-mony, and justice reigning in the Andes—it also meant that an ide-alized Inca Empire would be restored. Eventually Inkarrí was sometimes seen just as the restoration of the empire or its principles. In this way the concept of Inkarrí was not limited to the return of the Inca, but could be one and the same with the rebirth of a more just and harmonious world. Rumors of Inkarrí, increased during the latter part of the colonial period and were especially noticeable in the eigh-teenth century.[15]

There also emerged a growing belief in Gran Paititi, a hidden Inca society somewhere in Antisuyu, the jungle or lowlands to the east beyond where Manco Inca, Titu Cusi, and the first Túpac Amaru had resided while in resistance in Vilcabamba, became more prominent. In the late seventeenth century Christian missionaries heard accounts from indigenous people of the Incas and of a hidden city; one old Indian, when asked about Gran Paititi, responded it was the name of a river near where "a very large population" of Incas lived.[16] Clearly the Incas lived on, at least in the minds of some Andean peoples, in a homeland no longer centered in Cuzco. However, as Flores Galindo made clear, it is probably best to see beliefs such as Inkarrí and Gran Paititi as "small islands and archipelagos," for they were widespread but not continuous.[17]

The Inkarrí legend has many versions, but I have encountered none that remain unchanged from the colonial period. All seem to have been added to or updated over time. I have selected a representative version of Inkarrí, collected by the Peruvian novelist and ethnographer José María Arguedas, to share. Arguedas was reportedly "astonished" when in the mid-twentieth century he asked a group of Andean folk what they knew of the Inca and was given the following account of Inkarrí. The mythical forces and empire are personified in this account, as in others, and their meaning clearly extends to powerful, unknown forces that could be the Inca Empire in a personalized form.

> Inkarí rounded up the stones with a whip and commanded them. He drove them to the heights, and then he founded a city. . . .
>
> Inkarí enclosed the wind [and] tethered Father Sun. Thus Inkarí lengthened time; he made the day long, so that he could accomplish everything he had to do.
>
> After he had tamed the wind, he threw a golden staff from the summit of Great Osqonta mountain, saying, "May this establish Cusco." The staff . . . kept moving inland . . . until it reached the place where Cusco stands. We of today do not know how far that was. Atawallpa and the ancient ones, they knew.
>
> The king of the Spaniards seized Inkarí . . . and kept him prisoner somewhere. It is said that only Inkarí's head still exists. But from the head he is growing, growing down towards his feet. And when everything is complete, Inkarí will return.[18]

In the long period in which the Inca and the Inca world were becoming mythologized, the general tranquility of the realm and of the everyday interactions of colonial life, at least from the European viewpoint, led the Spanish to relax some of their fears of conspiracy and worship of pagan deities. By the late seventeenth century the Spanish state's and the Catholic Church's concerns with the Inca and with Andean religious practices had lessened. From Potosí to Lima to Cuzco, the Incas were allowed back into public celebrations such as parades. In a 1659 celebration in the Plaza de Armas in Lima there "were more than two thousand . . . [Indians and] the plaza seemed covered [*plateada*] with different flowers . . . [and] the Indians left well dressed and with '*muchas galas*' [great fanfare or glory]."[19] During the festivities a native Andean, acting the role of the Inca, was allowed to defeat all the other indigenous kings who then offered their allegiance (*ofrecieron las llaves*). Similar events were happening in Cuzco, the former center of Tawantinsuyu, the indigenous elite demonstrating their Inca heritage by wearing Inca clothing with pride in public celebrations. Thus, by the late seventeenth century "the long period of siege on the indigenous culture had ended and the Spanish opted for tolerance. In the sierra of Lima the extirpation of idolatries ceased. The evangelizers concluded that the Indian was Christian. . . . These circumstances, that evidently did not exist in 1555, permit the utopia to once again be public."[20]

It is in this context—the decline in civil and church oppression of Andean beliefs coinciding with the growth in the belief of the rebirth of the Inka—that the return of an Inca leader gathered credence and may have further inspired the second Túpac Amaru to view himself as the anticipated restorer of a more orderly and just Andean world.

In the mid-eighteenth century there erupted a rebellion in the central highlands and the nearby high jungle region of Peru. The movement was known by the name of its leader, Juan Santos Atahualpa. During the rebellion followers of Juan Santos Atahualpa referred to him as their "Inca," and he claimed descent from the Inca Atahualpa who had been executed by Pizzaro. As the Guamán Poma drawings suggest, the Inca Atahualpa was popularly thought to have been beheaded. In the syncretic conjuncture of Andean and Christian religions it is possible that he could have been viewed as having been "reborn" or "resurrected" in the form of Juan Santos. Be this the case or not, it was very clear that the "Inca"—Juan Santos Atahualpa—was respected. The defense of one community against the rebellion came apart when one of the indigenous defenders saw Juan Santos Atahualpa and shouted "this is our Inca." People even "kissed [Juan Santos's] hands and feet."[21] It was not just indigenous people who followed this new Atahualpa. Many mestizos also joined the movement, and the government feared the consequences of such popularity. The *corregidor* of Jauja cautioned, "[T]his problem has the deepest roots, . . . that the biggest enemy is the internal one in the highland Province, secretly favoring the Rebel. If we do not take other measures and precautions, we will be the target of further blows, with danger to the entire kingdom."[22] Showing their fear, and making others aware of the consequences, three Indians who were caught in a noncombatant situation were sentenced to hang "because it is clear that the land demands a speedy example, with notorious display . . . of the bodies or heads of the prisoners, so that horrified and intimidated by the punishment, the Indians [as well as] those who are not [that is, *castas* and dissident whites] abandon any thought that their vile inclination may have suggested."[23] Thus, in the late colonial period the growing identification with the Inca could lead to action by not only the elite, but also by those who were ready to turn to a now idealized Inca for their salvation. However, scholars such as John Rowe, referring to this phenomena as Inca nationalism, have warned against making too much of this enthusiasm or awareness, particularly for ordinary Andean people. Likewise, Flores Galindo raised a voice of caution when he suggested that for the average indigenous man or woman the ideas surrounding the "Inca" had less to do with a ruling family than it did with a more harmonious, ordered, and just world that came to be associated with the reign of the Inca.

It is in this political-cultural climate that José Gabriel Condorcanqui Túpac Amaru went about the process of converting himself into the Inca through both legal and symbolic means, as well as through his everyday actions. Like some others of royal Inca blood, Túpac Amaru and his wife Micaela Bastidas commissioned a portrait of themselves not in Spanish clothes, their everyday dress, but as Inca royalty. During the rebellion he wore Spanish-style clothes, but he also adorned himself with Inca symbols, especially that of a gold sun, which hung down from his neck for all his followers to see. An Arequipa newspaper in January 1781 gave this description of the Inca: "Túpac Amaru was riding a white horse, with embroidered and embossed trappings, a pair of large blunderbusses, pistols and sword, all dressed in blue velvet with gold braids on the front, his three-cornered hat, and over his attire an unco, like a bishop's rochet, sleeveless and richly embroidered, and around his neck a golden chain and hanging from it a sun of the same metal, insignia of the princes, his ancestors."²⁴

Túpac Amaru also capitalized on the aura and prestige of the Inca by seeking official and legal recognition as the heir to the Inca throne through descent from his namesake whom Toledo had beheaded in 1572. José Gabriel traveled to Lima to press his claim before the Audiencia (the high court), but the court never ruled on his claim to be the Inca heir. This mattered little, however, to his soon-to-be followers. They were much less interested than was the future rebel leader himself in what a court of Spaniards might say about Inca succession. At the same time that he was pressing his claim to be designated Inca, José Gabriel continued to exercise his authority as the kuraka of Pampamarca, Tungasuca, and Surimana and acted on behalf of other communities in his home territory of Canas y Canchis. For these people he sought exemption from forced labor in the mines of Potosí, the dreaded mita. He failed to achieve the exemption, but when he returned home to Canas y Canchis from Lima a local priest testified, "I noted the Indians looked at him with veneration, and not only in this village [Langui–Layo] but even outside the province of Tinta: the province, proud with his protection, imagined itself free from the mita obligation."²⁵ Did this veneration also stem from the fact that Túpac Amaru was now beginning to be seen by some as the reborn Inca who was acting on their behalf? Could they have been asking themselves if this was a first step in turning the world right-side up, of restoring social justice and Inca rule?

Central to any belief in the return of the Inca was faith in Andean gods and beliefs. The Inca, after all, had been a religious as well as a temporal leader. By the late eighteenth century, however, for most Andean indigenous people being religious meant being an observant Christian without having abandoned the Andean gods. This syncretism of religious practices ran deep. Even in Cuzco, a center of Andean Christianity, Christian symbols such as saints were often arrayed in Inca clothing during fiestas and Inca symbols such as that of the Sun God were included in public celebrations with the acquiescence of the Spanish. The bishop of Cuzco noted that the Indians "convince us that they adore the true God only when they see Him dressed like the Incas, whom they believed to be deities."²⁶

In the late eighteenth century it was Túpac Amaru's good fortune that circumstances in Canas y Canchis supported his indigenous followers' perceptions that this kuraka was both Inca and a defender of the Christian faith. Thus, he could not only call upon the ancestors and *apus* (mountain gods) of Andean tradition, but he could use his close ties to certain officials of the Catholic Church, such as the bishop of Cuzco, without appearing to be contradictory to any but the most ideological of his followers. Túpac Amaru's friendship with the bishop of Cuzco, Juan Manuel Moscoso y Peralta, may have developed in part because "bad blood" existed between Moscoso and the corregidor of Canas y Canchis, Antonio de Arriaga, just as it did between him and Arriaga. In fact, Túpac Amaru ended up launching the rebellion with the hanging of Arriaga. Moscoso, using his powers as bishop, did all he could to solidify his position and weaken that of the corregidor, including excommunicating Arriaga. In addition, local priests sympathetic to the corregidor were also excommunicated by Bishop Moscoso and removed from their parish churches in order to lessen Arriaga's public support and to assure that the public voice of the church was Moscoso's voice. As priests and civil officials took one side or another in the dispute, what was essentially a personal feud between a bishop and a corregidor ended up taking on much larger meaning. Túpac Amaru, who socialized with the bishop and who had his own rifts with Arriaga, was perceived as being solidly allied with the bishop and against the corregidor. In this situation those who opposed Moscoso were also likely to be antagonistic toward Túpac Amaru, but those who opposed Corregidor Arriaga were given further reason to support the kuraka. Seeing his closeness to the powerful church official, indigenous people and others could only assume that his influence with the church extended beyond those of most kurakas.

During the rebellion Túpac Amaru used religion effectively in an effort to bring people into the movement and maintain their loyalty. On the one hand, he sought to project an image of himself as acting on behalf of the Christian God by being a cleansing arm of the Spanish king. On the other hand, he also acted as the divine Inca, the spiritual leader of the Andean world. The utilization of these powerful symbolic inventories imbued this heir to the Inca throne with an authority, a majesty, that helped swell the ranks of his rebel army and gave his followers deeper faith in the righteousness of their leader and their cause.

Once the rebellion was initiated, Bishop Moscoso, despite his earlier relationship to Túpac Amaru, brought the full weight of Christian opprobrium down on the Inca and the movement he led. In the early fighting Túpac Amaru's army attacked the community of Sangarará, and some five hundred royalists took refuge in the church during the fighting. When the church was torched by order of Túpac Amaru, all those inside died. Following these events, Moscoso excommunicated the Inca.[27] While this action may have dissuaded some naturales from joining the rebellion and encouraged others to take up arms against the rebels, it had little effect on those people who were already in the rebel camp.

Some priests continued to support the rebel leader despite his excommunication. Gregorio de Yepes, the priest of Pomacanchi, tended to the rebels' religious needs, wrote letters of encouragement to the rebel leaders, and was "very passionate" in his support. He also supplied much-needed mules and stocks of copper. Yepes even compared Túpac Amaru to David who would slay the Spanish Goliath. He proclaimed that the Inca was an "instrument of the Lord . . . for the correction of many wrongs and abuses."[28] The priest of Pampamarca, Antonio Lopez de Sosa, had been close to Túpac Amaru since his childhood. The Inca's father died when he was quite young and Lopez de Sosa became not only his first teacher but, in the absence of young José Gabriel's father, a surrogate parent. It was most likely Lopez de Sosa who had actively promoted Túpac Amaru's entrance into San Francisco de Borja, the Jesuit school for kurakas' sons in Cuzco. This school was part of the colonial project to acculturate and educate the indigenous elite and the future Inca learned Latin as well as Spanish to complement the Quechua of his home and people. Lopez de Sosa also performed the marriage ceremony joining Túpac Amaru to Micaela Bastidas in May 1760. After the rebellion, relatives of Túpac Amaru claimed that it was Lopez de Sosa who had encouraged the rebellion by reading the kuraka's family tree to him and urging him not to tolerate bad treatment by corregidors. One of the relatives even declared that "the entire affair was the priest's fault, and that he should be punished for his sins." These priests— Lopez de Sosa and Yepes—were not the only Catholic officials to support Túpac Amaru. There were at least eighteen priests in the nearby region who aided the rebellion.[29] Having these Christians visible within the movement lent credibility and sacredness to Túpac Amaru and to the insurgency.

Although the Inca and most of his followers thought of themselves as Christian, not all the rebels shared these convictions. Some elements within the insurrection committed acts that were designed to offend Christian sensibilities or demonstrate the weakness of Christian divinities and thereby manifest the strength of Andean gods. This is similar to what those who wished to restore the Andean world had done in the Taki Onqoy movement a couple of decades after the Spaniards arrival in Tawantinsuyu in the sixteenth century. In the Taki Onqoy upheaval indigenous people claimed to have been filled with the spirit of Andean gods and argued that in order to triumph over the invaders they had to drive out all things European. During the Túpac Amaru rebellion some of his more radicalized followers sought goals parallel to those of the Taki Onqoy movement. In Calca, located in the Yucay Valley not far from Cuzco, rebels in the 1780 uprising gave no quarter to men, women, or children of European descent. One mestizo rebel killed a European woman, her husband, and children in a church. Having finished with the slaughter, the perpetrator, still in the church, violated the woman's corpse. The location and brutality of these acts appears to have been a challenge to, or defiance of, European Christian religion and an assertion of the power of the rebels and their beliefs over those of the Christians. In another instance, also in Calca, two Spanish brothers "were killed, their blood and hearts were consumed, their tongues cut off and their eyes pierced." Such mutilations, in keeping with ancient Andean ritual practices and punishments, were designed to either appropriate the power of the enemy or demonstrate their relative weakness next to the power of the rebels and their gods. Likewise, rebels in the region of Caylloma challenged Christian power. While killing Spaniards who had taken refuge in a church, they cried out that the "time of mercy is finished, there are no Sacraments nor God with any power."[30]

Cuzco was not the only region to rise in rebellion in 1780, and Túpac Amaru was not the only person to lead an insurrection. In the region near what is now Sucre, Bolivia, various members of the Catari (also Katari) family—Tomás, Nicolás, and Dámaso—led forces that challenged kurakas who were not serving the interests of the communities they governed, as well as attacking Spanish authorities and residents. Near modern-day La Paz, Bolivia, another rebel leader, Julián Apasa, was also in rebellion. He decided to augment his revolutionary credentials and appeal by linking himself to both the Túpac Amaru and Catari movements through his name, which he changed to Túpac Catari. The Túpac Catari rebels determined that certain Spaniards and Indians were outside the Andean (syncretic) Christian fold. As representatives of non-Christian forces these "enemies" were open to attack. In the Lake Titicaca community of Copacabana, royalist Spaniards who had been killed in the hostilities were said to be "excommunicated" or "demons." These dead, in keeping with Andean tradition for the treatment of criminals who violated standards of conduct, were left exposed rather than interred. The unburied dead could not regenerate, could not be reborn, unlike Túpac Amaru I or the Atahualpa of Guamán Poma's drawings. The offending, unburied Spaniards would never return.[31]

In other instances enemies were ritually mutilated. Some were beheaded, their blood drunk, their hearts removed, or their bodies dismembered. In the community of Juli, located on the shores of Lake Titicaca, royalist forces encountered numerous dead including the bodies of two caciques who had remained loyal to the Spanish, "their heads in gallows and their hearts extracted." Likewise, "the corpse of a cacique's wife was without blood, supposedly drunk by the rebels, according to the testimony gathered by the Spanish"[32] Whether these were acts of syncretic Christians against those determined to be un-Christian, or whether they were assertions of Andean religious authority over Christians or defeated enemies, is unclear, but they were part of the religious war that was fought by the forces of Túpac Amaru against the Spanish Christians and others considered foes.

In the first weeks of the rebellion a faction of Túpac Amaru's insurgent army questioned the need for Christian priests in their ranks. They told the Inca, "Thou art our God and Master and we beg thee that there be no [Catholic] priests from now on, molesting us." The Inca responded that this was not possible for "who would absolve us in the matter of death." For Túpac Amaru, Christian priests were necessary for the sacred duty of seeing his followers into the afterlife. Likewise, in Túpac Catari's forces in Bolivia, mass was held daily. In one instance Catarista rebels who did not demonstrate proper veneration for Our Lady of Copacabana were executed by their own people.[33]

At times the complex, syncretic nature of the rebels' Catholicism seemed to undermine the most basic of Christian beliefs, while still maintaining Catholic forms. For instance, Túpac Amaru was reported to have informed his troops on the eve of battle that only those who did not invoke the name of Jesus or confess before dying in battle would be resurrected after three days. In Puno a priest seemed to confirm that some rebels had turned from Christianity by observing that Indian rebels died "without taking unto their lips the Lord's sweet name."[34] Jan Szeminski argues that the "rebels believed that [with the rebellion] something changed in religion, some divinities lost their power, others gained. It seems that for the rebels the presence of an Inca precluded the presence, or power in Peru, of Spaniards and of Jesus."[35]

The Inca's legitimacy rested, in part, on his religious authority, Christian and otherwise, and he did much to enhance this authority before and during the rebellion. He and other rebel leaders, such as his cousin (sometimes referred to as his brother) Diego Cristóbal Túpac Amaru, presented themselves, and their followers, as the true Christians. The Inca, hinting at an afterlife, indicated that his followers who died "would have their reward." They, in turn, imbued him with "the power to raise the dead."[36] In the Quispicanchis community of Guaro, he informed the rebel army and the community that until then "they had not known God, nor had they understood who He is, because they have respected as God the corregidores, thieves, and the priests, but he was going to remedy this."[37]

Túpac Amaru and other rebel leaders also appealed to Andean religious tradition. To convey their messages and arouse their followers, they sometimes chose to speak at *huacas*, Andean religious shrines. When he could, such as after capturing the textile factory (*obraje*) in Pomacanchis (Quispicanchis, Cuzco), Túpac Amaru distributed cloth. While this may seem to be just part of the spoils of war, in the Inca realm woven items were highly regarded and weavings were used by the Inca to reward his followers, cement relationships, and demonstrate his power and largesse.[38] The syncretic nature of belief also manifested itself in the use of cemeteries, of both Christian and Andean importance, to persuade people to join the rebellion out of obligation to their ancestors, ancestor worship being a significant aspect in traditional Inca religion.[39] Thus, the Inca from Canas y Canchis drew on both Andean and Christian belief systems, and the syncretic mixture of these systems, to strengthen his position as leader. This allowed those who preferred to hear the Christian message to hear it, while those who sought Andean roots also could find inspiration in the Inca's words and actions.

Szeminski argues that for Indians who had awaited the return of the Inca, albeit a Christianized Inca, who would establish a new order, Túpac Amaru's arrival presented serious concerns.

The news that an Inca had reappeared obliged every Runa (person) to decide whether this was the Inca for whom everybody was waiting. If he was the Inca, everyone's duty was to follow him and kill the Spaniards, because the . . . [pachacuti], the cataclysm, had come, and the Spaniards' time was up. If, however, he was a false Inca, one should kill him and his followers, because the Spaniards' time would continue. In both cases, the chosen course of action was a religious duty.[40]

Certainly not all naturales saw Túpac Amaru as a Christian leader, nor the rebel army as "tramping out the vintage" of the Christian God. The bishop of Cuzco even reported that among Indians loyal to the crown there were those who did not loot the battlefield after an engagement because the dead rebels were excommunicated, outside the Christian fold, and therefore their possessions were believed to be tainted like their owners.[41] Both insurgents and royalists considered their work to be that of God. Thus, to a very great extent "the war between the Inca and his enemies was a war among Christians who accused one another of heresy and rebellion."[42]

The upheaval, however, also had very real causes based in economics and exploitation, as well as spiritual and governmental concerns, that had turned the world upside down. The rebel leader's actions in initiating the rebellion clearly demonstrated this. He executed Corregidor Arriaga and took funds that the Spanish had extracted from the people of Canas y Canchis through tribute. In Túpac Amaru's siege of Cuzco during the rebellion, in which he tried to avoid destroying the city or creating a situation in which his followers might wreak a terrible revenge upon the Spaniards, he wrote to the city council, explaining who he was and what were his motives.

Mine is the only blood that has come down from the Incas. the sovereigns of this realm. This has prompted me to seek by all possible means an end to abuses . . . against the unfortunate Indians and other persons, and against the provisions of the very kings of Spain, whose [beneficial] laws I know from experience have been suppressed and ignored . . . ever since the conquest here. . . . This is so notorious that I need no further proof than the tears that have flowed for three centuries from the eyes of my unhappy people. . . .

> My desire is that this type of official [*corregidor*, etc.] be
> abolished entirely; that their *repartimientos* [monopolies and
> extortions] shall cease; that in each province there shall be
> a chief magistrate [chosen] from the Indian nation itself
> [and] that in this city a Royal Audience be established with
> a resident viceroy presiding, so that the Indians may have
> ready access and recourse. That is the whole of my enter-
> prise for now.[43]

Despite the tremendous upheaval and massive mobilization of
indigenous people who supported the Inca and the thousands upon
thousands of deaths, neither the Cataris, Túpac Catari, nor Túpac
Amaru succeeded in wresting control from the Spanish. Their insur-
rections did not evolve into the cleansing pachacuti that would restore
the proper order of the world. The Andean highlands were not to be
ruled with justice and harmony by an Inca Empire that had been
"utopianized" in colonial indigenous dreams, as they were forced to
endure centuries of subjugation to and exploitation by Spaniards.

In their costly victory, the Spanish determined never to let such a
rebellion occur again. Having captured Túpac Amaru, they settled on
a brutal policy of annihilation against the Inca, his immediate kin, and
other rebel leaders. Given the vital importance of family in the
Andean world, it was only natural that when the rebel leader needed
people he could trust implicitly he had looked to his relatives. Thus,
many of Túpac Amaru's family were in the inner circle of the rebellion. His wife, Micaela Bastidas, enjoyed respect and a position of
leadership within the movement, man and wife being a unit and com-
plementing one another in Andean society. Her status was not just
ascribed, however, it was also achieved. Her competency expanded
her role in the course of the rebellion. She shared many of her husband's responsibilities and exercised sweeping authority on her own.
For her participation Micaela Bastidas, like much of the rest of the
family who were implicated in the insurrection, was to pay with her
life. She, like Túpac Amaru, was not only to be executed, but also dismembered. The body parts of several of the rebels were to be displayed throughout the region as a gruesome reminder and threat to
other potential rebels.

On May 18, 1781, the executions were carried out in the central
plaza of Cuzco where the first Túpac Amaru's head had been severed
from his body two centuries earlier. During the torture suffered by

Túpac Amaru before being executed, the Spanish had even dislocated the rebel leader's arm in an effort to get him to talk, but he would not. On the day of the executions the prisoners were confessed, heard mass, and were given communion.

> [Then] militiamen, armed with daggers and side arms, surrounded the large plaza; and the four sides of the gallows were circled by a body of mulattoes and soldiers from Huamanga, all having guns and fixed bayonets. Nine persons were to be put to death on that day: José Berdejo, a Spaniard and son-in-law of Francisco Noguera, the Inca's commander; Andrés Castelo, a captain; Antonio Oblitas, the Zambo who hanged Corregidor Arriaga in Tinta; Antonio Bastidas, a brother-in-law of Túpac Amaru; Francisco Túpac Amaru, an uncle; Hipólito Túpac Amaru, the twenty-year-old son of the Inca; Tomasa Titu Condemayta; Micaela Bastidas, the Inca's wife; and José Gabriel Túpac Amaru himself.
>
> All the prisoners wore handcuffs and fetters and came out at one time, one behind the other. They were put in sacks and dragged along the ground tied to the tails of horses. All were heavily guarded and accompanied by priests, who comforted them as they approached the foot of the gallows, where two executioners awaited them. Berdejo, Castelo, Oblitas and Bastidas were simply hanged. Francisco Túpac Amaru, a man almost eighty years old, and Hipólito had their tongues cut out before being hanged. The Indian woman Tomasa was garroted, or strangled with an iron collar or screw, mounted on a little platform with an iron wheel on it, never seen before in Cuzco. The Inca and his wife had to witness all these executions, and finally that of their oldest son. Then the Inca's wife, Micaela, dressed in the habit of the Order of Mercy, mounted the platform. Her tongue was to be cut out, but she refused to let the executioner do it; and so it was taken out after her death. She was also subjected to the garrote, but because she had a very small neck, the screw caused intense suffering without strangling her. The executioner then put a lasso around her neck and pulled it one way and another, all the while repeatedly striking her, until she died.

José Gabriel was then brought out to the center of the plaza. There the executioner cut out his tongue and threw him on the ground face down. He tied his hands and feet with four cords, fastened these to the girths of four horses, which four mestizos then drove in the four directions. Either the horses were weak or the Inca unusually strong, for he was not immediately torn to pieces, but remained suspended in mid-air, spider-like, for some time while the horses strained to pull him apart. The hard-hearted *visitador* [Areche] finally ordered the Inca's head cut off. At the same time he arrested the corregidor of Cuzco and another official for not providing suitable horses. The Inca's body was dismembered, as were the bodies of his wife, son, and uncle. Only the heads were removed from the bodies of the remaining victims. . . .

The Inca's youngest son, Fernando, a nine-year-old child, was exempted from capital punishment. With a chain on his foot and guarded by four soldiers, he was taken to the foot of the gallows and forced to witness the cruel deaths of his parents. His heart-rending shrieks resounded for a long time in the ears of the people who heard them. . . .[44]

The trunks of the mutilated bodies of the Inca and his wife were taken to the height of Picchu [mountain above Cuzco]. There they were thrown into a bonfire and reduced to ashes, which were scattered into the air and cast into the Huatanay River. The rest of the gruesome sentence was carried out to the letter. Hipólito's head was sent to Tungasuca, and his limbs were scattered in different places. Francisco's head was taken to Pilpinto, one leg to Carabaya, the other to Puno, and an arm to Paruro.[45]

His [Túpac Amaru's] head was to be sent to Tinta and kept on a gallows for three days and then put on a post at the entrance of the town. The same thing was to be done with one of his arms in Tungasuca, and the other arm would be exhibited in the province of Carabaya. One leg was to be sent to Livitaca in the province of Chumbivilcas, and the other to Santa Rosa in the province of Lampa. His houses were to be demolished completely and the sites publicly salted.[46]

The grisly executions did not end the insurrection. The rebellion, now led by Diego Cristóbal Túpac Amaru, continued until 1783 when he and his family signed a peace agreement and were pardoned. However, they soon fell afoul of Spanish "justice" and were brutally executed. Diego's mother was sentenced to be hanged, quartered, and burnt before his eyes. Diego himself had "pieces of his flesh torn off with red hot tongs" before being killed. To further disperse and weaken the family some ninety kin were taken to Lima in chains. One colonial official commented, "Neither the King nor the state thought it fitting that a seed or branch of the family should remain, or the commotion and impression that the wicked name of Túpac Amaru caused among the natives."[47]

Even the young Fernando, Túpac Amaru's son who had seen his parents and relatives executed before his very eyes, was exiled to Spain. Several died in a shipwreck off the coast of Iberia. Fernando and the others were made to live out their lives far away from their mountain gods and from the land where the Incas were revered and the name Túpac Amaru reverberated with hope for large segments of indigenous society.

The Spanish took no chances. They "cleansed," in the modern political sense of the term, the Andes of the Incas and their memory. Efforts were made to remove noble kurakas from their positions and to extinguish the use of "Inca" as part of family names. The Spanish tried to destroy or proscribe clothing, paintings and other works of art, literature, and history—such as Garcilaso's book—that extolled the Incas. Even the conch shells, or *pututus*, used to call people together were made illegal. It was suggested that Quechua be done away with by teaching Spanish, just as the Incas had sought to eliminate local languages, although serious efforts were not made in most of the Andes to accomplish this linguistic "cleansing."[48]

However, memory of the Inca did not die so easily, especially the idea of Inkarrí. On the day of his execution even nature seemed to warn that the beheading of Túpac Amaru was not to bring the closure the Spanish were seeking. One Spanish witness noted:

> Some things took place which seem to have been wrought by the Devil to confirm these Indians in their errors, omens, and superstitions. I say this because although it was a very dry time of year with fine days, that day dawned so overcast that the face of the sun was hidden . . . and at noon, when

the horses were stretching the Indian, a great squall of wind arose and then a downpour so fierce that everyone—even the guards—ran for cover. For this reason the Indians declare that heaven and the elements grieved at the death of the Inca.[49]

Like no other figure from the colonial past, Túpac Amaru lives on in the consciousness of many modern-day Peruvians, even if some of them—such as those who have benefited from the world as it is—do not always welcome his presence. Likewise, the idea of the rebirth or the regeneration of an Andean utopia, often rooted in a belief in Inca justice and social policy, is still a topic of conversation. Peruvians still struggle to achieve the all-too-elusive "good government" that Guamán Poma had desired and a more equitable, harmonious way of existing together. Sometimes this takes the form of Inkarrí, more often while the roots may have been with Inkarrí, the Inca and his rebirth remain more vague.

In modern accounts of Andean rebirth and regeneration there are tales of the children of the Inca—Inkarrí—returning in a manner that has a finality for Andean struggle, "Where can Inca's two sons be today? It is said that when the elder son is grown he will come back. And when he returns that will be *Punchaw Usiu*, the Last Day."[50] Another account, while seemingly more full of despair, may actually have great resonance for modern Peru.

There used to be gringos who . . . were slaves of Inkarí, and they worked without rest under his orders. But Inkarí was a good man. They say he governed the whole world: Huancayo, Cusco, the whole earth. And they say he built works so the water would stay on the heights.

In those days, because he did not wish it, nothing was baptized, nobody was baptized. The people didn't live in valley towns but up high in stone houses, to which the water came by the works of Inkarí.

Inkarí built Cusco . . . and there he lived, in a great and beautiful city all of stone. The whole world came to his palace, where he discussed and ordered everything.

When Inkarí and his people . . . died, they went down into the underworld; and the water descended to the low-lands, and was baptized.

The houses in the hills have no water anymore, only the stones remain.[51]

In the last couple of decades indigenous people have left, or fled, the sierra in tremendous numbers to escape the poverty, violence, and drought that has made life so extraordinarily difficult. They are reconstituting a new social order on the coast in which they increasingly have a say in national life. They have gone to where the water went, the coastal lowlands. They are making the water—the symbol of the life force of their world—their own as if Inkarrí had understood the future. To this point, however, there are no obvious indications of the Inca's body—symbolic or real—regenerating.

However, the image and symbolism of Túpac Amaru, far from disappearing as the Spanish had hoped, has been resurrected in the last few decades. The Left-leaning, reformist military government of Juan Velasco in the late 1960s and early 1970s, and the bicentennial of the rebellion, brought the Inca leader front and center in public consciousness. The government of Velasco used the image of Túpac Amaru in a way that equated the Inca with hopes for social and economic justice, and Quechua was even made an official language of Peru. Indeed, the plan for the 1968 coup and the government to follow was known as "Plan Inca."[52] Túpac Amaru became the military government's symbol of concern for, and action on behalf of, ordinary and poor Peruvians. To inaugurate his agrarian-reform program, General Velasco harkened back to the rebellion of 1780 and, using the words of Diego Cristóbal Túpac Amaru, vowed that "no longer shall the landlord feast on your poverty!"[53] But the Velasco government could not carry through on its hopes and promises and opposition in traditional sectors of power, including the military, saw to it that Velasco was removed from office. So while the Inca did return—if just through images and slogans—this rebirth once again did not result in the reign of Inkarrí.

Others were also aware of the history of the eighteenth-century Inca rebel and Andean utopian dreams. In the Río de La Plata region rebels took up arms under the name Tupamaros as they challenged the entrenched rulers of society in the 1960s and 1970s. In Peru, on May 18, 1980, a then little-known armed movement named Sendero Luminoso (Shining Path) made its first dramatic appearance on the Peruvian stage by destroying election results in the rural Andean community of Chuschi. The selected day, May 18, was the 199th anniversary of the execution of Túpac Amaru. The struggle between Sendero Luminoso and the government killed thousands, mainly indigenous peoples in the Andes who seemingly were supposed to be the beneficiaries, not the victims, of this insurgency. There was cataclysm as the brutal killing increased and thousands fled their Andean homes for refuge in provincial and coastal cities, but this too was far from a cleansing pachacuti that would reorder the world. It just brought more death and destruction. Another Peruvian revolutionary group took the name of Túpac Amaru—Movimiento Revolucionario Túpac Amaru (MRTA)—and contested for the hearts and minds of poor Peruvians and those others who dreamed of a more equitable world. Its goals were more in line with ideas of social justice, but it made little progress in a world already torn apart, like Túpac Amaru's body, by the brutal struggles of Sendero and the state.

Bolivia, too, still feels the impact of 1780. In October 2003 Aymara peoples, many with ties to the Katarista political movement or its ideas, laid siege to La Paz just as Túpac Catari had done in the early 1780s, and President Sanchez de Lozada was forced to resign. The Katarista party was organized in Ayoayo, the birthplace of Túpac Katari. An early segment of this political movement called itself the Fifteenth of November Movement in commemoration of the date Túpac Catari was executed.[54] The Bolivian scholar Xavier Albó wrote, reflecting on the history of his country over a decade before the events of 2003, "We have arrived at the final stretch of the great arc: from the Kataristas of 1980 to the Katari of 1780. It is evident that the Katari/Katarista nexus, spanning across two hundred years, has an ideological element: a unifying and mobilizing historical memory.[55] (See Illustration 2.4.)

As the new millennium begins a person of indigenous and Andean descent has been elected president of Peru and his wife, an European-born anthropologist, even invokes the images of the mountain gods, the apus. While listening to the president talk people may even sip on an Inca Kola (see Illustration 2.5). But times remain very difficult in Peru. The president, whose name is Toledo like the viceroy who executed the first Túpac Amaru, is struggling under the weight of office, the accumulated problems of an unequal, unjust society, and vicious, grinding poverty in a time of great economic difficulty. The heritage of the Inca, a sense of irony, and widespread doubts among Peruvians of all classes about the new president's capacity to govern much of Peru seems to share, are expressed in a

2.4   *Photo taken in Sucre, Bolivia, in 1992, showing a government poster stating "three years of peace, stability, and progress." Below this someone commenting on indigenous perspectives has painted "500 years of 'caca'" (Photo: Ward Stavig).*

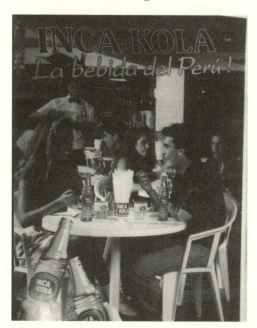

2.5   *Use of the term Inca is common in advertising and speech. Here a soft drink labeled "the drink of Peru" is named Inca Kola (Photo: Ward Stavig).*

political cartoon I saw in Peru. In this cartoon a journalist says to President Toledo that he has entered office like the Inca Pachacutec, that is to say, in triumph, and the journalist asks the president what he wants. Toledo, dressed as an Inca, answers that he does not want to leave office like Atahualpa (meaning dead). For now, at least, it seems that Inkarrí sleeps.

Notes

Parts of this chapter come from Ward Stavig, "Rebellion, Cultural Redemption, and Thupa Amaro," in *The World of Túpac Amaru: Conflict, Community, and Identity in Colonial Peru* (Lincoln: University of Nebraska Press, 1999). I wish to thank Lyman Johnson for his many fine suggestions.

1. John Hemming, *The Conquest of the Incas* (New York: Harcourt Brace Jovanovich, Inc., 1970), 448–49. Hemming cites several different colonial sources for his information and quotes, especially Martín de Murúa, *Historia general del Perú, Orígen y descendencia de los Incas* (1590–1611), ed. Manuel Ballesteros-Gaibrois, 2 vols. (Madrid: 1962, 1964); and Gabriel de Oviedo, "Relación de lo que subcedio en la ciudad del Cuzco cerca de los conciertos y horden que su Magestad mandó asentar con el Inca Titu Cuxi Yopanqui (1573)," in "Inédito sobre el primer Túpac Amaru," by C. A. Romero, *Revista Historica* 2 (Lima: 1907): 66–73.

2. Hemming, *Conquest*, 448–49.

3. Ibid., 449–50.

4. Ibid., 448.

5. Ronald Wright, *Stolen Continents. The "New World" Through Indian Eyes* (Boston and New York: Houghton Mifflin Company, 1992), 187.

6. *The Peru Reader: History, Culture, Politics*, ed. Orin Storn, Carlos Iván Degregori, and Robin Kirk (Durham, NC, and London: Duke University Press, 1995), 50.

7. Wright, *Stolen Continents*, 188–89.

8. Garcilaso de la Vega, "The Village Basis of Inca Society," in *Readings in Latin American Civilization: 1492 to the Present*, ed. Benjamin Keen, 2nd ed. (Boston: Houghton Mifflin Company), 30–31.

9. Alberto Flores Galindo, "In Search of an Inca," in *Resistance, Rebellion, and Consciousness in the Andean Peasant World, Eighteenth to Twentieth Centuries*, ed. Steve J. Stern (Madison: University of Wisconsin Press, 1987), 194–95, 202.

10. Rolena Adorno, *Guamán Poma: Writing and Resistance in Colonial Peru* (Austin: University of Texas Press, 1986), 61.

11. Adorno, *Guamán Poma*, 25–26.

12. Alberto Flores Galindo, *Buscando un Inca: Identidad y utopía en los Andes* (Lima: Instituto de Apoyo Agrario, 1987), 50–51.

13. Flores Galindo, *Buscando un Inca*, 67–68. Some paintings and other art work such as drinking vessels (*queros*) depicting the beheading of Atahualpa still exist. One has to suppose that many such artifacts and other things related to the rebellion were destroyed by the Spanish in the wake of 1780 in their effort to once and for all eradicated the Inca from indigenous memories.

14. Flores Galindo, *Buscando un Inca*, 49.

15. Flores Galindo argues that the term Inkarrí—from Inca and *rey* (king)—may have come from the time of Titu Cusi, heir to the Inca throne, who was in contact with nonindigenous peoples as well and who was to become Inca to the indigenous and rey to the mestizos. He also cites Franlin Pease as suggesting that the idea of Inkarrí began to spread in the early seventeenth century (*El Dios creador andino* [Lima: Mosca Azul, 1973], 50–51).

16. Flores Galindo, *Buscando un Inca*, 58–59.

17. Alberto Flores Galindo, *Europea y el país de los Incas: La utopía andina* (Lima: Instituto de Apoyo Agrario, 1986), 50, 67.

18. Wright, *Stolen Continents*, 279–80. Wright cites José María Arguedas and Alejandro Ortiz Rescaniere, "Tres Versiones del Mito de Inkarrí," in *Ideología Mesiánica del Mundo Andino*, ed. Juam M. Ossio (Lima: Ignacio Prado Pastor, 1973), 217–36. There are different accepted spellings of Inkarrí such as *Inkarí, Inkarri, Rey Inka*. Thus, the spelling in the quote is different and the author also did not italicize.

19. Flores Galindo, *Buscando un Inca*, 63–64.

20. Ibid.

21. Steve Stern, "The Age of Andean Insurrection, 1742–1782," in *Resistance, Rebellion, and Consciousness in the Andean Peasant World, 18th to 20th Centuries*, ed. Steve Stern (Madison: University of Wisconsin Press, 1987), 53.

22. Stern, "Age of Andean Insurrection," 55.

23. Ibid., 54.

24. Colección Documental de del Bicentenario de la Revolución Emancipadora de Túpac Amaru. Vol. 1, tomo V, no. 119, pp. 384–85. Copy of a chapter from the diary of Arequipa, dated January 4, 1781 [Copia de capitulo de un diario de Arequipa de 4 de enero de 1781].

25. Jan Szemi?ski, "Why Kill the Spaniard? New Perspectives on Andean Insurrectionary Ideology in the 18th Century," in *Resistance, Rebellion, and Consciousness in the Andean Peasant World, Eighteenth to Twentieth Centuries*, ed. Steve J. Stern (Madison: University of Wisconsin Press, 1987), 173.

26. Leon Campbell, "Ideology and Factionalism," in *Resistance, Rebellion, and Consciousness in the Andean Peasant World, Eighteenth to Twentieth Centuries*, ed. Steve J. Stern (Madison: University of Wisconsin Press, 1987), 116; Szeminski, "Why Kill the Spaniard?" 177.

27. Lillian Estelle Fisher, *The Last Inca Revolt, 1780–1783* (Norman: University of Oklahoma Press, 1966), 104.

28. Juan José Vega, "Los sacerdotes que lucharon por la patria," *La Republica*, "Domingo," Feb. 12, 1984, 4.

29. Scarlett O'Phelan Godoy, *Rebellion and Revolts in Eighteenth-Century Peru and Upper Peru* (Cologne, Germany: Bohlau Verlag, 1985), 225; Vega, "Sacerdotes que lucharon por la patria," 2–7.

30. Jan Szeminski, *La Utopia Tupamarista* (Lima: Pontificia Universidad Católica de Peru, Fondo Cultural, 1984), 19; Szeminski, "Why Kill the Spaniard?" 169.

31. Szeminski, "Why Kill the Spaniard?" 170; See also Jorge Hildalgo Lehuede, "Amarus y cataris: Aspectos mesiánicos de la rebelión indígena de 1781 en Cusco, Chayanta, La Paz y Arica," *Chungará* (Arica) 10 (March 1983): 117–38. In Chiapas during the Tzeltal revolt, Indians also saw themselves as the true Christians. See works by Robert Wasserstrom, "Ethnic Violence and Indigenous Protest: The Tzeltal (Maya) Rebellion of 1712," *Journal of Latin American Studies* 12 (1980): 1–19; and Kevin Gosner, *Soldiers of the Virgin: The Moral Economy of a Maya Rebellion* (Tucson: University of Arizona Press, 1992).

32. Szeminski, "Why Kill the Spaniard?" 170.

33. Ibid., 176–78.

34. Ibid., 177–78.

35. Ibid., 179.

36. Campbell, "Ideology and Factionalism," 126.

37. Szeminski, "Why Kill the Spaniard?" 168.

38. John Murra, "Cloth and Its Function in the Inca State," *American Anthropologist* 64 (1962).

39. Fisher, *Last Inca Revolt*, 95–96; Campbell, "Ideology and Factionalism," 126.

40. Szeminski, "Why Kill the Spaniard?" 190.

41. Ibid., 178.
42. Ibid., 191.
43. Wright, *Stolen Continents*, 197. The translation is by Wright. I have used it so that others may easily check sources. The letter was reproduced from Boleslao Lewin, *La rebelión de Túpac Amaru y las orígines de la emancipación americana* (Buenos Aires: Hachette, 1957), 464–65.
44. Fisher, *Last Inca Revolt*, 236–38.
45. Ibid., 237.
46. Ibid., 223.
47. Ibid., 379.
48. *Peru Reader*, "All Must Die," 157–61. Also see John Rowe, "El movimiento nacional inca del siglo XVIII," in *Túpac Amaru*, ed. Alberto Flores Galindo (Lima: Retablo de Papel Editores, 1976), 35–36.
49. Lewin, *Rebelión de Túpac Amaru*, 497–98.
50. Wright, *Stolen Continents*, 288.
51. Ibid., 282.
52. Abraham Lowenthal, "Peru's Ambiguous Revolution," in *The Peruvian Military Experiment: Continuity and Change under Military Rule*, ed. Abraham Lowenthal (Princeton, NJ: Princeton University Press, 1975), 33.
53. Wright, *Stolen Continents*, 285; Lowenthal, "Peru's Ambiguous Revolution," 37: Vega, "Sacerdotes que Lucharon por la Patria," 6.
54. Xavier Albó, "From MNRistas to Kataristas to Katari," in *Resistance, Rebellion, and Consciousness in the Andean Peasant World, 18th to 20th Centuries*, ed. Steve Stern (Madison: University of Wisconsin Press, 1987), 391.
55. Albó, "MNRistas to Kataristas," 412.

Chapter Three

Death's Patriots—Celebration, Denunciation, and Memories of Mexico's Independence Heroes:

Miguel Hidalgo, José María Morelos, and Agustín de Iturbide

Christon I. Archer

F ollowing months of incarceration in Chihuahua and fully aware that death would be his only avenue of escape, Father Miguel Hidalgo y Costilla (1753–1811) (see Illustration 3.1) received his sentence with resignation and a spirit of tranquility.[1] He had been insulted and abused by his royalist captors; stripped of his priestly rank, position, and clerical attire; and isolated from his friends and supporters. Rising before dawn on July 30, 1811, he ate a good break- fast, though he chided his guards for offering him a smaller-than- normal portion of milk.[2] Just because he was about to be killed, he saw no reason why they should provide him less than his normal serv- ing. Escorted from his cramped cell to the barren execution ground, Hidalgo talked with his guards and even distributed candies to the restless and uncomfortable soldiers who were to form his firing squad.[3] His status as a priest saved him from an even more dreadful, humiliating, and painful execution. After forming the firing squad, Hidalgo's guards blindfolded him and on command of *fuego*, large cal- iber musket balls slashed through his chest.

Even after Hidalgo was dead, the royalists were not content to grant him a peaceful burial. Enraged royalists proposed to make a spe- cial example of him. On orders, a soldier hacked off his head with a

3.1   *Father Miguel Hidalgo y Costilla (N. L. Benson Collection, University of Texas at Austin).*

machete for shipment and exhibition in the towns that initiated his rebellion.[4] They buried the rest of Hidalgo's corpse in a common grave. It remained there until 1824 when the new federal republic of Mexico brought his bones to Mexico City to venerate his life and to celebrate Independence Day on September 16, the day in 1810 that Hidalgo issued his epochal *grito* (cry) of Dolores. From this point forward, Father Hidalgo ceased to be a mere mortal and became a shining symbol and example for the new republic.

At the time of his death neither Hidalgo nor anyone else could have imagined that he would become a heroic icon whose statues, paintings, and murals would grace the walls of the Palacio Nacional in Mexico City and many other public buildings throughout the nation. Even in rural schools in the smallest of villages, Father Hidalgo—so controversial in life—became the great patriot, teacher, and guide.

Three Trials, Three Executions, Three Resurrections

It is important to follow first Hidalgo and then two other liberation leaders—José Maria Morelos and Agustín de Iturbide—in their lives and deaths to understand how these three key men of the independence epoch each underwent a gradual transformation from a discredited leader to a heroic symbol for a new nation.

Cura Miguel Hidalgo: Padre de la Patria

Following the disastrous Battle of Calderón near Guadalajara, during the retreat north and theoretically into the United States, the insurgent army commander Ignacio Allende deposed Hidalgo and left him powerless.[5] On March 21, 1811, in what was a quite audacious operation, the royalists baited a trap along the road by pretending to act as an insurgent honor guard. They disarmed and detained the rebel rear guard without violence, captured a picket force of sixty soldiers, and then overcame scattered resistance from the caravan of fifteen coaches that conveyed the insurgent hierarchy, their wives, and families. Allende attempted to fight but drew a hail of musket fire that killed his son. Father Hidalgo riding in the last coach some distance behind the others—the most valuable of all prizes—fell into royalist hands without firing a shot (see Illustration 3.2).[6] Caught by surprise, the main insurgent force of fifteen hundred troops that followed some distance behind the leadership either surrendered or fled. In a few minutes, royalist Indian lancers, including many Lipan Apache warriors, captured twenty-four cannon of different caliber, three mortars, and half a million pesos in coin and silver bars. They rounded up a total of 893 prisoners and either shot or ran through about forty insurgents who attempted to resist.[7]

The royalist troops escorted the caravan of insurgent prisoners to the town of Monclova were they were thrown into a squalid prison without sufficient food or water. Couriers raced south with the news that Hidalgo and his chief officers had been captured. In Mexico City, Viceroy Francisco Javier Venegas ordered church bells rung, artillery salvoes, and displays of fireworks that had been banned during wartime. In the meantime, the royalists moved Hidalgo and the most senior insurgent military leaders to Chihuahua, headquarters of Brigadier Nemesio Salcedo, comandante general of the Provincia Internas.[8] There, Salcedo set up a military commission headed by Angel Abella,

3.2   *The capture of Father Miguel Hidalgo in a royalist ambush, March 21, 1811 (N. L. Benson Collection, University of Texas at Austin).*

a peninsular Spaniard who had recently escaped death at the hands of the rebels, and in normal life was the chief administrator of the mail service at Zacatecas.[9] Needless to say, Abella was less than friendly toward the rebel leaders and toward Hidalgo in particular.[10]

Even before the military trials commenced, any solidarity among the insurgent leadership dissolved as Field Marshall Mariano Abasalo and others sought means to evade execution. Abasalo blamed Hidalgo for forcing him into the rebellion and took great pains to illustrate how during the insurrection he had saved many European Spaniards from certain execution. He implicated a number of less-well-known insurgent chiefs who on his evidence suffered execution by being shot in the back by royalist firing squads. Not withstanding defense arguments, the *consejo de guerra* (court martial) made short work of the insurgent generals, marshals, brigadiers, colonels, administrators, and professional bureaucrats, sentencing many to death by firing squad as traitors with attendant confiscation of their possessions and property. Those judged guilty of lesser offenses received lengthy sentences to hard labor in frontier presidios. Abasalo saved himself temporarily, but he perished from disease while locked up at Santa Catalina Castle at Cádiz in Spain.[11] The military court condemned to death six ecclesiastics captured with the insurgents, but the local bishop, Francisco Gabriel de Olivares, refused to defrock them. Despite his intervention, a year later at Durango, on July 17, 1812, soldiers escorted these prisoners in secret to a nearby hacienda where all of them were shot in the back by a firing squad.[12]

Because of his role as *exgeneralísimo* and his clerical *fuero* (privileged legal status), Hidalgo faced a rigorous two-track prosecution that dragged on well after the executions of Allende and the other major insurgent leaders. To begin with, Abella framed forty-two questions that Hidalgo responded to orally—some of his answers were in depth and others took up only a few sentences. Most certainly aware following the executions of his colleagues and associates that there could be only one possible verdict in his trial, Hidalgo made no effort to plead his innocence. He spoke clearly about his role and that of Allende, though regarding the initiation of revolution he described his associate as more active while he was much more passive. After the defeat at the Battle of Calderón, the two leaders had experienced a dramatic falling out. Finally, Allende removed Hidalgo from military command and stories circulated that he talked about poisoning his indecisive and muddled leader. For three days, May 7 to 9, 1811, Abella posed searching questions about Hidalgo's participation in the formative roots of the insurrection, attempting to learn about the major originators and seeking to illuminate the most egregious crimes committed by the rebels. The questions followed the brief period of insurrection from Dolores to Guanajuato, Valladolid (Morelia), Guadalajara, and finally to the flight of the insurgents to the north.[13]

Hidalgo admitted that he had assumed the rank of Captain General at Celaya. Though he claimed there were no formal orders, his officers addressed him as generalísimo, the political leaders *excelencia* and then *alteza* (highness) with others adding *serenísima* (serene highness). As might be expected, the military and ecclesiastical authorities focused on Hidalgo's use of the image of Nuestra Señora de Guadalupe and his refusal to submit to the commands of the Holy Tribunal of the Inquisition.[14] There were also questions raised about Hidalgo's role in the almost programmatic assassination of *gachupines* (European Spaniards) and some *criollos* (American-born Spaniards) without any form of trial or process. Hidalgo admitted that murders had taken place but insisted he had not been involved in the massacres at Guanajuato. At Valladolid, however, he accepted responsibility for the deaths of sixty gachupines and at Guadalajara where the total was close to 350 deaths.[15] There had been additional murders, but by that point Allende had taken command. Hidalgo recognized that these people had been executed without due process—removed secretly from the cities in the night to depopulated sites so the populace would not be aware of what was taking place. He claimed that the Indians and the lowest plebeian elements were the main proponents of the killings of gachupines.[16] Interrogated about the exact motives for the brutal assassinations and confiscation of property, Hidalgo agreed that these were the criminal acts committed by an army composed of Indians and the lowest social elements. However, the need for supporters for the revolutionary enterprise and the enthusiasm of plebeian elements prevented the insurgent leaders from having too many scruples about the means used to advance the cause.[17] In a word, the revolution and goal of independence transcended the means—fair or foul—required to reach the shining objective.

In the interrogation, Abella reflected the deep apprehension of all gachupines and criollos that the popular revolt came close to sweeping away the existing regime. The vortex of popular revolution—the power to overcome by the weight of numbers alone—presented a palpable danger for royalist leaders such as Félix Calleja and for all others who owned a stake in Novohispano (New Spain's) society. In confronting the symbolic Hidalgo and the instability of insurgent movements that followed, the royalists, including much of the criollo population, supported harsh counterinsurgency terror designed to kill popular aspirations as well as *cabecillas* (insurgent chiefs) and their *gavillas* (bands).

At some points, Hidalgo defended his actions effectively and at others he seemed to express remorse for the actions of those he had unleashed. Abella badgered him on several occasions about causing incalculable damage, destruction, and atrocities—particularly for having devoted such limited consideration to the consequences of his acts. Hidalgo defended himself by arguing that he believed the country to be in danger when Spain fell to the French. He insisted that any citizen had the right to act when the *patria* was at risk. Nevertheless, by the end of the interrogation and pained by the knowledge that many of his associates and comrades already had been dragged before royalist firing squads, Hidalgo expressed more remorse for what he had done and accepted responsibility. Following a harangue by Abella that summed up the terrible damages caused by the insurrection, Hidalgo recognized and confessed that the "enterprise" was unjust and impolitic. He admitted that the insurrection "has occasioned incalculable evils to religion, to customs, to the state in general, and particularly to America, to the degree that the wisest and most vigilant government will not be able to repair them for many years."[18]

Since the achievement of Mexican independence, the real meaning and depth of Hidalgo's remorse have been the subject for debate among historians. Confusing the issue further than the trial transcript at the Hospital Real in Chihuahua that most historians consider to be quite accurate, a manifesto dated May 18, 1811, attributed to Hidalgo and addressed to "Todo el Mundo" (Everyone) was a different matter. Claiming good provenance from Hidalgo in his prison cell at the Royal Hospital to Comandante General Nemesio Salcedo, the authorship of the document has been debated ever since it appeared on August 3, 1811, in the *Gaceta del Gobierno de México*. The manifesto carried with it signed certifications of authenticity from the Chihuahua religious authorities.[19] Alluding to the Prophet Jeremiah, who lamented the loss of his slain people, Hidalgo or much more likely an unidentified person writing without his knowledge, expressed enormous remorse, confessed his crimes, and abjured revolution. He called for insurgents everywhere in New Spain to throw down their weapons and to return to the Holy Mother Church, the king, and the royal government. He begged pardon for his excesses committed against religion and its ministers, expressing his horror at the bloodshed and the devastation that he wrought to the flourishing kingdom of New Spain. The writer lamented, "I see the destruction of this soil, that I have occasioned: the ruin of wealth that has been lost, the infinity of orphans whom I have left, the blood that with such profusion and temerity has been spilled, and that which I cannot say without feeling faint, the multitude of souls who for following me will be cast into the abyss of hell."[20]

As might be expected the conservative historian Lucas Alamán readily accepted the authenticity of Hidalgo's abjuration and recognition of the evils of his ways. Alamán was positive that no other hand except that of Hidalgo had been involved in the composition of the damning confession. He wished to erase the memory of Hidalgo and his anarchic attempt to attain the independence of Mexico. The curate of Dolores was someone to forget and not to celebrate. Alamán especially criticized the liberal historian Carlos María Bustamante for his effort to burnish Hidalgo's bloody reputation through concealing evidence that presented him in a bad light for abjuring his cause.[21]

Bustamante, of course, named Hidalgo in the title of his *Cuadro histórico de la Revolución Mexicana* as the founder and initiator of the independence epoch and the *padre de la independencia* (father of independence). Here was the embryo of the struggle between two political solitudes—liberal and conservative—that would be fought over and debated by politicians, journalists, historians, and the Mexican populace through the nineteenth century and in some respects up to the present.

As for the May 18, 1811, manifesto, the words did not appear to be at all like those of Hidalgo and the expressions failed to reflect his testimony just over a week before at the trial. If Hidalgo really abjured, it seems odd that the royalists did not make better use of the propaganda coup that such a confession would have produced.[22] By May 1811, the royalists had their hands full with proliferating insurgent bands that interdicted commerce and excelled at hit-and-run guerrilla-style warfare. Royalist commanders and administrators would have loved to propagate news of the abjuration of Hidalgo, the first and most evil of the cabecillas, and to use this information to appeal for a return of the former tranquility of New Spain.

With the evidence in hand, both the ecclesiastical and civil authorities moved to prepare final charges and to sentence Hidalgo for his multitudinous crimes. The court found him guilty of high treason and treacherous homicides committed in Valladolid and Guadalajara that were punishable by death and confiscation of his worldly possessions and properties. The auditor, Licenciado Rafael Bracho, recommended to Comandante General Salcedo that the method of execution must be the most ignominious that could be devised and even then no punishment could satisfy the thirst for public vengeance. He described Hidalgo as "the most atrocious of delinquents" and unworthy of any consideration. However, since he was also a priest, some reverence had to be shown to the church and its priests even when they were guilty of atrocious crimes. For lack of instruments in Chihuahua and of executioners who knew how to employ them, it was not possible to employ a garrote in his execution. On July 4, 1811, Bracho recommended that Hidalgo be shot by a firing squad at his prison or at some other location to be determined.[23]

The jurisdictional and communications delays between the ecclesiastical and civil authorities that kept Hidalgo alive longer than Allende and other senior insurgent leaders now ceased to save him. Between 6:00 and 7:00 A.M. on July 29, Hidalgo faced formal degradation under

Canon law. His sentence was read aloud, and he was made to suffer the ignominious and humiliating process of defrocking. Forced to kneel, as the sentence was read, he was stripped of his priestly ornaments and garments.[24] When this ceremony concluded, the ecclesiastical authorities turned him over to the civil power that already had sentenced him to death. On July 30, 1811, Hidalgo faced a royalist army firing squad (see Illustration 3.3).

In death, the legend of "the immortal Hidalgo" continued to grow. One of the greatest Hidalgo exponents, Carlos María Bustamante, took up and promoted the curate's cause as the initiator and immaculate symbol of national independence. As Bustamante proclaimed, "He [Hidalgo] raised the yoke from our necks" and overcame "the insupportable tyranny of the Spanish government and of those hated mandarins, who called the Americas 'Our Indies,' and its peoples 'Our Vassals.'"[25] Others such as Lorenzo de Zavala expressed similar admiration for Hidalgo but lamented the fact that his movement lacked organization and an underlying ideology. As Hidalgo himself had stated at his trial, Zavala commented, "Hidalgo worked without plan, without system, and without determined objectives." It was simply

3.3   *The execution of Father Miguel Hidalgo, Chihuahua, July 30, 1811.*
Note that the artist portrayed him incorrectly as being shot through the
back (N. L. Benson Collection, University of Texas at Austin).

not enough to raise the banner of the Virgen de Guadalupe and to "run from city to city with his people." In Zavala's opinion, the heroic Hidalgo needed to present the basis for a new social system, to organize and discipline his forces, and to avoid the horrors of assassinations and attacks directed against the European Spaniards and by association the criollo population. On the opposition side, Lucas Alamán and many other conservative Mexicans sought to denigrate Hidalgo's memory as a leader whose popular revolution stirred the popular classes to embrace chaos and a dangerous anarchy.

By October 1811, the preserved heads of Hidalgo and his commanders Ignacio de Allende, Juan de Aldama, and Mariano Jiménez had been shipped south to San Miguel for exhibition in the towns that they conquered and subsequently lost. However, the royalist commander Félix Calleja decided against exhibiting these trophies in the rebel towns of Dolores or San Miguel for fear that the remaining insurgent bands of the region might try to rescue and to venerate these remains.[26] As a consequence, the severed heads ended up on display in iron cages at the corners of the Guanajuato city granary (the *alhóndiga*) where they remained until 1821. The empty cages or more recently reconstructed facsimiles remain today hanging on the alhóndiga as powerful symbols of death and the horrors of the independence struggle. Although Hidalgo's insurrection was chaotic and unplanned, from the outset of independence his reputation advanced well beyond his record of success. He was the initiator, the inspiration, and the hope of the populace. In death, his bones would be venerated and the sites where he walked became places to be visited by pilgrims and travelers. Although conservatives and monarchists attempted to argue that the curate of Dolores was a very ordinary and unsuccessful figure, he became a key element in the fostering of Mexico's national identity. As a political symbol, the memory of Hidalgo's sacrifice was ready-made to use against nineteenth-century conservatism, monarchism, and foreign interventionism. In the twentieth century, new generations of Mexican revolutionaries traced their roots to Hidalgo and further solidified his inspiration.

Cura José María Morelos: Siervo de la Nación
Although Father José María Morelos y Pavón (1765–1815) (see Illustration 3.4) neither initiated Mexican independence nor brought it to a successful conclusion, he possessed the highest reputation among the *antiguos insurgentes* (old insurgents) and even today he is

3.4   *Father José María Morelos y Pavón (N. L. Benson Collection,
University of Texas at Austin).*

remembered by many as the real father of the Mexican nation.[27]
Lucas Alamán, who had little good to say about most of the leaders
who rebelled against Spain, described Morelos as "the most notable
there was among the insurgents."[28] The city of Valladolid was
renamed Morelia in his honor as well as the small state that was the
scene of the epic February to March 1812 siege of Cuautla Amilpas.
Unlike Hidalgo, who is well known by all Mexicans but little understood, Morelos was a decisive natural leader whose motives, aspirations, and plans for the future were thought out quite clearly. With
the outbreak of the Hidalgo Revolt, Morelos, the curate of
Nucupétaro and Carácuaro, did not wait for the visit of a revolutionary agent or commissioner; instead, he traveled to visit Hidalgo who
convinced him about the danger to New Spain posed by French revolutionaries and the grasping gachupines.[29] Morelos returned home
with a commission to raise troops along the Pacific coast and emerged
rapidly as an effective commander who could endanger the existence

of the Spanish regime. He began his career as an insurgent in territory that was not well defended by the royalists.[30] His early successes came at a time when the best forces of the royalist side concentrated their attention on Hidalgo's multitudes. Recruiting among the *pardo* and *moreno* (free black and mulatto) populace of the coastal districts and among criollo clans such as the Bravos and the Galeanas, Morelos organized a powerful regional rebellion based on a stronger foundation than that of Hidalgo.

By the end of 1811, Morelos had pushed toward the highlands of the Puebla region where rebel bands already operated, which would allow the new insurgency to challenge the main forces of the royalist side. On December 10, 1811, Morelos occupied and fortified the strategically important town of Izúcar.[31] The panicky royalists recognized that the province and city of Puebla were the real targets. Although Morelos appeared to have a strategic victory close at hand, he decided against risking a siege of Puebla and instead moved westward to keep open the routes to his bases close to the Pacific coast. It is quite possible that Morelos recognized that his forces lacked the artillery, organization, and logistical capabilities to besiege and to assault prepared fortifications. Instead, he occupied and fortified the town of Cuautla Amilpas, which was to become one of the principal battlegrounds of the independence struggle.[32] Although the insurgents captured Taxco and entered Cuernavaca, by this point Brigadier Félix Calleja moved his Ejército del Centro (Army of the Center) southward from the Bajío provinces through Toluca on his way to confront the new danger posed by Morelos.

By occupying and fortifying Cuautla and waiting for Calleja's army to finish off the rebels at Zitácuaro first before dealing with Morelos's forces, the insurgents gave up flexibility and mobility to adopt a "the last man standing is the victor" approach that favored the better armed and provisioned royalists. As Brian Hamnett pointed out, the insurgents lost their military initiative.[33] Nevertheless, the siege was a brutal and exhausting affair that Morelos ended on May 2, 1812, by breaking out of Cuautla to save his army to fight another day. Although Calleja and the royalist army received intense criticism from some royalist observers for failing to achieve an overwhelming victory, the truth of the matter was that Morelos suffered a bruising defeat and the loss of his reputation for invincibility.[34] Although Morelos did survive to rebuild his army and to occupy Oaxaca, Acapulco, and many other towns, his future as a general, legislator, and constitutional planner unfolded in peripheral regions off the beaten path and away from the major population centers of New Spain.

Against many divisions and squabbles within the insurgent movement, Morelos struggled to find consensus and to establish an effective and representative government. In 1813, the insurgent *junta gobernativa* (governing junta), a most difficult and quarrelsome body, agreed to commemorate the anniversary of Hidalgo's revolution on September 16. Also to be solemnized were the saints' days of Father Hidalgo (San Miguel) as well as that of Allende (San Ignacio), and that of the Virgin of Guadalupe, December 12. Finally, there were to be four new Mexican military orders—Nuestra Señora de Guadalupe, Hidalgo, el Aguila, and Allende.[35] Efforts were made to bestow upon Morelos the distinction of alteza, or highness, but unlike Hidalgo he rejected any special recognition of this sort. He adopted the more modest title of *siervo de la nación* (servant of the nation) and over the next two years served a congress better than it deserved.[36] On November 6, 1813, the Congress of Chilpancingo approved a declaration of independence drafted by Carlos María Bustamante. In 1814, the increasing pressure of royalist pursuers forced the congress to become an itinerant body. However, on October 22, 1814, at Apatzingán, the insurgent government proclaimed a provisional republican constitution. Based upon the French and American Constitutions, and the Spanish experience at Cádiz with the 1812 Constitution, the insurgent document was in reality a dead letter from the moment of its appearance.

Calleja and other royalist commanders recognized that the region of southern Valladolid province (today southern Michoacán) where Morelos operated could be attacked effectively from several directions. Recognizing their weaknesses, the insurgents decided to move the congress to Tehuacán that at the time was firmly in their hands. From there, they would be able to communicate freely with Veracruz, Oaxaca, and the Gulf coast where they expected to open communications with and to receive aid from the United States. Some rumors about the projected move leaked out and Viceroy Calleja ordered several royalist columns to conduct sweeping reconnaissance missions. One force of about six hundred well-armed troops commanded by Lieutenant Colonel Manuel de la Concha scoured the valley of Temascaltepec toward the province of Puebla. Joining up with another royalist force commanded by Lieutenant Colonel Eugenio Villasana, Concha discovered the insurgents near Tenango.[37] Once he learned that the main enemy force was near by, Concha pressed

his men forward in forced marches without much rest until they
crossed the Amacuzac River.

On November 5, 1815, royalist troops entered the village of
Tesmalaca where they sighted Morelos's rearguard withdrawing into
the hills. The members of the Congress, other officials, and their bag-
gage had gone ahead, thus they managed to escape. Pursued by royalist cavalry, a hastily formed insurgent battle line collapsed and
produced a precipitous flight.[38] Father Morelos and the small guard
force with him appeared to be surrounded, and he ordered his men
to disperse so that each might save himself. Morelos attempted to hide
but was captured by a royalist lieutenant, Matías Carranco, who earlier had served with the insurgents.[39] Recognizing his enemy captor,
Morelos was said to utter a famous line loaded with irony: "Señor
Carranco, I believe that we know each other" (see Illustration 3.5).[40]
In fact, like Hidalgo before him Morelos must have experienced the
cold chill of knowing that he was all but dead. The royalists celebrated
their great victory, and Concha thought no more about chasing the
much less interesting insurgent Congress.[41]

After forcing Morelos to witness the execution by firing squad of
thirty insurgent soldiers who had been captured in the battle,
Concha's troops marched him to Mexico City and to incarceration in
the secret prison of the Inquisition. Although Calleja may have wished
to parade his prize captive in public, the risks of such a show were too
great, and the entry into the city was made at dawn. Nevertheless,
there were enormous joyful celebrations in the capital and in other
royalist-dominated cities. Many on the royalist side were certain that
with the apprehension of Morelos, the most evil and persistent insurgent leader, the insurrection would soon collapse. This natural error
in thinking came home later to haunt the royalist side. Morelos faced
something of a rerun of Hidalgo's trial with both the ecclesiastical and
royal jurisdictions presenting their cases against him. The difference
was that Morelos's trials took place in Mexico City and were conducted with considerable pomp and ceremony by the most senior
officials rather than a hastily arranged affair in dusty, frontier
Chihuahua. This time both the accused and the accusers were very
important figures, and there was great public interest even though
most of the legal proceedings and the eventual execution took place
without advance publicity.

On the insurgent side there were loud lamentations in Tehuacán
where few made any pretense to disguise the disastrous impact of

3.5 *The royalist army capture of Father José María Morelos y Pavón (N. L. Benson Collection, University of Texas at Austin).*

Morelos's capture. Almost everyone viewed Morelos as "a common father" and they had dedicated themselves absolutely to his cause.[42] Attempting to put on a brave face, the insurgent government proclaimed that this terrible blow should be used to generate a desire for revenge on the battlefield and must not precipitate desolation and despair. The proclamation continued:

> Soldiers: You know better than anyone what you have lost. You know our Father Morelos, you accompanied him in his brilliant campaigns, you merited his most affectionate love, you partook with him in the glory of giving liberty to an afflicted America, and always he guided you by the road of honor and of victory. Ah! Consider him now in the midst of his rabid enemies, like a sheep in the claws of tigers and leopards, made the object of their scorn; mocked, outraged, wounded, and left to suffer a cruel death for you.[43]

Before Morelos even reached Mexico City, Calleja appointed Miguel Batallar, an *oidor* (judge) and *auditor de guerra* (judge advocate) of the Audiencia, to represent the royal jurisdiction, and he appointed Félix

Flores Altorre, the *provisor* (vicar general) of the archbishopric, to represent the ecclesiastical side. They were to cooperate in assembling the charges and in organizing the trial. Morelos received permission to appoint anyone he wanted as his defense attorney, but without contacts in the capital he accepted Licenciado José Quiles, an unknown young lawyer.[44] Recognizing that the judicial process could produce only one final result, unlike Hidalgo and Allende who had cast aspersions against each other, Morelos maintained a dignified and composed demeanor throughout his harrowing judicial ordeal. He dismissed the charges of treason, disloyalty to the king, and promotion of independence, arguing that at the time there was no king in Spain. Even when Fernando VII returned, Morelos was certain that he had been influenced by Napoleon and corrupted in his religious beliefs. Regarding executions of royalist commanders and bureaucrats, he defended himself by stating that insurgent bodies such as the Junta de Zitácuaro or the Congreso de Chilpancingo authorized all of these acts.[45] On the question of bloodshed, property damage, and other mayhem, he responded that violence and destruction always were the unfortunate accompaniments of revolution and warfare. Noting the published prohibitions and threats of the Inquisition and of bishops who fulminated against the insurgents, Morelos argued that he did not consider them valid since they could not impose their will on an independent nation. He spoke openly about his activities, named his associates, admitted having attempted to negotiate an alliance with the United States, and stated that a major purpose had been to purchase arms.[46] In spite of the impossibility of the situation, Morelos's defense attorney, Licenciado Quiles, made a valiant attempt to present his client's case.

The Inquisition formulated its own case against Morelos, presenting twenty-three charges that repeated previous matters considered by the court and dealt with issues of particular interest to the Tribunal and religious authorities. One charge criticized Morelos for having sent one of his three sons to study in the United States where he would learn the heretical maxims of Protestantism. Another sought to illuminate his licentious customs and suspected heresy. As with the previous trial, Morelos answered each charge clearly and concisely. He said that he had sent his son to the United States simply because there was no college where he would be safe in New Spain. On the matter of his personal life, he stated that while he had not been completely pristine for a priest, he had not acted in a scandalous manner.

As foreordained, the Tribunal of the Inquisition found Morelos guilty on all charges: he was a heretic; a persecutor and disturber of the ecclesiastical hierarchy; a profaner of the Holy Sacraments; an irreconcilable enemy of Christianity; and a traitor to God, the king, and the pope. In the unlikely possibility that he avoided execution in the royal jurisdiction for his litany of crimes, the Tribunal sentenced him to a life of exile and seclusion in Africa.[47]

The degrading or defrocking of Morelos took place at 8:00 A.M. on November 27, 1815, with about one hundred curious invitees present who were most anxious to view the rebel leader so famous for his evil deeds. Morelos had been found guilty of heresy, atheism, deism, materialism, hypocrisy, lasciviousness, and many other crimes. He arrived at the main chamber of the Holy Tribunal dressed up in clerical garb with a sacred chalice in his hands. A bishop pronounced the charges against him and at the same time ceremonially stripped him of his priestly adornments—cassock, vestments, and stole—even ordering his hair cut off to deface the clerical tonsure.[48] The accounts indicate that Morelos exhibited great fortitude and maintained his composure throughout this terrible ordeal.[49] Banished from the priesthood, the Tribunal of the Inquisition handed him over to the secular jurisdiction and into the custody of Colonel Concha and other army officers. A company of troops from the Provincial Infantry Regiment of Tlaxcala that had participated in his capture, transferred Morelos that night to a cell in the Ciudadela (the Citadel).[50]

There was no real need for additional judicial proceedings since Auditor Bataller already had demanded the death penalty by firing squad. He recommended that Morelos be shot through the back as a traitor, with the confiscation of his property, and the public display of his head in the Zócalo (the main square) of Mexico City. However, so as to obtain complete answers about Morelos's roles in the revolution, Viceroy Calleja ordered Concha to continue the interrogation process. Finally, on December 20, Calleja confirmed the death penalty, but in deference to the sensibilities of the clergy the execution was to take place somewhere outside of the capital. Morelos's body was to be interred immediately without severing his head for public exhibition. Such a tawdry display seemed unsuitable in the capital, and Calleja may well have feared that an exhibited head might become an object of veneration as well as for ghoulish curiosity. Instead, the viceroy proclaimed a new unrestricted royal amnesty offering rebels who surrendered the opportunity to serve with the royalist militia forces as volunteers.[51] The historian Carlos María Bustamante reported that many powerful persons including Calleja's criolla wife, Doña María Francisca de la Gándara, petitioned her husband repeatedly to pardon Morelos, but this was most likely apocryphal and formed part of later campaigns intended to glorify him.[52]

On December 21, Concha informed Morelos of his fate, and he was given blank writing paper in case he wished to pen a retraction or issue some exhortation. As in the case of Hidalgo, a document of this type did appear shortly after his death, but even Lucas Alamán, who insisted on the veracity of the Hidalgo document, stated that the writing style was foreign to that of Morelos.[53] Probably to maintain absolute secrecy concerning the execution, Concha informed Morelos that he would die in three days. However, at 6:00 A.M. the next day (December 22), Concha arrived and put Morelos in a closed coach that was guarded by a strong force of mounted troops headed for the sanctuary of the Virgin of Guadalupe. Recognizing the obvious meaning of this expedition, Morelos began to pray and prayed more fervently as the procession approached each plaza along the route, certain that they had reached the site where the sentence would be carried out. The procession finally arrived at the village of San Cristóbal Ecatepec outside the city at a military camp where the local commander had no advance knowledge about what was to transpire. Before the firing squad arrived, Morelos had time to pray and to consume a cup of broth. At 3:00 P.M. he took off his cloak and tied a white handkerchief to cover his eyes. Two soldiers bound his arms with their musket slings. He was taken out, ordered to kneel, and immediately shot four times through the back and another four times for good measure to extinguish any vestigial life. By 4:00 P.M. Morelos's body—wrapped in his own cloak—was interred in the parochial cemetery of Ecatepec.[54]

The following orgy of self-congratulation and bombast on the royalist side did nothing to tarnish Morelos's reputation, which became ever larger with his martyrdom. Even Lucas Alamán, who had little good to say about most insurgents, allowed that Morelos was the only one who might have been able to weld the dissonant insurgent chiefs together under one plan and system.[55] Alamán and Bustamante wrote their authoritative multivolume histories of the independence epoch later, and through their publications, political activities, and speeches, each played major roles in formulating how Mexicans would remember and celebrate the great men and women of Mexico's pantheon of heroes. Conversely, both historians and others identified the evil or unsavory figures who depending on politics, successes or failures in war, corruption, abuses of the population, and other reasons would be consigned to a black pantheon of enemies of the nation. Alamán may have viewed Morelos as the best of a bad lot, but his remark that if Spain had not lost Mexico in 1821 Calleja would have been recognized as the reconqueror or "the second Hernán Cortés," went a long way to explaining where his thoughts really lay.[56] He noted how Calleja had succeeded in defeating the cabecillas and their bands one after another until he captured the principal insurgent leader and conquered the entire country.[57] Writing after the Mexican-American War (1846–48), Alamán argued that the United States used the same method to overthrow Mexican defensive forces and even after that tragedy, the republic was still exposed to the divide-and-conquer maxim. However, he denied that the independence struggle was a war between nations as it had been represented; rather, "it was an uprising of the proletarian classes against that of property and civilization." Alamán concluded, "The triumph of the insurrection could have been the greatest calamity that might have befallen the country."[58] One of the great problems for Mexico, he insisted, was that a free press had been perverted by factions to the degree that instead of enlightening the nation, it had become "the most powerful instrument of deception and deceit."[59]

Alamán admitted that in large part he wrote his five volumes in response to Carlos María de Bustamante and other writers whom he felt had stolen the truth. For one thing, they caused the government to solemnize September 16 as the day to celebrate the launching of Mexican independence. In addition to the celebrations of this event in the capital, the state legislatures of Guanajuato and México ordered the erection of statues of Hidalgo at his birthplace in the town of Dolores, and at the site of the 1810 Battle of Monte de las Cruces near Toluca. In Alamán's opinion, these efforts celebrated a "deceit" that had been propagated by "the most immoral and atrocious means."[60] The actual achievement of independence was the work of others. Alamán wrote four volumes that sullied the reputations of Hidalgo and many other insurgent leaders—leaving Morelos a little credibility, but not a great deal. With only volume five left to write covering the entire second half of the war, Alamán sought to change the public view of independence and to advance a conservative interpretation that would answer the liberal popular views. As an historian of his own epoch and a man of strong views based on his family background, at times Alamán let his political philosophy overwhelm his historical acuity and brilliance. He failed or refused to understand that the revolution did not end under Calleja and that in the years after 1816, the royalist cause and its powerful military became exhausted against what was a broad-based peoples' struggle.[61]

Agustín de Iturbide: Emperor Without an Empire

It seems supremely ironic that Agustín de Iturbide, a whirlwind of terror for the royalist side against the insurgents, ended up not only as an emperor but also as a later claimant to the title as Mexico's liberator (see Illustration 3.6).[62] Indeed, his later proponents of conservative or monarchist views insisted that he should be accorded precedence over Father Hidalgo. Morelos, for all of his fame and importance, held the middle ground between the two would-be liberators. As a father figure for the Mexican nation, he could not compete with the Grito de Dolores of September 16, 1810, or Iturbide's triumphal entry into Mexico City on September 27, 1821, as the victorious commander of the Army of the Three Guarantees of the Plan de Iguala (see Illustration 3.7). Considering Iturbide's career, the term opéra bouffe comes to mind, but in this sanguinary epoch of Mexican history any comic elements were offset by tragedy. Whether it was true or not, Iturbide claimed that in 1810 Father Hidalgo offered him a commission as a lieutenant general. In his short autobiographical memoir, Iturbide stated that though he felt tempted as any young man of ambition who lacked experience might be (at twenty-seven years of age), he rejected Hidalgo's offer. He commented, "I declined it [the commission], however, because I was satisfied that the plans of the curate were ill contrived, and that they would produce only disorder, massacre, and devastation, without accomplishing the object which he had in view."[63] Iturbide went on to describe Hidalgo as a criminal who presided over the melt down of his country and failed to raise a hand to stop "the sufferings of his fellow citizens."[64] All of this is most interesting since Iturbide disseminated disorder and devastation for the royalist side—much of it in chasing down and executing those who had been swept up by Hidalgo's blandishments. In addition to pursuing insurgent leaders, including Morelos, in Guanajuato and Valladolid, Iturbide shared the affinity of many other royalist commanders who misused their wartime powers to destroy, to confiscate, or to appropriate by other means the wealth of the Mexican population. Beginning in 1816, he spent several years under indictment

3.6 *Emperor Augustín de Iturbide, 1822 (N. L. Benson Collection, University of Texas at Austin).*

without being able to convince the viceroy to grant him a formal court-martial so that he could prove his innocence. The story of how Iturbide emerged as emperor—even for a very short reign—is almost stranger than fiction. In a way, however, fate connected all three of these illustrious leaders of the independence era and they shared the same bloody end before firing squads.[65]

To understand the emergence of Iturbide, one must reexamine the second half of Mexico's War of Independence—moving away from the contemporary view of Alamán, other royalists, and the conclusion of many recent historians that in 1815–16 only a few insurgent bands remained in the field and peace was imminent.[66] In fact, the royalist side manned in large part by Mexican criollos and mixed-blood forces could not continue the struggle forever. Although the Spanish imperial government dispatched about ten to twelve thousand European expeditionary troops, over the next several years these units eroded owing to disease, desertion, and combat fatigue until they lost much of their fighting capacity. The final European regiment dispatched to

3.7   *Emperor Augustín de Iturbide and key supporters (N. L. Benson Collection, University of Texas at Austin).*

New Spain, the historic line Infantry Regiment of Zaragoza commanded by Brigadier Pascual de Liñan, arrived in 1817 and it soon suffered from being broken up to create separate detachments that ruined morale and encouraged desertions.[67] The multifaceted nature of the counterinsurgency struggle as in many similar wars then and today, compelled senior commanders to subdivide regiments and battalions for different missions and garrison duties that sapped efficiency and discipline. Not only did the endless struggle in New Spain consume company, battalion, and regimental funds, but the general economic depression caused by wartime disruptions, insurgent blockades, and banditry devastated the general tax base that over time was unable to bear the unmanageable burdens. Disease, homesickness, and the pure boredom of soldiers, who spent most of their time garrisoned in provincial towns, weakened any desire for dangerous campaigns, assaults, and sieges against tough rural-based guerrilla insurgents.[68] Adding to the confusion, Viceroy Juan Ruíz de Apodaca (1816–21) pursued broad amnesty programs that offered insurgent units a quick transition from rebel to royalist. A self-appointed rebel cabecilla who called himself a colonel or brigadier could apply for amnesty and reemerge as a more lowly but at least still living royalist militia captain. His officers and men simply continued their military duty, but now as royalist *patriotas* (patriots) assigned to tracking down their erstwhile former comrades.

In 1816, following a remarkably successful career in counterinsurgency duties that saw him promoted to colonel of the Provincial Infantry Regiment of Celaya and commander of the Army of the North and of the Intendancies of Guanajuato and Valladolid, Iturbide suddenly fell into official disrepute. He faced several charges citing him for abuses, corruption, and bad conduct. Although many senior royalist officers drew similar complaints for their marginal or even criminal malfeasance, for reasons that are still difficult to explain, Viceroy Calleja ordered Iturbide to Mexico City where he spent four years attempting without much success to clear his name.[69] Previously, even as a young and ambitious captain, Iturbide exhibited loyalty to his fellow officers, a willingness to press hard for his audacious military plans with senior commanders and even viceroys, remarkable energy and persistence, and an absolute dedication to the King. His self-promotion was quite shameless, but his string of battlefield victories underscored his developing reputation. In 1812, still early in his career, Iturbide boasted that he had fought in nine major actions—all of them more glorious than the description in the Reales Ordenanzas (Royal Ordinances) as "*distinguidos*" (distinguished).[70] He ingratiated himself with powerful well-placed patrons who watched over his career for years and overlooked or winked at his arbitrary and bullying tendencies. During convoy escort duties, Iturbide got to know Félix Calleja's wife, Doña María Francesca de la Gándara, who introduced him to the general. Thereafter, Iturbide referred to Calleja as "el hombre grande (the big man)."[71]

Iturbide was a man absolutely committed to his religion and to the absolute justice of his cause and the evil of insurgency, and he was intolerant of any criticism. Though he viewed himself as a man of destiny, at times he exhibited a dark side that marred his diplomacy and made him a bloody-minded and intolerant bludgeon of his opponents and enemies. His patron and commander, Brigadier Diego

García Conde depended on "the indefatigable Iturbide" and informed Calleja in 1813 that "nothing can fully reward this brave officer whose victories are innumerable."[72] However, in 1815, Iturbide attacked the curates of Guanajuato province for preaching pro-rebel sentiments and raising tithes to support insurgency. He introduced a brutal program to destroy small villages and isolated hamlets and conceived plans to concentrate the formerly dispersed population into communities protected by parapets and the guns of royalist forces. Anyone captured outside of the defended zones was to be declared a rebel and either shot or sentenced to forced labor.[73] Clearly, some quite powerful people in Guanajuato decided that Iturbide had gone too far.

During his years of unemployment in Mexico City, Iturbide worked to cleanse his reputation and to seek supporters. He came into contact with more politically active creoles who expressed frustration with the interminable war and with the inflexibility of Spanish rule. In these circles, political talk in the *tertulias* (coffeehouse or wine-bar discussions) would have covered a broad spectrum of possibilities. In 1820, the removal of King Fernando VII's absolutist rule and the unexpected restoration of the Spanish Constitution of 1812 produced what appeared to be a way to end the decade of conflict in New Spain. Viceroy Apodaca, now known as the Conde de Venadito, sought to declare a general amnesty to end hostilities in New Spain. However, some rebel gavillas such as those led by Vicente Guerrero and Pedro Ascencio in the rugged territory between Mexico City and Acapulco resisted all offers of conciliation. Frustrated by this intransigence, in November 1820, Apodaca appointed Iturbide to the post of comandante general al Rumbo de Acapulco (commander general of the Inland region toward Acapulco). During the four years since his political detractors had dispossessed him of his command of Guanajuato and Valladolid provinces, Iturbide said that he had made "the degrading metamorphosis from warrior to litigant," claiming incessantly that a most scrupulous and ample judicial investigation should be made of his conduct.[74] He blamed his trouble on the machinations of the rebels and insisted that he had strong support from prelates, officers, and various political groups. Iturbide stated that he felt anger toward his accusers who had destroyed his reputation and interrupted the progress of his military career. The origins of Iturbide's support for a new solution such as the Plan de Iguala and the formation of his Army of the Three Guarantees emerged from this background.

Iturbide's alliance with Vicente Guerrero and selection of the three guarantees of religion, independence, and union in the Plan de Iguala came at exactly the right moment to elicit widespread support. His broad alliance embraced war-weary criollos, who for years had paid the costs of heavy wartime taxation, officers and soldiers of the royalist army, who recognized that they could not win, and many insurgents, who also longed for peace. Combining this sentiment with the renewal of the constitutional system, a broad segment of the populace from all sectors proclaimed the Plan de Iguala and Iturbide as its commander. Alamán described Iturbide's 1821 campaign as a "promenade through the provinces."[75] Without significant fighting, in only six months New Spain simply collapsed of its own weight. The few remaining royalist troops, mostly European expeditionary soldiers who opted to return to Spain, ended up marooned in Mexico City and Veracruz.[76] On September 27, 1821, his thirty-eighth birthday, Iturbide and his Army of the Three Guarantees—a mostly royalist assemblage with some former insurgents—made their epochal entry into Mexico City (see Illustration 3.8). For his supporters, this date and not September 16 would mark Mexican independence.[77]

When events propelled Iturbide to victory, his popularity was enormous, making it quite obvious that he would become the leader of Mexico. Possibly, if the European Spanish expeditionary battalions had not been scattered in penny-packet garrisons across New Spain and if Captain General Juan O'Donojú had not arrived from Spain to sign the Treaty of Córdoba, the results of Iturbide's revolution might have been different. The treaty recognized a now-independent Mexican Empire as a constitutional monarchy that would offer the crown to Fernando VII, one of his three sons, or to a person designated by the Mexican Cortes (parliament).[78] When news arrived in February 1822, that Spain repudiated the Treaty of Córdoba and recognition of Mexican independence, Iturbide's supporters moved to press his candidacy to lead the new nation.[79]

In what may have been a completely staged occasion, on the night of May 1, 1822, the noncommissioned officers of Iturbide's old Provincial Regiment of Celaya conducted a "spontaneous" mass gathering that proclaimed their colonel the emperor of Mexico.[80] His popularity proved to be ephemeral, and his imperial reign endured for just ten months—May 1822 to March 1823. Almost immediately, Iturbide's characteristics as an extremely ambitious, arbitrary, and

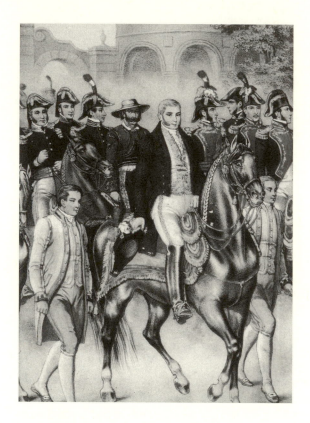

3.8   *Emperor Augustín de Iturbide's victorious entry into Mexico City,*
September 27, 1821 (N. L. Benson Collection, University of Texas at
Austin).

authoritarian commander who had fallen from grace returned in
other forms to bedevil him as a would-be emperor. After months of
acrimony and raging disputes, on October 31, 1822, Iturbide dispatched General Luis Cortazar to dissolve the Constituent Congress.
This maneuver outraged those who argued that the emperor had
taken too much power and was no longer following the Plan de
Iguala. To replace the Congress, Iturbide selected a group of forty-
five persons to serve on a new body called the Junta Nacional
Instituyente (National Founding Junta) that was to draft a new
Mexican constitution.

On December 2, 1822, at Veracruz, Brigadier Antonio López de
Santa Anna declared that Iturbide had become a despot and issued

the Plan de Veracruz as the basis for a revolt. On January 13, 1823, Vicente Guerrero and Nicolás Bravo slipped out of Mexico City secretly, renounced imperial rule, and launched another revolt in the south.[81] Although both of these uprisings did not develop into immediate dangers, the situation became more perilous for Iturbide. On February 1, 1823, General José Antonio Echavarrí and several other senior officers who commanded an army dispatched to put down Santa Anna's revolt instead declared the Plan de Casa Mata demanding the immediate restoration of the Congress. This new uprising precipitated a general insurrection by other commanders and army units to join the movement.[82] In March 1823, Iturbide recalled the Constituent Congress, but in the continuing state of unrest he abdicated and announced that he would leave the country.[83]

Accompanied by his immediate family, Iturbide departed for exile on March 30, 1823, and settled in Livorno, Italy. The Mexican government granted him a pension for life of 25,000 pesos so long as he stayed in exile, allowed him to carry his personal valuables, and paid his travel and resettlement costs. In fact Iturbide's sojourn at Livorno lasted for only a few months. On November 28, Iturbide left Livorno and arrived in London, England, January 1, 1824. There, he expressed his concerns about chaos in the Mexican provinces that might overturn independence. He indicated that his supporters begged him to return home.[84] After a visit of just over four months in England, Iturbide with his wife and two youngest children sailed for Mexico on May 11, 1824, aboard a chartered English vessel accompanied by a few attendants and a printing press.

During the voyage, Iturbide ran off a series of declarations and memorials warning Mexicans of the dangers that confronted them. He had no idea that on April 28, 1824, the Mexican Congress passed a draconian law of interdiction declaring the former emperor to be "a traitor outside law . . . and a public enemy of the state." Anyone who assisted him was a traitor to the Mexican Federation.[85] Arriving on July 14 at Soto la Marina on the coast of Tamaulipas, at first Iturbide's party made efforts to conceal their identity and said they were part of an Irish colonization scheme. According to the story an army corporal recognized Iturbide because of his equestrian dexterity and a Durango merchant who had known him in Mexico City confirmed the identification.[86] On July 17, the comandante general of the district, Felipe de la Garza, arrested Iturbide and conducted him to Soto la Marina. When Iturbide asked what was likely to happen, Garza informed him that he had been proscribed by the Mexican State and intimated that he could be executed in three hours. Absolutely horrified by this revelation, Iturbide asked to have his chaplain sent to him from his ship. Considering the importance of his prisoner, Garza showed some distress about applying the law and likely felt completely out of his depth. He decided to suspend any immediate execution and instead to escort Iturbide to Padilla the next day where the Tamaulipas congress was in session. If this situation was not sufficiently bizarre, according to Lucas Alamán, Garza spoke with his troops and informed them that Iturbide was not dangerous and that they would escort him to Padilla to obtain a clarification from the congress regarding the matter of proscription. In the interim, Iturbide was to be given his liberty and permitted to ride at the head of the column to Padilla. Later, Garza claimed that his purpose was to make Iturbide feel comfortable so as to obtain additional information about his real intentions.[87]

The next morning at Padilla, the congress upheld Garza's first interpretation—even though the commandant general argued that Iturbide could not possibly have known about his proscription. Nevertheless, the congressmen voted unanimously to uphold the law of the national government.[88] Now irreconcilably disconsolate, Iturbide received a second three-hour stay before he faced a firing squad. He asked a one-day deferral of the execution, but was given only until 6:00 P.M. that same evening. He had sufficient time to hear mass, to make his final confession, and to write some letters to his wife and family. He gave his watch and rosary to the priest who accompanied him and asked that some gold coins he had in his purse should be distributed to the soldiers of his firing squad. Escorted to the place of execution with his hands bound, Iturbide prayed the Apostles' Creed, kissed a crucifix, and on the command "fuego" he perished, shot once through the head and several times through the chest.[89] His body, shrouded in a Franciscan habit, was carried to a chapel and left overnight illuminated by four candles. The next morning, the congressional deputies, Garza, the soldiers, and the local people attended the funeral and interment in the ruins of an old church. Alamán commented about the irony of the fact that just two years previously, Iturbide had been crowned emperor in the Cathedral of Mexico City.[90]

Memory and Commemoration

It is remarkable that the big three of the Mexican independence epoch suffered such similar fates and that each of them became patriotic objects in the conflictive politics of nation building for succeeding generations. The royalist objectives of terrorizing the Mexican population and showing them body parts or hanging up the cadavers of insurgents achieved little in winning the hearts and minds of the populace. Hidalgo was not forgotten, but during the war years he did not emerge as an iconic figure representative of the nation. The royalists invoked his name only when their cause appeared to falter and commanders complained when something went wrong that Father Hidalgo would be pleased if he returned from the dead. Both Hidalgo and Iturbide held special positions since they initiated and completed the national independence movement that would be celebrated in the future. Following independence, the dates of September 16 (referring to 1810) for Hidalgo and September 27 (referring to 1821) for Iturbide became highly politicized and representative of republican or monarchist, liberal or conservative, federalist or centralist views. Morelos emerged safely from within the bloody conflict as a patriotic icon and recognized as *benemérito de la patria* (well deserving of the motherland). His reputation transcended the politics and ideological meanings of independence and the endless debates over decades about what kind of nation would replace colonial New Spain. Morelos's home city of Valladolid became Morelia, and like Hidalgo, he had a Mexican state named after him. His statues, some massive creations made of volcanic basalt such as that on Janitzio Island in Lake Pátzcuaro, are perhaps even more ubiquitous throughout the country today than those of Hidalgo.

Beginning in 1822, Mexicans of all origins and political inclinations commenced what became a lengthy debate about the merits of the great liberators of their new nation. For those who for various reasons refused to view Agustín Iturbide positively, the earlier revolutionary leaders now called the *antiguos patriotas* (old patriots) were the most deserving of remembrance and celebration. With the end of the insurgency, many who earlier served on the rebel side or secretly supported the goals of revolution now came out of the closet when it came to celebrating the feats of the first insurgents. Instead of promoting September 27 to glorify Iturbide's entry into Mexico City, the supporters of Hidalgo and September 16 gained the advantage. Contemporary historians such as Fray Servando Teresa de Mier and Carlos María Bustamante worked diligently to solidify the recognition of Hidalgo and Morelos as the truly great leaders of the independence movement.[91] On September 16, 1823, the bones of José María Morelos were moved from the parochial cemetery of Ecatepec and conveyed to the capital for public reburial and celebrations in the Cathedral of Mexico under the Altar of the Kings.[92] The same was done with the remains of Hidalgo, Allende, and other senior insurgent commanders. In addition, Congress ordered the names of these liberators to be inscribed in gold letters on the walls of the congressional hall.[93] With the overthrow of Iturbide and declaration of a federal republic under the Constitution of 1824, José Mariano Tornel, private secretary to President Guadalupe Victoria, pressed for government approval to celebrate Miguel Hidalgo's Grito de Dolores on September 16. Tornel encouraged a group of Mexico City residents to form an association to organize events called the Junta Cívica de Patriotas, later the Junta Patriótica.

In 1825, the celebration of September 16 commenced with processions of citizens to a heavily adorned platform in the Zócalo where an orator offered "an energetic discourse" followed by a speech by President Guadalupe Victoria. In the evening special illumination of the Alameda Park made it the venue for orchestras, allegorical paintings of independence themes, patriotic songs, and displays of fireworks.[94] The following year, with foreign legations invited to join the celebrations, the president first attended High Mass and then returned to the palace for a formal reception. When that event concluded, he and other dignitaries joined the crowd to listen to orators who spoke from a raised platform situated in the center of the square. To conclude the event, there was a grand military review involving four thousand well-dressed troops.[95] In the 1840s, Fanny Calderón de la Barca attended the same September 16 events that had been moved to the nearby Alameda Park. She described military parades and the attendance of many army officers, monks, priests, and ladies all in full dress. General Tornel, who years before had been instrumental in the launching of the commemorations, presented a speech. The trees were hung with garlands of flowers, and booths were erected in the Alameda. Calderón de la Barca viewed a magnificent procession and noted, "the line of carriages was so deep, that I thought we should never arrive."[96]

If, to the contrary, the conservative side assumed power, Iturbide replaced Hidalgo as the object of devotion and September 27 became the day for commemoration. In 1833, President Antonio López de Santa Anna obtained a congressional order for the remains of Iturbide to be exhumed at Padilla and shipped to Mexico City to be buried in the cathedral alongside the earlier heroes. Owing to a shortage of funds and general political effervescence, the project was not completed. Finally in 1838, President Anastasio Bustamante ordered Iturbide exhumed and transported to the capital. On September 25, there was a grand public welcome when the casket containing Iturbide's bones arrived at the entry to the city. It was taken to the Monastery of San Francisco to lie in state until October 24 when there was a solemn funeral at the cathedral. So as to avoid profaning Iturbide by placing his remains alongside those of Hidalgo, Morelos, and other insurgent chiefs, President Bustamante and pro-Iturbide elements were successful in their insistence that he should be interred in the chapel of San Felipe de Jesus. Lucas Alamán noted, "They [the insurgent chiefs] remained as separate in death as they had been in life."[97] However, Iturbide continued to have his strong supporters. When Anastasio Bustamante died in 1853, by a clause in his will, he asked his family to cut out his heart and to place it with the remains of Iturbide.[98]

Strange to say, the gulf between the two solitudes of independence took a new twist in the twentieth century. On July 19, 1924, the celebration of the centennial of Iturbide's death in Mexico City attracted a proclerical audience composed of the Knights of Columbus, Damas Católicas (Catholic Ladies), and other organizations, but no officials from the government attended. However, this was not to say that anticlerical politicians of the modern Mexican Revolution forswore the great clerical heroes of the War of Independence. On September 16, 1925, President Plutarco E. Calles was present when the remains of Hidalgo, Allende, Morelos, and the other great insurgent heroes were moved from the cathedral to the new monument on the Paseo de la Reforma with its great column crowned by the Angel of independence. During the public ceremonies, Calles informed the American historian Ernest Gruening that not all of the heroes made the trip across town. He commented, "I left Iturbide there (in the cathedral) among those of his kind, where he belongs."[99]

As might be expected, contemporary historians and journalists of the day through the nineteenth century played significant roles in promoting and discussing the great heroes of independence. With the nation passing through many crises caused by revolutions and coups, philosophical divisions between centralists and federalists, and battles between conservatives and liberals, the independence heroes became shining symbols that stood for real principles and for the spirit of dogged determination required to fight for liberties and national sovereignty. Invasions by Spain and France, the loss of Texas, and the overwhelming horror of defeat in the Mexican American War (1846–48) that cost the nation about half of its territory reminded Mexicans of the independence epoch and great leaders who even if flawed were worthy of great respect.

Writing his *Cuadro Histórico* in the 1840s, Carlos María Bustamante lamented the fact that Iturbide had not been able to divert himself from such a tragic end "so as at that moment not to embitter the memory of his triumphs!" He continued, "Iturbide has a right to our eternal gratitude, for the good that he accomplished, not for the great deal of bad: his ambition precipitated us into an abyss of evils, from which God only may know how we will escape."[100] Carrying his readers up to the 1840s and discussing the current state of affairs as he wrote his manuscript, Bustamante worried about the difficult situation of the nation caused by the criminal abuses of some army commanders, "who seduce gullible towns, assist factions, and destroy the constituted federal system."[101] Some appeared to want to adopt a centralized republic or even to restore the "odious empire of Iturbide by putting into place his first-born son." Speaking with great intuition and foreshadowing Mexico's bleak immediate future, Bustamante suggested that others might wish to sink the country into anarchy: "That may make necessary the intervention of a foreign power to subjugate us with the pretext of protecting us, or to establish the prince of a foreign lineage, thus reducing us to a servitude perhaps worse than in the past."[102]

Iturbide could have been "a magnanimous liberator," but instead of following the will of the people, Bustamante excoriated him for putting into motion the events and the system that made Mexico's postindependence decades a constant horror.[103] This was most certainly one way of remembering the liberator, but it put far too much blame on the shoulders of Iturbide or any other single individual. Depending on their politics, Mexicans looked back to the crucible of the independence epoch and the great liberators with a mixture of enthusiasm and bitterness. As late as 1891, Porfirio Díaz commented that had Morelos survived until 1821, Iturbide could not have grasped control over the independence movements. In his view, the nation would have been spared its internecine struggles and the war that cost it half of its territory.[104]

Had he lived long enough, Bustamante would have seen his predictions about discord, civil strife, intervention and renewed monarchy become realities. The War of the Reforma (1858–60) was a terrible conflict that pitted liberals against conservatives, and federalists against centralists. Since it was a civil war, the struggle produced all the horrors that Bustamante feared and more. When Napoleon III decided to restore monarchy to Mexico, even that part of Bustamante's nightmare came to fruition. As might be expected, the liberals during the Reforma epoch dominated by Benito Juárez embraced the Hidalgo and Morelos traditions and September 16 as the date of Mexico's birth. In 1864, when Maximilian of Habsburg arrived in Mexico, one might have thought that Iturbide's tradition would undergo a renaissance. Although conservatives who supported September 27 for the celebration of independence must have felt that victory was theirs, Maximilian wished to build an ecumenical independence monument shared by statues of Hidalgo, Morelos, and Iturbide. Siding with the liberal tradition of commemorating Hidalgo and Morelos, the emperor began the construction of the monument on September 16.[105] He visited Dolores, invoked Hidalgo's name, spoke of revolution, and ordered commemorative plaques to be put up at Hidalgo's house and at Morelos's birthplace. On September 30, 1865, the one-hundredth anniversary of the birth of Morelos, Maximilian presided over the unveiling of a fine marble statue of Morelos in Mexico City at the Plazuela de Guardiola.[106] He did not neglect Iturbide, transferring his remains on September 16 to a bronze sarcophagus in the cathedral. Conservatives expressed horror at the mixed messages that seemed to favor the liberal remembrance of the independence heroes and thus the liberal view of history. Nevertheless, Maximilian fulfilled Carlos María Bustamante's great fear that the descendants of Iturbide might one day inherit the throne. Childless in their own marriage, Maximilian and Empress Carlota went to great lengths to adopt two of Iturbide's grandsons.[107]

Although the Second Empire failed and Iturbide's grandsons were sent back to their family in the United States, by the late 1860s Hidalgo and Morelos won definitive victory in death and remembrance that they could not achieve in life. The liberal tradition and the commemoration of independence and its great insurgent leaders on September 16 pushed Iturbide and September 27 into the distant background. Although Iturbide continued to have his followers and still does today, as Timothy Anna pointed out in his recent study, most Mexicans subscribed to the demonization of their liberator and first emperor.[108] Of course, the vast majority of those who adopted Hidalgo and Morelos as father figures to be celebrated on September 16 also subscribed to a process of myth making that was akin to the stories about young George Washington and the cherry tree. Neither the insurgent leaders nor the tough royalist counterinsurgents involved in brutal warfare that raged in Mexico from 1810 to 1821 exactly fitted the stereotypes of nation planners or builders. In 1910, Mexico celebrated its centennial with grand flourishes of intellectual exuberance, public building, and the publication of works by scholars such as Genero García that opened the historical record to wider scrutiny. At the same time, the construction of the magnificent monument of independence symbolized the victory of the liberal perceptions of independence heroes and of September 16 as the date of commemoration. When President Calles moved the remains of the great heroes to the Paseo de la Reforma monument and left Iturbide behind in the cathedral, it was clear that the twentieth-century Mexican Revolution would continue to advance the liberal view of how memory should be molded to build the nation. Of course, one wonders if Curates Hidalgo and Morelos, Allende, and the other great insurgent chiefs rest comfortably amidst the torrents of traffic and cacophony of noise that swirl around their final resting place. In recent years, rural campesino protesters seeking justice, land reform, and better conditions set up temporary cardboard and plastic villages in the shadow of the monument that contains the heroes' remains. Although abandoned back in the cathedral, Iturbide may enjoy slightly more peace.

Notes

1. Hugh M. Hamill, *The Hidalgo Revolt: Prelude to Mexican Independence* (Gainesville: University of Florida Press, 1966), 137; and Christon I. Archer, "Bite of the Hydra: The Rebellion of Cura Miguel Hidalgo," in *Patterns of Contention in Mexican History*, ed. Jaime E. Rodríguez O. (Wilmington, DE: Scholarly Resources Inc., 1992), 50–69.

2. Carlos María de Bustamante, *Cuadro Histórico de la Revolución Mexicana iniciadada el 15 de Septiembre de 1810 por el C. Miguel Hidalgo y Costilla Cura del Pueblo de Dolores en el Obispado de Michoacán*, 3 vols. (Mexico City: Ediciones de la Comisión Nacional para la Celebración del Sesquicentenario de la Proclamación de Independencia Nacional, 1961), 1:200.

3. Ibid.; and Hamill, *Hidalgo Revolt*, 216.

4. Minuta de Comunicación del General Calleja al Intendente [de Guanajuato] Fernando Pérez Marañon, en que le ordena que exponga al público en Guanajuato las cabezas de los cuatro principales caudillos insurgentes, 14 October de 1811, in Género García, ed., *Documentos Históricos Mexicanos, obra conmemorativa del primer centenario de la independencia de México*, 7 vols. (Mexico City: Museo Nacional de Arqueología, Historia y Etnología, 1910–12), 6:111–12.

5. Hamill, *Hidalgo Revolt*, 206–7.

6. The major insurgent chiefs captured with Hidalgo were Ignacio Allende, Juan Aldama, Mariano Abasalo, and Mariano Jímenez. For the names of other religious and secular leaders, see Relación de los individuos aprehendidos en la derrota que padecieron los insurgentes en el paraje llamado de Bajan, el día 21 de Marzo de 1811, por las tropas del rey de la provincia de Coahuila, Monclova, 11 April 1811; and Noticia de los individuos aprehendidos en Acatita de Bajan en la provincia de Coahuila, que condujo a Chihuahua el teniente coronel D. Manuel Salcedo, gobernador de la provincia de Tejas, Monclova, 28 March 1811, in Lucas Alamán, *Historia de México desde los primeros movimientos que prepararon su independencia en el año de 1808 hasta la época presente*, vol. 2 (Mexico City: Imprenta de J. M. Lara, 1850), appendices 26–29.

7. Ibid., 175–77.

8. In 1811, Brigadier Nemesio Salcedo had served the Spanish army for almost fifty years beginning with expeditions against Algiers and first serving in the Americas under Lieutenant General Conde de Gálvez during the American and Bourbon War (the American Revolution). He took command of the Provincias Internas in 1801 and was to have been replaced owing to bad health when the Independence struggle broke out. Other active field commanders in the royalist army, such as Félix Calleja and José de la Cruz, often criticized older sedentary officers such as Salcedo for evading the dirty and dangerous work of commanding active forces. See Viceroy Félix Berenguer de Marquina to Antonio Cornel, no. 275, 27 July 1801, Archivo General

de Indias, Méjico [cited hereafter as AGI, Mexico], legajo 1459; and Archbishop Viceroy Francisco Javier de Lizana to Cornel, no. 60, 27 October 1809, AGN, Indiferente de Guerra, Correspondencia de los Virreyes, Series 1, vol. 243.

9. Alamán, *Historia de México*, 2:182–83.

10. Bustamante, *Cuadro Histórico de la Revolución Mexicana*, 1:176–77

11. Ibid., 1:190–91. Abasalo's wife dedicated her own life to saving her husband and family.

12. Ibid., 1:206–7.

13. *Proceso Inquisitorial y Militar Seguidos a D. Miguel Hidalgo y Costilla* (Mexico City: Instituto Nacional de Antropología e Historia, 1960), 218–48.

14. Luis Villoro, *El Proceso Ideológico de la Revolución de Independencia* (Mexico City: UNAM, 1967), 226–27, 231–32.

15. Ibid., 234.

16. Ibid., 234–35.

17. Ibid., 237.

18. Ibid., 247.

19. El Br. D. Miguel Hidalgo, Cura de Dolores, a Todo el Mundo, Real Hospital, Chihuahua, 18 May 1811, in Alamán, *Historia de México*, vol. 2, appendix, document 14, 51–54.

20. Ibid., 51.

21. Alamán, *Historia de México*, 2:201.

22. For additional thoughts on the 18 May Manifesto, see Hamill, *Hidalgo Revolt*, 213.

23. *Proceso Inquisitorial y Militar*, 273.

24. Alamán, *Historia de México*, 2:193–94

25. Bustamante, *Cuadro Histórico de la Revolución Mexicana*, 1:202.

26. Calleja to Cruz, San Miguel, 15 October 1811, AGN:OG, vol. 192; and Calleja to Nemesio Salcedo, Guanajuato, 24 July 1811, AGN:OG, vol. 188.

27. Although there is no definitive work on Morelos in English, for a positive overview, see Wilbert H. Timmons, *Morelos of Mexico: Priest, Soldier Statesman* (El Paso: Texas Western College Press, 1963). For what might be termed as the official scholarly view of Morelos as "father" of Mexico, see Ernesto Lemoine Villacaña, *Morelos, su vida revolucionaria a través de sus escritos y de otros testimonios de la época* (Mexico City: UNAM, 1965).

28. Alamán, *Historia de México*, 2:314.

29. Ibid., 313–14; and Timmons, *Morelos of Mexico*, 40–41.

30. Brian R. Hamnett, *Roots of Insurgency: Mexican Regions, 1750–1824* (Cambridge: Cambridge University Press, 1986), 142–49.

31. Bustamante, *Cuadro Histórico de la Revolución Mexicana*, 1:351–52.

32. In his research on this campaign and on the royalist defenses available at Puebla, Brian Hamnett concluded that Morelos missed an opportunity to capture the provincial capital and the significant resources of the region. This was a major miscalculation at a time when the main royalist armies were unavailable for duty in Puebla Province. As Hamnett pointed out, this window of opportunity soon closed (Hamnett, *Roots of Insurgency*, 156–59; also see Alamán, *Historia de México*, 2:433–35).

33. Hamnett, *Roots of Insurgency*, 160–61.

34. See Christon I. Archer, "New Wars and Old: Félix Calleja and the Independence Wars of Mexico, 1810–1816," in *Military Heretics: The Unorthodox in Policy and Strategy*, ed. B. J. C. McKercher and Hamish Ion (Westport, CT: Praeger, 1994), 50–52; and Christon I. Archer, "Years of Decision: Félix Calleja and the Strategy to End the Revolution of New Spain," in *The Birth of Modern Mexico, 1780–1824*, ed. C. I. Archer (Wilmington, DE: Scholarly Resources Inc., 2003), 125–50.

35. Alamán, *Historia de México*, 3:548.

36. Ibid., 3:56537. Alamán, *Historia de México*, 4:309–11.

38. Lemoine Villicaña, *Morelos su vida revolucionaria*, 142.

39. Ibid., 598.

40. Ibid., 312–13; and Bustamante, *Cuadro Histórico de la Revolución Mexicana*, 2:168–69. The line uttered by Morelos could be apocryphal, but its provenance through Bustamante, who was very well connected with the participants, makes it at least possible. Beyond the immediate meaning, the fact that Carranco changed sides from insurgent to royalist underscored the fluidity and movement within a civil war. The royalists used the offer of amnesties and other blandishments that attracted insurgents and infuriated those who remained loyal to their original cause. The insurgents expressed equal anger at the royalist name for their rural militias as patriotas. From the insurgent perspective, they were the patriots and Mexican royalists were the dupes and slaves of the Spanish oppressors.

41. Manuel de la Concha to Calleja, 13 November 1815, in Lemoine Villicaña, *Morelos su vida revolucionaria*, 598–603. The royalists claimed to have killed three hundred insurgents in the battle.

42. Bustamante, *Cuadro Histórico de la Revolución Mexicana*, 2:167.

43. Proclama del Gobierno insurgente, lanzada de Tehuacán, 17 November 1815, in Lemoine Villicaña, *Morelos su vida revolucionaria*, 607.

44. Alamán, *Historia de México*, 4:317.

45. Ibid., 4:317–19.

46. Declaración de Morelos, November 1815, in Lemoine Villicaña, *Morelos su vida revolucionaria*, 610–14.

47. Bustamante, *Cuadro Histórico de la Revolución Mexicana*, 2:172–75; and Alamán, *Historia de México*, 4:323–26.

48. Autillo y Degradación del Cura Morelos, 27 November 1815, in Lemoine Villicaña, *Morelos su vida revolucionaria*, 632–35.

49. Alamán, *Historia de México*, 4:326.

50. Bustamante, *Cuadro Histórico de la Revolución Mexicana*, 2:176.

51. Alamán, *Historia de México*, 4:331–32.

52. Bustamante, *Cuadro Histórico de la Revolución Mexicana*, 2:176–77. Bustamante added some dialogue in response to the *virreina*'s request, having Calleja state, "I would do it [pardon Morelos]; but do you want that tomorrow they will threaten to make me a prisoner like my predecessor Iturrigaray?" The supposed direct quotation referred to the overthrow of José de Iturrigaray in September 1808. Bustamante went on to state, "This race of vipers [the gachupines] counted the moments of Morelos' existence, and was not satisfied until he was dead: if they could have deprived him of eternal glory that he enjoys today, they would have done so." The attitude reflected the intense anti-Spanish political views expressed following independence. For more on the possible interventions of the virreina, see José de J. Nuñez y Domínguez, *La Virreina Mexicana: Doña María Francisca de la Gándarra de Calleja* (Mexico City: Imprenta Universitaria, 1950), 239–41.

53. Ibid., 332.

54. Alamán, *Historia de México*, 4:332–34; Report of Manuel de la Concha, Mexico City, 21 December 1815, in Lemoine Villicaña, *Morelos su vida revolucionaria*, 653; and Bustamante, *Cuadro Histórico de la Revolución Mexicana*, 2:78–79. Again, Bustamante offers additional information and dialogue apparently designed to set the scene for commemoration of Morelos's life. When the bullets hit Morelos and he fell to the ground, Bustamante has him uttering a scream that announced the end of Spain in America and that resonated in the hearts of *buenos americanos*.

55. Alamán, *Historia de México*, 4:335.

56. Ibid., 4:477.
57. Ibid., 4:721–22.
58. Ibid., 4:723.
59. Ibid., 4:724.
60. Ibid., 4:725.
61. Christon I. Archer, "Where Did All the Royalists Go? New Light on the Military Collapse of New Spain, 1810–1822," in *The Mexican and Mexican American Excellency in the Nineteenth Century*, ed. Jaime Rodríguez (Tempe, AZ: Bilingual Press, 1989), 24–43; and Christon I. Archer, "La Causa Buena: The Counterinsurgency Army of New Spain and the Ten Years' War," in *The Independence of Mexico and the New Nation*, ed. Jaime Rodríguez (Los Angeles: UCLA, Latin American Center Publications, 1989), 63–84.
62. On Iturbide, see William Spence Robertson, *Iturbide of Mexico* (Durham, NC: Duke University Press, 1952); and Timothy E. Anna, *The Mexican Empire of Iturbide* (Lincoln: University of Nebraska Press, 1990); and Timothy E. Anna, "The Role of Agustín de Iturbide: An Appraisal," *Journal of Latin American Studies* 17, no. 1 (May 1985): 79–110; and Timothy E. Anna, "Agustín de Iturbide and the Process of Consensus, 187–204," in *The Birth of Modern Mexico*, ed. Christon I. Archer (Wilmington, DE: Scholarly Resources Inc., 2003). In his works, Anna has made a valiant effort to reinterpret Iturbide's roles.
63. Agustín de Iturbide, *A Statement of Some of the Principal Events in the Public Life of Agustín de Iturbide written by Himself* (Washington, DC: Documentary Publications, 1971), 6.
64. Ibid., 8.
65. For studies in English on Iturbide, see the books noted above by William Spence Robertson and Timothy E. Anna.
66. Christon I. Archer, "Insurrection—Reaction—Revolution—Fragmentation: Reconstructing the Choreography of Meltdown in New Spain during the Independence Era," *Mexican Studies/ Estudios Mexicanos* 10, no. 1 (winter 1994): 63–98.
67. Archer, "La Causa Buena," 103–4.
68. See Christon I. Archer, "Politicization of the Army of New Spain During the War of Independence, 1810–1821," in *The Evolution of the Mexican Political System*, ed. Jaime E. Rodríguez O. (Wilmington, DE: Scholarly Resources Inc., 1993), 17–46; and Christon I. Archer, "Fighting for Small Worlds: Wars of the People during the Independence Era in New Spain, 1810–1821," *Cuadernos de Historia Latinoamericana* 6 (1998): 63–92.

69. Robertson, *Iturbide of Mexico*, 36–50.
70. Relación de Méritos de Agustín de Iturbide, 31 agosto 1812, AGN:OG, vol. 426. These battles included Las Cruces on 30 October 1810; Iguala, 3 and 4 July 1811; Acuichio and Sipemio, 7 and 14 September 1811; Valle de Santiago, 25 May 1812; the capture of Cabecilla Albino García, June 1812; Calpulalpan, against Cabecilla Chito Villagran and Padre José María Correa, June 1812; Valle de Santiago, 24 July 1812; and Salamanca, 7 August 1812.
71. Diario Militar particular de D. Agustín de Iturbide y Aramburu, el que lleva en sus expediciones desde la convalencia de la fiebre en que curó en Valladolid, y contrajó en la Tierra Caliente de dicha Provincia . . . , in *The Papers of Agustín de Iturbide*, Library of Congress, Washington DC, Ms. 15,338, roll 1.
72. Diego García Conde to Viceroy Calleja, 17 March, 1813, AGN:OG, vol. 900.
73. Iturbide to Calleja, no.443, Silao, 20 June 1815, AGN:OG, vol. 431.
74. "Instancia de Agustín de Iturbide," in Pascual de Liñan to Viceroy Venadito, no. 1089, 27 July, 1820, AGN:OG, vol. 502. Liñan was the *auditor de guerra* (judge advocate) of the army of New Spain. He passed Iturbide's petition to the viceroy without comment. Obviously, the matter was of such importance that the viceroy would handle it on his own. Also see Jaime E. Rodríguez O., "The Transition from Colony to Nation: New Spain, 1820–1821," in *Mexico in the Age of Democratic Revolutions, 1750–1850*, ed. Jaime E. Rodríguez O. (Boulder, CO: Lynne Rienner Publishers, 1994), 116–19.
75. Alamán, *Historia de México*, 5:348.
76. Archer, "Where Did All the Royalists Go?" 24–43.
77. See Rebecca Earle, "'Padres de la Patria' and the Ancestral Past: Commemorations of Independence in Nineteenth Century Spanish America," *Journal of Lain American History* 34, no. 4 (November 2002): 780; and Michael Costeloe, "The Junta Patriótica and the Celebration of Independence in Mexico City, 1825–1855," *Mexican Studies: Estudios Mexicanos* 13, no. 1 (winter 1997): 22–25.
78. Robertson, *Iturbide of Mexico*, 116; and for a thorough overview of these events, see Jaime E. Rodríguez O., *The Independence of Spanish America* (Cambridge: Cambridge University Press, 1998), 209.
79. Ibid., 171; and Anna, *Mexican Empire of Iturbide*, 58–60.
80. Anna, *Mexican Empire of Iturbide*, 61–62; Robertson, *Iturbide of Mexico*, 172–73.

81. Robertson, *Iturbide of Mexico*, 226.

82. Alamán, *Historia de México*, 5:717.

83. Robertson, *Iturbide of Mexico*, 246–48; Anna, *Mexican Empire of Iturbide*, 197–98; and Alamán, *Historia de México*, 5:740.

84. Robertson, *Iturbide of Mexico*, 283–84; and Anna, *Mexican Empire of Iturbide*, 231–32.

85. Alamán, *Historia de México*, 5:671.

86. Ibid., 5:793.

87. Ibid., 5:795.

88. Ibid., appendix, document 24: Extracto de las sesiones del congreso del Estado de Tamaulipas, reunido en la villa de Padilla, relativas á la ejecución de D. Agustín de Iturbide, 71–81.

89. Ibid., 5:797.

90. Ibid., 5:798.

91. Jaime E. Rodríguez O., "Vicente Rocafuerte," in *Historiogafía Mexicana*, vol. 3, *El Surgimiento de la Historiografía Nacional*, ed. Juan A. Ortega y Medina and Rosa Camelo (Mexico City: UNAM, 1997), 180.

92. Michael Costeloe, "The Junta Patrótica and the Celebration of Independence in Mexico City, 1825–1855," *Mexico Studies/Estudios Mexicanos* 13, no. 1 (winter 1997): 23; and Timmons, *Morelos of Mexico*, 166.

93. Alamán, *Historia de México*, 5:768–69.

94. Harvey Gardiner, ed., *Mexico, 1825–1828: The Journal and Correspondence of Edward Thornton Tayloe* (Chapel Hill: University of North Carolina Press, 1959), 80–81.

95. Ibid., 136.

96. Fanny Calderón de la Barca, *Life in Mexico during a Residence of Two Years in the Country* (London: J. M. Dent, 1913), 258.

97. Alamán, *Historia de México*, 5:802–3.

98. Carmen Vázquez Mantecón, *Santa Anna y la encrucijada del Estado: La dictadura (1853–1855)* (Mexico City: Fondo de Cultura Económica, 1986), 47.

99. Ernest Gruening, *Mexico and Its Heritage* (New York: D. Appleton-Century Company, 1936), 80.

100. Bustamante, *Cuadro Histórico de la Revolución Mexicana*, 3:342.

101. Ibid.

102. Ibid.

103. Ibid., 3:844.

104. Timmons, *Morelos of Mexico*, 167.

105. Robert H. Duncan, "Political Legitimization and Maximilian's Second Empire in Mexico, 1864–1867," *Mexican Studies/Estudios Mexicanos* 12, no. 1 (winter 1996): 56.

106. Ibid., 58–59; and Susan Hale, *Mexico* (New York: G. P. Putnam's Sons, 1888), 257.

107. Duncan, "Political Legitimization," 59–60.

108. Anna, *Mexican Empire of Iturbide*, 110–11.

Chapter Four

"Sometimes Knowing How to Forget Is Also Having Memory":

The Repatriation of Juan Manuel de Rosas and the Healing of Argentina

Jeffrey M. Shumway

Observers on the streets of Buenos Aires would have been duly impressed by the spectacle they saw on September 30, 1989. A procession, which included horsemen clad in nineteenth-century military uniforms, escorted the remains of Juan Manuel de Rosas toward the immaculate La Recoleta cemetery. The procession itself was symbolically enormous, for Rosas was perhaps the most famous and infamous figure of nineteenth-century Argentine history, and he had not stepped foot, alive or dead, in Argentina since going into exile in England in 1852. Also marching in the procession were descendants of Rosas, overcome with emotion and pride for at last bringing their hero home. Accompanying Rosas's descendants were the descendants of many of Rosas's enemies from the nineteenth century. Even though their ancestors detested, killed, and exiled each other, these families walked together as a symbol of national unification in 1989.[1]

Juan Manuel de Rosas was the governor of Buenos Aires Province and the leader of the Argentine Confederation from 1829 until his overthrow in 1852 (with a brief hiatus in the early 1830s). Following his defeat, he immediately left for exile in England, where he died in 1877, just shy of his eighty-fourth birthday. Rosas's supporters, both past and present, have praised him as an advocate of provincial rights, an icon of authentic Argentine culture, and a staunch defender of national sovereignty. To his critics he was a ruthless tyrant who ordered the murder or exile of his opponents and kept Argentina mired in backward tradition.[2] Many of the great liberal leaders of nineteenth-century Argentina, while in exile, fiercely opposed Rosas during his rule, and did so just as vigorously when Rosas himself went into exile. Bartolomé Mitre, soldier, historian, journalist, and future first president of the united Argentina, was a commander in the armies that defeated Rosas in 1852. Also accompanying the campaign that year was Domingo F. Sarmiento, author, educator, and another future president of the nation.[3] As a testament to their fame and stature, both Mitre and Sarmiento were buried in La Recoleta, the most distinguished *necrópolis* (cemetery) in the land, which also boasts the remains of most of Argentina's rich and powerful, including Evita Perón.

Bodies on the Move

On September 30, 1989, the remains of Juan Manuel de Rosas, as if to confront his old nemeses Mitre and Sarmiento, were finally returned to his home soil and placed in La Recoleta cemetery after more than a century of mortal and postmortem exile in England. But far from an act of confrontation between ancient enemies, the repatriation of Rosas served, for some, as an act of national reconciliation. For Argentina in 1989 was a country broken by decades of nauseating social and political bickering. Most recently, between 1976 and 1983, Argentines had suffered through a bloody military regime, driven by militant anticommunism, that conducted a "Dirty War" against all who were perceived as a threat to the nation. The military dictatorship left power only after leading the country into economic ruin and the humiliating Falklands/Malvinas War with England in 1982.[4]

After the return of democracy in 1983, Argentina faced enormous social and economic hardships as it tried to move on from the horrors of the dictatorship. Part of moving on was the trial and conviction of participants and leaders of the military dictatorship. However, those trials, and the general denigration of the military forces, brought on a new wave of military rebellions that threatened the fledgling democracy. These daunting challenges loomed before President Carlos Saúl Menem from the Peronist party, who took office in July 1989. Menem wanted to heal the wounds of his country, reconcile civilians and the military, and unify the nation, and he hoped that the repatriation of Juan Manuel de Rosas's body would help. After all, Rosas was once called "the restorer of the laws"; perhaps he could yet help restore the nation.

The repositioning of bodies was also taking place elsewhere. On a global scale, 1989 was a year when the graves of the famous and infamous, depending on one's perspective, were unusually active. This was especially the case in Eastern postsocialist Europe after the fall of the Soviet Union. Just as Eastern Europeans rewrote histories that had been dominated by Soviet ideology, so Argentina was attempting to emerge from its own bout with the cold-war contradictions manifested during the Dirty War. In Argentina and around the world, this transition meant erasing recent memories and resurrecting or reconciling with older ones. Repositioning bodies, as Menem and others did with Juan Manuel de Rosas, was a way to reorder the "cosmic universe" of values and identities.[5]

Restoring and reconciling Argentina would almost take a miracle, it seemed, and Menem did not hesitate to invoke the name of God in his quest. During his electoral campaign and his first few months in office, Menem sought to bridge the great divides that plagued the nation. By invoking God and using images from the life of Christ, Menem attempted to make his authority sacred as he took on the mantle of healer, even political savior. For Menem, the spirits and bodies of the dead across two centuries of Argentine history, if invoked correctly, might help lift the nation from the grip of death. By so doing, Menem tried to alter the collective memory of Argentine history and sought to redefine the nation's political and cultural family tree by reconciling archenemies of the past, including Rosas, Mitre, and Sarmiento.

Menem used these powerful symbols during the three most significant events of his early presidency: his inauguration, the repatriation of the body of Juan Manuel de Rosas, and the pardoning of convicted military personnel. It was the repatriation of Rosas, however, that provided the powerful story and symbol within which Menem could pursue his project of reconciliation. When Menem talked about forgetting past rancor regarding Rosas, he also provided a metaphor for healing societal wounds inflicted during the military regime. In the end, many Argentines were more willing to accept the repatriation of Rosas as a reconciliation with the remote nineteenth-century past and its contemporary legacy, but they proved more resistant to reconciling with the more recent tyrannies of the military dictatorship.

Since the nineteenth century Rosas's supporters dreamed of burying him in Argentina, and because he was such a controversial figure, the repatriation of his remains in 1989 meant different things to different people. This chapter, while offering an overview of different groups' views of Rosas and the repatriation, focuses on President Menem's use of the repatriation.

The Rise of Don Juan Manuel de Rosas

A dizzying array of historical symbols and images converged in the repatriation of Rosas. To grasp the most important convergences it is imperative to understand the basic contours of Rosas's rise to power, his rule, his exile, death, and legacy. Juan Manuel de Rosas was born on March 30, 1793, in San Miguel del Monte, in the province of Buenos Aires, to a family of some wealth. The late eighteenth and early nineteenth centuries were a time of transition for Argentina as Spanish colonial order gave way to an independent nation after 1810. Juan Manuel de Rosas flourished in the expanding ranching economy and also excelled as a militia commander. Such was Rosas's skill on horseback that it was commonly asserted that he could ride better than the gauchos who worked for him. (See Illustration 4.1.)

Rosas eventually involved himself in the politics of the day. Since 1810, Argentina had been divided by two main political factions, federalists and unitarians, labels that corresponded generally with conservatives and liberals elsewhere in Latin America. Federalists advocated strong provincial political rights and demanded the protection of provincial economic activities from excessive foreign competition. Many federalists also treasured their unique Argentine creole heritage, which consisted of a combination of Old and New World races and cultures bound together by the Catholic Church. Federalists stereotypically represented the interests of the interior provinces, those that did not benefit directly from international trade. Unitarians, by contrast, usually represented the interests of liberals from the port city of Buenos Aires (whose citizens are known as *porteños*). Unitarians promoted, among other things, reducing the power of the Catholic Church, instituting liberal free-trade policies, and creating a strong central government that could shape Argentina into a modern, secular nation like those emerging in the United States and Europe. These two factions struggled for dominance throughout the 1810s and 1820s.

4.1 *Juan Manuel de Rosas in his prime (Photo: Archivo General de la Nación).*

Although Rosas frequently refused to be labeled one way or the other, as a rancher and advocate of the rights of the Province of Buenos Aires, he ended up supporting the federalist cause. And Buenos Aires had many rights to protect, at least from a federalist perspective. The province was a geographic gem. Its fertile grasslands and strategically placed port made it the export-import center of the country, which also meant that the city controlled the lucrative customs duties. It was this "economic birthright" that Buenos Aires federalists sought to protect from proposed attempts to redistribute Buenos Aires's wealth to the other provinces. These proposals included plans to share the customs revenues among the provinces and detach the city of Buenos Aires from the Buenos Aires Province and make it into a federal capital similar to Washington DC for the United States, something Buenos Aires federalists saw as "decapitating" their province. The doctrine of federalism, then, served the federalists of Buenos Aires, Juan Manuel de Rosas among them, very well, while other provinces suffered.

Rosas experienced early success as a militia commander, but his interest in politics intensified when unitarian forces executed the federalist governor of Buenos Aires, Manuel Dorrego, in 1828. Rosas marshaled his forces and successfully laid siege to Buenos Aires. After a negotiated peace, the House of Representatives elected Rosas governor in 1829. After a brief hiatus from rule, Rosas returned to the governorship in 1835, and the legislature granted him broad powers. Rosas ruled with an iron fist and repressed public opposition. He forced many of his opponents into exile, while others were killed by his dreaded henchmen, the *mazorca*. One of his most infamous acts was ordering the execution of Camila O'Gorman, the daughter of a well-known family, and her lover, the priest Ladislao Gutiérrez. This and other misdeeds confirmed for many that he indeed was "the Caligula of the River Plate." Such abrasive epithets were hurled at Rosas in newspapers and other publications, all decrying the debacle of his regime (of course published by exiles in Uruguay, Chile, and Brazil, among other places).

Rosas faced many challenges during his governorship. Allies from the interior provinces constantly nagged him to protect their rights and help them develop trade and industry. But true federalism, in the Argentine sense, meant the protection of provincial rights from the encroachment of other provinces and the national government. Privileged to live in the wealthiest province, Rosas focused his federalism on protecting Buenos Aires's advantages.

Rosas also endured serious challenges to Argentine sovereignty from foreign powers. He performed admirably in staving off imperialistic advances of England and France. One of the most memorable confrontations came at the Vuelta de Obligado in November 1845, when a combined Anglo-French fleet tried to force open the Río Paraná to trade. Rosas put chains across the river to prevent the ships from passing, and ordered artillery batteries set up along the shoreline to shell the European vessels. Although the fleet finally made it successfully up the river, in the long run the English, with the most powerful navy in the world, were unable to keep the river trade open to their liking. These courageous acts brought Rosas praise from many segments of Argentine society that mistrusted European imperialism in Argentina. Rosas also received accolades from none other than General José de San Martín, the hero of independence and liberator of Argentina and Chile from Spanish colonialism. General San Martín so admired Rosas for his efforts that he gave Rosas the saber he had used in the independence wars. The battle at the Vuelta de Obligado became a symbol of Rosas's defense of national sovereignty, something that won him support at the time and endeared him forever in the hearts of Argentine nationalists. San Martín's acknowledgment of Rosas's patriotism would also not be forgotten. Besides a protector of national sovereignty, Rosas was seen by many as a defender of Hispanic-American identity in the hemisphere. As the British official Lord Howden explained, "They call it 'the great American system,' which is a determination never to admit the right of any European power to intervene, in hostility or protection, in the affairs of this Continent."[6]

The Fall, Exile, and Death of Rosas

While Rosas made some attempts to alleviate the plight of the interior provinces, his policies eventually fell short, and by 1850 his allies in the interior turned against him. In 1852, Rosas lost the battle of Caseros to Justo José de Urquiza, a federalist general from the province of Entre Ríos. Fleeing from the battlefield, Rosas boarded an English warship and sailed, ironically, for safety in Great Britain, where he would live the rest of his life. With Rosas out of the picture, exiled liberals returned in droves to Buenos Aires, where they embarked on an ambitious project of nation building. An essential part of that project was to erase, or at least denigrate, the memory of Rosas and his legacy. The new government confiscated all of Rosas's property and later convicted him of high crimes against the state. At the judgment, Félix Frías declared that "the name of Rozas will be stigmatized until the furthest generations in this country, and the sun of [the May Revolution] will have to shine many times before the blood, still wet in the city and countryside, dries up."[7] The famed writer José Mármol, imprisoned then exiled by Rosas in 1840, waxed poetic and prophetic in his denunciation of the toppled leader: "Not even the dust of his bones will rest in America."[8]

The issue of Rosas's memory would be important in another vital part of the nation-building project: the writing of a national history. Bartolomé Mitre, the vigorous young opponent of Rosas, future president of Argentina, and founder of the still-running newspaper *La Nación*, eagerly took up the task. In 1857 Mitre published a collection of biographies entitled *Galería de celebridades argentinas* (Gallery of Argentine celebrities), which helped establish the canon of "official" Argentine history. Mitre alluded to Rosas and spoke of other caudillos specifically in the introduction to the book.

> These men, truly distinguished in a negative sense, exercised tremendous influence over the destiny of the peoples of the River Plate. Their lives are devoid of transcendent incidents; they are the representatives of the domineering forces of barbarism, and their actions carry the seal of a primitive energy. These men can serve as a lesson for future Argentines. . . . Behold in them another series of historical portraits, terrible and threatening portraits which inspire horror, but can enhance by contrast the beautiful countenances of those who are become celebrated through their service, virtue, and intellectual endeavor.[9]

Perhaps it would have been too much to expect, so soon after Rosas's fall, for Mitre to use history as a tool of national reconciliation and unification, as some historians did in other parts of the Americas.[10] Instead, Mitre imposed historical exile on his enemies. For Mitre, Rosas and his gaucho hordes were so many phantoms that would haunt Argentina's future if the proper lessons of history were not learned. His ideas summarized the liberal interpretation then and in many ways continue to reflect the sentiments of many Argentines today. Rosas's supporters, by contrast, chafed under the weight of "official history." The mortal and postmortem exile of their hero was one of the great injustices of history.

Meanwhile, Rosas tried his best to start a new life in England. He chose to settle in Southampton, where he eventually bought a four-hundred-acre farm that included cows, goats, and horses. He stayed in contact with a few loyal friends in Argentina, but the trial, the confiscations, and the humiliation heaped on Rosas by his enemies increased the burdens of exile on the former governor. He was especially angered by rumors that he had stolen money while in office, something he vehemently denied. For a while he refused visits from his daughter Manuelita, who had followed him with her husband into exile, and he balked at accepting invitations from his English friends to go fox hunting and attend parties. After the first ten years of exile, however, Rosas seemed to settle into a comfortable pattern of living.

His passion for riding horses and showing off his gaucho tricks persisted to the end of his life.

Rosas's loss of stature was punctuated by his death and burial. He contracted pneumonia in early 1877, and it ultimately claimed his life on March 14, 1877, just before his eighty-fourth birthday. *The Times* of London published an obituary, which for many captured Rosas's character: "The general had become quite infirm from gout for some years, but he might be seen constantly riding about the grounds, and his greatest happiness seemed to be to sit on his horse and give orders to those employed. His love of what may be termed despotic command was so great that no one was allowed to speak a word except by way of acknowledgment of commands or in answer to questions."[11] He was buried without great fanfare in the Catholic cemetery of Southampton. Although Rosas's supporters may have mourned his passing, the official response to his death in Argentina was to suppress any veneration of his memory. Faced with the prospect of pro-Rosas demonstrations, the national government issued decrees in April 1877 that barred any public demonstration in favor of "the tyrant Rosas." On April 24 the government issued a statement aimed at honoring those who died at Rosas's hand: "It is appropriate that a strong people should honor the memory of those who died fighting against tyrants and in favor of liberty, and it is the government's duty to stimulate those manifestations of the people that promote civic pride by remembering and venerating patriots."[12]

The anti-Rosista nature of the official version of nineteenth-century Argentine history had powerful proponents. Nevertheless, by the end of the century, some scholars began to vindicate Rosas's memory. Ernesto Quesada, Adolfo Saldías, and others initiated a movement by scholars who later became known as "revisionists" for their attempts to buck the official history and tell the story of Rosas and his era in a positive light. Thus the battle between Rosista and anti-Rosista forces, though tilted heavily in favor of the latter, continued in the pages of history books and in the memories of the Argentine people.

The body of Rosas and the location of its final resting place also became a battleground. In his will, Rosas had anticipated the furor over his burial place. In the short term, he wanted to be buried in the Catholic cemetery of Southampton. However, once "my country recognizes, along with its government, the justice owed me for my services," he wrote, he wanted his body taken back to Argentina for a dignified though modest burial.[13] For Rosas's supporters in the nineteenth and twentieth centuries, the day of recognizing the governor's services was long overdue. For them, it was anathema for a true Argentine hero to be buried on foreign soil, and English soil at that![14] Anti-Rosistas, for their part, were happy to let stand Mármol's prediction about the dust of Rosas's bones never returning. The question took more than one hundred years to resolve.

The Rise of Revisionism and the Idea of Repatriation

Rosas supporters worked relentlessly to prove Mármol wrong and to repatriate their hero. They were aided by the growth in the 1920s and 1930s of the revisionist school of historiography that worked to rehabilitate Rosas's image. The Instituto Juan Manuel de Rosas was also founded in the 1930s for the same purpose. Revisionists naturally focused on Rosas's strong suit as defender of national sovereignty.[15] And while revisionism looked good on paper, Rosas's foreign burial ground continued to anger his supporters. Also in the 1930s, the Pro-Repatriation of Rosas Committee was established, and by the 1960s it had become quite active, even seeking the aid of exiled former president Juan D. Perón. An ardent admirer of Rosas, Juan Perón, along with his wife Evita, had governed Argentina from 1946 to 1955, when he was ousted by a military coup. Although exiled, Perón still had powerful contacts within the country.

Perón was, in many ways, similar to Juan Manuel: a military background; a popular base of power; strong nationalist sentiments; a life of exile (Perón's party had even been banned from fielding candidates in what was supposed to be a democratic system); and a denigrated memory in the official histories of the nation. Perón made his admiration for Rosas clear in his writings. "In protecting the Nation it is just as important to defend its future as to do justice to its past," wrote Perón in 1970 to Manuel de Anchorena, member of the pro-repatriation committee. Anchorena himself came from a family of ranchers and was related to Rosas. For Perón, Anchorena, and others, the injustices of the past included the anti-Rosista nature of official history. "Since I was a child," Perón continued in his letter, "my spirit has been repulsed by the fabricated 'histories' written by scribes of ignominy and rancor." Given the opportunity later in life to peruse documents in the National Archive, Perón found that "the extant documentation was totally unknown to me and it was covered by layers of dust which testified to its lack of use up to that point." Perón concluded that the history of Rosas, "like cheap music, has been written by amateur historians under contract. It has been necessary to await the action of the historical revisionists to know the reality hidden under the nefarious obscurity of lies." Perón went on to characterize the former governor in typical Rosista and Peronista fashion: "In the fight for liberation, Brigadier General Don Juan Manuel de Rosas deserves to be the archetype that inspires and guides us, because for more than a century and a half of shameful colonialism, he has been one of the few who knew how to honorably defend national sovereignty."[16]

When Perón returned to office again in 1973, after nearly twenty years of exile, he appointed Manuel de Anchorena as ambassador to England and gave him two specific charges: achieve a diplomatic solution to the issue of sovereignty over the Malvinas (Falklands) Islands, and repatriate the remains of Juan Manuel de Rosas. Anchorena was the right man for the job, for his admiration for Rosas perhaps exceeded even Perón's. "We should mention," Anchorena wrote in his memoirs of the repatriation, "that we consider the Restorer to be the most gaucho of all Argentines of all times. We have already indicated that he lived and died like a gaucho. Up to his last moments, as he made up his will, in his use of bolas and the lasso, and in spending even the last days of his life on horseback, he honored the verses of Martín Fierro."[17]

After receiving Perón's commission, Anchorena and others quickly went to work and shortly received permission from Great Britain to carry out the repatriation. By 1974, the National Congress of Argentina passed a resolution to repatriate Rosas's remains.[18]

The Breaking of Argentina

Times were hard in the Argentina of the mid-1970s. Perón died in 1974, leaving a country that was deeply divided along ideological lines to be ruled by his third wife, Isabelita. While leftist guerillas mounted kidnapping and assassination campaigns, right-wing anticommunist groups carried out their own war against perceived threats to the nation. It soon became clear that the presidency of Isabelita Perón could not survive. On March 24, 1976, the armed forces took over and initiated what they termed "the Process of National Reorganization," or *el proceso*. These were dark times for Argentina as a whole, as well as for the plans to repatriate Rosas. It is not clear if the generals or the repatriation committee instigated the pause, but just when Rosas's repatriation seemed imminent, it was put on hold.[19]

The military regimes that followed the coup of 1976 pursued a policy of national security that justified terror and murder for those labeled as enemies of the state. Thousands of alleged "subversives" were "disappeared" without a trace. From the military's perspective, they were stepping into an impossible situation and were forced to defend the nation.[20] For the thousands who died, and the families that mourned them, the proceso was a reign of terror.[21] It was a time when thinking certain thoughts and identifying with certain ideas were deemed as dangerous as carrying a weapon. Estimates of those killed or disappeared are as high as thirty thousand. Many, if not most, were tortured before they were killed. Others were drugged, taken up in airplanes, and dumped into the sea. Parents were killed and their children given up for adoption to be raised by military families or collaborators. Women taken prisoner while pregnant were usually allowed to give birth to their child before they were killed, and the child would then be given up for adoption. Still others were set free and later told their tales. One prisoner, Alicia Partnoy, remembered how her friend Graciela gave birth in prison and then was killed. Her son was given to one of her interrogators. "A new cry makes its way through the shadows fighting above the trailer. Graciela has just given birth. A prisoner child has been born. While the killer's hands welcome him into the world, the shadow of the life leaves the scene, half a winner, half a loser: on her shoulders she wears a poncho of injustice."[22] Disappearances such as these set off years of searching by family members, including grandmothers, who still today are looking for their lost and stolen grandchildren.

The proceso deeply wounded Argentine pride and identity. When public opposition mounted in the early 1980s, the military government sought to bolster domestic support through combative foreign relations. Argentine generals considered war with Chile, but finally settled on the Malvinas Islands dispute with Great Britain. It would, they hoped, be "the easiest war." They were wrong. After an initially successful invasion of the islands in 1982, the Argentine military suffered a quick and decisive defeat once the British arrived in force. In addition to the domestic political and economic crises, Argentina had now been humiliated in the international arena. The junta resigned in disgrace, and democracy returned to Argentina in 1983. The new president, Raúl Alfonsín from the reformist Radical Party, confronted the monumental task of managing the transition back to democracy. Perhaps he simply did not have time to deal with the issue of Rosas's repatriation, but the Pro-Repatriation Committee's petitions to start the process moving again went unanswered.[23] That Rosas served as a hero to Peronists, as well as to right-wing political groups who supported the military coup may have also inspired Alfonsín's inaction. Given the crisis facing Alfonsín such neglect is perhaps understandable, for he had more immediate demands to confront.

Among Alfonsín's most pressing problems was how to deal with the military leaders of the proceso and the thousands of cases of torture, murder, and disappearances. Who should be prosecuted? What about the concept of "due obedience," which supposedly shielded junior officers and staff members from the evils of their superiors? How could a country move on after such a crisis? The pressure surrounding these issues was immense from all sides. Victims wanted justice and retribution, yet Alfonsín could not afford to completely alienate the military either. He set up a National Committee on the Disappeared and, armed with its findings, put nine high-level military commanders on trial in 1985. Lower-level officers, the court decided, could invoke the concept of "due obedience," so long as they did not engage in acts deemed as "aberrant" and "atrocious." Seven of the nine were convicted and sentenced to terms varying from fifteen months to life in prison. Two were acquitted. Many other junior officers were put on trial in a process that took years. Finally, to avoid an endless parade of trials, and emphasizing the need to move forward as a nation, Alfonsín declared a *punto final*, or "final point," after which no more accusations could be brought against those involved in the military regime.[24]

In the end it was impossible to satisfy all parties. Human-rights activists and victims bemoaned what they saw as lenient sentences for only a handful of those who deserved prosecution. For them, the very idea of "punto final" was pitiful justice. Furthermore, military rebellions erupted around the country in protest of what some perceived as the relentless persecution and denigration of the military as an institution.[25] To make matters worse for Alfonsín, the Argentine economy plummeted during his tenure in office as hyperinflation reached astronomical levels. Such was the turmoil of the country that Alfonsín left office prematurely.

"Rise Up and Walk": The Healing Arts of Dr. Carlos Saúl Menem

All of these problems continued to loom before the new president, Dr. Carlos Saúl Menem, who took office in July 1989. Having served as the Peronist governor of the province of La Rioja, Menem boasted a long political history that included being imprisoned and tortured by the military government in the 1970s. Using his many gifts as a politician, Menem capitalized on the populist tradition of Peronism and effectively employed federalist symbols from the Rosas era.[26] Menem even groomed his sideburns in a way that evoked images of La Rioja caudillos such as El Chacho Peñaloza and Facundo Quiroga, Rosas's trusted ally. His inauguration parade also included many gaucho horseman. As he assumed office, Menem knew that he would need all the political prowess, all the symbolism, and all the charisma he could muster in order to bring Argentina out of the crisis of 1989.

"I would like to inaugurate this transcendental moment in which we live with a petition, a plea, with a call. I want my first words as president of the Argentines to be an oration to heaven, to our best efforts, to our most vital hopes. Before the eye of God, and before the testimony of history, I proclaim: Argentina, rise up and walk."[27] So did Menem open up his inaugural address on July 8, 1989. "The truth must be told once and for all," he continued. "Argentina is broken." Menem then introduced the main theme of his early presidency: the reconciliation of the nation. "I solemnly proclaim before my people, that this moment marks the beginning of a time of renewal for all Argentines. The country of 'everyone against everyone' is finished. The country of 'all for all' has begun."[28]

Menem highlighted the festering problem of civilian-military relations that he would strive to heal. The president strengthened his authority to act by recalling his own sufferings at the hands of the military. "Once upon a time, from the depths of my prison cell, from the depths of my suffering under torture, from the bitterness of my imprisonment, I pleaded to the most High of my necessity to dream of this moment. I asked Him to extend an open hand to my enemies before He closed off a bridge to my enemies. I asked for wisdom to build bridges of union instead of the passion to build walls of discord. Today I feel that that petition is beginning to be fulfilled." In this brief vignette of his experience in prison, Menem did not ask for vengeance, retribution, or even justice. Instead, he appeared to turn the other cheek toward some type of forgetting, or at least toward forgiveness. "We will never allow a confrontation between civilians and the military because both shape and nourish the essence of the Argentine people." It was now time to "move toward pacification, love, and patriotism. After six years of democracy we still have not overcome the cruel conflicts that divided us more than a decade ago. Between all of us Argentines we will find a definitive and final solution for those wounds that still wait to be closed. We will not agitate phantoms of dissent. We will serenade spirits."[29]

To build those bridges and to serenade the dead, Menem looked to the great men of the past. "There are San Martín, Bolívar, Artigas, Perón, and many others, telling us that our common frontiers should be bridges of union" that "strengthen our brotherhood and progress." Menem wanted to redraw the Argentine genealogical family tree, to displace Mitre's gallery of celebrities with a more inclusive pantheon. "I want to be the president of Rosas and Sarmiento" and of "Mitre and Facundo." This most unlikely coupling of historical enemies highlighted Menem's desire to bridge the gaps of Argentina's past. Where Mitre had created exclusion and division in the nineteenth century, Menem sought consensus and inclusion. Menem closed his inaugural speech the same way he began, with an invocation of deity: "A voice is raised today like a prayer, like a plea, like an inspiring call: Argentina, rise up and walk. Argentina, rise up and walk. Argentina, rise up and walk."[30]

The Repatriation and "Other Wounds to Close"

All of this healing, bridging, and closing of wounds would be a weighty task, even for the energetic Menem. He would need equally powerful healing tools. Fortunately for Menem, a potent tool waited in the wings. The Pro-Repatriation Committee had been longing for the moment to renew their efforts, aborted fifteen years earlier by the coup. Menem was their man. The decision to support the repatriation was consistent with Menem's Peronist perspective, since Perón himself had long before claimed affinity for Rosas. It also seemed like good political sense, since repatriating Rosas would allow Menem to address a number of issues that poisoned Argentine society: the long and bitter conflicts that separated Rosista and anti-Rosistas, nationalists and liberals, and the most vexing, the current gulf between the military and civilian society. Moreover, Menem hoped to renew relations with Great Britain. For all of these reasons, Menem encouraged the repatriation committee where Alfonsín had not, and very soon the British agreed to allow the exhumation and transfer of Rosas's remains.[31] (See Illustrations 4.2 and 4.3.) The plan was for the coffin to be removed from the cemetery in Southampton, loaded onto a plane, flown to France where the remains would be put into a new coffin, then flown to Argentina after stopovers in the Canary Islands and Brazil.

Rosas's supporters had long hoped to place Rosas's remains in the Cathedral of Buenos Aires, most notably the resting place of General José de San Martín, the great liberator who helped establish independence from Spain.[32] But whereas there was national consensus in support of San Martín's stature as a national hero, the legacy of Rosas continued to bitterly divide Argentina. The church had granted the committee permission to inter Rosas in the cathedral in 1974, but many things had changed since then. In 1982 Pope John Paul II decreed that no one would be buried in cathedrals except for popes, archbishops, and cardinals.[33] Still, in 1989 the committee hoped to bypass this regulation because the concession was received before the papal decree. To that end, Manuel de Anchorena sought an audience with the Papal Nuncio, Monseñor Calabresi. By Anchorena's own account, Calabresi rebuffed him. According to Anchorena, Calabresi

4.2   *President Menem meets with the Pro-Repatriation Committee (Photo: José María Soaje Pinto).*

4.3 *Members of the Pro-Repatriation Committee in front of Rosas's tomb in Southampton, England. From left to right: Eugenio Rhom, Juan Manuel Soaje Pinto, José María Soaje Pinto, Martín Garretón (Photo: José María Soaje Pinto).*

first informed him that Rosas did not deserve such a burial because he did not approach the level of General San Martín's greatness. Calabresi then added the clincher: "Next you will want to have Perón buried in the cathedral."[34] Although by his own profession Anchorena was a "practicing Apostolic Roman Catholic and I attend mass every Sunday," Calabresi's response deeply offended him, especially since the Nuncio was the representative of the Vatican, "a foreign state."[35] In the meantime the committee decided to place Rosas's remains in the cemetery of La Recoleta.[36]

While disappointed by the clerical obstacles to burial in the cathedral, the repatriation committee pressed forward. At 3:00 P.M. on

September 21, Rosas's body was exhumed in the Southampton cemetery. In his book chronicling the trip, Anchorena remembers the
moment with reverence. Tears filled his eyes as the Argentine flag was
placed over the coffin, the same flag that had flown over the Argentine
embassy in London at the time of the War of the Malvinas. After
boarding a plane, the commission headed for France. When they
entered French airspace, the captain opened a bottle of champagne,
everyone participated in a solemn toast, after which they all recited
the holy rosary. The French treated Rosas's remains like those of a
head of state: full military honors, the French flag at half staff, and a
red carpet. The repatriation team stayed in France for a few days as
Rosas's remains were transferred to a new coffin.[37]

Meanwhile, back in Argentina, the country prepared for Rosas's
return. How would the people respond to the return of one who had
been known to some as the "Restorer of the Laws" and to others as
"the Caligula of the River Plate"? Answers began pouring in by way
of newspaper accounts and editorials. In one of history's ironies, an
echo of the nineteenth century was heard from the newspaper *La
Nación*: the director of the newspaper in 1989 was Bartolomé Mitre,
direct descendant of Bartolomé Mitre, the first president of a united
Argentina (1862), the original founder of the newspaper, and committed foe of Rosas in word and deed. In an editorial of September
10, 1989, Mitre revealed his inheritance of nineteenth-century liberal
unitarianism. In the old days, Mitre argued, any discussion of Rosas
would "incite abrasive polemic and kindle old passions."
Nevertheless, he continued, *La Nación* had always been open to the
idea of repatriation, at least theoretically. When the idea of bringing
the governor back surfaced in 1934 the paper had stated that it was
"not opposed, for our part, that the bones of the exile of Southampton
return to rest in the womb of this country, which owes its most sober
hours to him." In 1974 the editors had again written that they did not
oppose the idea. "The judgment of history on his person and his government will not change because of it." If *La Nación* had not opposed
the idea before, reasoned Mitre, it would not do so now. "When over
a hundred years has passed" since Rosas's death, the repatriation
"should not provoke angry disputes." Nevertheless, Mitre clearly
stated that "for those who have followed a historical interpretation
that condemns despotism and tyranny in all forms," and for those who
value the freedoms that emerged after 1852, "the era of Rosas forms
a dark and painful history of the nation." These "ideals and values

should not be forgotten." Despite the clear opposition to the legacy of Rosas, the paper favored the idea of national reconciliation and repatriation. "Time, one way or another, heals wounds and allows for passed events to be seen in a spirit of reconciliation." And now, perhaps more than ever, after the recent decades of "stagnation and retrogression," it was time to embrace the "hope that liberty and harmony among men can put Argentina back on the path of economic and cultural growth."[38] This support, though quite qualified, surely pleased Menem, since *La Nación* represented a powerful voice of Argentine liberals.

Stronger manifestations of support came in from around the country as unions and other groups released official statements to the press. The Federation of Professionals from the province of Córdoba, the General Confederation of Workers (CGT), and many other groups lent their support to the move. Pro-Rosas groups in Córdoba established a "permanent commission of honor," with the stated purpose of "recreating the presence of the 'restorer of the laws,' placing him alongside the great men of his era, and searching for the historical truth." In addition, the commission hoped to "initiate an educational campaign to massively vindicate the necessity to unify our collective memory, resolving our past confrontations in a brotherly fashion."[39]

Others, however, opposed aspects of the repatriation. Notably, a voice of dissent emerged from Córdoba, in the interior of the country. Although the interior was traditionally a bastion of federalism, and even of Rosismo during certain times, the Buenos Aires-centered federalism of his regime ended up souring Rosas's relationships with many from the interior. As the following editorial in *La Voz del Interior* by Raúl Faure illustrates, Rosas had betrayed true federalism by favoring the province of Buenos Aires above the rest. Under the title "Not even the dust of his bones will rest in the homeland," Faure conceded that the prophecy of José Mármol would finally be disproved. However, Faure warned that Argentines should not place Rosas on par with General San Martín. The truth was that for more than two decades, Rosas "denied the country of regular government for the exclusive benefit of the province of Buenos Aires and its port city." It was that geographic reality which gave Buenos Aires the key to the treasures of Argentina, and Rosas held on to that key to the detriment of the rest. Glorifying Rosas without looking at the true history will do nothing to "pacify spirits."[40]

Faure also comprehended, as did many others, that in reconciling with Rosas, Menem sought to lay the foundation for reconciliation with the military.[41] Menem had already made his decision to pardon convicted military personnel and had hinted it would come in October 1989.[42] The issue of the pardons was much more divisive than the repatriation. The powerful La Unión Industrial Argentina expressed what many others thought as well: Menem had the right to reconcile with the military because he had suffered torture under the military. The union called the pardons "another step in the reconciliation of the Argentine family." After a mass attended by Menem on September 21, Monseñor Rodolfo Bufano told *La Nación* that he hoped the pardons would serve to "bring definitive peace" to the country. "I plead that God will illuminate not only the president . . . but all of us" and that "the pardons will truly be a solution and facilitate pacification."[43]

Others fiercely opposed the pardons, including Argentine and international human-rights organizations. Polls indicated that more than 70 percent of Argentines opposed pardoning. Alongside many newspaper accounts that traced the progress of the repatriation stood articles about masses of people organizing against the proposed pardons. Clearly, many Argentines understood that Menem was trying to use Rosas's repatriation as a prelude to grant amnesty. Human-rights advocates set up tables in all the major cities to collect signatures saying "no" to pardons. The Mothers of Plaza de Mayo heralded their slogan: "We will not forget, we will not forgive."[44] María Isabel Mariani, then president of the Grandmothers of Plaza de Mayo, wanted to collect one million signatures against Menem's proposal. In reality, she claimed, the opposition would be much more numerous, since "it is very rare to find anyone in favor of the pardons." The Ecumenical Movement for Human Rights also released a statement that challenged the idea of a new kind of memory. The movement rejected the notion of a pardon because the "Argentines' reconciliation should recognize a clear ethic that leads to a society with identity, memory, and historical coherence."[45] Youth groups also marched against what they saw as pernicious forgetfulness. On the eve of Rosas's arrival, as if they understood the connection between the repatriation and the pardons, numerous youth groups gathered in Córdoba under the banner of "No to pardons; nullify laws of 'punto final' and due obedience; judgment and punishment for Menéndez and other Killers." The end of their official declaration stated that "the youth of Córdoba maintain our promise to continue the fight against impunity and forgetting."[46]

Despite the strong opposition to the pardons, Menem and the committee must have felt satisfied that things were moving forward smoothly with the repatriation. During the stopover in France, Rosas's remains had been placed in a new coffin draped with the Argentine flag and with Rosas's red poncho over the top.[47] The final stage of the journey began on September 29. Leaving France, the military aircraft stopped in the Canary Islands and then landed in Recife, Brazil, at 2:30 A.M. the following day. At that moment Manuel de Anchorena felt "an ovation" swell up within him, one he thought would also be felt by millions of other Argentines throughout many generations: now that Rosas's remains were in America, "we had pulverized the ignominious judgment of Mármol." At 6:40 A.M. Argentine time, when the pilot informed them they had entered Argentine airspace, all present shouted "Long live the Fatherland!" and everyone joined in a rendition of the national anthem.[48] The party landed at the Fisherton airport in the city of Rosario, capital of the province of Santa Fe. There, at the Monument to the National Flag, Menem presided over the first official ceremonies of the repatriation. Conducting the ceremony at the monument in Rosario, instead of in the capital of Buenos Aires, paid homage to the flag as the "ultimate symbol of national unity" and also honored the ideal of federalism, which called for a broader and more equitable national culture, identity, and federal system.[49]

In his speech at the monument, Menem continued the themes of healing and national unity that had thus far characterized his brief presidency. "Is it possible to build a country upon hate among brothers? Is Argentina possible if we continue tearing ourselves apart with old wounds?" Is a glorious nation possible if we base it on the "false pillars of discord, disunion, and fratricidal conflict?" Without wanting to raise old hatreds, Menem encouraged Argentines to think of the history they will write of the future. "In that sense, as we welcome Brigadier General Juan Manuel de Rosas, we are also saying goodbye to an old country, wasted, anachronistic, absurd. . . . We proclaim that there is no more time or place for a country where thinking differently was cause for death and persecution."[50]

For Menem, "the principal sign of maturity" for Argentina is "to be capable of respecting an idea without persecuting another who thinks differently." With this thought Menem touched on the theme of intransigence that had been characteristic of Argentine society from its founding. "I am willing to pay all the political costs in the world in order that we again join hands, open our hearts, and leave our resentment behind." For this reason, Menem continued, "as we receive the remains and spirit of this Argentine, Brigadier General Juan Manuel de Rosas, I would like to quote a verse from José Hernández, which he made in a tribute to Domingo F. Sarmiento: 'Sometimes, knowing how to forget is also to have memory.'" Knowing how to forget meant having a "constructive memory" that would unite all Argentines.[51]

Following a Catholic "mass of national unity," Rosas's casket was loaded on to a naval vessel and began its journey to the city of Buenos Aires, perhaps a symbolic pilgrimage to unite the provinces with the port city (see Illustration 4.4). The government of the province of Buenos Aires had scheduled a ceremony at the Vuelta de Obligado, the site where in 1845 Rosas had fought the Anglo-French fleet trying to force its way up river. The Provincial Governor Cafiero wanted the vessel to stop there to honor Rosas's remains. Harking back to nineteenth-century conflicts between federalists and unitarians, Cafiero reasoned that it would only be fitting if Rosas stopped first in the province of Buenos Aires, before landing in the federalized capital.[52] While Anchorena agreed in principle with Cafiero, the logistics and timing of the trip made a stop impossible. Nevertheless, Anchorena found two loopholes that would allow the procession to continue with federalist honor intact: first, "the waters of the river run along the edge of the province of Buenos Aires," and second, "we should consider that the national capital was, at one point, provincial territory."[53]

Greeting the vessel when it docked in Buenos Aires, President Menem delivered a short address with direct implications for his future plans. "There are still wounds that need to be closed, and I, president of the Argentines, promise before God and my people that I will suture those wounds once and for all, so that we might march forth in national unity toward the nation dreamed of by Juan Manuel de Rosas, Justo José Urquiza, Sarmiento, Quiroga, Peñaloza, Güemes, and all the great men and caudillos born in this promised land."[54]

Awaiting Rosas's arrival was an impressive parade of national symbols that would accompany him along the fifty-five-block route to La Recoleta cemetery. A military carriage carried the casket and was escorted by an array of figures, including the General San Martín Regiment of Mounted Grenadiers. A symbolic formation of

4.4   *Rosas's remains under guard as they are transferred from Rosario downriver to Buenos Aires (Photo: Manuel de Anchorena).*

"unitarians," Rosas's ardent enemies during his reign, also marched in the procession, another statement of "forgetting the antagonisms of old." Along with Menem, his cabinet, and other government officials, the group included descendants of many of the great nineteenth-century generals who opposed Rosas in life.[55] Behind the Grenadiers followed an escort of the Federal Police dressed in uniforms from the Rosas era. In his memoirs, Anchorena added that although not many people knew it, the police were dressed in the uniform of the mazorca, Rosas's dreaded henchmen.[56] (See Illustration 4.5.)

Five thousand gauchos from throughout Argentina and Uruguay brought up the rear of the column. Members of the Pro-Repatriation Committee also participated in the procession. Manuel de Anchorena rode a horse, as did his son, who rode a "magnificent black horse" adorned with all the trappings of the Rosista era. Another beautiful animal, riderless, walked prominently in the parade, draped with the red poncho that symbolized the hosts of the Brigadier General.[57] Anchorena estimated that more than one million people lined up along the route to La Recoleta cemetery, although the television coverage was limited to the reception at the port and the entrance into

4.5   *Clad in period uniforms, horsemen escort the remains of Juan Manuel de Rosas through the Plaza de Mayo toward Recoleta cemetery (Photo: Manuel de Anchorena).*

the cemetery (see Illustration 4.6). President Menem, his wife, and descendants of Rosas then placed the remains of Juan Manuel de Rosas in the vault of the Rozas de Ezcurra family (Rosas spelled his last name differently than the rest of his family—see Illustration 4.7).

The prayer at the tomb highlighted the deep feelings felt by many Argentines on the occasion, although others surely winced at some references:

> We ask Thee that Juan Manuel's example be an inspiration to our youth, that they might turn away from the idols and foreign influences, and instead look to the holy heroes, and that they find in Juan Manuel the ideal gaucho and patriot. . . . We ask that Thou wilt grant us the grace to build an Argentina with an eye fixed on the deep roots and spiritual, cultural, and traditional values of our nation instead of looking to imported ideas from the outside, from the ideologies and empires that Juan Manuel confronted without conceding ground. . . . We plead for the souls of all those who died for their country, for Independence, in the wars

4.6   *The procession carrying the remains of Juan Manuel de Rosas to Recoleta cemetery (Photo: José María Soaje Pinto).*

4.7   *Rosas's resting place in the tomb of the Ortiz de Rozas family in Recoleta cemetery (Photo: Daryle Williams).*

of sovereignty, at the Vuelta de Obligado; for those who do not rest, but await, in the Malvinas Islands and in the frozen waters of the southern ocean. . . . May the firm and patriotic austerity and honor of Juan Manuel be an example to our men of government.[58]

Aftermath

As a whole, the ceremonies and burial went off smoothly. *El Clarín* noted that in Rosario and Buenos Aires, the ceremonies were surrounded by an "almost religious solemnity."[59] What followed was deep reflection of the larger meaning of the repatriation. Revisionist historians did not hesitate to challenge and expand the national historical consciousness with heavy doses of pro-Rosas interpretation of the ceremonies and past history. Surely the Rosistas saw it as an act of balancing the historical record that had been so long tilted against them. Fermín Chavez, prominent Rosista scholar, posed the following question: What did all the great supporters of Rosas see in him, whether they be San Martín and Alberdi in the nineteenth century or Perón and the revisionist historians of the twentieth century? Chavez answered: Rosas had strengthened the Argentine nation; he had preserved Argentina's territorial integrity; he was a victorious anticolonial leader who was seen as the leader of the American Party; he had represented the will of the people as seen in the plebiscite of 1835 (when he came back to power); and he had received the saber of San Martín, the great liberator, for his bravery in the 1845 battle at Obligado, which San Martín compared to the first war of emancipation. For these reasons Chavez agreed with Perón when the latter had praised Rosas as the "archetype" of national sovereignty.[60]

Other commentators stood on more moderate ground. As noted historian Félix Luna pointed out, debates over Rosas will always exist because those who value the ideal of liberty above all else will never accept Rosas, the absolutist dictator. By contrast, those who place national sovereignty above all will praise the "Restorer" for protecting the national territory and standing up to the aggression of England and France, the most powerful nations of the world at the time. Such discussion will continue for decades but will not produce anything new.[61] What was new, according to Luna, is that Argentines have ceased to argue militantly over these subjects and instead look at Rosas from a more distant view. People no longer referred to Rosas "simply as 'the tyrant,' just as no one attempts to hold him up as an ideal model." Instead, Argentines were trying to understand Rosas in the context of his era. The repatriation of Rosas was positive, Luna continued, because it diffused an issue that for so long was a volatile element in national debates between Rosas and anti-Rosista factions. "The ideal is that the repatriation not be used to absolve all that was condemnable in Rosas, nor that it be used to provoke anti-Rosista hysteria." For Luna and others, it appeared that the repatriation had succeeded, to a degree, for it allowed for a "more serene analysis of a man and his era that were instrumental in the formation of the Nation."[62] Others also noted the apparent maturity of the Argentine historical consciousness. One observer wrote that the current generation of Argentines, as opposed to their predecessors, "have relativized their vision of history. There are no more heroes or villains, and social processes (political, economic, cultural) have more influence than the actions of any one individual. History cannot be written in black and white."[63]

A week after the repatriation, President Menem issued decrees that effectively pardoned nearly three hundred convicted military personnel.[64] Human-rights activists in Argentina and around the world were outraged. "An assassin is an assassin despite any law or pardon," declared the Mothers of Plaza de Mayo. "Such crimes, deliberately planned and carried out, can't be pardoned. They are crimes against humanity and the assassins will commit them again."[65] The Mothers were joined by the Grandmothers of the Plaza de Mayo and other groups in their night marches protesting the pardons. A group of Mothers supported by the Human Rights Commission of Chivilcoy decided to take matters into their own hands by painting "Assassin" in front of the house and store of one of the Dirty War torturers.[66]

Menem was undaunted, and a few weeks later, on November 1, 1989, he delivered an address that echoed all the themes he had been expressing since he came into office, especially during the repatriation. "As president of all Argentines, I come to forever... forever, close a wound that for years has kept us down, frustrated, and hurt. ... I come to close an absurd chapter in the divisions between Argentines." The Argentine military, Menem continued, was not created to fail. "Today begins the reconstruction of the glorious armed forces of Argentina." No more will the armed forces represent "factions." "Glorious army of Argentina, forger of national independence, creator of the nation and defender of its flag: I call you to the battle that is the most difficult, the most valuable, the most honorable, the most patriotic. I call you to the battle of national reconciliation and reconstruction." As Menem was wont to do, he again closed invoking deity: "Under the protection of the Lord our God, we initiate this historic hour together."[67]

Conclusion

The crises of a downward spiraling economy, hyperinflation, and a social fabric shredded by the recent memory of a harsh and terrifying military dictatorship plagued the presidency of Raúl Alfonsín (1983–89), and continued to threaten the nation as Carlos Menem assumed leadership. In short, Argentina, it seemed, faced a life-or-death predicament. The cosmic nature of the problem called for an equally otherworldly solution. The parts of the solution were many. As he took office, President Menem summoned sacred authority when he invoked divine aid in closing the wounds of Argentina. He asked Argentines to reorder the way they remembered their national genealogies to make them more inclusive rather than exclusive. He did so by consciously forming unlikely historical pairings of individuals who in life hated each other. Menem attempted to graft together branches of the national genealogical tree of Argentina that had been growing apart since colonial times, and which had been further separated by wedges of historical exclusion and exile, and recurring national crises. In this sense Menem was asking for a change in the collective memory, but not necessarily an erasing of memories or beliefs about the past. For him, "sometimes knowing how to forget is also having memory" signaled a new kind of memory. This was not a memory that required one to abandon values, beliefs, and historical interpretations. Rather, knowing how to forget meant disagreeing without the rancor about Rosas and his legacy, as well as other divisions that had torn Argentine society throughout its history. In the more immediate context, Menem hoped that it meant moving forward by reconciling the nation with the military that had ravaged it for so many years. Knowing how to forget meant reconsidering and discarding the intransigent nature of Argentine society that had been the root of its most profound crises.

To help accomplish this cosmic task, Menem called on a cosmic yet contentious figure in the form of the body and memory of Juan

Manuel de Rosas. The polemical figure of Rosas, although appearing at first too divisive, proved a perfect symbol of reconciliation. To those who venerated him, his return was a vital step toward reconciling the years of historical injustice. For those who opposed the legacy of Rosas, allowing him to return provided a chance to forgive, or at least to tolerate. They allowed a prodigal son to return home, even if they did want to make sure that he did not garner more honor than he deserved. Whether as a martyr or as a sinner in need of redemption, Rosas served as an effective and affective symbol. Menem was able to get Argentines to reconcile, at least partially, with Rosas and his legacy, and in that sense the repatriation was a success. However, the same cannot be said for Menem's pardons. As the many human-rights protests surrounding the pardons demonstrated, even though Menem did issue the pardons, he failed to persuade the country to reconcile with the military dictatorship. For many Argentines, it was easier to consider forgiving and forgetting the remote past of Rosas than it was to reconcile with the recent history of military atrocities.

In the twenty-first century Argentina continues to face deep-rooted social and economic problems. The disintegration of its political and economic system at the end of 2001 hurled Argentina into perhaps the worst crisis in its history. In the meantime, civilian-military relations continue to simmer. During the last few years, pardoned military commanders have been rearrested, and Menem's pardons as a whole have been challenged by the new president, Nestor Kirchner, who took office in 2003.[68] And passions surrounding Juan Manuel de Rosas also continue to run high. In the early months of 2003 debates raged in Buenos Aires over the proposal to put Rosas's name on a section of Sarmiento Avenue in a prominent area of downtown Buenos Aires. One hundred and twelve people spoke during the community meeting, during which both Rosas and Sarmiento were accused of being tyrants, and where official history and revisionist history raised their polarized heads. As one descendant of Rosas commented, "We have been unable to incorporate our past, and that is why we are still a nation in convulsions."[69]

Back in 1989, essayist Julion César Moreno observed that since its founding Argentina has a history of "contentious character" and "recurring tendencies toward anarchy." He summarized events from the 1980s to highlight his point. "To emerge from a military regime and transition to democracy required a lost war (the Malvinas Islands), and when [Alfonsín's] constitutional government that emerged from that rupture was about to finish its term of office, another crisis hit, almost like an earthquake (the crises of hyperinflation and premature succession of power). The phantoms of the past continue with us."[70] It remains to be seen if Argentines can reconcile the phantoms of their past and create a more mature national consciousness, as Menem and others tried to do with the repatriation of Juan Manuel de Rosas.

Notes

I would like to thank Lyman Johnson, Donna Guy, and Osvaldo Barreneche for their comments on earlier versions of this chapter.

1. A statement in the title of this essay is attributed to José de Hernández, author of the epic poem *Martín Fierro*, as quoted by President Carlos Saúl Menem during ceremonies surrounding the repatriation of Rosas on September 30, 1989.
2. A good English standard for scholarship on Rosas is John Lynch, *Argentine Dictator: Juan Manuel de Rosas, 1829–1852* (Oxford: Clarendon Press, 1981), which has now been abridged as *Argentine Caudillo: Juan Manuel de Rosas* (Wilmington, DE: Scholarly Resources Inc., 2001). The original version is cited in this chapter. Volumes of scholarship in Spanish have dealt with the Rosas legacy, both negative and positive. For a useful anthology of anti-Rosas scholarship, see Bernardo González Arrilli, ed., *La tiranía y la libertad: Juicio histórico sobre Juan Manuel de Rozas* (Buenos Aires: Ediciones Libera, 1970). A more balanced collection of scholarship, both for and against, is *Con Rosas o contra Rosas* (Buenos Aires: Ediciones Federales, 1989).
3. For Sarmiento's critique on Rosas and his allies, see Domingo F. Sarmiento, *Life in the Argentine Republic in the Days of the Tyrants: Or, Civilization and Barbarism* (New York: Haffner, 1971).
4. The islands, known as the Falklands to the British and Malvinas to Argentines, lie off of the southeastern coast of Argentina. Argentina has always claimed them based on Spanish colonial claims, while the British have exercised control over the islands since the 1830s. Under disputed British sovereignty, Argentina invaded the Falkland/Malvinas Islands in 1982 and initially overwhelmed the small British force there, but crumbled quickly after the arrival of the full British force.
5. Katherine Verdery, *The Political Lives of Dead Bodies: Reburial and Postsocialist Change* (New York: Columbia University Press, 1999), 25.

6. Lynch, *Argentine Dictator*, 281, 293.

7. As quoted in González Arrilli, *La tiranía y la libertad*, 9, 11.

8. "Ni el polvo de sus huesos la América tendrá," as quoted in Manuel de Anchorena, *La repatriación de Rosas* (Buenos Aires: Distribuidora y Editora Theoria, 1990), 23. Mármol himself had suffered under Rosas's rule and was exiled from the country. He remembered the day of his exile as "the most mortifying day of my life," even though, for the moment, he felt some consolation in "seeing myself removed from the power of the tyrant" Rosas. See Alberto Blasi Brambilla, *José Mármol y la sombra de Rosas* (Buenos Aires: Editorial Pleamar, 1970), 278. Mármol's invectives against Rosas earned him the title of the "poetic hangman of Rosas."

9. As quoted in Nicolas Shumway, *The Invention of Argentina* (Berkeley: University of California Press, 1991), 191–92.

10. David Ramsay, contemporary historian of the American Revolution, is one such example. Ramsay saw history as a means to unify the fledgling United States of America. According to Lester H. Cohen, this "passion for unity" drove Ramsay to "invent a national past characterized by consensus" in order to "cultivate the political and moral consciousness of the present and future generations" of America. See David Ramsay, *The History of the American Revolution*, 1789, reprinted as 2 vols., ed., with a foreword by Lester H. Cohen (Indianapolis, IN: Liberty Classics, 1990), xvii–xviii.

11. *The Times*, 15 March 1877, 5. "Death of General Rosas," from facsimile in Anchorena, *Repatriación de Rosas*, 78.

12. As quoted in ibid., 77.

13. As quoted in Anchorena, *Repatriación de Rosas*, 35.

14. The English and the Argentines have a long history of animosity. The dispute over the sovereignty of the Malvinas/Falkland Islands, the English invasions of 1806–7, and pervasive English presence in the Argentine economy have all fueled bitter disputes, at least among certain parties, since at least the early nineteenth century.

15. From a statement by Alberto Nazario Alday, member of El Centro de Estudios Políticos Argentinos, in "Destacan 'la nobleza del gesto argentino," *La Voz del Interior*, 30 September 1989.

16. Juan D. Perón to Manuel de Anchorena, 8 January 1970, reproduced in Anchorena, *Repatriación de Rosas*, 32–33.

17. Anchorena, *Repatriación de Rosas*, 106. The bolas and the lasso were the preferred tools of the gauchos. Martín Fierro is the quintessential gaucho character in the epic poem of the same name written by

José Hernández in the late nineteenth century. The poem, for some, is the foundational piece of Argentine literature and identity.

18. As will be discussed later, one of the sticking points was Rosas's proposed resting place. Rosistas wanted him placed in the Cathedral of Buenos Aires, a motion that provoked resistance. After modifying the resolution to state that the final resting place would be determined later, the resolution passed into law on 26 September 1974. See Anchorena, *Repatriación de Rosas*, 59.

19. It is difficult to sort out why the repatriation did not go forward during the military regimes. In his book Anchorena does not offer any explanation as to why nothing was done during the years of the dictatorship regarding the repatriation. After mentioning the rise of the military in 1976, the next paragraph deals with the Alfonsín government in 1983. Perhaps the repatriation commission did not want to bring Rosas home under the guise of a military regime, since the image of a military dictator was exactly what Rosas supporters did not want to perpetuate. In addition, the military government was ardently anti-Peronist, and Peronists traditionally had great affinity for Rosas.

20. General Ramón G. Díaz Bessone justified military action because the country was involved in a war, albeit a civil war. The general compared the Argentine military's actions during the dictatorship with the U.S. bombing of Hiroshima and Nagasaki; the execution of thousands of collaborators by the French resistance during WWII; as well as Abraham Lincoln's response to the secession of the southern states of the United States. See Díaz Bessone's *Testimonio de una década* (Buenos Aires: Círculo Militar, 1996), prologue.

21. For more details on the activities of the military regimes, see CONADEP's *Nunca Más: The Report of the Argentine National Commission on the Disappeared* (New York: Farrar, Straus, Giroux, 1986); and *The Politics of Anti-Politics: The Military in Latin America*, revised and updated version, eds. Brian Loveman and Thomas M. Davies Jr. (Wilmington, DE: Scholarly Resources Inc., 1997), chap. 15.

22. Alicia Partnoy, *The Little School: Tales of Disappearance and Survival in Argentina* (San Francisco, CA: Cleis Press, 1986), 121–24.

23. In June 1984, Manuel de Anchorena, president of the Popular Pro-Repatriation of Rosas Commission, presented a note to the president of Argentina saying that everything was ready for the repatriation. According to Anchorena, "this note was registered in

the desk of in and outgoing correspondence, but it was not answered by the government of Dr. Alfonsin" (Anchorena, *Repatriación de Rosas*, 60).

24. For a more detailed discussion of the prosecution and defense of members of the military, see the introduction to CONADEP's, *Nunca Más*.

25. Alfonsín did what he could to placate the military, such as granting salary raises and budgets for modern equipment. Nevertheless, military unrest continued. For more on military rebellions during this time period, see Deborah L. Norden, *Military Rebellion in Argentina: Between Coups and Consolidation* (Lincoln: University of Nebraska Press, 1996).

26. His political prowess also made the electorate overlook his Syrian ethnicity, a problem for many Argentines unaccustomed to the idea of a non-European and a questionable Catholic in office. Menem converted from Islam to Catholicism as a boy, out of deep spiritual conviction, according to his memoirs. See Carlos Saúl Menem, *Universos de mi tiempo: Un testimonio personal* (Barcelona: Plaza y Janés, 1999). His Middle-Eastern and Muslim background, however, give many Argentines pause.

27. *Mensaje presidencial del Dr. Carlos Saúl Menem a la Honorable Asamblea Legislativa*, 8 July 1989 (Buenos Aires: Secretaría de Prensa y Difusión Presidencia de la Nación República Argentina, 1989).

28. Ibid.

29. Ibid.

30. Ibid.

31. "El retorno de Rosas," *El Clarín* (Buenos Aires), Saturday, 23 September 1989. The only stipulation English authorities made was that no reporters or large crowds come to the cemetery in Southampton, since it was a very respected tourist site and had been closed to burials since World War I.

32. Anchorena suggested that his remains could be placed to the side of one of the altars or in one of the chapels (Anchorena, *Repatriación de Rosas*, 52).

33. "Acerca de la sepultura de Rosas," *La Nación*, 5 September 1989.

34. While Rosas may have supported the church, Perón, in his later years, got into major battles with the Catholic hierarchy over his social policies. Such was the animosity that Perón's followers burned church property in 1955.

35. Anchorena, *Repatriación de Rosas*, 94.

36. That the committee to repatriate wanted to place Rosas in the cathedral highlights a number of important points about their view of the former governor. First of all, he is a national hero who deserves an honored place in the pantheon of Argentine history. Secondly, the importance of the Catholic faith to many nationalists is paramount, and having Rosas interred in the cathedral would unify their vision of Rosas as a national and spiritual leader.

37. Anchorena, *Repatriación de Rosas*, 22.

38. Bartolomé Mitre, "La repatriación de los restos de Rosas," *La Nación*, 10 September 1989.

39. "Crearon una comisión permanente de homenaje," *La Voz del Interior*, 30 September 1989.

40. Raúl Faure, "Ni el polvo de sus huesos la patria tendrá," *La Voz del Interior* (Córdoba, Argentina), 25 September 1989.

41. "Exumaron los restos de Rosas," *La Nación*, 22 September 1989.

42. *La Voz del Interior*, 30 September 1989.

43. "Exumaron los restos de Rosas," *La Nación*, 22 September 1989.

44. Marguerite Guzmán Bouvard, *Revolutionizing Motherhood: The Mothers of the Plaza de* Mayo (Wilmington, DE: Scholarly Resources Inc., 1994), 209.

45. "Comenzó recolección de firmas por el 'no,'" *La Voz del Interior*, 30 September 1989.

46. "Marcha y festival contra el indulto," *La Voz del Interior*, 30 September 1989.

47. "Los restos llegan a París," *El Clarín*, 23 September 1989.

48. Anchorena, *Repatriación de Rosas*, 20, 21, 27.

49. As stated by Julio Mero Figueroa, Menem's man in charge of the repatriation. See "Misa por los restos de Rosas," *El Clarín*, 13 September 1989.

50. Menem, speech delivered on 30 September 1989.

51. Ibid.

52. The original idea was for the expedition to stop and take part in the ceremony at Obligado, where a soldier from each branch of the armed forces would present President Menem with a piece of the chain used to block the passage of the English fleet in 1845. This was one detail of the planned voyage that did not come off exactly as planned since Menem was not even there and the ship did not make the stop. "La repatriación de los restos de Rosas," *La Nación*, 18 September 1989.

53. Anchorena, *Repatriación de Rosas*, 103. Although the remains of Rosas

continued downriver, the governor of Buenos Aires carried on with the planned ceremony anyway.

54. Menem, speech delivered 1 October 1989.

55. "Prometió Menem cerrar las heridas del pasado," *La Voz del Interior*, 2 October 1989.

56. Anchorena, *Repatriación de Rosas*, 105. Anchorena also implied that most people did not realize that these were uniforms of the mazorca, "the secret police of Rosas. Even the Interior Minister, who wanted to "erase any hint of federalism or of the color red in the return of the Restorer," did not notice or understand.

57. Regarding the symbolic importance of the horse, Anchorena added, "Rosas conquered the deserts of the South, defended the sovereignty of our nation, and completed the campaign of our national emancipation, all on horseback. The country was built on horseback. There, in this parade, in the thousands of mounts were found all of the types and markings of the criollo horses; and there were also some with the brand of Don Juan Manuel de Rosas as well: the Southern Cross" (Anchorena, *Repatriación de Rosas*, 110).

58. As quoted in ibid., 112–14. Multiple readings are possible for this prayer. First of all, since the prayer was given in honor of Rosas's repatriation, the priest surely chose words that would honor the former governor. They text of the prayer, however, does have political and cultural implications. As for the reference to things "foreign," one of the main nationalist critiques of both the liberal and the leftist movements was that they were based on a doctrine foreign to Argentine soil—Marxism—that needed to be eradicated. The prayer could also have been a warning to beware the rising tide of neoliberalism—another foreign concept—that swept Latin America in the 1980s and 1990s. Those who "wait" in the Malvinas Islands and the southern ocean refer to those killed in the Malvinas/Falklands War with Great Britain in 1982, including the cadets on the naval cruiser *Belgrano*, sunk by a British submarine outside of the war zone. Notably, and almost surely intentionally, the prayer says nothing of those who died during the "war against subversion," as the military also called the Dirty War of the 1970s. On the one hand, the proceso was not a fight for sovereignty in the traditional sense, and hence may not have deserved specific attention in the context of this prayer. On the other hand, military leaders and their civilian supporters did believe that national sovereignty was at risk from Marxist rebels who, armed with a foreign, and hence un-Argentine,

ideology, threatened the country. So another reading of the prayer might find reference to those felled during the proceso in the phrase that decried an Argentina that looked to ideas imported from the outside.

59. "Entre la solemnidad y la sencillez," *El Clarín*, 2 October 1989.
60. Fermín Chavez, "Lo que vió San Martín," *El Clarín*, 1 October 1989.
61. Félix Luna, "Un acto de madurez," *El Clarín*, 1 October 1989.
62. Ibid.
63. But the writer cannot resist taking a shot at Rosas by comparing him unfavorably to Sarmiento. Sarmiento benefited the nation much more than Rosas ever did. Although both men understood that Argentina could not be ruled by a small elite, Rosas chose the route of paternal populism, a "national caudillo," while Sarmiento chose to educate the masses and shape them into builders of a modern nation. See Julio César Moreno, "¿Una opción del presente?" *La Voz del Interior*, 5 October 1989.
64. Although the vast majority were pardoned for acts committed during the Dirty War, the pardons also included participants in the post-1983 military rebellions, as well as those convicted of wrongdoing during the Malvinas/Falklands War. These pardoned individuals did not include many of the highest level commanders convicted. However, Menem pardoned them soon after another military rebellion in December of 1990. See Norden, *Military Rebellion in Argentina*, 140–41.
65. Guzmán Bouvard, *Revolutionizing Motherhood*, 209–10.
66. Ibid.
67. Menem, "Documento de reivindicación del ejercito Argentino," 1 November 1989.
68. "Argentine Congress Likely to Void 'Dirty War' Amnesties," *New York Times*, 20 August 2003.
69. Quote of Juan Manuel Soaje Pinto, in "A Street Battle Rages in Argentina's 150 Years War," *New York Times*, 14 August 2003.
70. Moreno, "¿Una opción del presente?"

Chapter Five

The Mortal Remains of Emiliano Zapata

Samuel Brunk

On April 10, 2001, during the eighty-second commemoration of the death of Emiliano Zapata, Mayor Matías Quiroz Medina of Tlaltizapán, Morelos, called for the transfer of the "mortal remains of the caudillo of the south, to bury them in the mausoleum that Zapata ordered constructed in 1914 for himself and his generals." Quiroz Medina added that Tlaltizapán was not just another town. Along with the mausoleum, it possessed "the blood of the caudillo fixed in the clothing he wore when he died," as well as the best maintained museum of Zapatismo in the state. Moreover, he contended, the people of Tlaltizapán "venerate and respect the history that permits us today to have free governments, clear thoughts, and a country with dignity." For all these reasons, he believed, Zapata's place was in his mausoleum "at the feet of father Jesus." A second speaker from the local government provided context for Quiroz Medina's last comment by indicating that Zapata was a man of great faith who often attended the local church in the atrium of which his mausoleum had been built. This official also pointed out that other important leaders of the movement—Emigdio Marmolejo, Jesús Capistrán, Pioquinto Galis—had been buried there, and that Zapata should be permitted to "rest with his compañeros, who are waiting for him."[1]

In Cuautla, meanwhile, where Zapata's bones lay beneath a statue erected for them in the late 1980s, there were several ceremonies in his honor. The city government turned out early in the morning to deposit a floral wreath at the monument. Moments later the governor of Morelos, Sergio Estrada Cajigal of the National Action Party (Partido de Acción Nacional, PAN), arrived with other representatives of the state government to commemorate Zapata. They, too, left a floral offering. Shortly thereafter a scuffle broke out between representatives of the governments of Cuautla and Ciudad Ayala (previously Villa de Ayala). Both entities wanted to control the ceremony soon to be enacted by leaders of the Party of the Institutionalized Revolution (Partido Revolucionario Institucional, PRI). Unfortunately for anyone hoping for order or decorum, pilgrims from the town of Tepoztlán, Morelos, arrived during the spat and performed their own brief ceremony, which reverberated with cries of "Zapata vive, la lucha sigue, sigue" (Zapata lives, the struggle continues, continues). Ultimately, the folks from Ciudad Ayala won the field. They got their sound equipment and speakers' table set up just before the head of the National Peasant's Confederation (Confederación Nacional Campesina, CNC) and the leader of the state PRI arrived to make their speeches to a conspicuously small group of onlookers. One speaker claimed that in coming elections the PRI "will be the alternative that Zapata wanted."[2]

As if these events at Cuautla and Tlaltizapán were not enough, in the village of Chinameca, Governor Estrada Cajigal, who had made his way south from Cuautla, presided over the official, national tribute at the hacienda where Zapata had been assassinated in 1919. During that ceremony Secretary of Agrarian Reform María Teresa Herrera Tello, there to represent President Vicente Fox of the PAN, insisted that Fox knew that Zapata stood for a commitment to social justice, "which will be taken up again by the federal government." Fox was not, she added, "trying to cancel the history of Mexico."[3]

Zapata was surely spinning in his grave. What did it all mean: the references to blood and body and Jesus Christ, the flowers and the boosterism, the claims and the monuments? Perhaps the most obvious part of the story involves political changes that had recently taken place in Mexico. After two decades of growing pluralism in a country once dominated by a single party, the PRI, in the summer of 2000 Fox finally turned the PRI out of the presidency it had occupied (under several names) for seventy-one years. The PRI was completely identified with the Mexican Revolution (1910–20) in which Zapata participated. The PAN, however, was formed in 1940 by Catholics and other conservatives in opposition to much of the revolutionary agenda. It had, therefore, never embraced the legacy and the myth of Zapata, which were deeply important to many Mexicans. With Fox in power it was an open question whether the revolution would persist even as rhetoric and symbol, which was all that remained of it.

In short, the 2001 version of the annual celebration of Zapata's death and accomplishments was clouded by political competition—and a political sorting out—of a kind never before witnessed in Mexico. The PRI could no longer control commemorations at Cuautla as it had once done, certain that all participants would march in lockstep, but if the PAN wanted a place in the feeding frenzy at Zapata's table—and Herrera Tello suggested that it did—it had some explaining to do about its traditional posture toward him. And then there were the other political players: the Party of the Democratic Revolution (Partido de la Revolución Democrática, PRD) on the left, with its strong appeal to the nation's campesinos; the Zapatista Army of National Liberation (Ejército Zapatista de Liberación Nacional, EZLN), Maya Indian rebels who took Zapata's name when they rose up in armed opposition in 1994 and still held territory in uneasy stand-off in the southern state of Chiapas; and myriad other organizations operating on local, state, and national levels around the country. On this day, most sought to make the case that Zapata was on their side, but apparently none of those cases was entirely compelling, for even Zapata's three surviving children went their separate ways. Both Diego and Ana María Zapata maintained their allegiance to the PRI, while Mateo Zapata exhibited his appreciation of the PAN by attending the ceremony at Chinameca.[4]

Another part of the story, of course, is Emiliano Zapata himself. In early 1911, Zapata and a small group of campesinos from in and around his home village of Anenecuilco, Morelos, joined a broad rebellion against the regime of longtime dictator Porfirio Díaz. For them, taking arms against Díaz meant fighting to stop expanding haciendas from infringing on their land and water rights. It also meant fighting for local liberties—for the right to make many of their decisions for themselves, decisions that had increasingly been taken out of their hands during Díaz's long rule. Together, land and liberty were critical to the preservation of the rural culture that Zapata and his collaborators valued. Zapata soon took over the leadership of this movement and Díaz, surprisingly, quickly fell. Zapata then began to discover, however, that land reform was not high on the agenda of leaders of the many other groups that had joined the revolution. In November 1911, this realization prompted him to produce, with the help of local schoolteacher Otilio Montaño, the famous Plan of Ayala, with which he laid out his demands to the nation and struck out on his own revolutionary path. The civil war deepened as one faction battled another, and Zapata continued to fight for his principles for nearly a decade in this conflict that became known as the Mexican Revolution. In the process, he developed a national program and a national reputation. Then, on April 10, 1919, he was killed in an ambush at the hacienda Chinameca by revolutionaries loyal to Venustiano Carranza, who had been trying since 1915 to consolidate national power from Mexico City. Zapata was far from being a national hero when he died, but his program captured imaginations in this largely rural country, and his clarity and consistency with regard to his goals—unrivalled by any of his revolutionary competitors—would be at the center of the hero cult that soon grew up around him.

The final part of the story beneath the events of April 10, 2001, concerns the way in which that hero cult developed. For most people death and that which is considered sacred have been intimately related. Death is among the several moments of passage in an individual's life that are usually marked by ritual. It is sacred, perhaps, because it is understood as an occasion when the heavens and the earth meet as the deceased moves between them. Some scholars have contended—convincingly, I think—that it is the most important of those moments, even the very source of religious feeling, because of the fear that it generates, the mystery that presses for some sort of explanation.[5]

To remember their dead, most human societies have practiced forms of ancestor worship. An ancestor cult, of course, need amount to nothing more than a family coming together to remember an ancestor who has died, praying before an altar in the home, making a visit to a grave site. Some dead, by contrast, are of lasting significance for people outside their family circles. These might be tribal elders or national presidents, religious figures, artists, war heroes, entertainers—the possibilities are numerous—but those who fit in this category are generally considered to have (or have had) charisma. Max Weber defined charisma as "a certain quality of an individual personality by virtue of which he is set apart from ordinary men and treated as endowed with supernatural, superhuman, or at least specifically exceptional powers or qualities." Others have suggested that charisma derives from being near the center of power or important events. In the Christian context, the word means the "gift of grace."[6] Those dead whose value to the living transcends their families serve as ancestors to communities—tribes, villages, regions,

nations—which unite around their memories. Often still conceptual-
ized as heads of families, founding fathers, for example, these sacred,
charismatic dead become part of the cultural glue that holds societies
together. The ancestors of nations, in particular, have lately drawn a
great deal of scholarly attention. In his book *Imagined Communities*,
Benedict Anderson demonstrates that people have been able to
"imagine" national communities by conceiving a historical unity for
a given population based on shared ancestors and other cultural
roots.[7] As symbols of national identity, such ancestors are frequently
also agents of state power because government officials employ them
in the effort to persuade the people they seek to rule of the legitimacy
of their regimes.

These general observations are born out in Mexico. That Mexico
has a well-developed tradition of ancestor worship is especially
evident each year on the Days of the Dead, the first two days of
November, when families remember their departed by building
elaborate altars and feasting at their graves. Mexico also possesses a
sizeable pantheon of national heroes: Aztec resistance leader
Cuauhtémoc; the Virgin of Guadalupe; such leaders of the independence movement as Miguel Hidalgo and José María Morelos; the head
of the mid-nineteenth-century liberal reform, Benito Juárez; and various founding fathers of the "revolutionary," twentieth-century state.

It is my contention, of course, that Zapata is just such a Mexican
ancestor; indeed, he is among the most prominent of them. If he was
not a national hero at the time of his death, he was a hero in the
regional arena, both before and after his death, due to his persistent
expression of peasant demands.[8] On the national scene, in 1920 a
short rebellion removed Carranza from the presidency and ended a
decade of revolutionary fighting. Almost immediately, during the
brief, interim presidency of Adolfo de la Huerta, the men who now
ruled Mexico started to cast Zapata in a more heroic mold. They recognized that he was the best symbol of land reform available, and they
also realized that in order to consolidate their power they needed such
a symbol. Zapata would help them express their intentions to address
the agrarian issue, which may have been the single most important
revolutionary demand. Whether they truly had such intentions—
some did, and some did not—they began to borrow ideas from
Zapata's local cult, sponsor and attend commemorative events, and
evoke Zapata's spirit in their speeches. Zapata would not have supported many of their policies—like the drive to centralize governance,

which cut against his demand for liberty—but, after all, they would not have needed to exploit his image if they were willing to do all that he asked. Thus did Zapata gradually rise, due to his own record and the political aspirations of others, to the top of the Mexican pantheon.

But what, precisely, was the role of Zapata's body within this ancestor cult? Zapata's remains have played several major roles. First, his body was crucial to the establishment of the cult. The way in which the corpse was scrutinized in the time between death and burial was at the root of one of the cult's main religious manifestations: the belief that someone else had died in Zapata's place. In this line of thinking Zapata's survival enabled him, much like Christ, to return to help those who had faith in him. Zapata's cadaver was also of great value in that the site where it was buried became sacred ground and thus the place where rituals devoted to his memory were first undertaken on anniversaries of his death. The establishment of this sacred ground meant that claims made over his remains—largely those of the state, which controlled the rituals—probably gained from them a certain degree of holiness, or at least legitimacy, of their own. Despite the significance of the place where Zapata was buried, as the century progressed that site gradually lost some of its initial advantages. Interestingly, this seems to be testimony to the original power of the remains in establishing the cult. As the cult gathered adherents and spread, copies of the body proliferated and were appropriated by people unwilling, generally on political grounds, to let the state control the way Zapata was remembered just because it had his bones.

Over Zapata's Warm Corpse

By the time Zapata was killed his movement had endured nearly four years of declining fortunes. In late 1914 Zapatista troops occupied Mexico City, and for some months they ran a national government there in conjunction with the faction headed by Francisco "Pancho" Villa. It seemed then that Zapata and Villa were destined to win the revolution, but by the summer of 1915 they were on the ropes, and in early 1916 Carranza's Constitutionalist army was able to invade the state of Morelos. For Zapata that meant a return to a more decentralized, defensive guerrilla warfare. It also meant growing turmoil within his ranks and between Zapatista fighters and civilians as resources were stretched to—and beyond—the breaking point. Zapata sought to change his luck with a diplomatic onslaught designed to cultivate allies, including discontented Constitutionalists who might help him beat Carranza. The search for allies led him to a Constitutionalist colonel, Jesús Guajardo, who was reputedly unhappy with Pablo González, the general in charge of pacifying Morelos. After some testing of the waters, Zapata met Guajardo on April 10 at the hacienda Chinameca. According to Salvador Reyes Avilés, author of the official Zapatista report of Zapata's death, Zapata ordered ten men to follow him and rode toward the hacienda, where Guajardo waited. As he approached the gate, wrote Reyes Avilés, "the guard appeared ready to do him the honors. The bugle sounded three times, the call of honor, and when the last note fell silent, as the General arrived at the threshold, in a manner most treacherous, most cowardly, most villainous, at point-blank range, without giving him time even to clutch his pistols, the soldiers who were presenting arms fired their rifles twice, and our general Zapata fell never to rise again."9

The language of Reyes Avilés may have started the process of loading the corpse with meaning, but the Constitutionalists had the body. They threw it over the back of a horse and rode north to Cuautla. There Pablo González, who had helped set the trap, waited with witnesses who were prepared to identify the cadaver before a judge. Once that was done, the body was "injected" so that photographs could be taken the following day. "Those that desired to or might doubt" could thus see "that it was actual fact that the famous *jefe* [chief] of the southern region had died."10 In the early hours of April 11, the injection finished, the body was presented to the public at the police station. It remained on display for nearly twenty-four hours, and thousands came to look.11

In that looking began perhaps the most remarkable part of Zapata's posthumous saga. The Constitutionalists understood that the stakes were high. So did various Mexico City-based newspapers, which suggested that the body also be displayed in the capital to calm metropolitan fears of the southern Attila. After all, this was not the first time there had been rumors of his demise. Carranza took the position, however, that to do that "would be to do honor to his [Zapata's] unhappy memory."12 Instead, González sent the photographs to the papers. In the most striking of these pictures, excited young soldiers propped up the bloated head of the corpse so the camera might leave no doubt (see Illustration 5.1). The bloodstained clothing Zapata had been wearing also apparently made its way to the city, where it was placed for a time in the showcase in front of a newspaper building facing the

5.1 *Carrancista soldiers showing off Zapata's corpse, April 10, 1919
(Archivo General de la Nación, Mexico City, Archivo Fotográfico
Díaz, Delgado y García).*

Alameda Central, a downtown park.[13] Back in Cuautla, the viewing
done, just after five in the afternoon on April 12, Zapata's remains were
"placed in a pine box, without paint," and carried to the cemetery
while a movie camera recorded the scene. González, ironically,
presided over the event, accompanied by other Constitutionalist
officers. The pallbearers were men who had been jailed as Zapatistas,
some of whom had helped identify the corpse. Also in the procession
were three of Zapata's female relatives, probably sisters and a cousin,

but they have been variously identified—one is sometimes described as his mother though she was long dead. Zapata's body was placed in a simple grave site marked with a wooden cross that indicated his name and the day of his death. González ordered the gravediggers to bury the body deep, so "Zapatista fanatics" would not try to move it.[14]

"With respect to Zapata's corpse," reported the Mexico City daily *Excélsior* on April 12, the Zapatista captives of the Constitutionalists who were asked to identify it "said they did not remember having seen that man before." At first "no one imagined that the cadaver, bathed in blood and still warm" was that of Zapata, but then, "with terror painted on his face," one prisoner made the identification. This article added that as Zapata's body made its journey from Chinameca to Cuautla, "men, women, and children had emerged from the humble huts of the hot country" to watch the procession. "All of those that contemplated the cadaver agreed in asserting that it was that of Emiliano himself . . . and began to recall the outrages they had suffered at Zapata's orders."[15] In describing the funeral, though, on April 14 the same paper noted that the locals were "dismayed and demoralized" by Zapata's death, adding that "many, before viewing it [the body], doubted that the man they judged invincible had died." *Excélsior* also indicated that the Carrancistas in Cuautla had had similar doubts. On hearing that the body was on the way, they had taken precautions, "given the possibility that Guajardo had fallen into the hands of Zapata . . . and it was the rebel leader who approached Cuautla with his troops." Still, the author of this article was quick to point out that when Guajardo and his soldiers arrived, "all of the doubts were dispelled."[16] In general, the papers of the capital asserted that it was Zapata's body, that his death meant the end of Zapatismo, and that his life could effectively be summarized as that of a "roving marauder" who suffered from "idiosyncratic personal cowardice."[17]

Something was fishy. González, an arrogant and grasping invader from the perspective of most Morelenses, had taken great pains to inject, photograph, and display what he insisted was Zapata's body. He seemed concerned that it might not stay put. Then there were those Mexico City journalists. For a decade they had expressed their nearly uniform opposition to Zapatismo and, over and over again, gotten even the simplest details wrong. Now they continued their name-calling and backed the Constitutionalist line as they could be expected to do, but not without expressing their doubts—however fleeting—about the reality of Zapata's demise. What were they all worried about? Was there evidence that it might not be Zapata? A prudently distrustful Morelense could only be thankful that so many locals had gone to see the cadaver.

A 1919 *corrido* (folk song) entitled, "Most Important Revelations of the Family of the Deceased Emiliano Zapata," proves that rumors that Zapata had not died surfaced almost immediately.[18] This corrido, urban in origin and anti-Zapatista in attitude, indicates that "someone revealed in secret/ that the dead man was missing/ a mole above the mustache" that Zapata had. In a 1928 publication, Carlos Reyes Avilés, brother of the scribe who wrote the official report of events at Chinameca, told of having met an old man in late 1919 who would not accept that Zapata had died. Then, in 1930, anthropologist Robert Redfield published a more detailed account of this train of thought, based on fieldwork he had done in 1926 and 1927 in Tepoztlán. "I know he had a scar on his cheek," one of Redfield's Zapatista informants told him, "and the corpse that was brought back from Chinameca had no scar. I saw it myself." "Some say," this man added, "that he [Zapata] is in Arabia, and will return when he is needed. For myself, I think he still lives." Redfield also wrote that this argument was taken up in another corrido of the period. "The singers have circulated," the bard asserted, "a phenomenal lie/and everyone says that Zapata already/rests in peace in eternity." But this was not the case. Rather, "since Zapata is so experienced/alert and intelligent/he had thought beforehand/to send another man in his place."[19]

In the decades that followed, the lasting significance of the viewing of the body periodically reached print. In 1938 a newspaper article written for the anniversary of Zapata's death described an exchange in Yautepec, Morelos, during which a local doctor averred that some who had examined the corpse claimed it was missing the wart Zapata had on his left cheek. The doctor volunteered that this was because the wart had been removed by a bullet—the rationalist's interpretation.[20] In 1952, a piece in the journal *Historia Mexicana* indicated that many locals believed the body lacked a "mark that looked like a little hand," a birth mark, that Zapata had on his chest.[21] In 1968 a journalist spoke to a group of Zapatista veterans who speculated on the subject. Their doubts about Zapata's demise, the report explained, were due to the claim that the most renowned identifier of the body, Eusebio Jáuregui, had immediately cried out that it was *not*

Zapata, "basing his claim on specific signs that he knew perfectly." This explained why Jáuregui was executed the following day. Among the stories offered at this gathering was that a compadre of Zapata's, his double, "offered to impersonate him." Some of these men claimed to have seen Zapata shortly after Chinameca, "before he left the country"; others declared they saw him later, after he returned.[22] Yet another suggestion, offered the following year, was that it was difficult to recognize Zapata because the way he was thrown over the horse for the trip to Cuautla made the blood rush to his head, swelling it.[23] Whether people believed Zapata died at Chinameca, they returned to the corpse for much of their evidence.

More than fifty years after the ambush, in the early and middle 1970s, researchers from the Instituto Nacional de Antropología e Historia (INAH) undertook an oral history project that recorded the impressions of aging revolutionaries. In these interviews the story of Zapata's survival received its fullest treatment, and again the body was a central issue. One veteran pointed out that while Zapata was missing a finger, the body presented as his "had its fingers complete." Another old Zapatista noted not only the finger but his belief that Zapata had had a black mole that the corpse was missing, as well as a scar on his calf where a bull had gored him before the revolution. Some now claimed that Zapatista sympathizers had told the Carrancistas the body was Zapata's to avoid being beaten or killed. One interviewee described a group that saw the remains crying, for Constitutionalist ears, that they were "orphans" now that "their father had been fucked" and saying theatrical goodbyes—it was a way of avoiding, presumably, Jáuregui's end. But later, this witness added, "the word spread."[24]

Accounts of such reactions to the body continue until the present. In 1996 *Excélsior* reported on the ancient Zapatista Emeterio Pantaleón, who stated, "We all laughed when we saw the cadaver. We elbowed each other, because the jefe was smarter than the government." Pantaleón then added material that had by then become conventional, referring to the finger, the mole, the scar.[25] Though his advanced years made it just plausible that he had really visited the corpse, there was no danger that stories of Zapata's trickery at Chinameca would die with Pantaleón and whatever other last representatives of his generation were still around: also in 1996, a far younger and much more educated resident of Morelos explained to me that it was quite possible that Zapata had avoided the trap.

The passing of accounts of Zapata's body from one generation to the next was not the only way in which they traveled; by way of those newspaper and journal articles they also moved into Mexico's urban culture. Although the idea that Zapata lived was never embraced by national officials, its urban manifestations are nearly limitless. For example, in acclaimed crime novelist Paco Ignacio Taibo's *An Easy Thing (Cosa Fácil)*, first published in 1977, detective Hector Belascoarán Shayne accepts a client who is looking for Zapata. The client's story begins with what was supposedly Zapata's murdered body, "laid out on the ground and the flies eating at his eyes." He argues, however, that Zapata had escaped and in the late 1920s joined Augusto César Sandino to fight the gringos in Nicaragua. "If you look carefully," the man contends, "you can see him in some of those old pictures [of Sandino], kind of off to the side in one of the corners, like he doesn't want to be seen, almost like he isn't even there." In the course of his investigation, Belascoarán Shayne has occasion to detail the indications that Zapata might have survived. There was the finger he had lost when a pistol exploded in his hand, the usual mark on his chest and wart on his cheek, and the compañero who looked very much like him. There was also the fact that his horse, who "loved him tremendously," did not recognize the body. Belascoarán Shayne wanted badly to believe that Zapata was still alive and to look into his "living eyes" to learn "if the country the old revolutionary had once dreamed of was still possible."[26] At the end of the novel, it appears, that is exactly what he does.

What emerged from the remains of Zapata, then, was a complex messianic drama. Zapata was a Christ figure or—perhaps a closer association—he followed in the tradition, important in Iberia, of the "hidden king" who had only apparently died and would eventually return to establish a golden age. For Christ, of course, the body at the time of death was a critical concern and the same has been true for many hidden kings: there were also difficulties in identifying the corpse of Portuguese King Sebastian, who ostensibly died in battle in 1578 but subsequently became the object of a powerful cult.[27]

Zapata's case fits into broader messianic patterns in other ways as well. Newspaper coverage at the time of his death, for instance, sought to modify outrage over the way he had been killed by suggesting that he had learned of the plot beforehand and tried to turn the tables on his assassins.[28] Perhaps building out of that story, local tradition consistently included the notion that Zapata had survived, either because he simply had a premonition or because he was warned. That is a common element in stories of this kind.[29] One INAH subject stated that a crying woman told Zapata of the trap just before he was to enter the hacienda at Chinameca.[30] The man sent in his place is variously identified: Jesús Delgado, who traveled with him and pledged to die for him if necessary; Agustín Cortés, who had a large moustache like Zapata, but "was bigger and fatter"; Joaquín Cortés, a compadre from Tepoztlán; Jesús Capistrán, a member of Zapata's staff and, again, a compadre.[31] Some interviewees even supplied the words with which the double persuaded Zapata to make the switch. "I will only be missed by my family," reenacted one, "but you, compadre, would be missed by the whole country."[32]

Zapata's post-Chinameca life had a detailed trajectory, as Taibo's novel illustrates. His travels took him most often to Arabia, apparently because he had had a compadre of Arab descent, who was often mentioned in the stories. He frequently moved back and forth, however, between the familiar world and the distant, exotic one. In the 1970s, for instance, Zapatista veteran Serafín Plasencia Gutiérrez asserted that Zapata had gone either to Hungary or Arabia, where he learned "certain languages and was doing well. They loved him like a god." Later, Zapata returned to Morelos and had a girlfriend in Cocoyoc; he dressed like a ranchero to call on her. Ultimately, though, he stopped visiting his home state. "The Arabs no longer let him come," Plasencia explained, "because he had many enemies: all of the *hacendados*, all of the politicians, everyone here in Cuautla was against him." He had died twenty or thirty years prior to the interview, "in his bed, over there in Arabia."[33] Emeterio Pantaleón, meanwhile, testified that Zapata lived a year in a cave close to a volcano. He then went to Tepoztlán, where he had a girlfriend. Still later, with a compadre and his wife Josefa, he went to Acapulco, where he boarded a warship bound for Arabia. There he died in 1967.[34]

Finally, Zapata's continued existence meant that he could return to help those who believed in him—the messianic punch line. Writing in the late 1920s, American historian Frank Tannenbaum stated that the "Indians" of southern Mexico, "will to this day tell a stranger that Zapata's spirit wanders over the mountain at night and watches over the Indians and that he will return if they are mistreated." In particular, Zapata stood guard in those mountains to be sure that no one would try to take away campesino lands.[35] Although Tannenbaum makes the post-Chinameca Zapata spirit rather than flesh, the sense of possible salvation is the same.

For many Morelenses, then, Zapata's warm corpse proved that he was too strong and too smart to be ambushed. In doing that the body played a critical role in the launching of the cult, helping to make Zapata a point of discussion, a subject of interest, and a symbol that local, regional, and national identities could eventually form around. Whether Zapata died in 1919 remains something of a mystery in Morelos—a mystery that people sometimes take seriously. People have killed each other, one old Zapatista stated, fighting over whether Zapata died at Chinameca.[36]

The Body's Place

Discussion of creating a monument to honor Zapata's memory started during the 1920s. In 1927, the newly formed National Peasant's League (Liga Nacional Campesina), acting on the proposal of its delegates from Morelos, announced a plan to build a monument to the "Martyr of Chinameca" somewhere in his home state. The monument was to be financed by contributions from the nation's campesinos, through the purchase of a pin bearing Zapata's portrait and the slogan, "tierra y libertad" (land and liberty). The Liga advocated a pyramid constructed of stones that would be sent from all of the nation's *ejidos* (collective landholdings) and other peasant communities and organizations, each stone engraved with "a dedication or thought alluding to our agrarian struggle." Atop the pyramid would stand a statue of Zapata, in which he would appear "supported on a mauser in the serene and self-confident bearing of one who is conscious of his strength." At his side there was to be "a giant sickle," also bearing the "land and liberty" motto. The preliminary sketch of the monument was done by world-famous muralist Diego Rivera, who also offered to make the model and oversee work on the project. The Liga desired to avoid "the vulgarities of bourgeois art," and its leaders believed that this design—"very Mexican and very campesino at the same time"—would accomplish that goal.[37] Although those who made these plans did not mention it, their conviction concerning the suitability of their project probably owed much to the mausoleum Zapata had ordered built in Tlaltizapán, which took the form of a small step-pyramid with neoclassical elements, painted mustard-yellow.[38] (See Illustration 5.2.) The Liga did not indicate, however, whether its monument was to house Zapata's remains.

5.2   *The mausoleum in the churchyard at Tlaltizapán (Photo: Sam Brunk).*

The monument the Liga envisioned never came to fruition, but the idea of honoring Zapata was in the air, and by late 1931 work on a statue was underway. This statue was to be placed in one of Cuautla's main plazas, which was called the Plaza del Señor (Plaza of the Lord) due to the presence there of the Church of the Señor del Pueblo. To make the plaza suitable for Zapata, a committee had formed to undertake its "beautification," which included the "establishment of a garden, benches and electric lighting, all of the most refined, modernist taste." Still, not everything would be modern: the renovations were to leave space for the traditional fair of the second Friday of Lent, for which Cuautla was regionally renowned. Thus was a new layer of revolutionary meaning being superimposed on a place with older associations in a way that again paired Zapata and Christ.

Most importantly, this statue was being built to contain Zapata's remains, and on April 10, 1932, the thirteenth anniversary of his death, Zapata was exhumed and reburied. Cuautla woke on that day, claimed *Excélsior*, as it did on days of "great celebrations." *Agraristas* (proponents of agrarian reform) began to arrive from around the state to a city adorned with triumphal arches that were decorated with slogans and portraits of Zapata (see Illustration 5.3). At dawn, federal forces with their military bands "traversed the principal streets," playing marches, and in general there was "greater solemnity" than on the previous anniversaries due to the intention of moving the body. Jefe Maximo Plutarco Elías Calles, the power behind the presidency, did not attend the commemoration as expected, but many other important officials did. Vicente Estrada Cajigal, grandfather of Sergio Estrada Cajigal and head of the Department of the Federal District, presided over the commemorative event, officially representing both Calles and President Pascual Ortiz Rubio. It was he who, as governor, had initiated work on the statue. The acting governor of the state, José Urbán Aguirre, was also present, as were governors of other states, congressmen, and, of course, peasants and their representatives. The official newspaper of the revolution, *El Nacional*, characterized those present, in a front-page article dedicated to the event, as the leaders of "our social movement."[39]

The ceremony began with a parade of agraristas, federal forces, and government officials in their dark suits. Zapata's remains were taken from where they lay—beneath a "sentimental" marble angel with drooping wings that had been placed over his grave sometime in the early 1920s—and put into a small black box "with some incrustations of gold."[40] (One Zapatista veteran who witnessed the ceremony later testified that the bones fit nicely.) The box was carried the short distance to the plaza by Zapatistas Emigdio Marmolejo and Andrés Pérez, one dressed in the everyday, white *calzones* of the Morelos peasantry, the other in his military uniform (see Illustration 5.4). As Zapata's body was placed in a cavity in the base of the statue, a bugle sounded honors three times, recalling Chinameca in 1919, where the sounding of honors was the signal to fire as Zapata entered the hacienda gate. A police band then struck up the funeral march, and Estrada Cajigal followed by unveiling the plaque that renamed the square the Plaza of the Revolution of the South. The dedication of the statue followed. The work of Moisés Quiroz, it depicted a serious, sympathetic Zapata on horseback, dressed in his *charro* best, and beside him a man that *El Nacional* identified as a "humble Indian."[41] Zapata's figure bent slightly to rest its hand on the young campesino's

5.3 *Commemorating Zapata's death, April 10, 1928 (Centro de Estudios sobre la Universidad, Universidad Nacional Autónoma de México, Archivo de Gildardo Magaña, photographs).*

shoulder, apparently listening and offering advice or consolation in what can only be described as a paternalistic manner. Then the politicians spoke. Although his true feelings about Zapata were at best mixed, Estrada Cajigal gave a "panegyric to the southern hero." Urbán spoke too, assuring the crowd, "Zapata is with us, converted into ideas, to make us better, and he lives in the heart of the people that extols and exalts him." Finally, flowers were laid at the base of the statue on behalf of various states and officials. Leaving a lamp burning at the site, the prominent visitors and their retainers then retired to "an orchard on the outskirts" of town for lunch.[42]

Zapata's remains had been moved, but they were not exactly laid to rest. The article in *Excélsior*, in the fall of 1931, which outlined plans for the Cuautla monument, indicated that this commemoration of Zapata on the part of the inhabitants of Morelos would be "without prejudice to the one of a national nature that was being considered for the hacienda of Chinameca, the place where [Zapata] was sacrificed."[43] Given the importance of death to hero cults in general

5.4   *Moving Zapata's remains to the new statue, April 10, 1932 (Centro de Estudios sobre la Universidad, Universidad Nacional Autónoma de México, Archivo de Gildardo Magaña, photographs).*

and to that of Zapata in particular, it is not surprising that many people felt that Chinameca had the greatest claim to a *national* Zapata memorial. But more than merely seeking some form of monument to Zapata, those who made claims for Chinameca also often argued that Zapata's body should rest there as well. In October 1931, the state legislature of Guerrero (a state somewhat closer to Chinameca than to Cuautla) asked that the national government designate the days on which Zapata was born and died, respectively, as days of celebration and mourning, and that national, state, and local governments together purchase what remained of the hacienda of Chinameca, locate a statue of Zapata there, and move his body to that monument. This request apparently did not receive a final answer until 1936, when the Ministry of the Interior ruled that Zapata had already received enough honors, including, by then, the official addition of his days of birth and death to the ritual calendar. The ministry added that Zapata was already honored "in all of the nation's communities" on April 10, but it did not explicitly address the idea of moving his remains so as to make Chinameca a special focus of pilgrimage on that day.[44]

Those who sought to gain for Chinameca a more prominent role in commemorating Zapata did not give up. In 1939 the practice began of honoring him there a day late, on April 11, so as not to be overshadowed by the Cuautla ceremonies. In the spring of 1940, officials and citizens of Chinameca wrote to President Lázaro Cárdenas (1934–40) to remind him that it was in Chinameca that Zapata had died and to request, again, a statue to commemorate that event. In a recent visit to their village, they claimed, Cárdenas had promised them such a monument, which "would perpetuate his [Zapata's] enormous sacrifice and remind us with veneration of the agrarian cause for which he happily offered his life." In expressing their hopes that Cárdenas would comply with this promise before leaving the presidency at the end of the year, the letter resorted to flattery, indicating that he was the only agrarista president Mexico had ever had. On this occasion Chinamecans did not request Zapata's remains. Perhaps they had decided it was best to take one thing at a time.[45] Although the Cárdenas regime indicated that a monument was being planned, in 1941 the Chinamecans were at it again with a manifesto that charged, "not even a stone has been raised in this village to justify the place where the body of the southern hero fell." By the following year, however, things were looking up. Chinameca was then in a position to invite President Manuel Avila Camacho to the unveiling, at an April 11 commemoration, of a bronze bust of Zapata provided by the government of Morelos. It would be erected "precisely in the place where [Zapata] fell dead."[46]

The subject of moving Zapata to Chinameca also came up in 1965. This time the governor of Morelos, Emilio Riva Palacio, and the state legislature agreed that in the future April 10 would be observed at Chinameca, where Zapata, "victim of a betrayal, was assassinated, and that his remains should be moved to Chinameca from the place in which they were located." The people of Morelos, the act read, "have manifested their desire that the epic deeds realized in the Morelian campaign be commemorated precisely where they took place, so that our children and youth do homage to our heroes in a way that is historically true." Strangely, the act also indicated that in the future, August 9, the ostensible day of Zapata's birth, would be celebrated at Chinameca too, though birth celebrations had always before been the province of Anenecuilco, where he was born. The government of

Morelos had decided, in other words, to place all of the commemorative focus of Zapata's cult on the place where he died, yet more evidence of the importance of death to Zapata's memory.[47]

Not surprisingly, many in Cuautla were unhappy with this decision. An editorial in the Cuautla newspaper *El Eco del Sur* asked what reason there could possibly be, after Zapata's remains had reposed so long in Cuautla, for "casting them aside in the rough, inhospitable ground of Chinameca." Why should he be taken from the place "where he was known so well and is still venerated and respected."[48] Ultimately, arguments such as these won the day, or they have until the present. Chinameca did, however, receive a new, more impressive statue to the memory of Zapata's bloody demise, and commemorations there of the day of his death have gradually grown to rival those of Cuautla.

Tlaltizapán, another town in Morelos that has believed it had a right to Zapata's bones, has based its arguments largely on the establishment of his headquarters there and his consequent decision to honor the village in which he had chosen to spend so much time with the pyramid meant for his movement's illustrious dead. This claim was strong enough that the Constitutionalists may have briefly discussed burying him there in 1919.[49] Two decades later, in 1939, a "Committee for the Transfer of the Remains of the Caudillo of the Revolution of the South, Divisionary General Emiliano Zapata" was circulating a petition, supported by the state legislature, to move the body to Tlaltizapán. The argument, at least as it was put to Cárdenas, was simply that Zapata should rest in Tlaltizapán because the mausoleum he built there demonstrated that such was his desire. In the plaza at Cuautla, the committee contended, the remains were "isolated from those of the group of dead Generals that belonged to his [Zapata's] staff." Prominent Zapatistas who still lived, the letter implied, also hoped to see Zapata at Tlaltizapán; indeed, the committee was headed by Zapata's nephew, Gil Muñoz Zapata, a Tlaltizapán resident who had fought in the revolution. The committee conceded that the lack of a highway leading to Tlaltizapán could be an obstacle but noted that Governor Elpidio Perdomo, a Zapatista, was working to get a highway built. Perhaps that was part of the reason that other towns in southern Morelos—Tetecala, Tlaquiltenango, Amacuzac, and Jonacatepec—also supported the initiative. This letter ended with the hope that Cárdenas's affinity for Zapata would prompt him to intervene in the issue, and Cárdenas apparently did take some early steps in support of the initiative before he left office.[50]

So far, though, Tlaltizapán has had to settle for building an infrastructure for Zapata's cult without possessing the body. Like Chinameca, Tlaltizapán was trying to regularize its commemorations by at least the 1940s. Those events could, and did, incorporate the mausoleum, and in 1944 two commemorative plaques were added to that structure.[51] Also in 1944, the federal government purchased the old house and mill complex Zapata had used as headquarters. The Zapatista Front—an organization created in 1940 by Zapatista veterans and their families, which worked to unify the veterans, spread the Zapatista creed, and guard Zapata's reputation—then began the push to have the headquarters converted into a library, museum, and medical dispensary. Unfortunately, the process was slow: by 1955 the local chapter of the Front had started work on the building, paid for by the sugar mill, named after Zapata, in nearby Zacatepec, but the museum was not inaugurated until 1969.[52] The "blood of the caudillo fixed in the clothing he wore when he died" has surely been the museum's most celebrated holding since then, but there is much doubt about the authenticity of that exhibit. In the 1990s one newspaper account indicated that "the clothing he wore when they killed him, they say, has come to form part of private collections of ex-officials." A second national paper offered a painstaking analysis of the clothing on display, noting that the supposed bullet holes were far too small. Also at the museum, on the patio, stands a bronze bust of Zapata, "on a pedestal built of stones, giving the impression that it is a trench behind which one finds the caudillo."[53]

The competition in Morelos for Zapata's remains seems to have been driven by one part practicality and one part pride. Part of the motivation was that there would be public works projects connected to the body, as Tlaltizapán recognized in angling for a highway to facilitate the pilgrimage to Zapata's shrine. State and national politicians made promises to Morelenses on April 10, and the community where Zapata was buried was bound to get its share and more. There were obviously commercial benefits too: a highway would increase trade year around, but with or without one, April 10 would be a good day for local merchants. On the pride side of the equation, having the remains would put a community, its inhabitants, and their revolutionary experiences on Mexico's map.

But it was not just a matter of competition between different towns within Morelos. I have argued elsewhere at length that much of the lasting power of Zapata's cult comes from the way in which he has served, simultaneously, as ancestor of local or regional communities, on one hand, and of Mexico's national community, on the other.[54] A 1970s interview with Prospero García Aguirre reflects the tension that the claims of differently conceived communities could generate, as well as the depth of feeling some veterans had with regard to Zapata's place of burial. If Zapata had truly died at Chinameca, García Aguirre said, adopting the present tense for effect, "they embalm him, take him to the United States, pass him through wherever, and come bury him at Tlaltizapán . . . because he designated it as his ultimate home, right? In Tlaltizapán he has his monument; they buried him like a dog [in the] cemetery [at Cuautla], like a dog."[55] At least in the mind of this Zapatista, Zapata's corpse—if it *was* his corpse—was entitled not merely to national but international interest and acclaim. The body's final resting place, however, was a moral issue, and García Aguirre believed it should be emphatically, specifically, local. What he did not say, but what the behavior of many Morelenses suggested, was that part of the reason that national and international acclaim was crucial was because it would redound to the credit of the villagers who fought alongside Zapata and the region that had nurtured him. If the body remained in the national sphere much of that credit, much of its value for the inhabitants of Morelos, would be lost, along with its connectedness to specific events, locales, and people of the state.

Given Zapata's growing significance for the national community, it is not surprising that there has been considerable discussion about whether he should continue to be a Morelense for all eternity. The alternative to keeping him in his home state has revolved around a structure called the Monument to the Revolution. This monument was completed in Mexico City in 1938 on the iron frame that was all that existed, when the revolution broke out, of a Porfirian building intended to house the federal legislature. Its goal was to symbolically unify a revolution that had been, in fact, a bloody encounter between diverse factions. A single monument devoted to the abstract notion of the revolution would, its creators apparently hoped, help break down persistent regional and ideological differences and contribute to making the revolution understood as a coherent, national movement—a movement that was, of course, to be directed and controlled by the revolutionary elite that had emerged at the national level. It made sense from this nationalizing and state-building perspective to move Zapata's body to this building. There it would join the bones of its colleagues: between 1942 and 1976, Francisco Madero, Francisco "Pancho" Villa, Venustiano Carranza, Plutarco Elías Calles, and Lázaro Cárdenas were placed in the four massive piers of the edifice, which together support its huge dome.[56]

Carranza's body was the first to be moved to the new monument, in 1942, and despite the fact that Carranza and Zapata had been mortal enemies and that Carranza had colluded in Zapata's assassination, discussion began shortly over whether Zapata should rest there as well.[57] In 1946, Avila Camacho's office responded to a request for a new Cuautla statue in a highhanded fashion, indicating that a new statue was a moot point, because "the Federal Government is promoting the project of moving to the Monument of the Revolution erected in this capital the remains of those who have offered distinguished services to the Fatherland."[58] The names of Zapata and Carranza had, in the service of national unity, already been inscribed in gold together in congressional chambers. Pairing them in everlasting sleep probably seemed like the next logical step. Still, the federal initiative did not go anywhere at this time.

The most protracted discussion of moving Zapata's remains to Mexico City took place in the 1970s. At the Cuautla commemoration of Zapata's death in 1971 a campesino got the opportunity to speak, something that did not happen often at these events, which were wellscripted and dominated by the rhetoric of PRI officials. Supposedly taking the podium "outside of the program," Facundo Salazar Solís rose briefly to propose the transfer, and his idea was "received with thunderous applause by the thousands attending." The secretary general of the National Peasant's Confederation, Alfredo B. Bonfil, then stood to offer his organization's support of the initiative. Also quickly backing the motion was the Zapatista Front. Several of Zapata's children were present as the request was made and, despite their frequent disagreements with the regime, Zapata's sons Mateo and Nicolás soon came to support it as well. Moving Zapata's body to the capital would, its proponents claimed, reflect and emphasize Zapata's national and international significance.[59]

Four days later *El Nacional* weighed in on the issue. Telegrams, it indicated, had been pouring into the headquarters of the National Peasant's Confederation from all over the nation to support the suggestion "of the campesinos of Morelos" that Zapata's remains be moved to the capital. The League of Agrarian Communities of the state of Oaxaca, for instance, called on President Luis Echeverría to heed the appeal to honor Zapata in this way, noting that it was a great coincidence that Zapata might be moved just as the current regime's new agrarian legislation, with its great benefits for campesino families everywhere, was being promulgated. Another organization, *El Nacional* reported, took the position that Zapata was worthy of the honor as the "true caudillo" of the agrarian movement, which was the essence of the revolution.[60] Elsewhere in the national media there was indignant repudiation of the accusation that honoring Zapata by moving him to Mexico City was intended as a substitute for action on agrarian reform.[61]

Meanwhile, *El Campesino*, the official organ of the Zapatista Front, argued that "it is not just" that Zapata's remains were not at the monument. Noting that the Front had raised this idea two years earlier to no avail, one editorial contended that Zapata had, after all, given the revolution its "basic ideology." Echeverría's agrarian reform law was merely the fulfillment of Zapata's plan, and Zapata's ideas had been translated into all major languages and honored in other nations. The editorial conceded that some people emphasized that Zapata was from Morelos and should remain there, but it insisted that since he was an international figure he should go to "the place that has been chosen as the most sublime site for present and future generations to do homage to the most distinguished men of the Revolution." Zapata's failure to take his place at the monument was now especially problematic since the body of Cárdenas, "the standard-bearer of the agrarian cause for which Emiliano Zapata gave his life," had just been placed there. The leaders of this Zapatista organization, it would seem, were trying to carve out a more visible place for themselves and their cause at the national level through a highly politicized sacrality.

It was not just national opinion, though, that favored the move. On April 18 the Cuautla newspaper *Polígrafo* printed an article that traced the postmortem history of Zapata's body. It referred to Zapata's death as an act of betrayal and noted that "the cadaver still smelled of powder and blood, and already of decomposition" when they took it to the cemetery two days later. The author of this piece took the position that with a move to the Monument of the Revolution, "the national campesino will have taken a transcendental step in favor of his agrarian hero; but surely Cuautla will lose one of its characteristic and typical festivities of the last forty years."[62] Five days later another piece in the same paper argued that Zapata, like those already present at the monument, had made Mexico better. He had given the revolution social content, and there had been many improvements for the peasantry. While some campesinos were still poor and miserable, in those cases Zapata represented the ongoing challenge. For all those reasons he belonged in Mexico City.[63]

In 1979 Nicolás and Mateo Zapata confirmed their willingness to permit the transfer of their father's remains in light of the agrarian policy of President José López Portillo, which, they declared, had made Mexico's campesinos the "objects of justice."[64] Not everyone, however, agreed. In October of that year, at the First Meeting of Independent Agrarian Organizations, which took place in Milpa Alta in the Federal District, peasant organizations not connected to the huge, state-affiliated National Peasant's League came out against the nationalization of Zapata's body. They were just in time, because Zapata's move to the capital had been scheduled for the following November 20, Revolution Day. This was the ideal day, from the national government's perspective, to place his remains in the Monument to the Revolution because on this anniversary the revolution is evoked and venerated as a coherent movement. The primary argument of the peasant organizations was that it was unacceptable for Zapata to be placed next to Carranza. "All of Cuautla will watch and keep guard that this accord is respected," claimed one representative, "the general always wanted to be in the land where he was born, buried at the side of his generals."[65]

A flurry of commentary followed. Morelos Governor Armando León Bejarano weighed in immediately, asserting that moving Zapata "is not an official request, but an old desire of the sons of the hero" that no Zapatista organization could oppose. The implication was that agreeing to the transfer was a litmus test of true Zapatismo, and León Bejarano was not above suggesting that people were appropriating Zapatista identity with scarce justification. He added that the government, though neutral, was willing to grant Mateo's condition— Nicolás had just died—that Zapata not be placed with Carranza, but rather in the crypt of the agrarian reformer Cárdenas. As far as León Bejarano was concerned, it was now up to Mateo.[66]

An editorial in *Excélsior*, meanwhile, supported those who sought to keep Zapata in Morelos. Author Javier Blanco Sánchez wrote that if it was true, as he heard, that the citizens of Cuautla were dead set against the transfer of Zapata, "it would be the first gesture ever of provincial rebellion in defense of the right to possess a historical treasure." This, he believed, would be a positive step because letting the locals keep the remains of national heroes would foment patriotism. He also noted that León Bejarano's statement that moving Zapata to Mexico City was an old dream of his sons was nonsense. Rather, they had initially opposed the measure. In the same edition of *Excélsior,* a cartoon depicted a group of campesinos tilting the Monument to the Revolution into the air while one of them announced, "We prefer to take the monument to the remains of Emiliano."[67]

The representatives at the Milpa Alta meeting had sent a message to Mateo Zapata who, though a participant in the formation of independent peasant organizations, did not attend that gathering. While they respected Mateo's decision to authorize Zapata's transfer, they argued that the remains "are the patrimony not of his family, but of the entire people."[68] On November 20, Zapata's body stayed where it was partly because, as he indicated in an interview on that day, Mateo Zapata had adjusted his stance. He had at first agreed to moving his father, he said, "on the condition that the federal government implement the Plan of Ayala." Clearly he had decided that that condition had not been met.[69] Instead, in the late 1980s the remains were placed beneath a new monument at Cuautla. This towering statue depicted Zapata standing alone, propping up a gun with one hand and in the other holding the Plan of Ayala. He looked much like a latter-day Moses, with the Plan of Ayala supplanting the Ten Commandments. (See Illustration 5.5.)

There were specific reasons, of course, for the timing of national initiatives to appropriate Zapata's body. In the 1940s the idea made sense within the larger trajectory of revolutionary consolidation, as well as in a context in which the social reformism of Lázaro Cárdenas was yielding to the economic priorities of the Mexican Miracle decades (1940–70). While Cárdenas had taken revolutionary action, Avila Camacho and his successors were more inclined to do homage than to act on social issues. In the 1970s the political motives were of a more defensive nature. In the wake of the 1968 massacre of student protesters at Mexico City's Plaza of Tlatelolco, guerrillas began to operate in Mexico, some of them using Zapata's image (as had the students). The political and economic stability of the miracle years was starting to corrode, and the uneasy Echeverría administration adopted a populist style in the hope of making itself palatable to those who opposed the PRI regime. Under such circumstances, the national

5.5 *The statue that presently houses Zapata's remains (Photo: Sam Brunk).*

government apparently hoped to tighten its grasp on Zapata and send a message of revolutionary unity by getting his body into the Monument of the Revolution.

Why then was the transfer not accomplished in the 1970s? Ultimately, it was thwarted by Zapata's resurrection. The government's Zapata as founding father had presided, since 1940, over the pursuit of rapid industrialization to the detriment of policies intended to help campesinos, who remained the poorest segment of Mexican society. During that time Zapata was resurrected rhetorically over and over again to support government actions, but there were also rhetorical hints at a more ominous sort of resurrection—ominous at least for the PRI. In April 1962, for example, the Cuernavaca weekly *Presente* indicated that the hypocrisy of that year's death day speeches was so bad that "it appeared that the equestrian statue of the caudillo moved."[70] This kind of grumbling flowered into open, coordinated protest in 1972, when hundreds of peasants from Tlaxcala and Puebla marched on Mexico City to commemorate Zapata's death. In the years since, April 10 has become a day of predictable ritual protest, as evidenced by the delegation from Tepoztlán that arrived at Cuautla in 2001.[71] The rising tide of dissent in Zapata's name, the anger over PRI authoritarianism that stirred the student protesters of 1968 and was deepened by the Tlatelolco massacre, and the increasingly effective organization of labor and peasant groups not connected to the PRI combined to make the nationalization of Zapata a touchy issue. The Milpa Alta meeting reflected these trends, and the increased militancy around Zapata dictated that the government had to be cautious on the issue, as shown by León Bejarano's profession of official neutrality. All this spelled victory for the position advocated at Milpa Alta.

Zapata was resurrected, then, in the sense that he was no longer caught in "the hollowness of the towering monuments or the frozen metal of the statues," as Taibo's Belascoarán Shayne puts it.[72] He was no longer the straight man for government policy that he had become during the Miracle. But whether the remains were in Mexico City or Morelos, the state still did control them, which meant nothing it considered improper could happen at the podium in Cuautla on April 10. Those who have turned April 10 into a day of ritual protest and who, since the 1994 uprising of the EZLN, have wrested Zapata away from the central government, have done so without the body. Perhaps that means that in the last three decades, even as the way in which Zapata should be remembered has drifted to the very center of national politics, the importance of his body has diminished.

Before we rush to that conclusion, though, one last facet of the fighting over the bones demands consideration, and that is the sense in which Zapata's body has proliferated over the years. Aside from the blood in the clothing at the Tlaltizapán museum, Zapata's remains have not multiplied as have those of saints in Europe, where claims to fragments of such notables as St. Francis of Assisi are legion.[73] Instead, Zapata's body has merely been imitated. As evidenced by the examples of Tlaltizapán and Chinameca, not having the remains did not keep communities from seeking to honor Zapata, and to do so they frequently recreated the body in stone or bronze. In Mexico City veneration of Zapata certainly muddled through without the corpse. There, April 10 commemorations began around 1930; they often took place at the Monument to the Revolution after that structure was completed. This was not sufficient, however, for the Zapatista Front, which in 1946 launched a campaign for a major statue in the capital, preferably along the fashionable Paseo de la Reforma, which already contained several monuments central to Mexico's historical memory.[74] The Front went begging for years before the city's large equestrian statue of Zapata was finally unveiled, in November 1958, at Huipulco. Though Huipulco fell short of the Paseo in terms of location, it did become a significant center of Zapata ritual. Zapata's presence in the capital was important in fashioning his image in that urban artists and writers, like Taibo, were increasingly inclined to play with his memory, with the result that he became hip in the 1970s. Along with his good looks, which made him perfect icon material, this explains much of his commercial and pop culture success. Another statue that became a regional rallying point on April 10 was the one at Cuatro Caminos in Michoacán, which Cárdenas initiated to commemorate his agrarian reform in his home state.[75] In life Zapata had never been to Michoacán, but that was beside the point. Elsewhere in Mexico—in every corner of Mexico—though the statues were smaller, the outcome was similar: these reproductions of the body both reinforced the cult and gave it new avenues of expression.

Another way in which Zapata's body proliferated was in the simulation of the cadaver, or its trappings, at provincial commemorations. This occurred at least during the 1950s in the state of Guerrero, where Zapata had enjoyed substantial support during his lifetime. On April 10, 1951, in Apango, Guerrero, an honor guard was mounted before "a simulated body of General Zapata."[76] A year later, the "humble peasants" of Zotoltitlan, Guerrero, "constructed a catafalque where the casket of the southern jefe was simulated" during a fourteen-hour "vigil for the caudillo." According to *El Campesino* it was an "imposing" act in which "among copious flowers and the mourning veils, large candles constantly burned."[77] Village politics swirled around a similar catafalque in Tlalchapa, Guerrero, in 1955. The head of the local Zapatista Front complained that the municipal president neither attended the ceremony nor offered his support, and that the head of the ejido arrived late with "an insignificant floral offering."[78]

In more recent years the bodies have also multiplied at ritual protests. During the 1980s, April 10 marchers sometimes carried crucified peasants—perhaps representing Zapata, perhaps not—as visual commentary on government policies. In the 1990s, the identification of the crucified figure with Zapata became explicit. In 1997, for instance, *Excélsior* identified such an image as "a 'Zapata' crucified by NAFTA."[79] On a more somber note, some of the participants in the 1999 commemoration in Tlaltizapán traveled a short distance outside of town to San Rafael. There they honored Marcos Olmedo, who was killed in San Rafael on April 10, 1996, in an encounter between pilgrims and police charged with keeping them away from where President Ernesto Zedillo was presiding over "an agrarian act."[80]

Zapata's actual remains have probably come to matter less than they used to. At Huipulco, at Chinameca, at Apango, the imitations of the body carried with them enough of the original body's sacredness to give commemorations the necessary gravity. For those who marched in protest on April 10, in an increasingly urban and secular Mexico in which sacrality of all kinds was at something of a discount, a crucified Zapata made the political point well—better, in fact, than the old bones could. But if Zapata's bones mattered less, that was a reflection of their success. They had established the cult on a firm footing that allowed it to grow and expand, and they remained the point of reference for the metaphorical bodies that materialized across Mexico. The body's lasting value was reflected in the fact that the imitations mattered, whether for religious reasons, for political ones, or—as was usually the case—for both kinds of reasons together.

Conclusion

The villagers of Morelos who extracted a story with messianic implications from Zapata's cadaver displayed their sense of the dead body as a revealer of mystery, an at least temporary bridge between this life and another, between what is known and what is believed, between the concrete and the abstract. Practices on the Days of the Dead demonstrate that many Mexicans understand ancestors to be mediators between the earth and the heavens, and the corpse is an ancestor in the making at a critical moment of passage.[81] We might add, though the locals probably would not have, that Zapata's remains were the passageway between Zapata as material individual and Zapata as embodiment of communities that are increasingly abstract, increasingly imagined, the larger they become. In his wonderful novel on the life and death of Argentina's Evita Perón, Tomás Eloy Martínez attributes to a president of that nation the quote: "We are all that [Evita's] corpse. It's the country." Elsewhere, Martínez describes Evita's body as having grown too large because of all the anger and expectation it had come to contain.[82] As reflected in the boosterism of Tlaltizapán and Chinameca—spiced with emotional claims about what Zapata would have wanted—communities soon started to compete over Zapata's corpse. Controlling the bones was valuable in Zapata's case because there has been rough agreement about what he represents. The contest has always been over who can claim him, over which community he centers, who defines that community, and whose interests or policies would thus benefit from association with the bones. Ultimately, people who could not control the body learned to make do with copies, but this is not necessarily a reflection of the body's declining power: that those who sought Zapata's blessing for their causes so often made their political points with or near simulations of his body is compelling evidence of its lasting power as a source of the cult.

In basic function Zapata's bones are not markedly different from the bones of noteworthy ancestors in other places. Nina Tumarkin, for example, contends that the embalmed corpse of the Soviet Union's Vladimir Lenin demonstrated his saintliness, his immortality, and his lasting power through its incorruptibility. The mausoleum on the Red Square where his body was exhibited was the center of his cult, which was a useful prop for the young Soviet state.[83] In her analysis of the recent politics of dead bodies in Eastern Europe, Katherine Verdery finds that reburying and honoring the remains of the famous evokes cosmic concerns and "uses their specific biographies to reevaluate the national past." She also notes that because of their materiality, corpses, unlike mere ideas, can be placed and thus "localize" a claim.[84] In *Fallen Soldiers*, meanwhile, George Mosse argues that European practices of honoring the war dead made the two world wars into sacred experiences, thus helping to justify unprecedented numbers of deaths, and placed the fallen-soldier cult at the center of nationalist thought. He adds that war monuments needed proximity to the dead to serve as places of pilgrimage.[85] In all of these cases, then, the body is somehow sacred, can pass that sacredness on to the place where it is buried or exhibited, and can for that reason play an essential role in beginning a hero cult. In each of these cases, too, the body becomes a tool with which to make political claims. Finally, we should note that each of these three authors indicates at least the rhetorical presence of the notion of rebirth or eternal life.

But how bodies do what they do and what they can mean differ from case to case, which is another way of saying that Zapata's body is unique because of the historical and cultural context through which it moves. No other culture duplicates Mexico's attitude toward death and the dead, reflected not just in the Days of the Dead, but in the more general artistic tradition featuring the *calavera* (skull or skeleton). Octavio Paz, Mexico's most renowned twentieth-century poet, wrote that the Mexican is intimate with death; she or he, "jokes about it, caresses it, sleeps with it, celebrates it; it is one of his favorite toys and his most steadfast love."[86] In terms of historical context, Lenin's situation is comparable to that of Zapata in that both died at the end of periods of revolutionary warfare in which it was perhaps predictable that their bodies would quickly be employed, by mythmakers, in service to new, revolutionary states. Even here, though, the differences are profound. The treatment of the two corpses, of course, was different. Lenin was an intellectual who died in power; he led a communist revolution, which broke with a dynastic past. Zapata was far more a man of the people. He died while still fighting in a revolution that simply deepened some facets of the liberal tradition established in Mexico in the middle of the nineteenth century. And, most importantly perhaps, though he presented the nation with powerful arguments on behalf of his cause, he led what was largely a regional movement and never got a firm grasp on national power. None of the other bodies mentioned in this chapter, whether Mexican or not, comes close to displaying a comparable tension between local and national meanings and claims. Zapata's body excels here because of its context, and in that tension, I think, lies the lasting power of his cult.

Notes

The research on which this chapter is based was funded by a grant from the University Research Institute at my wonderful home institution, the University of Texas at El Paso, and two summer research fellowships from the University of Nebraska. I would also like to thank Lyman Johnson for proposing this topic and for his valuable comments on an earlier draft. Finally, for crucial help and encouragement in Mexico, thanks are due to Javier Flores and, as always, Laura Espejel.

1. "Buscará Tlaltizapán recuperar los restos de Emiliano Zapata," *Unión de Morelos* (Cuernavaca), 11 April 2001. The traditional definition of a caudillo is a strong leader on horseback who uses military force to compete for regional and national power.

2. "Autoridades y el PRI disputaron ayer la tumba de Zapata," *Unión de Morelos*, 11 April 2001.

3. "Conmemoración plural," *Unión de Morelos*, 11 April 2001.

4. *Unión de Morelos*, 11 April 2001.

5. See Walter Burkert, *Creation of the Sacred: Tracks of Biology in Early Religions* (Cambridge, MA: Harvard University Press, 1996), 31–32; John Eade and Michael J. Sallnow, "Introduction," in *Contesting the Sacred: The Anthropology of Christian Pilgrimage*, ed. J. Eade and M. J. Sallnow (London: Routledge, 1991), 6 on Mircea Eliade; and Emile Durkheim, *The Elementary Forms of the Religious Life*, trans. Joseph Ward Swain (New York: Free Press, 1965), 56–57.

6. Max Weber, *On Charisma and Institution Building*, ed. S. N. Eisenstadt (Chicago: University of Chicago Press, 1968), 48; Clifford Geertz, "Centers, Kings, and Charisma: Reflections on the Symbolics of Power," in *Rites of Power: Symbolism, Ritual, and Politics Since the Middle Ages*, ed. Sean Wilentz (Philadelphia: University of Pennsylvania Press, 1985), 13–38; and Michael Conniff, "Introduction: Toward a Comparative Definition of Populism," in *Latin American Populism in Comparative Perspective*, ed. Michael Conniff (Albuquerque: University of New Mexico Press, 1982), 21.

7. Benedict Anderson, *Imagined Communities: Reflections on the Origin and Spread of Nationalism*, rev. ed. (London and New York: Verso, 1991), 4–12.

8. We should not assume, though, that Zapata's status as regional hero was automatic. For the argument that there was probably a rethinking of Zapata at the time of his death, see Samuel Brunk, "Remembering Emiliano Zapata: Three Moments in the Posthumous Career of the Martyr of Chinameca," *Hispanic American Historical Review* 78 (1998): 467–68.

9. Salvador Reyes Avilés to Gildardo Magaña, 10 April 1919, in *Documentos históricos de la revolución mexicana*, 27 vols. ed. Isidro Fabela and Josefina E. Fabela (Mexico City: Editorial Jus, 1970), 21: 313–16.

10. González to Carranza, Cuautla, 10 April 1919, in Centro de Estudios Históricos del Agrarismo en México, *El ejército campesino del sur (ideología, organización y programa)* (Mexico City: Federación Editorial Mexicana, 1982), 218.

11. *Excélsior* (Mexico City), 11 and 12 April 1919; and, for the photographs, Enrique Krauze, *El amor a la tierra: Emiliano Zapata*, Biografía del Poder, no. 3 (Mexico City: Fondo de Cultura Económica, 1987), 120, 122.

12. *El Demócrata* (Mexico City), 11 April 1919.

13. Jesús Silva Herzog, *Una vida en la vida de México*, 2nd ed. (Mexico City: Siglo XXI, 1975), 71; Gilberto Rubalcaba, "Cómo ocurrió el drama de Chinameca, Morelos," *El Nacional* (Mexico City), 10 April 1953.

14. Rafael Sánchez Escobar, *El ocaso de los héroes: Como murieron algunos connotados revolucionarios* (Mexico City: Casa de Orientación para Varones, 1934), 54, 152; Gustavo Casasola, *Hechos y hombres de México: Emiliano Zapata* (Mexico City: Casasola, 1994). Porfirio Palacios, *Emiliano Zapata (datos biográficos e históricos)*, 2nd ed. (Mexico City: Centro de Estudio Históricos del Agrarismo en México, 1982), 194; *Excélsior*, 31 March 1965, 13 April 1919.

15. *Excélsior*, 12 April 1919.

16. *Excélsior*, 14 April 1919.

17. *Excélsior*, 11 April 1919; *El Demócrata*, 11 April 1919.

18. Catalina H. de Giménez, "Importantísimas revelaciones de la familia del extinto Emiliano Zapata," in C. H. de Giménez, *Así cantaban la revolución* (Mexico City: Grijalbo, 1990), 383–85, 195.

19. Robert Redfield, *Tepoztlán, A Mexican Village: A Study of Folk Life* (Chicago: University of Chicago Press, 1930), 202–3.

20. Salvador Martínez Mancera, "Perdura en el sur la leyenda de que E. Zapata no ha muerto," *El Universal Gráfico* (Mexico City), 13 April 1938.

21. Mario Gill, "Zapata: su pueblo y sus hijos," *Historia Mexicana* 2 (1952): 294–95.

22. *El Campesino* (Mexico City), 31 May 1968.

23. *Excélsior*, 11 April 1969.

24. Interview with Carmen Aldana, conducted by Laura Espejel, Tepalcingo, Morelos, 2 and 30 March 1974, Programa de Historia Oral, Instituto Nacional de Antropología e Historia and Instituto de Investigaciones Dr. José María Luis Mora (hereafter cited as PHO), Z/1/32, p. 73; interview with Serafín Plasencia Gutiérrez, conducted by Laura Espejel and Salvador Rueda, Mexico City, 13 and 20 September 1974, PHO-Z/1/59; interview with Prospero García Aguirre, conducted by Laura Espejel and Salvador Rueda, Tlatenchi, Jojutla, Morelos, 16 August 1975, PHO-Z/1/17, pp. 11–18; and

Alicia Olivera, "¿Ha muerto Emiliano Zapata? Mitos y leyendas en torno del caudillo," *Boletín del Instituto Nacional de Antropología e Historia*, época II, 13 (1975): 45.

25. *Excélsior*, 10 April 1996.

26. Paco Ignacio Taibo II, *An Easy Thing*, trans. William I. Neuman (New York: Penguin Books, 1990), 4–6, 47–48, 99. I would like to thank Christopher Boyer for bringing this source to my attention.

27. Carole A. Myscofski, "Messianic Themes in Portuguese and Brazilian Literature in the Sixteenth and Seventeenth Centuries," *Luso-Brazilian Review* 28 (1991): 79–80.

28. *El Demócrata*, 13 April 1919.

29. For the class of Russian princes who, Christlike, foresaw and embraced their own deaths, see Nina Tumarkin, *Lenin Lives!: The Lenin Cult in Soviet Russia* (Cambridge, MA: Harvard University Press, 1983), 6, 84.

30. Interview with Prospero García Aguirre, PHO-Z/1/17.

31. Interview with Prospero García Aguirre, PHO-Z/1/17; interview with Carmen Aldana, PHO-Z/1/32, p. 73; interview with Agapito Pariente A., conducted by Alicia Olivera, Tepalcingo, Morelos, 2 March 1974, PHO-Z/1/29, pp. 16–19; interview with Andres Avila Berrera, conducted by Laura Espejel, Atatlahucan, Morelos, 15 May 1973, PHO/1/53, p. 36.

32. Olivera, "¿Ha muerto Emiliano Zapata?, 50.

33. Interview with Serafín Plasencia Gutiérrez, PHO-Z/1/59, pp. 87–89.

34. *Excélsior*, 10 April 1996.

35. Frank Tannenbaum, *The Mexican Agrarian Revolution*, 1929, reprint ed. (New Haven, CT: Archon Books, 1968), 161.

36. Interview with José Lora Mirasol, conducted by Laura Espejel, Mexico City, 2 and 4 October 1973, PHO-Z/1/14, pp. 46–47.

37. *Primer congreso de unificación de las organizaciones campesinas de la república* (Puebla, Mexico: S. Loyo, 1927), 69–73. I would like to thank Tom Benjamin for pointing me to this source.

38. See Policarpo B. Arellano to Zapata, Tlaltizapán, 17 July 1915, Archivo General de la Nación, Mexico City, Archivo de Zapata (hereafter cited as AZ) 19:3:56; and Bibiano A. Trejo to Zapata, Tlaltizapán, 5 April 1915, AZ 7:4:33.

39. *Excélsior*, 31 March 1965, 10 April 1932; *El Nacional*, 10 April 1932; interview with Vicente Estrada Cajigal, conducted by Eugenia Meyer and Alicia Olivera, 15 and 27 February 1973, and 5 and 13 March 1973, Cuernavaca, PHO/4/12, pp. 47–48.

40. *El Universal*, 11 April 1924; Carleton Beals, *Mexican Maze* (New York: Lippincott, 1931), 22; *Polígrafo* (Cuautla), 18 April 1971.

41. A charro is a Mexican horseman best identified by his manner of dress, which includes such elements as a broad sombrero; a short, embroidered jacket; and tight pants, often with buttons down the sides.

42. *El Nacional*, 11 April 1932; *Excélsior*, 10 and 11 April 1932; interview with Professor Juventino Pineda, conducted by Carlos Barreto M., 7 August 1974, PHO-Z/1/57, p. 29; Thomas Benjamin, *Mexico's Great Revolution as Memory, Myth, and History* (Austin: University of Texas Press, 2000), 126, 129. The photograph of the two pall bearers standing in front of the statue with the box comes from the Centro de Estudios Sobre la Universidad/Archivo Histórico de la Universidad Nacional Autónoma de México, Archivo de Gildardo Magaña, photographs, box 20, no. 0690. For Estrada Cajigal's view of Zapata see the interview of Vicente Estrada Cajigal, PHO/4/12.

43. *Excélsior*, 20 November 1931.

44. Report from the "Primera Comisión de Gobernación," Mexico City, 17 November 1936 to Honorable Asamblea, Centro de Estudios de Historia de México, Condumex, Mexico City, Archivo de Jenaro Amezcua, VIII-3, 9:852.

45. Ayudante Municipal of Chinameca, Ignacio González, et al. to Cárdenas, Chinameca, 2 March 1940, Archivo General de la Nación, Mexico City, Archivo de Lázaro Cárdenas (hereafter cited as ALC), 562.2/22; Oficial Mayor, Encargado de la Secretaría General de Gobierno, José Urbán to Juan Gallardo Moreno, Oficial Mayor de la Secretaría Particular de la Presidencia de la República, Cuernavaca, 22 May 1940, ALC, 562.2/22.

46. Manifesto of the Frente Revolucionaria de Chinameca, Morelos y Pueblos Circunvecinos Pro-Estatua de Emiliano Zapata, Chinameca, 14 March 1941, Archivo General de la Nación, Mexico City, Archivo de Manuel Avila Camacho (hereafter cited as AAC), 135.21/21; Secretary General Jesús Flores López of the Frente Revolucionaria de Chinameca, Morelos y Pueblos Circunvecinos Pro-Estatua de Emiliano Zapata to Avila Camacho, Chinameca, 11 March 1942, AAC, 135.21/21; Carlos J. Sierra Brabatta, *Zapata: Señor de la tierra, capitán de los labriegos* (Mexico City: Departamento del Distrito Federal, 1985), 89.

47. "Trasladarán a Chinameca los restos del líder agrarista Emiliano Zapata," *Excélsior*, 31 March 1965; *Periódico Oficial de Morelos* (Cuernavaca), 10 March 1965.

48. *El Eco del Sur* (Cuautla), 11 April 1965.

49. *El Demócrata*, 12 April 1919.

50. Diputado Miguel H. Zúñiga to Cárdenas, Cuernavaca, 18 February 1939, ALC, 562.2/22; Presidente Municipal Ausensio Barreto, et al. to Cárdenas, Jonacatepec, Morelos, 20 February 1939, ALC, 562.2/22; Juan Gallardo Moreno to Manuel Moreno, 21 March 1939, ALC 562.2/22.

51. President of the Municipal Committee of the Zapatista Front Gregorio Castañeda Domínguez, et al. to Avila Camacho, Tlaltizapán, 25 July 1944, AAC, 135.21/134.

52. Secretary General de Gobierno, Ernesto Escobar Muñoz to Luis Viñals Carsi, Sub-Jefe del Estado Mayor Presidencial, Cuernavaca, 2 August 1944, AAC, 562.4/321; *El Campesino*, 1 September 1949, 1 January 1955, 31 August 1969.

53. *Excélsior*, 10 April 1995; *La Jornada* (Mexico City), 10 April 1999.

54. Samuel Brunk, "Zapata's Eyes," in *Heroes and Hero Cults in Latin America*, ed. Samuel Brunk and Benjamin Fallaw (forthcoming).

55. Interview with Prospero García Aguirre, PHO-Z/1/17, pp. 11–18.

56. Benjamin, *La Revolución*, 117–36.

57. Sierra Brabatta, *Zapata*, 84.

58. Oficial Mayor Robert Amorós G. to Higinio Peña Ch., Mexico City, 24 January 1946, AAC 562.2/67.

59. *El Campesino*, 30 April 1971; *Excélsior*, 11 April 1971.

60. *El Nacional*, 14 April 1971.

61. *Día* (Mexico City), 18 April 1971.

62. *Polígrafo*, 18 April 1971.

63. *Polígrafo*, 23 April 1971.

64. *El Nacional*, 25 August 1979.

65. *Excélsior*, 15 October 1979.

66. *Excélsior*, 16 October 1979.

67. This is not unlike the argument made by Avner Ben-Amos, "The Sacred Center of Power: Paris and Republican State Funerals," *Journal of Interdisciplinary History* 22, no. 1 (1991): 45–46.

68. *Excélsior*, 15 October 1979.

69. *Excélsior*, 21 November 1979.

70. *Presente* (Cuernavaca), 15 April 1962.

71. For a fuller discussion of the rise of ritual protest in Zapata's name, see Brunk, "Remembering Emiliano Zapata," 477–85.

72. Taibo, *Easy Thing*, 6. For Zapata's adoption by students in 1968, see Elena Poniatowska, *Massacre in Mexico*, trans. Helen Lane, 1975,

reprint ed. (Columbia: University of Missouri Press, 1984), 32, 41.

73. Katherine Verdery, *The Political Lives of Dead Bodies: Reburial and Postsocialist Change* (New York: Columbia University Press, 1999), 28.

74. Barbara A. Tennenbaum, "Streetwise History: The Paseo de la Reforma and the Porfirian State, 1876–1910," in *Rituals of Rule, Rituals of Resistance: Public Celebrations and Popular Culture in Mexico*, ed. William H. Beezley, Cheryl E. Martin, and William E. French (Wilmington, DE: Scholarly Resources Inc., 1994), 127–50; José G. Parrés, Secretary General of the Zapatista Front, to Avila Camacho, Mexico City, 6 April 1946, AAC 562.2/67; Miguel Alemán to the Secretaría de Hacienda y Crédito Público, Mexico City, 12 February 1952, Archivo General de la Nación, Mexico City, Archivo de Miguel Alemán, 934/32124; *El Campesino*, 1 September 1949; President of the Zapatista Front Benigno Abúndez, et al. to Ruiz Cortines, Mexico City, 11 February 1956, Archivo General de la Nación, Mexico City, Archivo de Adolfo Ruiz Cortines, 135.21/35.

75. *El Campesino*, 30 April 1969, 30 April 1971.

76. *El Campesino*, 1 June 1951.

77. *El Campesino*, 1 May 1952.

78. *El Campesino*, 1 May 1955.

79. *Excélsior*, 11 April 1985, 1989, 1997, 1998.

80. *La Jornada*, 11 April 1999; Carlos Monsiváis, "Crónica de Tepoztlán," *La Jornada*, 15 April 1996.

81. See Elizabeth Carmichael and Chloe Sayer, *The Skeleton at the Feast: The Day of the Dead in Mexico* (Austin: University of Texas Press, 1991), 14, for the idea of ancestors as mediators.

82. Tomás Eloy Martínez, *Santa Evita*, trans. Helen Lane (New York: Random House, 1997), 136, 365.

83. Tumarkin, *Lenin Lives!*, 3, 169, 173.

84. Verdery, *Political Lives of Dead Bodies*, 20, 27–31.

85. George L. Mosse, *Fallen Soldiers: Reshaping the Memory of the World Wars* (New York: Oxford University Press, 1990), 6–7, 99.

86. Octavio Paz, *The Labyrinth of Solitude: Life and Thought in Mexico*, trans. Lysander Kemp (New York: Grove Press, Inc., 1961), 57, 59.

Qué nos ha costado más,	What has cost us more
Se pregunta la Nación:	Asks the nation:
La patita de Santa Anna	The leg of Santa Anna
O el brazo de Obregón? . . .	Or the arm of Obregón? . . .
	—Mexican saying

Chapter Six

The Arm and Body of a Revolution:

Remembering Mexico's Last Caudillo, Alvaro Obregón

Jürgen Buchenau

On July 17, 1989, the Mexico City newspaper *El Universal* published a story about the commemoration of the sixty-first anniversary of the assassination of General Alvaro Obregón Salido, president of Mexico from 1920 to 1924 and the country's most successful military leader of the twentieth century. As every year, the celebration was to take place at the Monumento al General Alvaro Obregón—Mexico City's preeminent monument to a modern national leader—located at the place of his death near Avenida Insurgentes in the bustling suburb of San Angel (see Illustration 6.1). Normally, the occasion was given to extended oratory of officials of the ruling Partido Revolucionario Institucional (PRI) to the perfunctory applause of their minions. This year, however, the newspaper reported, there had been a prelude the day before the July 17 celebration. During an "inspiring, but overlong ritual," government officials had removed from the monument and cremated the remains of Obregón's badly decomposed arm that had been severed by a hand grenade on June 3, 1915, during one of the decisive battles of the Mexican Revolution. This arm, which now "inspired pity instead of patriotic sentiments," had served as a powerful symbol in Mexico. During the thirteen years that followed his injury, Obregón had become Mexico's military and political leader, serving as head of the army under Venustiano Carranza (1917–20), as president, and as the mentor of his successor, Plutarco Elías Calles (1924–28). When the officials cremated the arm and deposited the ashes inside the monument, it appeared, the last severed body part of the revolution was laid to rest.[1] At the precise historical moment when President Carlos Salinas de Gortari enjoined Mexicans to "reform the Revolution" and let go of old slogans, the cremation and reburial of these ashes seemed like an appropriate political symbol to mark the passage of a long era.

Unfortunately, *El Universal* had jumped the gun on the story, and the frayed lump that was once the caudillo's arm was still—as it had been for forty-six years—in a fluid-filled vial inside the Monumento Obregón. But a dispute among the general's descendants had combined with public outcry over incinerating a piece of the revolution to cancel the ceremony.[2] It was not until November 16, 1989, that Obregón's descendants had the arm cremated and replaced with a marble replica. The ashes ended up with the rest of the general's remains in his grave in Huatabampo, Sonora, rather than in the Monumento Obregón. In the end, there was no newspaper account of the actual cremation of the arm or the disposition of the ashes. Many Mexicans only learned of these deeds through an article in the *Wall Street Journal*.[3]

This vignette demonstrates the ongoing symbolic significance of the dismemberment and death of Alvaro Obregón to the Mexican political elite. Existing studies of hero cults and martyrdoms in Mexican history have focused on those slain leaders who represent the oppressed in the collective historical consciousness. For example, the torture and execution of Cuauhtémoc at the hands of the Spanish conquistadors still captivates Mexicans almost five centuries after the conquest.[4] If the last Aztec emperor thus became the first inductee into a pantheon of murdered national heroes, the Wars of Independence in the early nineteenth century provided more martyrs. Even though Miguel Hidalgo and José María Morelos were only two of several leaders of the independence movement captured and executed by Spanish colonial authorities, their stance on behalf of the Mexican rural poor and their refusal to compromise with the elite made them into national icons.[5] The Mexican Revolution of 1910, which ushered in Mexico's latest cycle of violence on a national scale, created new heroes that

6.1   *The Monumento al General Alvaro Obregón (Photo: Jürgen Buchenau).*

became larger in death than they had been in life. Once again, the postmortem symbolism of Emiliano Zapata and Pancho Villa, the leaders of the agrarian coalition defeated by Obregón's armies, towers over that of other revolutionaries. To be sure, Mexicans fondly remember Francisco I. Madero, the leader of the revolutionary coalition against the Old Regime of Porfirio Díaz who was assassinated in a counterrevolutionary coup in February 1913. But Madero was a wealthy landowner interested in political democracy rather than the social reforms that would have benefited the poor majority in Mexico. Zapata, who had mobilized the indigenous peasants of his native state of Morelos against Díaz to the rallying cry of "land and liberty," was the only revolutionary leader truly committed to land reform, and he stuck to his principles through Madero's ill-fated presidency, the dictatorship of Victoriano Huerta, the war between the factions, and, finally, the presidency of another wealthy landowner, Venustiano Carranza. The April 1919 assassination of Zapata at the hands of Carranza's hired guns assured not only the end of the Zapatista faction, but also Zapata's place in the pantheon of national heroes.[6]

Carranza himself, gunned down by Obregón supporters sixteen months later, is a far lesser hero despite his own violent death. Finally, Pancho Villa, a rustic caudillo who once commanded the largest army ever in Mexico, is remembered less for his military role or his vague political principles than for attacking the United States and getting away with it. After Villa's forces attacked a small border town in New Mexico on March 9, 1916, U.S. President Woodrow Wilson sent a so-called Punitive Expedition into Mexico to capture him, but Villa eluded the invading army for more than a year until Wilson had it withdrawn in failure. When Villa died in an ambush linked to Obregón in July 1923, three years after the end of revolutionary violence, he too joined the pantheon of national martyrs.[7]

Like Villa and Zapata, Obregón joined a series of Mexican national heroes to become larger in death than in life through political martyrdom. But in a political culture that associates victory with oppression and corruption, and defeat with heroism, Obregón is definitely a lesser figure in a world of heroic political ancestors. In contrast to the postmortem careers of Cuauhtémoc and Zapata, which are explored elsewhere in this volume, the tale of Obregón's arm and body is a distinctly unheroic and unromantic one. Most significantly, his faction won the Mexican Revolution and hence assumed responsibility for all that has gone wrong with it since. In addition, Obregón himself had played a villain's role more than once: his faction was widely held responsible for Carranza's and Villa's deaths. Winning the revolution and killing fellow heroes obviously could not help Obregón's postmortem political career.

A forgotten aspect of Mexican hero cults, the memory of Obregón must therefore be understood in a framework different from that of other Mexican leaders such as Hidalgo and Zapata. Just like that of Zapata, the death of Obregón spawned commemorative celebrations that served as a ritual of rule, a significant discursive framework in which members of the ruling party debated the nature of the revolution. But unlike the memory of Zapata, for purposes of public consumption, the speeches read at the commemorations of Obregón's death needed to address the actual achievements of the revolution rather than the unfulfilled promise that resided in its vanquished martyrs. In yearly celebrations at the Monumento Obregón, speakers reinterpreted his career and his legacy to reinvent a revolution that served as the base of legitimacy of the ruling party. Orators made Obregón into an agrarian reformer, a centrist pragmatic, and, finally, an anticommunist, in accordance with their political objectives. Displayed to the curious gaze of visitors in a glass jar since the July 1943 celebration, Obregón's arm became a silent witness to these ceremonies.

The One-Armed Caudillo, 1915–1928

The morning of June 3, 1915, started like many others for General Alvaro Obregón. Thirty-five years old, the head of the Constitutionalist army was more than halfway through his five thousand miles of military campaigns that had begun in 1912 against the rebellion of Pascual Orozco. His campaign against Villa had entered its decisive phase. Considered by many Mexicans the inventor of the foxhole and trench warfare, Obregón had already guided his well-equipped, if undermanned forces to an impressive victory over Villa's Gold Shirts near the city of Celaya in the central Mexican state of Guanajuato, and he was ready to deal his foe a decisive blow. That morning, Obregón and his men claimed a position at the nearby hacienda of Santa Ana de Trinidad, the observation tower of which provided a magnificent vantage point to watch troop movements. At nine o'clock, they observed the rapid approach of enemy artillery toward their position, and Obregón decided to attack immediately. As his troops charged toward the enemy, a grenade knocked several of them to the ground and ripped off the caudillo's right arm.[8] As an eyewitness reported, Obregón got up and shouted at his troops: "Let's go, guys! Long live Mexico! Long live the Revolution!"[9] Bleeding profusely and certain of his impending death, the general then took out his pistol and attempted to put a bullet through his heart. Only the fact that the magazine of the pistol was empty kept the caudillo alive. It was his closest brush with death until that fateful day in July 1928, a time when he had survived all of his major adversaries.[10]

As we have seen in preceding chapters, the remains of several important Latin American leaders have become subject to a politics of the body. In this fashion, the postmortem veneration of an Eva Perón or a Cuauhtémoc took the form of a fetishization of their remains, and stealing the hands of a Juan Perón or the head of a Pancho Villa amounted to an affront to the hero cults of those leaders.[11] Likewise, a severed limb of a leader has much to tell us about the culture of leadership in a society. If leadership is primarily civil and institutional in character, the limb will not mean much in the political and symbolic discourse, and it will probably be discarded and eventually forgotten even if the physical handicap of the surviving leader serves as an important reminder. However, the creation of a personality cult of a military leader, as in the case of Latin American *caudillismo*, will allow that leader's faction to imbue the severed limb with significance of its own. Like the bones of a medieval saint, such a limb, if lost in battle, can then become a sacred commodity for the leader's supporters, and even the fetishistic embodiment of national sovereignty.[12] Such was the case with Obregón's arm. In the recollection of one of the eyewitnesses of the battle, "the arm . . . was passed around among Obregón's officers, who looked at it as something sacred, as a relic, as it indeed would be later on in the admiration of the people."[13]

In a comparison that sheds light on an interesting similarity between Mexican and U.S. Southern political culture, a somewhat similar fate befell the left arm of Confederate General Stonewall Jackson, who, like Obregón, was a hero to his cause. Injured in northern Virginia by a North Carolina contingent that fired on his troops in the mistaken belief that they were Union forces, Jackson had his arm amputated in the wee hours of May 3, 1863, and died of pneumonia a week later. Wrapped in cloth, the arm was interred near the site of this accident, twenty-seven miles away from Jackson's grave. The site where the arm was buried did not have a marker until 1903, and only in 1921 was the arm reinterred in a box and a plaque placed on the site. But today, the site draws two thousand visitors per year, even though, unlike in the case of Obregón, the injury was a result of friendly fire rather than the deeds of the enemy. It is noteworthy that a Confederate political culture that has persisted for almost 140 years after its cause was lost resembles the Mexican one in its fascination with martyrdom, sacrifice, and the severed limb of one of its leaders.[14]

As Obregón and his supporters knew well, even in Mexico the status of a severed limb as a sacred commodity could be ephemeral once a public reappraisal of a caudillo or the cause that he championed occurs. Thus, an important precedent in Mexican history discouraged Obregón and his aides from making a public spectacle of the severed arm. In 1838, in the midst of Mexico's prolonged time of troubles marked by a succession of caudillos in the National Palace, a French fleet blockaded the port of Veracruz in order to exact payment of 600,000 pesos worth of claims held by French citizens against the Mexican government. The smallest item on the list, but the one that led Mexicans to label the subsequent conflict the "Pastry War," was the claim of a French baker. On November 27, Mexico's foremost caudillo, Antonio López de Santa Anna—then in retirement from national politics at his hacienda at Manga de Clavo, within earshot of Veracruz—heard the distant rumblings of cannon that accompanied the French attack on the fortress of San Juan de Ulúa. Charged by President Anastasio Bustamante with repelling the French, Santa Anna mounted his white horse to meet the invaders. As the Mexican armies forced the French to return to their ship, a French cannonball severed the caudillo's left leg below the knee. The sacrifice of a limb initially proved beneficial to Santa Anna's career. Widely blamed for the disastrous Mexican defeat at San Jacinto more than two years earlier, a battle that led to the independence of the Republic of Texas, the caudillo again became a national hero. But Santa Anna went too far in manipulating public sympathy over the loss of his leg. On September 27, 1842, he gave what remained of his leg a state burial, complete with an urn, a mausoleum, and a twelve-gun salute.[15] Over the next decade, however, Mexico suffered political instability and economic crisis, leading to the seizure by the United States of half of the national territory. During this time, the leg became a symbol of Santa Anna's vanity and the bankruptcy of caudillo rule. Not surprisingly, upon the end of the Santa Anna era with the triumph of the Plan of Ayutla of 1854, the victorious Liberals removed the leg from its mausoleum and waved it around during their procession through Mexico City. In Santa Anna's own words: "A member of my body, lost in the service to my country, dragged from the funeral urn, broken into bits to be made sport of in such a barbaric manner. . . . In that moment of grief and frenzy, I decided to leave my native country . . . for all time."[16]

For our twentieth-century caudillo, Obregón, who considered himself the harbinger of a new and better era, a burial with military honors invited unwelcome comparisons with one of the most vilified personages in nineteenth-century Mexican history. Not surprisingly, Obregón and his aides decided to keep the arm away from the public and use the image of its "sacrifice" in more subtle ways. His physician, Enrique C. Osornio, placed the arm in a formaldehyde solution and kept it in his office in the provincial capital of Aguascalientes rather than seek the creation of a shrine. The limb remained out of public view, and the caudillo never discussed the loss of his arm in his official speeches. Instead, he implicitly promoted the idea that he had sacrificed it for the good of the nation. Photographs show him in military uniform, with the right sleeve shortened to draw attention to the missing arm. Without mentioning his arm directly, Obregón repeatedly referred to "sacrificio" as a necessary attribute of a Mexican political leader.[17] (See Illustration 6.2.)

The caudillo also referred to the loss of his arm in more oblique ways that sought to further his image as a down-to-earth, popular leader. As his political star rose, leading him all the way to the Mexican presidency, Obregón liked to talk about the loss of his arm, and even made light of the way his men found it on the battlefield. As he told the Spanish novelist Blasco Ibañez in a 1919 interview, one of his aides found the arm by holding a gold coin in the air. "Immediately from the ground," Ibañez recalled Obregón as saying, "rose a species of bird with five wings. It was my hand that, upon feeling the nearness of a gold coin, abandoned its hiding place to grab it

6.2   *Statue of Obregón inside monument (Photo: Jürgen Buchenau).*

with a devastating impulse."[18] Conscious that this admission of corruption might be used against him, however, the caudillo defended himself against charges of thievery and corruption in the very same interview, again referring to the loss of his arm to make his point. "Here we are all a little bit thieves," he said. "But I have only one hand, while my opponents have two of them."[19]

Popular lore, however, contributes another view, one that emphasizes the human cost of a political career that claimed the lives of Carranza, Villa, and dozens of lesser political and military figures. As an anonymous rhyme cited in the newsweekly *Proceso* goes:

Si con una sola mano	[If with only one hand
A tantos ha asesinado	He has assassinated so many
Con dos hubiera dejado	With two hands he would have left
Vacío el suelo mexicano	The Mexican soil empty][20]

A joke current in the 1920s proclaimed the caudillo as untrustworthy, since he did not have the right hand necessary to swear an oath. An important outlet for popular frustration with Mexican politics in general, jokes such as these indicate the existence of a popular discourse that viewed Obregón as the most successful of a series of venal landowners who had turned into revolutionary leaders. This popular discourse contradicted an official one that emphasized Obregón's sacrifices for the nation.[21] (See Illustration 6.3.)

The mutilation had an adverse long-term effect on Obregón as well. As one Mexican historian has pointed out, the caudillo and his wallet fattened simultaneously in the five years that followed the loss of his arm. As his hacienda "La Quinta Chilla" grew from 450 to 9,000 acres, and as his business became an international operation that sent chickpeas to distant California, Obregón began to eat without inhibition. His growing girth was accompanied by an increasing obsession with both his health and his wealth. Throughout the years 1916–20, the caudillo visited a series of U.S. hospitals, each time mingling his medical appointments with meetings with U.S. importers and bankers. Obregón's jokes about his arm thus masked his concern with an aging body. In 1920, barely forty years old, he already felt like an old man.[22]

By then, Obregón had acquired a political persona that was ruthless, pragmatic, and capable of compromise, but distinctly nonideological. Like so many other caudillos, Obregón was a survivor who

6.3   *Marble replacement for Obregón's arm in monument (Photo: Jürgen Buchenau).*

had triumphed through force and opportunism, frequently changing allegiance to his political benefit. In early 1917, Obregón had aligned himself with the left wing within the victorious Constitutionalists—the alliance that had defeated the agrarian coalition of Villa and Zapata—and he had strongly supported the inclusion of economic nationalist and anticlerical articles in the new constitution. Nonetheless, he remained loyal to President Carranza, the wealthy landowner and a conservative within the revolution whom he had joined in the Constitutionalist alliance, and he served as secretary of war under Carranza until he sensed his own opportunity. After a rebellion ended in Carranza's assassination, he first promoted close ally Adolfo de la Huerta to the interim presidency, then assumed the reins of power himself in December 1920. In the words of Martín Luis Guzmán, the famed chronicler of Pancho Villa and a political adversary of Obregón's, the caudillo "did not live on the ground of everyday sincerities, but on a tableau: he was not a person . . . but an actor. His ideas, his beliefs, his sentiments were those of the . . . the-ater, to shine before an audience."[23]

As president and thereafter, Obregón continued this pattern of for-saking ideology for pragmatism. He recognized the fact that Mexico remained in turmoil after a decade of war. Facing first the lack of U.S. diplomatic recognition, and then the destructive rebellion of former comrade-in-arms de la Huerta, he adroitly moved to implement some of the promises of the revolutionary constitution to peasants and workers while reassuring foreign investors and those landowners who would cooperate with him. He established a rural education program, selectively parceled out hacienda land to peasants, and promoted the growth of labor unions in Mexico. But he avoided tackling the thorny issue of the foreign domination of the oil industry, and his land reform stopped well short of satisfying peasant demands. In 1925–26, his ally and handpicked successor, the fellow Sonoran Plutarco Elías Calles, forged policies designed in part to gain political significance by por-traying himself as a genuine reformer. Calles confronted the Catholic Church in Mexico, a confrontation that led to the suspension of all public religious ceremony and the persecution of outspoken govern-ment opponents among the clergy. He also elevated the supposedly radical labor leader Luis N. Morones to a cabinet position and signed into law an ambitious Petroleum Law that forced all oil companies to apply for confirmatory concessions that drastically increased the tax-ation of their product. But just as these measures appeared to put Calles in the position to eclipse the power of his mentor, two events vindicated Obregón. The Cristero Revolt in western Mexico—a rebellion of peasants disenchanted with the attack against the church—challenged government authority. At the same time, a severe economic crisis forced Calles to retreat from implementing the Petroleum Law and patch up relations with the United States. His loss of political luster in turn benefited Obregón when he ran for a second term to replace Calles, who was ineligible for reelection under the terms of a constitution designed in part to prevent the reestablishment of a long-lived dictatorship à la Porfirio Díaz. At that time, in July 1928, no one knew what to expect of the one-armed caudillo—and this after more than a decade as the country's foremost military and political figure. He had shown himself to be a brilliant military leader, a capable entrepreneur, and a good administrator, but he had also demonstrated that his political decisions were neither motivated by ideals nor a clearly defined program of action.[24]

In this, Obregón represented the drift of postrevolutionary Mexican politics: brawn rather than brain, practice rather than ideals, and—although a succession of regional revolts such as the Cristero Revolt still limited central authority—the beginning of its Caesaric, or Napoleonic dissolution into what historian Enrique Krauze has called the "imperial presidency" of post-1940 Mexico.[25] In the allusion of one Mexican public intellectual to Suetonius's work *Lives of the Caesars*, Obregón was the first of thirteen power-hungry and dishonest Mexican Caesars, "men and monsters at the same time."[26]

The Ancestor of the Institutional Revolution, 1928–1943

As it turned out, Obregón committed a tragic error when he ran for and won another term as president in a country where "effective suffrage, no reelection" had served as the rallying cry of the revolution. In the afternoon of July 17, 1928, shortly after his second election, Obregón attended a lavish luncheon in his honor in the patio of a restaurant in San Angel. While waiters refilled wine glasses and brought one sumptuous course after another, a young artist named José de León Toral made rounds drawing caricatures of the guests. At last, he approached Obregón and asked him whether he would like to see his artwork. When the president-elect consented, Toral pumped five bullets into his head and thus ended the life of Mexico's last caudillo, an end that was also an important beginning. Six weeks later, President Calles proclaimed during his final address to the Mexican congress that the assassination marked the end of the era of the caudillos and the beginning of the era of institutions, a speech that presaged the creation of the party that ruled Mexico for the rest of the century.[27] As Mexican historian Arnaldo Córdova has pointed out, perhaps a bit hyperbolically, Obregón's death was the "most decisive event in the political development of [Mexico] in the postrevolutionary era."[28] As Córdova might have added, this was all the more so because the general had already sacrificed a limb for the revolution.

Obregón's assassination touched off one of the wildest waves of rumors and speculation ever experienced in Mexico City. Based on interrogations under torture of Toral and other suspects, President Calles concluded that the crime was the work of Catholic radicals bent on avenging the government's campaign against the church over the past four years.[29] But the word on the street implicated the government itself in the assassination. Some blamed the death on labor leader Luis Morones, a Calles ally who had always been jealous of Obregón's influence over and friendship with the president. Others accused Calles himself of masterminding the plot, pointing to the fact that the president desired to escape the shadow of his mentor and sponsor. Although most historians eventually accepted Calles's version of the story, the circumstances of the assassination have yet to be fully elucidated.[30]

In the immediate aftermath of the assassination, the speculation over both the perpetrators of and the motives for the crime shaped the discourse over Obregón's memory. Was he the victim of religious fanatics opposed to Calles's attack on the Catholic Church, an attack that had led the clergy to suspend almost all religious ceremonies in Mexico? Had he died because of his own ambition to win election to a second term? Or was he the target of a sinister plot hatched by Calles and his allies, a group that had become increasingly conservative and repressive during the president's last two years in office? The mystery of the events of July 17 gave many possible meanings to Obregón's death and, hence, to his life.

What was clear, however, was that the assassination led to sweeping changes in Mexican national politics. Most immediately, it renewed the question of the presidential succession. In late 1927, Calles's obvious support for Obregón's candidacy over those of his rivals Francisco Serrano and Arnulfo Gómez had led to the summary execution of these two presidential hopefuls to clear the way for Obregón to prevail at the polls. Obregón's death threatened to provoke revolts by other political rivals such as former Education Secretary José Vasconcelos, especially in case President Calles used the crisis to prolong his term in office. After a silence of six weeks, however, Calles used the occasion of his last annual address to Congress to quell these suspicions. Under no circumstances, he proclaimed, would he serve as president again.[31] Mexico, he stated, had entered the transition from a "country of one man" to a "nation of institutions and laws."[32] In one fell swoop, Calles had not only silenced many of those who had suspected his involvement in the murder, but he had also begun his behind-the-scenes rule as *jefe máximo* (highest chief). During what would later be called the Maximato, Calles continued to play a significant role in national politics and built up the Partido Nacional Revolucionario (later called the Partido de la Revolución Mexicana, or PRM, which in 1946 became the Partido Revolucionario Institucional, or PRI). He remained the jefé máximo until President Lázaro Cárdenas shook off his tutelage in 1935 and exiled Calles the following year.[33]

The political realignment that followed Obregón's death replaced *caudillismo*—rule by a strongman—with a ruling party. The PNR promoted a set of ideas that enshrined the protagonists of the Mexican Revolution as fathers of the nation and elided the significant differences among them. First, the revolution was permanent (*la revolución hecha gobierno*). Second, the crisis touched off by the assassination required national unity and the forging of a revolutionary family. Third, the PNR (and later PRI) represented this effort at national unity and permanent revolution (*la revolución hecha partido*). Fourth, monuments would propagate this official version of the revolution among the Mexican population (*la revolución hecha monumento*).[34]

The monuments to the fallen heroes of the revolution thus promoted an official version of Mexican history that held that the revolution was unitary rather than a heterogeneous process made by conflicting forces. One monument in particular—the Monumento a la Revolución, inaugurated in 1938—served as the official memorial of the revolutionary family, eventually commemorating Madero, Zapata, Villa, Carranza, Calles, and Cárdenas. This monument united Zapata with the man who had ordered his assassination (Carranza), and Calles with the very president who exiled him (Cárdenas).[35]

In light of the purpose of this monument, Obregón's omission appears most surprising. In Linda Hall's words, he was "the primary revolutionary hero, the embodiment of the Revolution."[36] As the last casualty of the revolutionary turmoil, his role was that of a unifier, what one U.S. historian has called the "great compromiser of Mexico's time of troubles."[37] The lore of the revolution made him the "undefeated caudillo of the revolution," slain only when the bullets of an assassin "did in a few minutes what armies and weapons had not been able to accomplish in many long years of war."[38]

Obregón did not become the centerpiece of the Monumento a la Revolución, however, because the memorialization of the caudillo had already taken a different course by the time the Monumento a la Revolución opened. His family had ordered his body to be interred in Huatabampo, Sonora. Until the 1931 inauguration of a monument in nearby Navojoa, the principal "homenajes" took place there, far from Mexico City.[39] In front of family and close friends, the Sonora state government used July 17 to remind its inhabitants of the crucial role of their state in the Mexican Revolution and to emphasize the theme of national unity. Meanwhile, in the capital, the proposal of a group of university students under the leadership of Obregón's friend Alfonso Romandía Ferreira that a monument be erected on Mexico City's posh Paseo de la Reforma had failed.[40]

It had failed in large part because the national government had grander plans for Obregón's memory in Mexico City. Long before the Monumento a la Revolución was completed, the symbolism of Obregón's violent and highly public death—a symbolism that aided Calles's attempt to achieve an ideological unification of the revolutionary leadership—inspired the construction of a monument at the site where he was shot. In 1934, President Abelardo Rodríguez commissioned plans for the Monumento al General Alvaro Obregón. Designed by architect Enrique Aragón and sculptor Ignacio Asúnsolo, the monument evoked a blending of Mexico's distant past and present. Inaugurated in 1935, the monument looks like an ancient temple. Outside, two sculpture groups represent triumph and sacrifice, respectively. Inside, two fierce twentieth-century guerrillas guard the entrance. Once inside, visitors found a life-size bronze statue of a one-armed Obregón, and the original floor of the La Bombilla restaurant on which the bullet holes from Toral's pistol remain visible (see Illustration 6.4). Each July 17 since 1935, the Asociación Cívica General Alvaro Obregón, founded to preserve and promote the memory of the slain caudillo, sponsored annual celebrations of Obregón's life and death at the monument that remains Mexico's closest approximation of the Invalides in Paris.[41] The Mexican national government always sent important representatives to these celebrations: former presidents, cabinet members, and highly ranked officers in the military. One of these politicians, Obregón's old friend Aarón Sáenz Garza, formerly secretary of foreign relations and governor of Nuevo León and later an industrialist and landowner, was also the most important figure within the Asociación Cívica General Alvaro Obregón. Sáenz Garza's dedication speech at the monument on July 17, 1935, mentioned three key sectors of the PNR—peasants, workers, and soldiers—as mainstays of Obregón's support: "In the place of your sacrifice, the Fatherland consecrates to your memory this reminder made into stone. In it are also figures that represent those who accompanied you in battle: the peasant, the worker, and the soldier."[42] What Sáenz did not mention was that the Obregonistas themselves represented a fourth sector: the new class of landowners and industrial capitalists that had emerged victorious in the revolution.[43]

6.4   *Original floor of "La Bombilla" restaurant inside monument (Photo: Jürgen Buchenau).*

The Monumento Obregón turned what had previously been a relatively low-key ceremony into public ritual on a grand scale. The new monument shifted attention away from Obregón's birthplace on the northern periphery of the nation to the place of his death, and, more importantly, to the center of political power. Two groups shared responsibility for these more public commemorations of Obregón's assassination: the caudillo's family, friends, and comrades-in-arms; and the leadership of the PNR. Had the monument opened during the Maximato, the fact that these two groups shared many members would have made it easy for the organizers to orchestrate an impressive show of national unity. Lázaro Cárdenas's ouster of Calles, however, complicated the ritual, making a sharp distinction between the Obregonistas, most of whom remained loyal to Calles, and Cárdenas's new PNR leadership. The Callistas agreed on a version of history that saw both Obregón and Calles as leaders who fulfilled the promise of the revolution. Cardenismo, however, constituted in large part a rejection of the Calles years. As Cárdenas redistributed forty-two million acres of land to the Mexican peasantry; as he mobilized peasants and workers in a politics of the masses under his own tutelage; and as he nationalized the foreign-owned oil industry, he became a revolutionary hero in his own right and claimed the mantra of the defender of the revolution from Calles.[44] In order to preserve Obregón's role in the revolutionary pantheon during this period of social and economic reform, the Obregonistas needed to claim their fallen hero as a precursor to Cardenismo.

The July 17 memorial discourses of the years 1935–40 demonstrate this pattern. Orators at the monument now portrayed Obregón as a social revolutionary who paved the path for Cárdenas, a supposition that implied that Calles had betrayed or at least stalled the revolution. In 1935, even Sáenz Garza proclaimed Obregón a "protector of the working-class movement" and claimed that his friend "laid the groundwork for new justice in the distribution of land."[45] After Sáenz Garza's speech, which amounted to an endorsement of the new order in Mexico, the Cárdenas administration turned the July 17 event into a show that ultimately included more than one thousand invited guests each year.

The Cárdenas years, however, soon proved an anomaly. As early as 1941, only seven months after Cárdenas had handed over power to Manuel Avila Camacho, the rhetoric of social revolution had given way to a developmentalist agenda that focused on the industrialization of Mexico—a process in which Sáenz Garza and other Monterrey entrepreneurs played leading roles. With the acquiescence, if not open support of President Avila Camacho, the Asociación Cívica General Alvaro Obregón refashioned the image of the slain caudillo as that of a moderate, and even as that of an anticommunist. The most striking evidence of this shift came with the speech of Alfonso Romandía Ferreira, a friend of Obregón's and longtime advocate of the Monumento who used the occasion of his speech on July 17, 1941, to lambaste Cardenismo. As the speaker exhorted the audience, "the ceremonies with which nations honor their heroes would not be worth much . . . if one did not use the occasion to remember these men's views about the great national issues" of the day.[46] In his view, Cárdenas destroyed national unity by pitting the campesino against his landlord, and the worker against his boss. In clear reference to the Cardenistas, he declared that Mexico had "found many destroyers; great distributors of land; great expropriators of private wealth; great thieves of public wealth."[47] Obregón, he believed, organized rather than expropriated agricultural production; educated rather than indoctrinated rural Mexicans; and, most importantly, displayed decorum that Romandía Ferreira found lacking in the Cárdenas regime. "We have left," he announced "the authentic path of the revolution."[48] This speech cited numerous other transgressions against the "true Mexican Revolution" represented by Obregón and Calles. While no other speaker ever came close to writing another diatribe against the left-wing of the Mexican Revolution, Romandía Ferreira's speech, which was reprinted in all major Mexico City newspapers, set the tone for the following years. Mexico's involvement in World War II as an ally of the United States and the fears provoked by the beginning of the cold war discredited radicals on the Right and Left, and led to the Mexican government's renewed attempt to achieve national unity.[49] Obregón emerged as the one revolutionary leader who, even in death, represented the new official version of the revolution, one that rejected all of the "isms" that had given rise to the totalitarian regimes in Germany, Japan, and the Soviet Union. He became the sum of the revolution's tendencies. Through the cult associated with his memory, the government encouraged its citizens to venerate the other murdered revolutionaries as well.[50]

A Decomposing Arm and a Disintegrating Revolutionary Myth, 1943–1989

It was in this atmosphere of national unity during World War II, almost three decades after the caudillo's mutilation at the Hacienda de Santa Ana, that Obregón's friends in the Asociación Cívica decided to connect the severed arm with the political culture of their time. On the occasion of the fifteenth anniversary of Obregón's assassination in 1943, the caudillo's private physician, Enrique Osornio, took the vial containing the arm from his study and solemnly placed it into a new, specially designed niche inside the Monumento Obregón. As if to deflect attention from the decomposing arm, the onlookers at the ceremony were then treated to a lecture on "General Obregón and Public Hygiene" by one of Osornio's colleagues.[51] This public display of the arm claimed for the Monumento Obregón the mantle of the principal site of this particular hero cult. It became a tourist attraction as the only place in Mexico where a body part of a political leader was on display. Meanwhile, the unpretentious grave site of Huatabampo where the caudillo's ashes resided (and, by extension, the circle of relatives and acquaintances who lived in Sonora rather than the capital) found itself marginalized in this hero cult. The display of the arm in the Monumento Obregón thus completed the recentering of the caudillo's memory away from the periphery where he had lived most of his life and to the national capital.

In the words of a Mexican historian, the arm also "infused charisma into a bureaucracy that insistently called itself revolutionary" despite the fact that this bureaucracy steadily moved away from revolutionary ideas.[52] To the degree that postrevolutionary reconstruction yielded to the "institutional revolution," the oxymoron enshrined in the new name of the party (PRI, or Party of the Institutional Revolution), the regime needed this charisma to continue to lay claim to a revolutionary heritage that it had in fact abandoned. It was no coincidence that the reappearance of the arm in public led to increased references to Obregón's hands and arms on the part of memorial speakers. For instance, in 1945, the Yucatecan poet Antonio Médiz Bolio, a close friend of the slain caudillo, referred to these body parts four times in a fifteen-minute speech, anthropomorphizing Mexico as a body.[53]

Thus, after Avila Camacho, the last of the revolutionary generals to head the Mexican state, gave way to his civilian successor, Miguel Alemán Valdés, the late 1940s witnessed the final steps toward the apotheosis of Obregón as a revolutionary hero. On July 17, 1950, Luis L. León, a close friend of both Obregón and Calles who had given the funeral oration at Calles's burial five years before, announced that the "Revolution is a sacred movement. . . . To defame the great revolutionaries is to insult and betray the revolution."[54] He called on all revolutionaries "of all the 'isms' to express solidarity with our great movement and to always know how to defend it," and he asked his audience to defend "not only Obregón, but also the triumphs, the greatness, and the accomplishments of all the dead leaders of the revolution."[55]

Not surprisingly, not everyone within the Asociación Cívica General Alvaro Obregón, a small group that included the caudillo's surviving friends as well as members of his immediate family, was happy with this interpretation. Notable among the detractors was Humberto Obregón, son of the fallen caudillo, who expressed unhappiness that entrepreneurs such as Sáenz had seized control of the memorial discourse. In a scathing letter, Obregón asked Sáenz to relinquish his role in an association devoted to the memory of "a caudillo of a revolution of extreme leftist tendencies."[56] He accused Sáenz of having become like the people his father had fought all his life: a "group of plutocrats" that resembled the inner circle of the Old Regime of dictator Porfirio Díaz.[57]

This document eloquently demonstrates the continuing battle over the legacy of the revolution and of Alvaro Obregón in particular. For President Calles, the death of Obregón had offered an opportunity to forge national unity by fomenting the myth of a single, unified revolution. For him, the fallen caudillo was the most useful symbolic representative of this revolution. Cárdenas, by contrast, had posited Obregón as a precursor to his own efforts at social reform. He sought to make a sharp contrast between the idolized, martyred Obregón and Calles who seemed to still threaten a return to boss rule from his exile. Romandía Ferreira and Luis L. León resisted the Cardenista reinterpretation and reinvented Obregón as a father figure opposed to radical ideologies. Finally, Humberto Obregón's opposition to Sáenz and the other directors of the Asociación Cívica highlights the fact that by 1950, the public commemoration of the revolution had become a stale ritual that served the interests of elites interested in industrial capitalism rather than the concerns of agrarians and labor.[58]

Therefore, twenty-five years after Obregón's assassination, the debate about the nature of the Mexican Revolution and the caudillo's place in it lost much of its currency. For the generation that came of age during the so-called Mexican Miracle of the 1950s and 1960s, the revolution was little more than a historical artifact. During these years, state-sponsored industrialization yielded promising results: economic growth rates topped 8 percent annually, and the peso entered a twenty-two-year period of stability vis-à-vis the U.S. dollar. By 1960, the revolutionary past seemed a mere prologue to the country's journey toward inclusion among the world's most industrialized nations, an event promised and predicted annually by the PRI's ideologues. Mexico, these politicians proclaimed, was no longer an underdeveloped country, but one "en vías del desarrollo," in the process of development. In this atmosphere, revolutionary caudillos like Obregón were portrayed as father figures who had propelled Mexico toward a better future, but who were no longer role models for the country's new civilian and bureaucratic leadership of university graduates. Thus, the annual celebrations of July 17 remained a major event on the PRI calendar, since the party continued to draw its legitimacy from Obregón and the other revolutionaries. But the annual ceremony was marked by boilerplate speeches celebrating the party's achievements rather than a reflection on Obregón's memory.[59]

The lesson was not lost on the Mexican public, and press coverage of the event became lackluster, and sometimes overtly critical. For instance, in 1954, an editorial in the newspaper *Novedades* asked: "Obregón, was he a hero? To conquer laurels at the expense of one's brothers is not a triumph, but defeat. . . . Those who died were those from below, those proletarians of the countryside and the city that now . . . have become . . . *braceros* [Mexican workers in the United States]."[60] Mexicans, the editorial argued, had become tired of both the promises of a perfect revolution and the assertion that Obregón had helped bring democracy to Mexico.[61] Twenty years later, the disillusionment with the revolution was general enough that not even the orators attempted to draw an idealized picture. At the 1974 commemoration, Senator Alejandro Carrillo labeled Obregón "one of the great constructors of the nation," but admitted that the Mexican Revolution, just like any other major social upheaval, had not reached all of its goals.[62]

The arm inside the vial slowly decomposed as the myth of revolution faded. Imperfectly preserved and damaged by light inside the monument, the arm lost all natural color. It also began to disintegrate, beginning from the point where the grenade explosion had severed it. Frayed nerves and tendons began to protrude from the limb, which had shriveled until a ghastly white hand seemed to sit on an indistinct mound of pale flesh. Just as the PRI's insistence that it represented the ideals of the Mexican Revolution met with growing cynicism and ridicule among the country's youth, so the revolting spectacle of the caudillo's arm made a mockery of the idea of preserving the spirit of a revolution in a generation more familiar with Michael Jackson than with Emiliano Zapata. Comments by visitors ranged from "not very presentable," in the words of one of the caudillo's sons, to "pretty gross," as a Chicano visiting Mexico City remarked.[63] Not surprisingly, Obregón's descendants decided in the mid-1980s that the arm should be cremated and reunited with the caudillo's ashes in Huatabampo, where a large number of family members continued to reside.[64] In deference to the Asociación Cívica and its connection with the Mexican government, however, the family never made their wish public, hence avoiding a debate on the issue.

Nonetheless, some Mexicans opposed the plan to remove the last physical vestige of the revolution from the Monumento Obregón. The arm was one of the few remaining symbols of a bygone era. In the minds of many older Mexicans, the romantic appeal of this era lingered in the "lost decade" of the 1980s—a decade marked a debt crisis, sharply declining real wages, the financial devastation of the middle class, and the flight of millions of rural inhabitants to urban shantytowns and across the U.S. border.[65] At a time when neoliberal technocrats such as Salinas de Gortari (president from 1988 to 1994) sacrificed the PRI's old rhetoric as a part of their attempt to bring Mexico out of its economic doldrums according to the precepts of international lending institutions, the public would have suspected that the cremation of the arm was the decision of the government rather than that of the Obregón family. In the Salinas era, removing the arm would therefore draw attention to the fact that the Mexican government had given up on its attempt to use the revolution for political capital. Not surprisingly, the aging caretaker of the monument said in an 1989 interview that the arm had "become a part of history and to take it away would be to change history a little bit."[66]

Meanwhile, regional differences in the remembrance of Obregón added another wrinkle to this debate. The inhabitants of the caudillo's home state had long resented the fact that the Monumento Obregón was not only the principal site at which the Mexican state paid homage to the victor of the revolution, but also the repository of an arm that had been severed from its owner long before that owner met his death at La Bombilla. Many Sonorans wondered why the arm was not displayed at the battle site in Guanajuato, or, better yet, cremated alongside and mingled with Obregón's ashes in Huatabampo. In 1988, as if to emphasize this claim on the whole revolutionary rather than the one-armed martyr, the city of Ciudad Obregón, located one hour north of the caudillo's birthplace, built a statue of Obregón on horseback with both of his hands firmly on the horse's reins (see Illustration 6.5). These most recent Sonoran statue contrasts with the earlier representations of the one-armed caudillo, such as the most famous one in the Monumento Obregón.

Hence the story ends with a whimper with the unpublicized cremation of the arm on November 16, 1989, a cremation about which no details were released to the general public. A debate over the last mortal relic of the revolution was not in the interest of either the Mexican government or the vast Obregón clan with its Mexico City

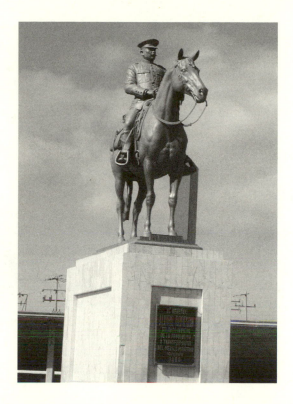

6.5   *Statue of General Obregón (pre-injury) in Cuidad Obregón, Sonora (Photo: Jürgen Buchenau).*

and Sonora branches. The swift action of the Obregón family stole the chance of groups of revolutionary veterans to march on Mexico City's main square, the Zócalo, and precluded a national debate on whether the ashes of the arm should repose with the rest of Obregón in Sonora (see Illustration 6.6) or with the monument in Mexico City. Always a better military leader and tactician than a politician, Obregón himself would have appreciated the end of his arm's political career.

Obregón's piecemeal transition out of the world of the living into the realm of the dead created two separate postmortem cults: that of the arm and that of his body. The arm still represents Obregón's victories on the revolutionary battlefield; his masculinity and military prowess. The body, by contrast, represents one of the most important members of the Mexican revolutionary family, a precursor of the institutional revolution and unifier of divergent political tendencies.

6.6   *Obregón's tomb in Huatabampo, Sonora (Photo: Jürgen Buchenau).*

In terms of lasting political symbolism, the assassination of the caudillo in 1928 proved to be a more significant loss than the loss of his arm in 1915. Strikingly, however, the arm would prove to be the last physical reminder that connected Obregón in particular and the Mexican Revolution in general to a Mexican political culture that had grown increasingly cynical about the "sacrifice" of this particular life—or any human life for that matter—to a cycle of violence that had fallen short of delivering the political and social change that many Mexicans had hoped for.

Notes

I thank Víctor Macías for bringing to my attention the saying that forms the epigraph of this chapter. I also appreciate the help of Norma Mereles de Ogarrio, director of the Fideicomiso Archivos Plutarco Elías Calles y Fernando Torreblanca in Mexico City. I gratefully acknowledge the financial support of UNC Charlotte and the Southern Regional Education Board.

1. *El Universal*, 17 July 1989.

2. *Proceso*, 24 July 1989.

3. "If Only the General Could Have Ruled on the Fate of his Arm: Revolutionary Hero Lost Limb in Battle, and it Surfaces as Issue" *Wall Street Journal*, 28 November 1989.

4. See Lyman Johnson's chapter in this volume.

5. See Chris Archer's contribution to this volume.

6. See, for instance, Samuel Brunk's contribution to this volume; and Ilene V. O'Malley, *The Myth of the Revolution: Hero Cults and the Institutionalization of the Mexican State, 1920–1940* (New York: Greenwood Press, 1986).

7. Friedrich Katz, *El asesinato de Pancho Villa*, Boletín 32 (Mexico City: Fideicomiso Archivos Plutarco Elías Calles y Fernando Torreblanca, 1999).

8. Alvaro Obregón, *Ocho mil kilómetros en campaña*, 1917, 2nd ed. (Mexico City: Fondo de Cultura Económica, 1959), 370–71.

9. Elías L. Torres, "Cómo perdió el brazo Obregón," in Archivo Histórico General y Licenciado Aarón Sáenz, Mexico City (hereafter AHAS), exp. 183/1641.

10. Obregón, *Ocho mil kilómetros en campaña*, 371.

11. See also the other essays in this volume. For a theoretical appreciation of the politics of the body and its application to postcommunist Eastern Europe, see Katherine Verdery, *The Political Lives of Dead Bodies: Reburial and Postsocialist Change* (New York: Columbia University Press, 1999), esp. 1–22.

12. Claudio Lomnitz, *Deep Mexico, Silent Mexico: An Anthropology of Mexican Nationalism* (Minneapolis: University of Minnesota Press, 2001), 94.

13. "La tragedia de Obregón," *Zócalo*, 24 August 1952, in AHAS, exp.183/1641.

14. "Misplaced Body Parts: Stonewall Jackson's Arm," *The Washington Post*, 7 August 2001. I thank Karen Cox for pointing me to this source.

15. Lesley Byrd Simpson, *Many Mexicos*, 4th rev. ed. (Berkeley: University of California Press, 1967), 242–48.

16. Quoted in Lomnitz, *Deep Mexico*, 90.

17. Alvaro Obregón, *Discursos del General Alvaro Obregón* , 2 vols. (Mexico City: Talleres Gráficos de la Nación, 1932).

18. Enrique Krauze, *El vértigo de la victoria: Alvaro Obregón* (Mexico City: Fondo de Cultura Económica, 1987), 62–63.

19. Quoted in ibid.

20. Quoted in "La mano de Obregón perdió su última batalla," *Proceso* 663 (17 July 1989): 47.

21. Samuel Schmidt, *Humor en serio: Análisis del chiste político en México* (Mexico City: Aguilar, 1996), 114–19, 170–71.

22. Krauze, *Alvaro Obregón*, 58–59.

23. Martín Luis Guzmán, *La sombra del caudillo* (Mexico City: Ediciones Botas, 1938).

24. There is to this date no in-depth study of Obregón's years as president. For his career as a revolutionary, see Linda B. Hall, *Alvaro Obregón: Power and Revolution in Mexico, 1911–1920* (College Station: Texas A&M University Press, 1981). Nor is there a scholarly biography of Calles after 1920, a void that will be filled by this author's *Architect of the Institutional Revolution in Mexico: Plutarco Elías Calles* (manuscript in preparation).

25. Enrique Krauze, *La presidencia imperial: Ascenso y caída del sistema político mexicano, 1940–1996* (Mexico City: Tusquets Editores, 1997).

26. Jorge Aguilar Mora, *Una muerte sencilla, justa, eternal: cultura y guerra durante la revolución mexicana* (Mexico: Ediciones Era, 1990), 10. Mora's list ends with the José López Portillo administration (1976–82), a regime vilified for its authoritarianism and corruption. Suetonius's collective biography, of course, describes the careers of twelve Caesars.

27. Address to the Mexican Congress, 1 September 1928, quoted in *Plutarco Elías Calles: Pensamiento político y social*, ed. Carlos Macías Richard (Mexico City: Fondo de Cultura Económica, 1988), 240–43.

28. Arnaldo Córdova, *La Revolución en crisis: La aventura del maximato* (Mexico City: Cal y arena, 1995), 23.

29. Plutarco Elías Calles, "A la nación," Fideicomiso Archivos Plutarco Elías Calles y Fernando Torreblanca (hereafter FAPEC), Fondo Alvaro Obregón (hereafter FAO), fondo 11 serie 060100 expediente 2, inventario 5046.

30. See Krauze, *Alvaro Obregón*, 205; Enrique Klaus, *Plutarco Elías Calles: Reformar desde el origen* (Mexico City: Fondo de Cultura Económica, 1987), 136. Even Calles's opponent José Vasconcelos later concurred, albeit not without elevating Toral to hero status. José Vasconcelos, *El proconsulado* (Mexico: Ediciones Botas, 1939), 22–23.

31. Plutarco Elías Calles, "Informe de gobierno del 10. de septiembre de 1928," in *Declaraciones y discursos políticos* (Mexico City: Cuadernos de causa, 1979), 167–68.

32. Ibid., 167.

33. Córdova, *Revolución en Crisis*, 31 and passim.

34. Thomas Benjamin, *La Revolución: Mexico's Great Revolution as Memory, Myth, and History* (Austin: University of Texas Press, 2000), esp.131.

35. Ibid.

36. Quoted in ibid., 33.

37. David C. Bailey, "Obregón: Mexico's Accommodating President," in *Essays on the Mexican Revolution: Revisionist Views of the Leaders*, ed. George Wolfskill and Douglas W. Richmond (Austin: University of Texas Press, 1979), 82.

38. "Discurso pronunciado por el Lic. Aarón Sáenz," Monterrey, N. L., 17 July 1929, FAPEC, FAO, fondo 11, serie 060400, gaveta 33, expediente 2, inventario 5129.

39. FAPEC, FAO, f. 11, s. 060400, gaveta 33, exp. 2, inv. 5129.

40. "Un monumento al General Alvaro Obregón en el Paseo de la Reforma," *El Universal*, 26 July 1928.

41. Departamento del Distrito Federal, *Monumento al General Alvaro Obregón: Homenaje nacional en el lugar de su sacrificio; prospecto*, in FAPEC, FAO, f. 11, s. 060400, gav. 33, exp. 7, inv. 5134.

42. Aarón Sáenz, "Discurso pronunciado en la solemne inauguración del monumento erigido a la memoria del señor General Alvaro Obregón, 17 de julio de 1935," FAPEC, FAO, f. 11, s. 060400, gaveta 33, exp. 8, inv. 5135.

43. For the "revisionist" critique of the new ruling party, see David C. Bailey, "Revisionism and the Recent Historiography of the Mexican Revolution," *Hispanic American Historical Review* 58, no. 1 (1978): 62–79. For postrevisionist criticism that does not invalidate this key point, see Gilbert M. Joseph and Daniel Nugent, "Popular Culture and State Formation in Revolutionary Mexico," in *Everyday Forms of State Formation: Revolution and the Negotiation of Rule in Mexico* (Durham, NC: Duke University Press, 1994), 5–15.

44. Arnaldo Córdova, *La política de masas del cardenismo* (Mexico City: Ediciones Era, 1974).

45. Aarón Sáenz, "Discurso pronunciado en la solemne inauguración del monumento erigido a la memoria del señor General Alvaro Obregón, 17 de julio de 1935," FAPEC, FAO, f. 11, s. 060400, gaveta 33, exp. 8, inv. 5135.

46. Lic. A. Romandía Ferreira, "Discurso," 18 [sic] July 1941. FAPEC, FAO f. 11, s. 060400, gaveta 33, exp. 13, inv. 5140.

47. Ibid.

48. Ibid.

49. Steve Niblo, *Mexico in the 1940s: Modernity, Politics, and Corruption* (Wilmington, DE: Scholarly Resources Inc., 1999), 1–74.

50. Cf. O'Malley, *Myth of the Revolution*, 114–32, which overlooks the Obregón cult as a unifying force.

51. FAPEC, FAO, f. 11, s. 060400, gaveta 33, exp. 15, inv. 5142.

52. Claudio Lomnitz, "Elusive Property: The Personification of Mexican National Sovereignty," in *The Empire of Things: Regimes of Value and Material Culture*, ed. Fred R. Myers (Santa Fe, NM: School of American Research Press, 2001), 128.

53. "Discurso pronunciado por el Lic. Antonio Médiz Bolio," FAPEC, FAO, f. 11, s. 060400, gaveta 33, exp. 17, inv. 5144.

54. "Discurso pronunciado por el Sr. Ing. Luis L. León . . . ," 12–13; FAPEC, FAO, f. 11. s. 060400, gaveta 33, exp. 22, inv. 5149.

55. Ibid.

56. Humberto Obregón to Aarón Sáenz, Mexico City, 7 June 1950, FAPEC, FAO, f. 11. s. 060400, gaveta 33, exp. 22, inv. 5149.

57. Ibid.

58. On the postrevolutionary state and the cultural project of the PRI state, see Arthur Schmidt, "Making it Real Compared to What? Reconceptualizing Mexican History Since 1940," in *Fragments of a Golden Age: The Politics of Culture in Mexico Since 1940*, ed. Gilbert Joseph, Anne Rubenstein, and Eric Zolov (Durham, NC: Duke University Press, 2001), 25–33.

59. FAPEC, FAO, f. 11. s. 060400, gaveta 33, exp. 22–37, inv. 5149–61.

60. "¿Cada año, el 17 de julio, hay cátedra de obregonismo?" *Novedades*, 23 July 1954.

61. Ibid.

62. "Ninguna Revolución en el Mundo Ha Alcanzado Todas sus Metas: La Mexicana no es Excepción," *El Nacional*, 18 July 1974.

63. "Some Still See Decaying Display as Piece of Revolutionary History Farewell to Arm?" *Los Angeles Times*, 11 September 1989.

64. Ibid.

65. Nora Lustig, *Mexico: The Remaking of an Economy*, 2nd rev. ed. (Washington DC: Brookings Institution, 1998), chap. 3; Alma Guillermoprieto, *The Heart that Bleeds: Latin America Now* (New York: Vintage Books, 1995), esp. 47–67 and 237–58.

66. "Some Still See Decaying Display" *Los Angeles Times*, 11 September 1989.

Chapter Seven

Digging Up Cuauhtémoc

Lyman L. Johnson

On September 26, 1949, a crowd of locals seeking relief from everyday chores stood in hushed silence outside the Church of Santa María de la Asunción in Ixcateopan (alternatively spelled Ichcateopan) in Guerrero, Mexico. Their ranks had been integrated by a small number of newspaper journalists, politicians, and visiting dignitaries. This unlikely mix of witnesses grew in number while a team of investigators under the command of Eulalia Guzmán of the National Institute of Anthropology and History (INAH) pursued their excavation beneath the church's main altar in the hope of discovering the final resting place of Cuauhtémoc, the last Aztec *tlatoani* (ruler). Cuauhtémoc had heroically defended the Aztec capital of Tenochtitlán from the Spaniards and was later captured, cruelly tortured, and finally executed by Hernán Cortés. This tragic figure had grown in stature after Mexican independence, becoming a potent symbol of selfless sacrifice and heroism in the face of impossible odds. From the first day of the excavation on September 21 the size of this vigil had fluctuated in response to the arrival and departure of visiting dignitaries including the governor of Guerrero, Baltasar Leyva Mancilla, his entourage, and a handful of officials from the national government in Mexico City. The restless character of this official ebb and flow reflected both the widespread hope that Guzmán and her colleagues would succeed and the fears of the politicians that the entire enterprise would fail and their presence would brand them as gullible fools.

At four in the afternoon the team of investigators working beneath the main altar signaled that they had uncovered powerful evidence that the church sheltered a significant burial, perhaps the remains of the Aztec ruler. Eulalia Guzmán was hurriedly called to the site and the search for Cuauhtémoc's remains moved forward with renewed energy as the crowd outside the church quickly grew. Copper plates, one of which appeared to carry a variant of the Mexican ruler's name, Coatemo, and the dates 1525 and 1529 were found and soon after skeletal remains were uncovered.[1] As Eulalia Guzmán, deeply moved and with tears in her eyes, walked outside to announce the discovery of this evidence her conviction and joy were broadcast throughout the town by the church's bells. As reported by one of Mexico City's major newspapers, "There is no doubt that it is the tomb of the king [Cuauhtémoc]."[2]

Farmers from the surrounding fields and pastures, shopkeepers from the plaza a block away, and a string of dignitaries from the state capital and even from Mexico City hurried to Ixcateopan to celebrate the discovery. Even the U.S. embassy rushed to establish a presence, sending, among others, technicians to record the final stages of the dig and an unlikely representative from the Hoof and Mouth Disease Commission. Little patience was required of the witnesses as work in the church ended with the announced discovery of skeletal remains.[3]

Neither this discovery nor the resulting patriotic furor had been adequately anticipated by Guzmán's superiors. Academic bureaucrats at the INAH in Mexico City had been surprised by news of a recently uncovered cache of documents and oral traditions that connected Cuauhtémoc to Ixcateopan, Guerrero. On February 2, 1949, the parish priest of Ixcateopan, David Salgado, was shown a remarkable collection of documents by the patriarch of a long-established local family, Salvador Rodríguez Juárez. Rodríguez Juárez claimed the documents, along with corroborating oral testimony, had been passed from generation to generation since time immemorial. The Juárez branch of the family had been significant locally since the late nineteenth century as landowners and as political officeholders. Rodríguez Juárez had lived for a time in Mexico City after the Mexican Revolution and returned to Ixcateopan claiming to be a medical doctor, although his credentials are now dismissed as forgeries.[4]

News of the documents led the INAH to send Eulalia Guzmán to Ixcateopan, charging her with evaluating both the documents and the testimony of Rodríguez Juárez and other village elders. Was it possible that Cuauhtémoc was buried beneath the altar of the parish church? (See Illustration 7.1.) According to the compelling narrative and documents provided by Rodríguez Juárez in 1949, Cuauhtémoc's

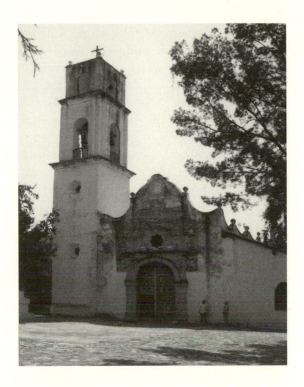

7.1   *The church of Santa María de Asunción in Ixcateopan, Guerrero, where Eulalia Guzmán claimed to have discovered the remains of Cuauhtémoc (Photo: Lyman L. Johnson).*

remains had been rescued from the site of his execution in Honduras by loyal servants.[5] Cuauhtémoc's retainers then carried his corpse to Ixcateopan because this had been his birthplace and the place where he had passed part of his youth at "the palace of his grandparents."[6] Once returned to Ixcateopan, Cuauhtémoc's remains were hidden until reburied under the main altar of the Church of Santa María de la Asunción in 1529 by order of the famous Franciscan missionary and indigenous advocate, Fray Toribio de Benavente, known commonly as Motolinía.[7]

The documents and the story they told provoked immediate criticism from historians in Mexico City. Working from typed or photographic copies, rather than the originals, critics pointed out a series of problems, among them that the documents did not conform to sixteenth-century handwriting or forms of writing dates. The Motolinía signature itself was suspicious. More suspicious still, there was no convincing contemporary evidence that Motolinía had been in Mexico, specifically in Ixcateopan, around the time of the alleged reburial of Cuauhtémoc. These criticisms seemed to disappear from the press in March as Eulalia Guzmán worked to defuse objections by suggesting to the press that the documents conserved by Salvador Rodríguez Juárez were copies of originals made in 1777 and not the sixteenth-century originals. She went on to claim that local oral history traditions provided corroborating support for the documents.[8]

Although her INAH superiors had assigned a trained archaeologist to supervise the excavation, the expert was very slow to arrive. Guzmán, apparently fearful of a botched excavation, urged INAH to send another archaeologist, but this plea was ignored, thus leaving her on her own. The governor of Guerrero and other state officials pressured Guzmán to begin the excavation immediately in order to resolve the issue of Cuauhtémoc's remains. She tried to buy some time by hiring locals to break down the altar and prepare the site, but in the end the excavation proceeded rapidly with little concern for traditional archaeological practices.[9] It is clear that the presence in Ixcateopan of powerful, well-connected politicians put overwhelming pressure on Guzmán to move quickly. Nevertheless, Guzmán's professional ambitions, ambitions difficult to realize without political sponsorship, made successful resistance to these pressures unlikely.

Once the decision was made to move forward without waiting for the arrival of the archaeologist, the workforce of untrained locals pushed forward quickly, even working on Sunday. Evidence suggests that Guzmán was unable to exercise full control at the site, with military and civilian officials and even members of the Rodríguez Juárez family directing workers at times. The lack of professional discipline, the absence of notes and photos, for example, would later cause Guzmán serious problems when her results were reviewed by critical experts, but the euphoria that accompanied her "discovery" of Cuauhtémoc's remains on September 26 seemed to sweep aside questions about the legitimacy of the documents and the chaotic and rushed nature of her excavation.[10] In the popular rush to celebrate Cuauhtémoc's patriotic legacy there were few questions. Didn't the discovery of the bones and related grave goods confirm the legitimacy of the documents?

News from Ixcateopan swept across the nation, and the small town was predictably transformed in the resulting wave of patriotic fervor.

The church was unofficially rechristened by visiting reporters and politicians as a "national patriotic sanctuary" and, alternatively, as the resting place of the "héroe más limpio de la historia" (the purest hero of history), "the fallen eagle," or the "young grandfather."[11] In the enthusiasm of the moment, practical concerns to preserve the site from contamination mixed in promiscuous and unpredictable ways with symbolic acts. Eulalia Guzmán and state officials moved with dispatch to secure the site, artifacts, and human remains from the enthusiasms of a crowd deeply moved by patriotic passions. On a more practical level, fears that the "treasure of Cuauhtémoc" might be located near the burial led state officials to post a small garrison of rural guards in Ixcateopan.[12] The useful and the symbolic fused predictably in the decision to decorate the excavation with Mexican flags and have the governor of Guerrero join the first honor guard posted at this now hallowed site.[13]

There was little room for skepticism as the remarkable story was broadcast across Mexico. Mounting popular enthusiasm was propelled in large measure by the eagerness of politicians from Mexico's ruling party, the PRI (Party of the Institutionalized Revolution, or Partido Revolucionario Institucional), to uncritically endorse the legitimacy of Guzmán's claims. Both in Guerrero and especially in Mexico City the immediate link between the reported discovery of Cuauhtémoc's remains and the political arena was predictable given the proven symbolic utility of the martyred ruler. Cuauhtémoc was already a well-established popular symbol whose image and reputation had been usefully attached to everything from patriotic rituals to breweries.

Ixcateopan prepared itself for its much anticipated, and apparently inevitable, future as a major tourist destination. One plan called for the construction of a monument to Cuauhtémoc built on the scale of the national capital's monument to Mexican independence erected in 1910 on the eve of the Mexican Revolution by the government of Porfirio Díaz. Another advocated the construction in Ixcateopan of a museum devoted to Cuauhtémoc and the theme of indigenous resistance in Mexican history. Foreshadowing these future transformations, a patriotic crowd of nearly ten thousand gathered in Ixcateopan to celebrate the Día de la Raza (Day of the Race) on October 12. This holiday had been celebrated since 1918 to recognize Mexico's place in the Iberoamerican world. In 1949, following the discovery of Cuauhtémoc's remains, the holiday was recast to celebrate Mexico's indigenous past alone.[14] The town's compact plaza was overwhelmed and thousands spilled out onto the central street as buses and cars unloaded patriotic pilgrims who hoped to enter the church and catch a glimpse of Cuauhtémoc's remains. It must have seemed that the master narrative of Mexican history, a history of indigenous oppression and resistance given potent formulation in the works of Diego Rivera and the other muralists, had gained in Ixcateopan the perfect relic to infuse this story with corporal reality.[15] Certainly local boosters, especially the Rodríguez Juárez family that had guarded the documents and oral traditions, hoped to see their town floated to national prominence as a patriotic pilgrimage site by its historical association with Cuauhtémoc.

Mexico's first fifty years of independent existence had been fractured by civil war and foreign interventions. The traumatic loss of Texas in 1836 was followed by the loss of California and much of the nation's northwest at the end of the Mexican-American War in 1848. These terrible defeats led Mexican political leaders to self-consciously examine the nation's past to find appropriate heroes to hold up as examples. With half its national territory already lost to the United States, Mexico's very existence as an independent nation was challenged by a French invasion in 1862. The French and their conservative allies in Mexico imposed Maximilian of Habsburg, as emperor. Mexican forces led by President Benito Juárez (no relation to the Ixcateopan family that produced the documents) forced a French withdrawal and then captured and executed Maximilian in 1867. Victory put in place a political leadership with a renewed commitment to invigorating Mexican patriotism through a studied use of historical example.

One component of this effort was the identification and celebration of Mexican heroes whose lives (and deaths) would educate citizens for the task of building a modern nation. In practical terms this meant celebrating Miguel Hidalgo and José María Morelos as the progenitors of independence. It also meant embracing Benito Juárez, who successfully led resistance to the French, as the nation's virtuous shield against foreign invasion.[16] Both Hidalgo and Morelos died as victims of Spanish oppression, executed by firing squads after being captured. Benito Juárez, although he had been a divisive political figure during his life, proved to be an irresistible symbol because of his defeat of the French. Collectively these heroes taught that patriotism was in essence resistance to foreign domination. The logic of this heroic sequence led inexorably to a deeper embrace of Cuauhtémoc.[17] The usefulness of the martyred Aztec ruler was evident even before the achievement of independence. José María Morelos invoked the memory of Cuauhtémoc and other Aztec leaders in 1813 in a speech to delegates to the constitutional convention, suggesting that Cuauhtémoc "celebrate this happy moment in which your sons have united to avenge the crimes and outrages committed against you and free themselves from the claws of tyranny and fanaticism that were going to grasp them forever."[18]

However, the celebration of a patriotic hero from the indigenous past created some difficulties for leaders of an independent Mexico.[19] By the end of the nineteenth century, the cultural values of the elite were derived unambiguously from Europe, not the indigenous past. The language of political, economic, and cultural life was Spanish and the material culture was unapologetically imitative of Europe and the United States. Indeed, the central objective of economic and political policy after 1870 was the modernization of Mexico, seeking to install the industrial world's streetcars and gas lights as well as factories and extractive industries, like mining and petroleum. Nevertheless, the symbolic value of the indigenous past was irresistible. While pursuing land policies and cultural practices that endangered the very survival of Mexico's large indigenous population, the elite worked to harvest indigenous history for useful symbols of Mexican identity.

By identifying with the Aztecs, Mexico's nineteenth-century leaders were able to portray the bloody and destructive independence struggle (1810–21) as the reassertion of a national identity that had been temporarily suppressed by the Spanish conqueror Hernán Cortés. When they linked the Mexican nation to the ancient Aztecs, the nation's political leaders forged a single transcendent historical narrative. Mexico's defeat of the French, its earlier resistance to the imperial aggressions of the United States, and the achievement of independence from Spain were now portrayed as a serial redemption from the originating injustice of the Spanish Conquest. In this narrative Cuauhtémoc became the symbolic "young grandfather," the patriotic progenitor, of Hidalgo, Morelos, and Juárez.[20]

This patriotic narrative was literally written in stone through the erection of impressive new monuments in Mexico City and elsewhere. Cuauhtémoc was given pride of place. Although a bust had been placed in Mexico City in 1869, the government of Porfirio Díaz decided in 1876 to erect an impressive statue of Cuauhtémoc on the Paseo de la Reforma, the capital's major thoroughfare. Vicente Riva Palacio, Díaz's minister of development, was primarily responsible for this monument. Completed and dedicated in 1887, the statue represented a complicated deconstruction of Cuauhtémoc's life.[21] The statue itself was a heroic representation of the defeated ruler with spear held aloft ready to launch at Mexico's enemies. Cuauhtémoc is depicted in the neoclassical style (see Illustration 7.2), his Aztec robes reminiscent of ancient Rome or Greece. The image proved so popular that the postrevolutionary government of Alvaro Obregón placed a smaller copy of this statue manufactured by Tiffany in Rio de Janeiro as part of Mexico's contribution to the 1922 World's Fair that marked the centennial of Brazilian independence.[22]

The stone pedestal evoked some of the greatest architectural glories of the indigenous past, the ruins of Teotihuacán, Mitla, and Palenque. It also presented two remarkable scenes from the life of Cuauhtémoc. The first portrayed the captured Cuauhtémoc being

7.2 *The statue of Cuauhtémoc in Mexico City erected in 1887 during the presidency of Porfirio Díaz (Photo: Lyman L. Johnson).*

presented to Cortés (see Illustration 7.3). Cuauhtémoc places his
hand on Cortés's knife, asking his captor to take his life, suggesting
that death was preferable to life as a captive. The second shows
Cuauhtémoc and a kinsman undergoing torture at the hands of
Cortés, who believed they had hidden treasure, this torment foreshadowing Cuauhtémoc's later cruel execution (see Illustration 7.4).
The bronze bas relief depicts Cuauhtémoc's feet coated with oil and
put into a fire. The hero is portrayed as calm and transcendent while
his kinsman shows the terror and pain of this terrible torment. Here
the preferred qualities of the fallen Aztec ruler are made clear: sto-
icism, honor, bravery, and nobility.[23] As one witness to the inauguration of the monument put it, "In Cuauhtémoc we do not see the
last descendant of the Aztec kings . . . [instead] we view in him the
hero of the fatherland . . . Cuauhtémoc conquered, Cuauhtémoc
imprisoned and enchained, Cuauhtémoc powerless to defend his
throne by means of arms, defended it suffering valiantly the wicked
and terrible torments. . . . [providing] with such heroic sacrifice [a]
most solemn protest against usurpation which later should produce

7.3　*A bronze relief located on the pedestal of the Cuauhtémoc statue. The
captured Cuauhtémoc places his hand on the dagger of Hernán Cortés,
expressing a desire to die rather than live as a captive
(Photo: Lyman L. Johnson).*

7.4   *A second bronze relief located on the pedestal of the Cuauhtémoc
      statue. Cuauhtémoc calmly endures torture at the hands of the
      Spaniards, while his kinsman tortured at the same time reacts in pain
      (Photo: Lyman L. Johnson).*

its greatest and most precious fruits."[24] Here was the essential
Cuauhtémoc, the noble victim who suffered the brutal cruelty of the
oppressor stoically and patiently.[25] This was the Cuauhtémoc Eulalia
Guzmán sought beneath the altar in Ixcateopan.

    The discovery of Cuauhtémoc's remains provided Eulalia Guzmán
with an instant celebrity that rescued her from the relative obscurity
of her long apprenticeship within the institutions of Mexican archaeology and history as it simultaneously elevated the town of Ixcateopan
to national prominence. Mexican intellectual culture in 1949 was a
traditional patriarchy dominated by powerful men who sustained a
steady stream of publications by organizing the efforts of "equipos"
(teams of subordinates, many of them women). Guzmán had effectively begun her career as a useful and undemanding associate of the
archaeologist Alfonso Caso.[26] Following the publication of a successful book that had argued forcefully for a separate and distinct indigenous aesthetic in 1932, she was rewarded with a position as head of

the Department of Archaeology at the National Museum. She also gained the plum assignment of cataloging pre-Hispanic manuscripts in Europe.[27] But it was the remarkable events in Ixcateopan that gave Guzmán the opportunity to stand alone in the national spotlight, recommended for an honorary doctorate from the National Autonomous University of Mexico (UNAM) and granted the Mérito Cívico medal from the national government shortly after the excavation in Ixcateopan. With this new attention, her schedule filled with invitations to speak to civic, business, and political groups.[28]

As news of Guzmán's extraordinary discovery spread, school children in Mexico City were mustered by school administrators to stand as guards of honor in front of the Cuauhtémoc statue on the Paseo de la Reforma. Thousands more marched in well-organized celebrations of Cuauhtémoc's full reintegration in Mexico's pantheon of heroes. Schemes for appropriately marking Eulalia Guzmán's momentous discovery flowed from every direction. One successful proposal called for the renaming of the location of the bones Ixcateopan de Cuauhtémoc. Another urged that Cuauhtémoc be officially designated as "symbol of Mexican nationality" by legislation. Mexico's intellectual and artistic communities were equally swept along by this emotional tidal surge. The performing arts center, Bellas Artes, commissioned a ballet based on the life of Cuauhtémoc, plays for both children and adults were written, and Diego Rivera was enlisted to produce a portrait of the heroic martyr that would be reproduced and given to elementary students throughout Mexico.[29] In the euphoria of the moment the Colegio Militar proposed moving the hero's remains to Mexico City, "the place Cuauhtémoc had heroically defended."[30] But this idea was immediately checked by Guerrero state authorities who instinctively resisted the loss of this valuable relic to the capital.

The Ixcateopan excavation had occurred in a remarkable context of discoveries of patriotic relics. On November 24, 1946, bones unearthed at Hospital de Jésus in Mexico City were turned over to a team of experts from INAH who determined that they were the skeletal remains of Hernán Cortés, the conqueror of the Aztecs. On March 26, 1947, a date roughly coinciding with the centenary of the American invasion of Mexico, the remains of Mexico's young military martyrs who had thrown themselves off the battlements rather than surrender to the invading Americans, Los Niños Héroes (the young heroes), were discovered and authenticated by another commission of experts. Once authenticated, these remains were then reburied with full military honors at the Colegio Militar. Unwilling to leave this event in the hands of mere academics, President Miguel Alemán had the sacred bones authenticated subsequently by congressional act. The Catholic Church joined the rising tide of patriotic celebration, providing the Niños Héroes with a burial mass at Mexico's most sacred religious shrine, the Basilica of the Virgin of Guadalupe.[31] In a nearly perfect trifecta of exhumation, the bones of Mexican and American soldiers who fell at the battle of Padierna in 1847 were uncovered and identified shortly after the emotional recovery of the bones of the Niños Héroes. This context of near-miraculous exhumations had heightened public awareness of Cuauhtémoc in Mexico, generating a public anticipation for the discovery of his remains.

Although Cuauhtémoc and Mexico's indigenous past had proved useful in the nineteenth century, the Mexican Revolution (begun 1910) had given birth to a deeper and more passionate attachment of Mexican identity to the indigenous past. This desire to recover and celebrate the indigenous past, referred to as *indigenismo*, was more an enthusiasm of the new governing elite than a coherent agenda pursued by indigenous groups.[32] Many of Mexico's most consequential reforms of the 1920s and 1930s were politically justified as the righting of ancient wrongs imposed by the Spanish Conquest, wrongs symbolized by the torture and execution of Cuauhtémoc in numerous speeches by politicians and intellectuals. This symbolic connection between the sixteenth-century conquest and Mexico's twentieth-century social reforms was made explicit in the reinvention of the indigenous *ejido* (agricultural collective) as a tool of land reform, in enhanced academic investment in archaeology and indigenous language study, and in the heroic and patriotic appropriation of Aztec history by Mexico's famous muralists, including Diego Rivera, José Clemente Orozco, and David Alfaro Siquieros, among others.

These evocations of the indigenous past in the 1920s and 1930s meant that the 1946 exhumation of Cortés's remains occurred in an inhospitable political environment. As a result, efforts were made by those in charge to avoid exciting the anger of anti-Spanish political factions. Indeed, any public celebration of Iberia's contribution to Mexican identity was recognized as dangerous during this decade.[33] Resentment of Spaniards and of Spain's contribution to Mexican history had remained an active component of Mexican political life from the time of independence. In fact, the arrival of the remains of the great patriots of the independence era, Hidalgo and Morelos, in Mexico City in 1823, provoked a patriotic frenzy. Hearing rumors that a mob planned to desecrate the remains of Hernán Cortés, prominent conservatives had acted quickly to hide the great conqueror's bones.[34] With the passage of time the remains had been "lost" in the sense that only a small number tied to the Spanish embassy in Mexico City knew their location. Although the discovery of the location in 1946 was noted in newspapers and gave heart to some conservatives and Hispanophiles, the work of the academic commission that authenticated the remains and the official reburial were managed carefully to avoid re-igniting popular Mexican resentment of Cortés and of Spain.[35]

Passion for Cuauhtémoc was most intense on the Mexican Left, a diverse mix of political inclinations with a long history of fratricidal conflicts. Despite differences on policy issues, the Left had generally found the indigenous past, specifically the Aztec past, useful when portraying Mexican history as a single long struggle against oppression; in this transformation Cuauhtémoc's martyrdom anticipated the later martyrdoms of Hidalgo, Morelos, Los Niños Héroes, and the tragic figures of the Mexican Revolution, Francisco Madero and Emiliano Zapata. This unlikely repackaging of the bloody-handed Aztec aristocracy with their passions for military conquest and human sacrifice as a Mexican pre-proletariat required a symbolic vocabulary that necessarily emphasized the tragic fall of Tenochtitlan and the redemptive suffering of Cuauhtémoc. This symbolic nomenclature with its instinctive rejection of Spain provided the context for Eulalia Guzmán's struggle with her critics.

With news of the discovery in Ixcateopan, Jorge Acosta, chief archaeologist at INAH, and Alfonso Caso, Director of National Institute of Indigenous Studies, visited the site with other members of INAH. This was not a hostile delegation. Caso, for example, had been Guzmán's supervisor during her early archaeological excavations in Oaxaca. While publicly enthusiastic, the experts were not fully convinced by the evidence. Some of this reticence resulted from the early criticism of the documents. But even a brief stay in Ixcateopan made the INAH commission aware of problems that grew out of Guzmán's decision to push ahead with the excavation without waiting for the arrival of the trained archaeologist. There had been no traditional site discipline as Guzmán and her team excavated. They had not used string grids to mark out the site and provide reference points to fix the location of artifacts, a standard practice, at the church. With these doubts in place the officials returned to Mexico City, still publicly supporting Guzmán's results.[36]

On October 14, two days after the celebration of the Día de la Raza in Ixcateopan with its focus on the recovery of Cuauhtémoc's remains, the INAH commission delivered its opinion to the Mexican public.[37] In an economical, unemotional prose the commission stated that the documents provided by the Rodríguez Juárez family were forgeries, that the two copper plates recovered from the site were also likely forgeries, and that the burial location itself could not be confidently dated.[38] More devastating still, the INAH commission deconstructed the remains, asserting that what the public had taken to be the sacred relics of their beloved Cuauhtémoc were in fact the aggregated bones of as many as five individuals.[39]

As this frontal assault on her achievement was made public, Eulalia Guzmán, originally trained as a schoolteacher rather than as a historian or archaeologist, signaled clearly both her independence from INAH superiors and her political sophistication. Moving quickly, she temporarily disarmed the academic experts by acknowledging again to sympathetic newspaper journalists that the documents were eighteenth-century "copies" of the originals. The documents were genuine, she asserted, but were not the originals. These, she claimed, had been lost generations ago. The questions raised by the INAH experts, therefore, were off the mark. She also repeated her claim that local oral traditions found among the local *ancianos* (elders) corroborated the documents as had the discovery of the bones themselves. Her dismissal of the commission's work as superficial and rushed received broad public support.

Politicians and intellectuals also proved eager to dismiss the commission as a collection of Hispanophiles, while major newspapers and periodicals invested buckets of ink in stirring the public's anger. One writer asked, "Is a cold, indifferent truth more valuable than a lie or mere ignorance full of passion, stimulating and forceful?" Other supporters sought to denigrate Guzmán's critics as "antipatriotic and anti-Mexican" or as "official wise men, possessed by Malinchismo." By the 1950s Malinche, Doña Marina the indigenous woman who served as Cortés's translator and mistress, had become a common term of contempt used to describe someone willing to betray the nation. Refusal to accept the legitimacy of the remains, these critics suggested by their use of "Malinchismo," was the equivalent of selling out the nation. Others saw both the commission's negative decision and the resulting slow trickle of anti-Guzmán articles in the press as the work of Yankee Imperialists. The communists wondered publicly if this outrage could be setting the stage for efforts to illegally reelect Alemán as president of Mexico. The attack reached its full expression in a published statement made by Mexico's most famous artist, Diego Rivera, on November 21, 1949: "If tomorrow the country people, the sublime Indians that guard the remains of their chief with rifles in their hands, seized these negators [the commission members], lined them against a wall in Ichcateopan and shot them, they would have undertaken a work of patriotic and historical justice."[40]

Many were troubled when they compared the INAH process for verifying the remains of Cortés with that used to examine the remains of Cuauhtémoc. Wasn't it clear that a different, less rigorous, standard had been used to authenticate the remains of the cruel Spaniard than used to dismiss those of his martyred victim, Cuauhtémoc? Certainly, Guzmán and her allies found this comparison useful on many levels. Guzmán herself had criticized the differing standards used in the two cases and gone on to compare the two men, Cuauhtémoc, the perfect hero, and Cortés, the perfect villain. Guzmán's was well-known among intellectuals for her rejection of Mexico's Iberian heritage and for her deep hostility to Cortés.[41] In conversation with the reporter Angel Torres y Gonzalez, she claimed to have an unpublished manuscript proving the famous five letters of Cortés were filled with self-serving fraud.[42] In a separate incident Guzmán had stood before a painting of Cortés and said, "Your face is as false as are your letters."[43] Before the Ixcateopan excavation, Guzmán had protested the findings of the INAH authentication of the Cortés remains and, without having examined the bones herself, argued that the hated Cortés was a syphilitic dwarf. The fact that two of those associated with the INAH decision about Cortés were appointed to the team evaluating the Ixcateopan find gave the results the appearance of a vendetta.[44]

With public anger at the boiling point, Eulalia Guzmán acted with dispatch to mount a successful campaign to discover scientific support for her conclusions among Mexico's intellectuals. The *jefe* and *subjefe* of the military laboratories (Laboratorio Central de la Industria Militar) publicly rejected the "science" of the commission's evaluations. More consequential was the decision of the Banco de México to organize an independent examination of the site by its own experts, the remains, associated artifacts like the copper plates, and the documents. The results published serially between November 1949 and August 1950, unambiguously supported Eulalia Guzmán.[45] The bank's experts found the documents convincing and the oral traditions collected by Guzmán to be legitimate. The copper plates, according to this group of friendly experts, were of the appropriate period and the oxidation genuine. The most telling anomaly of the site, the discovery that the bones were from five or more individuals, was reinterpreted as reinforcing evidence, since noble men of era, it was asserted, were commonly buried with retainers.[46] As support for the legitimacy of the Ixcateopan discovery grew, public events celebrating Cuauhtémoc and invoking his memory proliferated. Plans went forward for the construction of a monument in Ixcateopan, and the decision was made to rename a street in Mexico City for Cuauhtémoc. The national lottery initiated a nationwide advertising campaign with the slogan "Confíe usted en los huesos y en su suerte" (Have confidence in the bones and in your luck).[47]

With the controversy now fully developed, the character of Eulalia Guzmán attracted national attention. Both her supporters and detractors mined her personal history for revealing details. The essential elements of her biography were soon well known. She was born in San Pedro Gorda, Zacatecas, in 1890 and had graduated from normal school in 1910. Guzmán had lost her job because of her support for Francisco Madero in 1913, but had been rewarded after the triumph of the revolution with a number of education positions in the 1920s, including that of primary school inspector and later deputy head of the Department of Primary Education. In these positions, she had continued her education, gaining a *maestría en filosofía* in 1943 and a *título* in archaeology in 1945. She was described as woman of the people with her roots in the rural lower middle class. Among her family members singled out for attention was her grandfather, an Indian whose command of Spanish was limited. She was portrayed as humble and without guile, a short and stout woman with the hint of a moustache on her upper lip. One reporter who had interviewed her noted that she worked in the patio of her home using a rough bench as a desk and writing with a pencil on the backs of memos saved from the office trash.[48]

For Eulalia Guzmán Cuauhtémoc was Mexico's ideal hero. She described him as "el héroe mas puro" (the most pure hero), "gran rey, valiente guerrero" (the great king and valiant warrior), and "ejemplo de heroísmo y valor y sobre todo, como gran patriota" (the example of heroism and valor and more than anything else as a great patriot).[49] This passionate advocacy drew some powerful politicians to her cause, prominent among them was former president Lázaro Cárdenas (1934–40) who chaired a committee of supporters and even traveled to Ixcateopan, in support of Guzmán. As the Left organized to support Guzmán and, more importantly, to fortify the symbolic status of Cuauhtémoc as the revolution's bridge to Mexico's Indian origins, the Right took aim. Guzmán, they pointed out, had defended her work in the pages of the communist publication, *Cultura Soviética*, and had been publicly lauded by the Mexican Communist Party. One letter to *Excélsior* dismissed her and "her bones" by placing her in a sentence with the labor leader Vicente Lombardo Toledano and with an easily dismissed cadre of intellectual straw men identified by the author as "little creole rabbis who campaign for a Soviet peace"[50] The U.S. embassy made this same connection, reporting in 1951 that, "Guzmán . . . es una mujer de tendencias izquierdistas" (Guzmán is a woman with leftist tendencies).[51]

The secretary of public education, Manuel Gual Vidal, had quickly distanced himself from the controversial and unpopular decision of the INAH commission and the firestorm of protest that inevitably followed. Early in 1950 the secretary created a new and larger commission rather than face having to choose between public support for Eulalia Guzmán and the official academic world as represented by the INAH group. This effort to settle the controversy by requiring a reexamination of the evidence by a new commission coincided with the Mexican government's decision to dedicate the coming year to the memory of Cuauhtémoc, a decision that signaled clearly the wishes of the politicians. The new commission, its members selected to establish a clear distance from INAH, signaled its recognition of these expectations with the decision to stand as an honor guard at the Cuauhtémoc monument on the Paseo de la Reforma before its first meeting.[52] No member of this second commission could have had any illusions about the expectations of the public or the politicians.[53] Known as the Gran Comisión (Great Commission), or as commonly identified by the press the *super sabios* (super wisemen), the members worked for a full year before coming to a conclusion.

When in February 1951 the second commission published its results, the hopes of Guzmán and her supporters were again frustrated. The commission endorsed the findings of its predecessor, rejecting explicitly the alternative reconstructions of the skeletal material proposed by a member of the Banco de México team.[54] As had happened previously with the earlier INAH report, one member of the commission broke ranks. José Gómez Robleda not only refused to sign the final report of the Gran Comisión, he went on to publish a comprehensive report of his own that supported the authenticity of the Guzmán excavation.[55] The unpopular nature of the second commission's judgment was, perhaps, best signaled by the decision of the secretary of education, Manuel Gual Vidal, to pay for the publication of Gómez Robleda's 173-page rebuttal of the commission's report, but to refuse to publish the official commission's report itself.[56]

Beginning with the report of the original INAH Commission in October 1950, academic opinion in Mexico had generally opposed Eulalia Guzmán's position. With the second commission's hostile report there was no longer much likelihood that any of the academics associated with the nation's major universities or research institutes would swim against this tide. Guzmán and her supporters had to fight their battles in the press or in political arenas rather than in academic settings. Despite the very public and very aggressive support offered Guzmán from the Banco de México's experts and from the second commission's lone dissenter, Gómez Robleda, too many anomalies had to be explained in order to accept the Church of Santa María de la Asunción as the final resting place of Cuauhtémoc. Even President Miguel Alemán carefully distanced himself from Guzmán and her supporters by staying away from the ceremony celebrating the second anniversary of the Ixcateopan discovery.

The lingering controversy and the political ill will that had informed every effort to resolve the competing claims about Ixcateopan led the Mexican government to create a third official commission in 1976.[57] The decision to look again at the Ixcateopan discovery was made by the administration of Luis Echeverría. Echeverría had taken an interest in numerous indigenous questions and had extravagantly appropriated indigenous symbols for political ends.[58] Once again the commission membership was suggested by the director of INAH and once again the commission operated in a supercharged political environment. Eulalia Guzmán had continually agitated on behalf of her work after 1951, publishing a polemical analysis of the work of the first two commissions in 1973.[59] In this she argued that few members of the first two commissions had actually visited Ixcateopan; their work, she suggested, was superficial and politically motivated. Frustrated by what she regarded as persecution, she even compared herself to Galileo Galilei who had been threatened by the Inquisition for his assertion of a heliocentric universe.[60] Although she had never asked explicitly for a new commission, she refused to accept the decisions of the official commissions and continued to press for vindication. By 1976 the government of Mexico had its own reasons for resurrecting Guzmán's claims. Eduardo Matos Montezuma, one of the new commission's two archaeologists, later wrote that the government of Mexico had been facing a chaotic economic situation, paused on the brink of monetary devaluation, when it decided to revisit the controversy of Ixcateopan. He also pointed out that the state government of Guerrero, which had also lobbied very hard for a new commission, "remain[ed] in constant social agitation and exist[ed] practically in a state of siege."[61] The commission members should have been forewarned, only one result was expected.

The third commission began its investigation with a full review of the work of the two prior official commissions as well as the numerous publications generated by the Banco de México experts and by Guzmán and her supporters. It also examined all the notes, site photographs, and other materials from Ixcateopan produced by Eulalia Guzmán and her assistants since 1949. Following the earlier disappointments, Guzmán and her allies had continued to work to prove the legitimacy of her original claims. She had conducted a number of new excavations in Ixcateopan, although she had been disappointed with the results in the church and nearby locations, finding neither the "treasure of Cuauhtémoc" nor the "palace of his grandparents." Guzmán, eighty-six years old in 1976, and her chief local informant, Salvador Rodríguez Juárez, had more recently revealed an apparently rich harvest of previously unknown documents, including some pictographs with the clear appearance of indigenous authorship, as well as oral history testimonies developed through her small army of informants and supporters in Ixcateopan. As the third commission's work proceeded, its archaeological team also conducted a limited schedule of new archaeological research in Ixcateopan focused on sites recommended by Eulalia Guzmán.

The human remains unearthed by Guzmán's team in 1949 had drawn skeptical attention from archaeologists and physical anthropologists from the outset. Once the skeletal remains had been extracted from beneath the altar of the Church of Santa María de la Asunción, Guzmán had temporarily halted further excavation. The remains had been sealed and guarded by local and state authorities until the arrival of officials from INAH. From the beginning these remains raised troubling questions. As determined in 1949 by the INAH team, the human remains unearthed by Guzmán had come from at least five different individuals. The skull was from a woman and some of the other bones appeared to be those of children. The second commission (the Gran Comisión) had concurred, although some discrepancies can found in the two reports.[62]

Although Guzmán and her allies had tried to defend each component of the evidence uncovered in Ixcateopan, she defended the skeletal remains with ferocity against the experts (see Illustration 7.5). From her perspective, it was the skeleton itself that made Ixcateopan a sacred place and connected Cuauhtémoc to Mexico's other venerated historical figures, especially Hidalgo, Morelos, Juárez, and the recently sanctified the heroes of the Mexican Revolution like Madero and Zapata. The bones made Ixcateopan (indeed Mexico) important, not the reverse. As a result, Guzmán had offered a series of possible explanations for the unlikely mix of bones identified by the experts. Her first theory was that the bones uncovered beneath the altar were those of a "herald" buried to signal Cuauhtémoc's location, but this theory was abandoned quickly because it subverted her argument for the sanctity of the church.[63] She had then produced the explanatory argument that she would stick to until the end. She noted that multiple burials were common in the Aztec era and that the previously unexplained mix of bones in Ixcateopan included both those of Cuauhtémoc and those of servants sacrificed to accompany the *tlatoani* to the afterlife.

Given the dismissive evaluation of the human remains by the second commission, the very fact that there was a controversy twenty-five years later was a testament to the resilience and endurance of Eulalia Guzmán. The third commission went through this physical evidence and Guzmán's theories like a freshly sharpened scythe through a wheat field. They concluded that "the human remains belong to eight individuals buried at different times and in different ways." Moreover, they identified some of the dental and cranial remains as those of a mixed race young adult buried well after 1529.[64] This was a devastating judgment, since the absence of a plausible skeleton that could be exhibited as the authentic Cuauhtémoc undermined the very coherence of the story that located both the birth and burial of the last Aztec ruler in Ixcateopan.

7.5   *The purported remains of Cuauhtémoc located in church of Santa
María de Asunción in Ixcateopan. Critics claimed the skeleton was
constructed from the remains of eight separate individuals
(Photo: Lyman L. Johnson).*

The documents displayed to the village priest in 1949 by Salvador
Rodríguez Juárez provided the foundation for Eulalia Guzmán's
claim that Cuauhtémoc was buried in Ixcateopan. Before this revelation no important archaeologist or historian had claimed that
Ixcateopan had any direct connection to Cuauhtémoc. These documents and the testimony of Rodríguez Juárez and a handful of his
allies had provided a compelling provenance, detailing how this
archive had been passed down across the generations and opening the
possibility that the biography of Cuauhtémoc would have to be
amended. If the documents could be proved authentic then Guzmán's
alternative interpretation of the confused skeletal evidence, the possibility of multiple burials of retainers, was also plausible.

However, the documents that outlined the reburial of Cuauhtémoc
by the Franciscan friar Motolinía had drawn focused criticism even

before the discovery of the bones on September 26, 1949. By the time the second commission (Gran Comisión) initiated its examination early in 1950, the original cache of documents had been supplemented by additional documents provided by Rodríguez Juárez, but these would be dismissed by the experts as well. Silvio Zavala, one of the influential scholars who served on the INAH commission, had been unyielding in his dismissal of the original documents and the copper plates found in the grave. He acknowledged that if the documents and copper plates were genuine they would provide strong circumstantial evidence in support of the legitimacy of the excavated human remains, despite the confusion of bones identified by the experts. But he and the other commission members rejected every piece of documentary evidence provided in 1949. Zavala's summary of the commission's examination noted that the Motolinía signature was a crude copy from a publication of the nineteenth century and that the other documents were exposed as forgeries by numerous and obvious errors in spelling and in the style of letters and numbers. He believed they were probably composed in the nineteenth century, during the lifetime of Salvador Rodríguez Juárez's grandfather, Florentino Juárez.[65] This judgment was accepted by the Gran Comisión that examined a somewhat larger number of documents.

In the twenty-five years that separated this dismissal from the appointment of the third commission in 1976, Eulalia Guzmán and Salvador Rodríguez Juárez, the Ixcateopan patriarch, had "discovered" additional documents culled from church and household archives. Although the Rodríguez Juárez family denied the third commission's experts full access to their papers, there were still more than twenty new documents to be examined in 1976, including three pictographic documents containing glyphs and architectural details that appeared to have indigenous authors. The fact that these documents had appeared late in the game and were so closely connected to the Rodríguez Juárez clan guaranteed that they would be closely scrutinized.

In the end, the third commission's judgment followed closely Silvio Zavala's categorical dismissal of the original cache of documents in 1950, finding that all the documents that connected Cuauhtémoc to Ixcateopan were forgeries. The only exceptions were a small number of documents that were unrelated to the purported burial of Cuauhtémoc in Ixcateopan such as pages of the parish register and pages from old books. The commission then went on to brand as frauds the all documents produced since 1949. However, because the evidence suggested that this scheme was ongoing some members of the third commission decided that Salvador Rodríguez Juárez was the principal author of the entire scheme. This meant rejecting or amending Silvio Zavala's theory that most of the original documents had been produced in the nineteenth century.

Commission member Luis Reyes García significantly revised the summary opinion of the earlier commissions by suggesting, "the twenty-eight documents now known that come from the collection of Salvador Rodríguez Juárez . . . are apocryphal and written after 1917; some of them reveal, by their content that they were written in the decade of the 1940s and two documents were written after 1950."[66] Among the many examples of sloppy forgery identified by Reyes García was a document claimed by supporters to be written in the seventeenth century that contained a reference to a five peso coin with the image of Cuauhtémoc that was not minted in Mexico until 1947.[67] He and his colleagues also dismissed as obvious frauds the pictographs that allegedly described the repatriation of Cuauhtémoc's body to Ixcateopan following his execution. Nearly everything was wrong with these documents. The documents included numerous anachronistic architectural details and the glyphs purportedly produced by indigenous scribes were distinct from those found on authenticated local records. Finally, the commission decided that the inscriptions on the two copper plates found during the church excavation also dated from the recent past, even if the copper itself might have dated from the colonial era.[68]

While the first two commissions had suggested that Florentino Juárez had probably authored the fraudulent documents and artifacts in the 1890s, Luis Reyes García and his colleagues on the 1976 commission believed that Salvador Rodríguez Juárez, his grandson, had produced most of the documents in the 1940s. It is clear from the tone of this report that the late appearance of more than a dozen "new" documents, including the pictographs and the oral testimonies collected by Guzmán's allies, had undermined whatever credibility the original records and testimonies had retained. The members of the 1976 inquiry thought they saw a clear pattern where each generation of questions posed by academic experts in Mexico City resulted in the production of new "discoveries" at Ixcateopan. After examining these new forgeries, Reyes García backtracked to the original group of documents presented in 1949 and found numerous similarities among the errors in orthography and script in the two groups of documents. This he took to indicate that a single author had produced everything and that author had to be Salvador Rodríguez Juárez. In coming to this conclusion, he ignored the possibility that Rodríguez Juárez "discovered" his grandfather's fraudulent documents and then later produced more, using the original forgeries as models, when confounded by the decisions of academic experts.

The historian Josefina García Quintana, another member of the third commission, followed the opinion of Zavala and the earlier commissions less critically in a book published after the work of the third commission was completed. She decided that the fraud had been planned in the 1890s. She tracked the story backward to its likely origin in the nineteenth-century enthusiasm for the Aztec past and for Cuauhtémoc in particular.[69] Although much of the actual research was conducted by José Ortiz Monasterio and not acknowledged, the conclusions became generally known through García Quintana's publication. Silvio Zavala had suggested in 1950 that Vicente Riva Palacio, the important nineteenth-century liberal politician who had been instrumental in erecting the statue of Cuauhtémoc in Mexico City, might have helped create the fraudulent documents.[70] Scholars associated with the 1976 inquiry conducted a thorough examination of the Riva Palacio correspondence and other contemporary records but were unable to demonstrate a clear link to the Ixcateopan "fraud."

García Quintana did uncover a circumstantial case that connected Florentino Juárez and other prominent figures in nineteenth-century Ixcateopan, like Juárez's nephew José Jaimes, to the cresting enthusiasm for Cuauhtémoc manifested by Riva Palacio and others in Mexico City. Both local men were tied indirectly to groups that celebrated Mexico's Aztec origins and Cuauhtémoc's exemplary role in the defense of Mexico, including the Free Masons. For example, Masonic lodge Aztecas número 2 had endorsed Cuauhtémoc "as the representative of the race and defender of liberties" in 1893. No less a figure than Porfirio Díaz, the long-serving dictator of Mexico (1876–80, 1884–1911) whose government had erected the statue of Cuauhtémoc in Mexico City, had both sponsored the cult of Cuauhtémoc and led efforts to unify Mexico's Masonic structure. It seemed likely to García Quintana that the documents shown to the parish priest of Ixcateopan in 1949 by Salvador Rodríguez Juárez had been concocted by his grandfather Florentino Juárez and a kinsman, José Jaimes (nephew of Florentino). Jaimes had been an active Mason tied to both regional Masonic leaders and to Mexico City's enthusi-asts for the cult of Cuauhtémoc.[71] She wrote, "It is perfectly explained that the politically and economically dominant group of Ixcateopan had manipulated [facts] . . . to its own benefit, improving on a [local] tradition of a king interred in the church."[72] Once the burial, documents, copper plaques, and the rest were in place, why was the planned "discovery" delayed to 1949? Juárez's own journals provided by his grandson in 1949 suggest that he actually tried to launch this scheme in the 1890s but was thwarted by the lack of inter-est shown by Díaz and by own his declining political power in Ixcateopan.[73] It is also likely, as argued by García Quintana, that the beginnings of the Mexican Revolution and the death of Florentino Juárez in 1915 interrupted these plans and delayed Ixcateopan's asso-ciation with Cuauhtémoc for five decades.

With the physical remains and documents disposed of the third commission's experts went on to demolish Guzmán's often cited "tradición oral" collected, she claimed, from Ixcateopan's oldest res-idents. As time had passed, Guzmán had inflated the importance of these testimonies. In 1976, the team's trained oral history experts were sharply critical of Guzmán's methods in collecting and reporting these testimonies, noting that the interviews had not been adequately recorded or transcribed. In her own publication, Alicia Olivera de Bonfil noted the existence of three distinct oral traditions relative to Cuauhtémoc in Guerrero. The only two that made specific references to Cuauhtémoc and to Ixcateopan were narrowly associated with the Rodríguez Juárez family and probably dated from the twentieth cen-tury.[74] Even these traditions had been hopelessly tainted by the flood of experts, politicians, and enthusiasts of various stripes who had vis-ited Ixcateopan embellishing local legends with concocted evidence in an effort to promote the Ixcateopan "discovery."

What little support for Guzmán's work in Ixcateopan was left was demolished by the third commission's archaeologists who found no corroboration for the belief that Cuauhtémoc was born in Ixcateopan. Published results of archaeological research carried out in Guerrero since 1950 as well as the work of Guzmán and her assistants were sup-plemented by new research conducted by the commission's two archaeologists. They concluded that there was no evidence that Ixcateopan had been a place of consequence before the arrival of the Spanish. Ixcateopan's population was probably no more than five hun-dred at the time of Cuauhtémoc's birth, a time when the Aztec twin capitals of Tenochtitlán/ Tlatelolco probably housed a population of 150,000.[75] Was it likely that the Aztecs would find their ruler in such an obscure place? Most historians of the period had always held that Tlatelolco, not Ixcateopan, had been the birthplace of the martyr.[76] Any asserted connections between Ixcateopan and the Aztec state were tenuous at best, according to these experts.

They also dismissed the idea that the Church of Santa María de la Asunción could have been the burial place for Cuauhtémoc. Not only was there no evidence that placed the Franciscan friar Motolinía in Ixcateopan in 1529, the third commission's examination of the church and the altar under which the bones were uncovered also suggested that neither the building nor the altar existed at the time of the presumed burial of Cuauhtémoc. Instead, Ixcateopan's first church had probably been constructed on a different site with the Church of Santa María de la Asunción being built after 1550, more than two decades after the purported burial of Cuauhtémoc.[77]

In the end the third commission's official report suffered the same fate as that of the second commission; it was shelved by a different, but equally embarrassed and unhappy, secretary of education.[78] Nevertheless, its comprehensive rejection of the "discovery" proved to have greater traction than had the dismissals of its predecessors. In part this was the result of the publication of a number of influential books by the commission members, detailing the case against the Ixcateopan remains. The unwillingness of academic experts to validate the research of Guzmán, no matter how carefully these experts were vetted by politicians, was now undeniably clear. Realization of this unforeseen fact finally exhausted the desire of Mexico's politicians to provide a foundation of scientific certainty to support the patriotic ardor of Guzmán and other Ixcateopan boosters.[79] The accumulated weight of repeated rejection at the hands of experts and the desire of the Mexican political class to avoid public disappointment meant that Guzmán and the other supporters of the Ixcateopan exhumation would now operate without official support outside the state of Guerrero.

Despite the powerful blows dealt to the supporters of Guzmán, the local cult of Cuauhtémoc has endured in Ixcateopan. The month of February is devoted to the veneration of the martyred Aztec tlatoani. Each day of the month is assigned its celebratory act while local dignitaries stand guard at the site of Eulalia Guzmán's 1949 discovery. The discovery itself is celebrated at the church, now converted

into a memorial, on September 26. Inside the church are the purported remains of Cuauhtémoc protected in a crystal casket designed
by Diego Rivera. Guzmán died in 1985 at age ninety-five.[80] Her name
has been immortalized in Ixcateopan in the plaza and a nursery school.
Ixcateopan has also become a pilgrimage site marked by heroic statuary of the immortal Cuauhtémoc (see Illustration 7.6). The annual
ritual calendar draws both representatives of indigenous groups from
the U.S. and other Latin American nations and left-leaning intellectuals who routinely find in the life and martyrdom of Cuauhtémoc
convenient lessons for the deconstruction of imperialism and
racism.[81] This enduring round of ritual and celebration in Ixcateopan,
however, seems to an outsider pinched and defensive, the emotional
and intellectual content stripped of spontaneity and passion by the

7.6 *The statue of Cuauhtémoc in Ixcateopan erected after the purported discovery of his remains by Eulalia Gúzman. In this representation the
young Aztec tlatoani is accompanied into battle by his iconic double, an
eagle (Photo: Lyman L. Johnson).*

long and bitter debate about the 1949 excavation and the findings of the three government commissions.

Guzmán's long effort to prove that Cuauhtémoc was born in and later buried in Ixcateopan survived her death and has endured. The government of Guerrero wholesales this story in its publications and Web sites.[82] Moreover, her version of events has won a completely unforeseen victory on the Internet. Searches using Cuauhtémoc, Ixcateopan, or even Aztec as keywords produce a succession of favorable references to the story told in the original documents revealed in Ixcateopan in 1949 and to Guzmán's initial report on her excavation.[83] It would appear that the less-constrained character of the Internet, without editorial boards or institutional authority, has proven a much more hospitable environment for Guzmán's populist campaign than the world of scholarly journals and books. Of particular interest is the fact that the hostile reports and publications of the three official commissions are almost completely absent from this arena, neither cited nor quoted.

On the national stage, however, the heroic image of Cuauhtémoc retains its potency (see Illustration 7.7). This topic cannot be explored with any real thoroughness here, but the very ubiquity of Cuauhtémoc demands some attention. Why Cuauhtémoc? From monuments, place names, and heroic murals to mundane images adorning beer bottles, sailboats, and restaurants, Cuauhtémoc is found nearly everywhere in Mexico. This symbolic ascendancy suggests a great complexity in the symbolic messages associated with Cuauhtémoc. The popularity of Cuauhtémoc in political and commercial settings follows inevitably from a deep political identification of modern Mexico with the Aztec past, although evidence suggests that official support of this cult has waned since 1976 (see Illustration 7.8).

This is not to say that modern Mexican culture does not have a sophisticated understanding of the nation's complex indigenous past. But modern politics uses, and requires, simple images suitable for mass consumption. The highly edited and repackaged history of the Aztecs now popular in Mexico has stripped the story of the Spanish Conquest of its complexity, demonizing Cortés's indigenous allies like the Tlaxcalans or Doña Marina and focusing on the Aztec defense of Tenochtitlán. Cuauhtémoc's brief reign as tlatoani usefully represents the heroism of Tenochtitlán's defenders while his experience of torture and execution exposes the cruelty and injustice of Spanish colonial rule.

7.7 *A typical modern romantic representation of Cuauhtémoc. This one is
located in the sanctuary of Santa María de Asunción in Ixcateopan near
the casket (Photo: Lyman L. Johnson).*

Cuauhtémoc was certainly brave, in a culture that expected nothing less, but he clearly failed to protect the debilitated Aztec state, his
patrimony. In the end, he failed and was captured. His legacy then is
not victory, but endurance in the face of terrible cruelty, a stoic heroism. The iconography recognizes this clearly. It is his patient suffering that is celebrated on the pedestal of the statue on the Paseo de la
Reforma (see accompanying illustrations) and in the famous portrayal
of Cuauhtémoc's torment by David Siquieros. These experiences of
torture and martyrdom were also central to the story told by Eulalia
Guzmán and her supporters. The anger expressed by Guzmán and
her supporters only makes sense when we recognize that her academic critics were seen as denying Cuauhtémoc's redemptive suffering and his political meaning while they denied the legitimacy of the
Ixcateopan grave.

7.8   *A mosaic of Cuauhtémoc with an eagle created by the famous artist Juan O'Gorman at La Posada de la Misión in Taxco, Guerrero (Photo: Lyman L. Johnson).*

The same symbolic vocabulary evoked on behalf of Cuauhtémoc is commonly used in representations of Hidalgo, Morelos, and Juárez and more recent heroes like Emiliano Zapata (see the essay by Samuel Brunk in this volume). What explains this representational leverage? The answer may have been suggested in the debates that swirled around Eulalia Guzmán. Forced by her academic opponents to reinvent or recontextualize her initial claims, Guzmán found a firm foothold in a representational discourse that subtly folded the life and death of Cuauhtémoc with that of Christ. These symbolic connections between Christ and Cuauhtémoc continue to be made in Ixcateopan and elsewhere when the life of the tlatoani is recalled. Key to the success of this device was the implicit nature of this metaphor. The ingredients disassemble themselves for us effortlessly once this connection is made. In the revisionist version of Eulalia Guzmán, Cuauhtémoc's patient suffering of torment, his martyrdom at the hands of Cortés, the actions of his followers who reconnected him with his family and with his birthplace by returning his remains to Ixcateopan, and, importantly, his insertion within the Christian community through reburial by Motolinía made the connection to the life of Christ inevitable.

Certainly, all the anticipation that preceded Eulalia Guzmán's 1949 discovery, the emotional transport affected by her happy news, the predictable character of the ceremonies and rituals evolved with remarkable speed to mark this propitious event echoed the embedded behaviors, the reflexive inclinations of the Mexican religious experience. Once unleashed, the cult of Cuauhtémoc was enfolded in the well-established trope of Christian martyrdom. Cuauhtémoc's purity was emphasized. Even though he was married and some historical accounts claimed he had fathered a child with a servant, Guzmán and most other enthusiasts argued, unconvincingly, that the tlatoani died a sexual innocent, pure and uncontaminated by the low desires of the merely human. This was unlikely given the existence of "Houses of Joy" where Aztec military men were given access to prostitutes.[84] To Guzmán and her supporters, Cuauhtémoc was also equally free from greed, pride, ambition, and envy.[85] He was, then, the perfect antithesis of what many Mexicans thought was the corruption and selfishness of the political leadership that had disappointed Mexicans' hopes. Here perhaps we find the utility of Eulalia Guzmán's discovery as well as the endurance of the symbolic Cuauhtémoc.

Notes

I would like to thank colleagues who read and commented on earlier versions of this essay. Paul Gillingham knows more about the purported discovery of Cuauhtémoc's remains in Ixcateopan than anyone else. He is currently working on a book on this topic and generously shared his insights with me. I also want to thank William Beezely, Samuel Brunk, Jürgen Buchenau, John Chasteen, William French, Michael Gonzales, Donna Guy, Sonya Lipsett-Rivera, and Xóchitl Medina for their comments and suggestions.

1. Eulalia Guzmán "Las pruebas científicas de la autenticidad de la tumba de Cuauhtémoc," in *La Supervivencia de Cuauhtémoc*, ed.

Héctor Martínez and Eulalia Guzmán (Mexico City: SDN, 1987), 39–48. See also Angel Torres y Gonzalez, *La tumba de Cuauhtémoc* (Mexico City: Ediciones Nacionalidad, 1950), 112–13.

2. From an article in *Excélsior*, 27 September 1949, quoted in Alejandra Moreno Toscano, *Los hallazcos de Ichcateopan 1949–1951* (Mexico City: UNAM, 1980), 91.

3. See Eulalia Guzmán, *Letter to Jaime Torres Bodet and Short Papers on the Tomb of Cuauhtémoc* (Mexico: Typescript w/o publisher, 1950), 2.

4. This information was generously provided by Paul Gillingham.

5. There was little agreement about where Cuauhtémoc was executed or whether he was transported to Ixcateopan. See Pedro Vega Martínez, *La ruta trágica de Hernán Cortés Coatzacoalcos—Las Hibueras* (Villahermosa, Mexico: Universidad Juárez Autónoma de Tabasco, 1991); and William Brito Sansores, *Cuauhtémoc murió en la zona Maya* (Mérida, Mexico: Instituto del Instituto Yucateco de Antropología e Historia, 1971).

6. An elaboration of this story was published by José Gómez Robleda, *Descubrimiento de la tumba de Cuauhtémoc* (Mexico City: Secretaría de Educación Pública, 1952), 18, where he provides numerous undocumented details such as the fact that the body was wrapped in fine textiles and carried only at night to avoid detection.

7. Alfonso Quiroz Cuarón, *Ichcateopan la tumba de Cuauhtémoc, Héroe supremo de la historia de México* (Mexico City: Aconcagua Ediciones y Publicaciones, S.A., 1973), 1.

8. Moreno Toscano, *Hallazcos de Ichcateopan*, 90–92.

9. This interpretation of the excavation follows the research of Paul Gillingham, who after reading an earlier draft provided me with additional sources. He bases his opinion on a letter from Eulalia Guzmán to Ignacio Marquina, 21 September 1921, INAH, Archivo Eulalia Guzmán, caja 9, exp. 45, and on articles carried in *La Prensa*, 24 and 26 September 1949.

10. This irregularity in organizing the dig was later brought up by Eduardo Matos Moctezuma, a member of the third official commission in 1976 who noted this context in the prologue of his book (*Informe de la revisión de los trabjos arqueológicos realizados en Ichcateopan, Guerrero* [Mexico City: UNAM, 1980], 26–27).

11. "Fallen Eagle" is a translation of the word "Cuauhtémoc" while "young grandfather" evokes the idea that although Cuauhtémoc died young he was the patriarch of the nation of Mexico. See a discussion

of these terms in Octavio Paz, *The Labyrinth of Solitude: Life and Thought in Mexico* (New York: Grove Press, 1985), 83–84.

12. Cuauhtémoc had been tortured by Cortés who believed that Aztec treasure had been hidden from the victorious Spaniards. Some in 1949 believed, with little evidence, that somehow this treasure had been removed to the burial site in Ixcateopan and buried near Cuauhtémoc.

13. Moreno Toscano, *Hallazcos de Ichcateopan*, 12.

14. Wigberto Jimenez Moreno, "Los hallazgos de Ichacateopan," *Historia Mexicana*, 12, no. 2 (October–December 1962), n 4, 180.

15. See Leonard Folgarait, *Mural Painting and Social Revolution: Art of the New Order* (Cambridge and New York: Cambridge University Press, 1998), as well as his *So Far from Heaven: David Alfaro Siqueiros' March of Humanity and Mexican Revolutionary Politics* (Cambridge and New York: Cambridge University Press, 1987). See also the chapter "Indigenism and Social Realism" in Dawn Ades, *Art in Latin America* (New Haven, CT: Yale University Press, 1989).

16. These themes have been impressively explored by a number of authors. See Rebecca Earle, "'Padres de la Patria" and the Ancestral Past: Commemorations of Independence in Nineteenth-Century Spanish America," *Journal of Latin American Studies* 34 (2002): 775–805; and Pedro Santoni, "'Where Did the Other Heroes Go?': Exalting the *Polko* National Guard Battalions in Nineteenth-Century Mexico," *Journal of Latin American Studies* 34 (2002): 807–44.

17. For detailed coverage of this topic, see Josefina García Quintana, *Cuauhtémoc en el Siglo XIX* (Mexico City: UNAM, 1977), 20–24.

18. The speech was prepared by Carlos María Bustamante. See D. A. Brading, *The First America* (Cambridge and New York: Cambridge University Press, 1991), 580–81, 636–37.

19. For a broader view of this topic, see Rebecca Earle, "Creole Patriotism and the Myth of the 'Loyal Indian,'" *Past and Present* 172 (2001).

20. See the excellent essay by Barbara Tannenbaum, "Streetwise History: The Paseo de la Reforma and the Porfirian State, 1876–1910," in *Rituals of Rule, Rituals of Resistance*, ed. William H. Beezley, Cheryl English Martin, and William E. French (Wilmington, DE: Scholarly Resources Inc., 1994), 127–50.

21. García Quintana, *Cuauhtémoc en el Siglo XIX*, esp. 12–29.

22. This is the discussion of the statue and of Mexican participation found in Mauricio Tenorio-Trillo, *Mexico at the World's Fairs* (Berkeley: University of California Press, 1996), 200–219.

23. Enrique Krause, *Mexico Biography of Power: A History of Modern Mexico, 1810–1996,* trans. Hank Heifetz (New York: Harper Perennial, 1997), 25–27. Krause emphasizes the statue's elaboration of Cuauhtémoc's suffering at the hands of Cortés.

24. This discussion follows closely Barbara Tannenbaum, "Streetwise History," 135–42; quote on 140.

25. The power of this image is perhaps best signaled by the decision to use the alleged date of Cuauhtémoc's torture as the date to announce the competition for the design of the monument. García Quintana, *Cuauhtémoc en el Siglo XIX,* 25.

26. See *http://www.saa.org/Publications/oaxaca* for a brief biography of Caso, who was the founder and first Director of National Institute of Anthropology and History (founded in 1939). Eulalia Guzmán was his associate in a number of his excavations of Monte Alban in Oaxaca.

27. I want to thank Paul Gillingham for this background information on Eulalia Guzmán.

28. Moreno Toscano, *Hallazcos de Ichcateopan,* 14.

29. Diego Rivera had already used Cuauhtémoc in a number of his most famous murals, including his mural painted in the stairwell of the National Palace in Mexico City. See Moreno Toscano, *Hallazcos de Ichcateopan,* 107.

30. The events summarized above were described by Moreno Toscano, *Hallazcos de Ichcateopan,* 13.

31. Jimenez Moreno, "Hallazgos de Ichacateopan," 165–66.

32. This topic is discussed by Alan Knight in "Racism, Revolution, and *Indigenismo*: Mexico, 1910–1940," in *The Idea of Race in Latin America, 1870–1940,* ed. Richard Graham, (Austin: University of Texas Press, 1990), 71, 113.

33. My discussion of the discovery of the remains of Cortés follows closely the firsthand account of the senior investigator. Alberto María Carreño, *Hernán Cortés y el Descubrimiento de Sus Restos* (Mexico City: [s.n.], 1947).

34. Among the most important participants in this effort to protect the remains from the mob was Lucas Alamán, *Historia de México desde los primeros movimientos que prepararon su independencia en el año de 1808 hasta la época presente,* vol. 2 (Mexico City: Imprenta de J. M. Lara, 1850), 308–10.

35. The documents indicating the burial location of Cortés were brought to Alberto María Carreño by a Spaniard and a Cuban, both with ties

to the Spanish embassy. Carreño himself was a well-established historian. See Alamán, *Historia de México*, 303–5, for the explanation of how the documents were delivered to Carreño.

36. See Moreno Toscano, *Hallazgos de Ichcateopan*, 98–99.
37. The INAH commission members were: Dr. Silvio Zavala, Dr. Eusebio Dávalos Hurtado, Prof. Javier Romero, Prof. Carlos Margáin, the architect Alfredo Bishop, Lt. Colonel Luis Tercero Urrutia, Major Roberto Tapia, and the photographer Luis Limón. Wigberto Jimenez Moreno, "Hallazgos de Ichcateopan," 169; and Angel Torres y Gonzalez, *Tumba de Cuauhtémoc*, 134–41.
38. See Jimenez Moreno, "Hallazgos de Ichacateopan," 169–70.
39. The INAH Commission's reports were published in *Revista Mexicana de Estudios Antropológicos* 11 (1950): 197–295.
40. Moreno Toscano, *Hallazgos de Ichcateopan*, 132–37.
41. See Eulalia Guzmán, *Una visión crítica de la historia de la conquista de México-Tenochtitlán* (Mexico City: UNAM, 1989), for a comprehensive presentation of this perspective.
42. In an article in *Excélsior* on 29 September 1949, Guzmán elaborated on this manuscript, offering the working title, "Rectificaciones a las cartas de Cortés." Moreno Toscano, *Hallazgos de Ichcateopan*, 94–95.
43. Ibid., 59–61.
44. This information was generously supplied by Paul Gillingham.
45. Eulalia Guzmán, *Pruebas y dicámines sobre la autenticidad de los restos de Cuauhtémoc* (Mexico City: Imprenta Arana, S.A.: 1962), 3. The Banco de México financed reports were supplemented between March 1951 and March 1952.
46. Ibid., 128–29.
47. Moreno Toscano, *Hallazgos de Ichcateopan* , 17.
48. This discussion summarizes Angel Torres y Gonzalez, *Tumba de Cuauhtémoc*, see for example 50–51.
49. Moreno Toscano, *Hallazgos de Ichcateopan*, 108–9.
50. Ibid., 190.
51. Ibid., 32.
52. Ibid., 17.
53. The members of the Gran Comisión were: Alfonso Caso, Pablo Martínez del Río, Julio Jiménez Rueda, Manuel Gamio, J. Joaquín Izquierdo, Pedro C. Sánchez, Rafael Illescas Frisbie, Manuel Toussaint, Arturo Arnaíz y Freg, and Wigberto Jiménez Moreno. This larger commission represented all of Mexico's major historical and archaeological institutions, except INAH, which was seen as hostile

to Guzmán after its report. Jiménez Moreno, "Hallazgos de Ichcateopan," 171–72.

54. Jiménez Moreno, "Hallazgos de Ichcateopan," 176–78, provides a good summary of newspaper coverage of the controversy that followed the publication of this report.

55. His opinion is expressed at length in *Dictamen acerca de la autenticidad del descubrimiento de la tumba de Cuauhtémoc en Ixcateopan* (Mexico City: Secretaría de Educación Pública, 1952).

56. One commission member bitterly complained of the attacks against the group, see Jiménez Moreno, "Hallazgos de Ichacateopan," 177–78.

57. The commission members were: Dr. Luis López Antúnez, Arturo Romano Pacheco, Dr. Luís Alberto Vargas, Dr. Ramón Fernández Pérez, Eduardo Matos Moctezuma, Juan Yadeun, Sonia Lombardo de Ruiz, Luis Reyes García, Luis Torres Montes, Dr. Juan Antonio Careaga, Alicia Olivera de Bonfil, Josefina García Quintana, and Dr. Alejandra Moreno Toscano. Mentioned in Sonia Lombardo de Ruiz, *La Iglesia de la Asunción de Ichcateopan en relación a la autenticidad de los restos de Cuauhtémoc* (Mexico City: Universidad Nacional Autónoma de México, 1978), 81. The appointment of the new commission is found in *Diario Oficial*, Tomo CCCXXXIV, no. 19, 15 January 1976, 15.

58. I gratefully acknowledge Xóchitl Medina for her guidance on the Echeverría administration and the Ixcateopan controversy.

59. Eulaia Guzmán, *Ichcateopan, la tumba de Cuauhtémoc: Héroe supremo de la historia de México* (Mexico City: Aconcagua, 1973). Guzmán argues that the struggle to validate the burial location of Cuauhtémoc was similar to President Lázaro Cárdenas's successful expropriation of the foreign oil companies in 1938 (18).

60. Guzmán, *Letter to Jaime Torres Bodet*, 9.

61. Eduardo Matos Moctezuma, a commission member, noted this context in the prologue of his book, *Informe de la revisión*, 7–8.

62. See the report of the Gran Comisión in *Revista Mexicana de Estudios Antropológicos*, tomo XI, 200–201. These results are summarized comparatively with those of the Banco de México study by Eulalia Guzmán and José Gómez Robleda, eds. in *Pruebas y dictámines sobre la autenticidad de los restos*, 5. Gómez Robleda was the dissenting member of the Gran Comisión. They claim the commission found remains from four individuals.

63. The third commission in fact found that Guzmán had secretly excavated another church in Ixcateopan, perhaps in hope of finding a less

problematic set of remains. See Matos Moctezuma, *Informe de la revisión*, 28–29.

64. Ibid., 41.

65. See Zavala's summary in "Síntesis del dictamen sobre los documentos y la inscripción de Ichcateopan," *Revista Mexicana de Estudios Antropológicos* 11 (1950): 290–95.

66. Luis Reyes García, *Documentos manuscritos y pictórios de Ichcateopan, Guerrero* (Mexico City: UNAM, 1979), 51.

67. Ibid., 49–51. Reyes García repeats the judgment of the first two commissions that the Motolinía documents, claimed by Guzmán to have been eighteenth-century copies, were, in fact, produced later. The new documents produced subsequent to these commissions were also dismissed by him as fabrications (50).

68. Matos Moctezuma, *Informe de la revisión*, 41.

69. Josefina García Quintana, *Cuauhtémoc en el Siglo XIX* (Mexico City: UNAM, 1977).

70. See Zavala, "Síntesis del dictamen," 293–95, for the suggestion of Vicente Riva Palacio's role in the fraud. Riva Palacio was tied to the state of Guerrero through his mother, the daughter of the independence-era hero Vicente Guerrero and through numerous political connections.

71. García Quintana, *Cuauhtémoc en el Siglo XIX*, 28–30, for the ties between the masons and Cuauhtémoc, and 41–42, for the biography of José Jaimes.

72. Ibid., 49–51.

73. This convincing theory was offered by Paul Gillingham to the author.

74. Ibid., 124–25.

75. Matos Moctezuma, *Informe de la revisión*, 36–37.

76. Eulalia Guzmán published a revisionist family history for Cuauhtémoc that asserted the Ixcateopan evidence for his birthplace in Guerrero. See Guzmán, *Genealogía y biogarfía de Cuauhtémoc*, esp. 31–36.

77. Sonia Lombardo de Ruíz, *La iglesia de la Asunción de Ichcateopan en relación a la autenticidad de los restos de Cuauhtémoc* (Mexico City: UNAM, 1978), 82–83.

78. Eduardo Matos Moctezuma notes this with some bitterness in *Informe de la revisión*, 7–8. He also notes the political nature of the debate, repeating earlier charges that Eulalia Guzmán pursued her argument in communist and other leftist publications.

79. Again the government refused to "accept" the decision or publish the commission's findings. As a result a number of books and articles were published by the participants. See, for example, Alicia Olivera de Bonfil, *La tradición oral sobre Cuauhtémoc* (Mexico City: UNAM, 1980); and Luis Reyes García, *Documentos manuscritos y pictórios*. In addition, four other commission members published books that have already been cited: Josefina García Quintana, *Cuauhtémoc en el Siglo XIX* ; Eduardo Matos Moctezuma, *Informe de la revisión de los trabajos arqueológicos realizados en Ichcateopan;* Sonia Lombardo de Ruíz, *La iglesia de la Asunción de Ichcateopan*; and Alejandra Moreno Toscano, *Los hallazcos de Ichcateopan 1949–1951*.

80. Until 1970 Eulalia Guzmán served as "encargada de los archivos históricos del INAH."

81. Francisco Vidal Duarte, *Ixcateopan* (Chilpancingo, Mexico: Instituto Guerrerense de la Cultura, 1987), 33.

82. *www.guerrero.gob.mx/dominios/gobierno/divisiónpolitica/Ixcateopan.htm.*

83. A small sampling includes *www.jornada.unam.mx/1999/feb99/990223/cul-soltero.html; www.webpuente.com/epo302/anahuac.html;* and *www.toltecayotl.org/articulos/escribir.html.*

84. See Inga Clendinnen, *Aztecs, An Interpretation* (Cambridge and New York: Cambridge University Press, 1991), 164–65.

85. Moreno Toscano, *Hallazgos de Ichcateopan*, provides a wonderfully useful compendium of articles from *Excélsior* that fully illustrates this symbolic appropriation.

Chapter Eight

Life and the Commodification of Death in Argentina:

Juan and Eva Perón

Donna J. Guy

A s Argentine novelist Hugo Ezequiel Lezama pointed out after Juan Perón's hands had been cut off and stolen, "This is a diabolical country. What would happen to us if we couldn't use death as a way to discharge political passions?"[1] This paper explores the significance of Juan and Evita's deaths from a historical perspective informed not only by cultural and political history in Argentina, but also by religious practices involving popular saints. It argues that Eva Perón, both before and after her tragic death at a young age and the subsequent theft of her remains, became eminently marketable as a popular saint, while Juan Perón, wildly charismatic before his death, lost the charisma associated with him during life. This occurred after his tomb was desecrated and his hands cut off. Therefore his death and subsequent dismemberment were unable to catapult him into popular sainthood. Nevertheless, rumors about his purported Uruguayan and Swiss bank accounts commodified his body in different ways as people wondered how they could access those accounts.

Whatever people thought about the political couple, Eva and Juan's deaths in 1952 and 1974, respectively, had mystical powers of their own. Even before Eva died, through official discourse and popular practices, she had already developed a cultlike following in Argentina. Much like recent phenomenon of public reaction to the death of British Princess Diana, Eva brought a personal connection from government to the people that had not been seen before. In

Argentina supporters called Eva *La Dama de la Esperanza* (the Lady of Hope), and even though this label did not emerge from the working classes, it resonated with their desire to make contact with Eva. She personally became aware of peoples' problems at her offices in the Eva Perón Foundation, founded in 1948, and during her many orchestrated appearances. Her devotees forgave her penchant for expensive French clothing and jewels and her desire to wreak vengeance on her political and social opposition.

Argentines from all over the country wrote to her pleading for her intervention and help in the most mundane matters. A few examples of this voluminous correspondence should give an idea of her charismatic powers. In October 1947, a single mother, J. N. Z., wrote to Eva, with a simple salutation: "*Respectable señora*," [Respected Lady]," (a salutation her enemies were loathe to bestow). The woman petitioned Eva for help because, "I know you are very good and you are my only hope." J. N. Z. felt terribly isolated. Her parents didn't know she had given birth, and she had left her baby at the Foundling Home because he was suffering from diphtheria. She had to reclaim the child within three days or lose custody of him, but she could not ask her parents for help. The letter was sent bureaucratically to what remained of the Sociedad de Beneficencia, the organization of elite women who operated the largest state orphanages in the country. The child was allowed to stay in the orphanage and the young mother received periodic updates and pictures of him. The accompanying paperwork indicated that Evita's secretaries had acted on this request.[2]

In this letter Eva was asked to intercede because of her "good" qualities and because she was in a position to help. Since September 1946 the Sociedad de Beneficencia had been placed under control of the national government, and this had been popularly attributed to Eva Perón. It is no wonder that the anguished mother wrote to her, although Eva did not personally intervene in either matter.[3]

On July 3, 1949, Francisco Luna, a twenty-eight-year-old public servant discharged from his job in Salta, wrote to Eva in search of justice. Evidently the letter was intended for both Peróns to read as it began: "My dear leaders, father of all the poor, I direct myself to you with the goal of asking a great service in favor of God and the Virgin of Ledesma who battled against Tyranny and it has to do with our Patria. Our mother Evita, I direct myself to you and to [Juan Perón] our beloved Leader to tell you my sad story." The author had lost his job working in a police station because of accusations brought against him by a Spaniard who had sent a letter to the Ministry of the Interior. Francisco accused the Spaniard of being a "capitalist" and "not of our kind." In his letter to the Peróns Francisco identified himself as a poor man with two children struggling to make a living to support his family. He pleaded with the Peróns for help. Significantly he equated the couple to God and the Virgin, something that had been part of official rhetoric, but interpreted their identification to include a regional official patron saint. It is unclear from the subsequent paperwork whether he was reinstated, but clearly Fernando, like thousands of other Argentines, believed Eva could work miracles that included returning him to his job.[4]

In her later years, Eva worked tirelessly through her foundation to provide welfare for the poor, the elderly, and particularly for children. She established schools, orphanages, an old-age home, and even a miniature city that included scaled-down versions of congress, the government house, the post office, and so on. In many of the negative stories attributed to Eva, supposedly she "volunteered" rich people to give large sums of money to the poor. If a rich person attended her audience with the people at the Eva Perón Foundation and Eva ran out of checks, she asked the rich to supplement her largesse, just as she enforced so-called voluntary contributions to her organization from labor unions and even from other charities. From this perspective, she was a female Robin Hood. At the same time, her cruel death from uterine cancer drained her of energy while she was never told of the nature of her illness. Every time her U.S. cancer specialist, Dr. George Peck, saw her, she was sedated so that she would neither be able to ask questions nor see that a U.S. doctor was treating her, as she was rabidly anti-American.[5]

When Eva died at age thirty-three of cancer in 1952, an entire nation went into mourning for thirteen days. Millions of Argentines went to Buenos Aires to view her body, and dozens, perhaps hundreds, died in the crush of the crowds. Soon there was an official movement to beatify her, one rebuffed by the Catholic Church, and some called her Santa Evita.[6] Children in the public schools during the remainder of Perón's time in office said this prayer:[7]

> Our little Mother, thou who art in heaven,
> good fairy laughing amongst the angels . . .
> Evita, I promise to be as good as you wish me to be,
> respecting God, loving my country;

> taking care of General Perón; studying
> and being towards everyone the child
> you dreamed I would be; healthy, happy,
> well-educated and pure in heart.

Significantly, in this poem Juan had already been demoted to more secular position as a nonhero in need of Eva's protection. Indeed, by this time, portraits of her commonly imitated depictions of the Virgin Mary.

Eva's body was exhibited initially at the Ministerio de Trabajo y Previsión (the Ministry of Labor and Welfare) and then taken to the national congressional building during the wake that lasted two weeks. Later she was carefully embalmed and plastified by the Spanish mortician Pedro Ara so that she could be displayed indefinitely and valued as a relic. It was this plastified corpse that was robbed from its resting place in the building of the Argentine Confederation of Labor by the military on November 23, 1955. The cult of her body had become such a threat to the military government that overthrew Perón in 1955 that they kidnapped her body, shocking her followers.[8]

Eva's body then went through a long, circuitous journey. For several months it moved about the city of Buenos Aires unceremoniously carried in a florist's delivery truck. It ended up in the house of one Major Arandía. Caring for the body seemed to have unnerved the major, who accidentally killed his pregnant wife while defending their home from what Arandía thought was an attack by pro-Peronist supporters. The body then remained in the office of the man who had stolen her body from its original resting place, Lt. Col. Carlos Moori Koenig, head of military intelligence. More relaxed than Major Arandia, Moori Koenig showed the cadaver to visitors as if it were a valuable trophy. Finally, under pressure from General Pedro Aramburu, author of the theft, plans emerged to move the body. The military had a great fear of a Peronist guerrilla group called the Montoneros. Every time Eva's body was moved, these left-wing Peronists would find its resting place and mark it with flowers. In fact, General Aramburu was eventually kidnapped and assassinated by the Montoneros in 1970 for the theft of the body.

Once the body had been plastified by Dr. Ara, the only way to destroy it was through cremation. While military officials discussed this, the Catholic Church intervened to prevent cremation, which was not approved at the time. Instead, Vatican officials suggested burial in an undisclosed place because Eva's mother was promised by Argentine military president Lonardi that her daughter's body would be given a Christian burial. The promise was made while the mother was in exile at the Ecuadorian embassy in Buenos Aires. Eva's corpse was taken by ship to Germany and then to Milan, Italy. There she was interred in a cemetery under a false name with the help of a religious community who cared for her tomb.[9]

For years no one outside of the religious group and a few military men knew the whereabouts of Eva's body, and that time period coincided with the brutal repression of Peronism and years of military dictatorship. During this period, Eva was imagined by the Peronists in many ways: as a saint, a revolutionary, and a heroine. The Montoneros claimed that "si Evita viviera, sería Montonera" (if Evita were alive, she would be a Montonera). More recent depictions of "si viviera Evita" have imagined her as a body builder and a political picketer (*piquetera*), opposing the policies of the Peronist government of Eduardo Duhalde, as a single woman who would not tolerate patriarchy, and as a woman who would have kept Isabelita (Perón's third wife) from marrying Juan Perón.

While in exile, Perón did nothing to deter the cult of Evita. At the same time, however, it was more difficult to maintain his own heroic cult as he aged and took on a new wife, Isabelita Martínez de Perón, who tried to look like Eva, but never won the hearts of the Peronists. In 1971, following the kidnapping of General Aramburu, Eva's corpse was returned to Juan Perón in Madrid, and at his Puerta de Hierro residence, the corpse remained with Juan and his new wife. There her plastified body was repaired by experts. During the next few years Eva remained in Spain as Juan explored the possibilities of returning to Argentina and its complex politics.

On June 20, 1973, Juan's second return led to a shooting spree at the Ezeiza airport by opposing political groups. He was subsequently elected president. After the death of Juan Perón in July 1974, Juan was buried in his family's plot in the middle-class Chacarita cemetery. Eva's body remained in Spain, so left-wing Peronists again intervened, this time robbing the body of General Aramburu from his crypt in the fashionable Recoleta cemetery to demand the return of Eva's body. Her remains finally came home in 1976, and she was buried in Recoleta cemetery in her family's crypt under lock and key to keep robbers away (see Illustration 8.1). And Aramburu's body was also returned to Recoleta.[10]

8.1 *Evita plaque in the Recoleta cemetery (Photo: Donna Guy).*

From that time onward, people have left plaques and offerings on the tombs of Juan, Pedro, and Eva, but most frequently at Eva's. Her mausoleum is the favorite and is called, appropriately, *la tumba sin paz* (the tomb without peace). These incidents have been recalled in scholarly and literary works and in several movies including the Hollywood version with Madonna. Eva's tomb has become a popular spot for foreign tourists in Buenos Aires as well as for the local faithful that remember her with great fondness and hope for her intercession with their problems.[11]

During his lifetime, Juan had developed strong bonds of loyalty with his supporters among the military, the working class, and others who took up the Peronist cause. As a young man he cut a dashing figure, resembling Carlos Gardel, the popular tango singer who died tragically in a plane crash in 1935. After 1944 Eva helped to develop a personality cult around Perón through her constant adulation of her husband the president. Even as early as February 1947, when Eva was beginning to give political speeches, she showed her total devotion to Perón. At a soap factory meeting she commented:[12]

> You all know perfectly that Coronel Perón, from the Secretariat of Labor and Welfare, struggled for the welfare and the happiness of all the working classes and he continues to work to make you each day happier and prouder to be among the true creators of this great, happy and powerful

country. I, the most modest and insignificant collaborator that General Perón has, have placed myself in the struggle to embrace the flag of the working class, the same one that Perón and Colonel Mercante, today governor of the vigorous province of Buenos Aires, embrace.

As Maryssa Navarro and Nicolas Fraser put it, Eva's florid language, derived from her earlier career playing roles in soap operas, "made the notions of love and loyalty to Perón vivid and urgent. . . . They also played a large part in the progressive elevation of Perón to divine status. Eva's cult of Perón . . . by 1949 . . . was institutionalized and Evita was its priestess."[13] The massive rallies and demonstrations, added to new school textbooks that deified both the Peróns, further instilled the cult of Juan's personality among Argentina's youth. This demagogic hero worship of Juan, along with strong repression of his opponents, led his enemies to refer to the cult of Perón in a disparaging way. For example, in 1955 Raúl Damonte Taborda (pseudonym, COPI), a humorist and playwright who left Argentina to live in Paris, scathingly named his 1955 exposé *Ayer fue San Perón* (Yesterday Was Saint Perón) to indicate that the tyrant who presumed to be sanctified was no longer in power.[14]

After his overthrow in 1955, Perón continued to maintain leadership of his party and his followers even while in exile. He was constantly sending messages with visitors so that no one could contest his authority. To combat any attempts by his followers to dictate policies, Perón recorded his thoughts on tape recorders. No one could presume to represent Perón in Argentina without his personal authorization. Nevertheless, by the time he returned in 1973, the nation had changed. Eva was no longer around to rally the masses. And Juan was an old man fighting youthful militants whom he chastised just before his death. When he died, after a brief, chaotic, and violent period in office, that aura began to dissipate, as the public sought other popular saints.

The trajectory of Juan Perón's body in death was not as fortunate as that of Eva's, even though it was carefully buried in the Perón family crypt. Perón had not obtained permission to be buried in Recoleta. Before his death Perón had explicitly asked that this body not be embalmed; however, a Japanese specialist embalmed the former president because Perón was too valuable a commodity to discard. Once he died, as Damian Nabot and David Cox have pointed out, his body also "was transformed into the merchandise of others." His body became a valuable commodity, like that of Eva Perón, despite his stated objections.[15] Indeed, on June 23 1987, even with all kinds of security measures that included a series of locks to prevent the body's theft, thieves entered the tomb. They carefully cut off his hands and stole, among other things, a poem written to him by his widow Isabelita that mentioned his hands.[16] The robbers initially demanded eight million dollars to return the hands and several other symbolic articles taken from the tomb, but the ransom was never paid because Peronist leader Vicente Saadi, leader of the Saadi family dynasty in Catamarca Province, refused to pay the ransom, and Eduardo Duhalde, soon to be Peronist president of Argentina, claimed that "people like General Perón are not valued for their bones, but rather for the ideas they left behind."[17] The hands detached with an electric saw, to this day, have never reappeared.[18]

Efforts to determine the authors of the crime, the ransom's significance, and the whereabouts of the hands have all been fruitless. Ever since the theft of Perón's hands there have been a series of murders or unexplained deaths surrounding witnesses to the event. The accidental deaths of the judge and his associates who spent years trying to prosecute the case have been viewed as highly questionable. As they investigated it became evident that the keys to the tomb had been stolen, and that powerful people in Argentina and perhaps in Italy were implicated, but no one was ever charged. Most of the researchers have attempted to determine who committed the crime.[19] And while crowds demanded justice when they found out about the desecration, over time people became less interested in justice and more interested in jobs.

The stories of Juan and Evita's bodies, their political cults during life, fears of their bodies after death, and, in the case of Juan Perón, dismemberment, provided the basis for the commodification of their bodies and the cult of their personalities. In 2002 the new Evita Museum opened in Buenos Aires where visitors could look at the material proof of her existence, purchase memorabilia, and carry them out in paper bags emblazoned with her picture. Eva's portrait can be purchased as a refrigerator magnet, along with that of Che Guevara (but not of Juan), and some of her jewelry has recently been sold at public auction for exorbitant prices. In one case, the auction of her jewel studded pin of the Argentine flag sent prices soaring from an early estimate of US$80,000 to more than US$800,000 by an unidentified bidder.

The commodification of Juan Perón has traveled a different, less successful, course. At the time of his death, tens of thousands of people flocked to his funeral. In the interior of Argentina workers commandeered trains and busses to get to Buenos Aires to pay their respects. It seemed that Perón's body would be revered as much as Evita's. In his case, however, public preoccupation with his body initially ended when the theft of his hands went unpunished. Perhaps that was all that was necessary to steal, as they resonated all the power at his disposal. His hands were always raised as part of Perón's greetings to the masses. Hugo Ezequiel Lezama, no friend of Perón, noted that Perón had commented after World War II that he would cut off his hands rather than sign the Treaty of Chapultepec, although he eventually signed this regional hemispheric treaty, and that he once said he would cut his hands off before accepting the rank of general, and again Perón kept his hands and became a general. To Lezama, Perón's hands were unimportant to Perón compared with his principles.[20] Yet those same hands once had the ability to caress Eva, greet the working class, and sign legislation.

Rosana Guber is one of the few people who have contemplated the cultural significance of the theft. She viewed the debate about the hands as symbolic of efforts to promote democracy, at the same time that Peronism divided the body politic after 1983. At the mass of mourning held in Buenos Aires after the hands had been discovered missing, posters were raised by Perón loyalists that said: "YOUR HANDS ARE THE HANDS OF THE PEOPLE."[21] Unlike Guber, I believe the theft of the hands became a catalyst to destroy the symbolic cult of Perón. Without his hands to venerate, the rest of his body became less important. The theft of his other symbols of power including his sable mantle destroyed his symbolic access to authority. Equally important, the robbery and desecration forced people to think about the meanings of the past, including the ways that Perón wielded power.[22] And, without his hands, his value in popular religiosity diminished. In practical terms, the cult of Eva's body continued while that of Perón dissipated. No matter how many flowers were placed on his tomb, and how many visitors came, he was dismembered, and, politically, he was on the way to being replaced by Menemist Peronism.

The disappearance of Juan's hands took place just before the 1988 elections of Peronist Carlos Saúl Menem as president of Argentina. During his campaign Menem symbolically placed himself under pictures of Juan and Evita to form a Peronist political genealogy that transferred popular Peronist authority to him. Once in power Menem transformed Peronism into a conservative party that privatized what Perón had expropriated for the people and celebrated himself rather than Perón. Whereas Perón had supported the return of nineteenth-century dictator Juan Manuel de Rosas's body to Argentina, Menem not only accomplished the task, he also attempted to restore Juan Manuel de Rosas as a popular cult. In this way Menem ironically and symbolically demoted Perón in the pantheon of political heroes who could unite the nation and replaced him with the Federalist Rosas. By returning the bones of the nineteenth-century charismatic leader, both conservatives and nationalists now could revere the early leader whose body, and now his reputation, was intact. The restoration of the cult Rosas represented as much of a theft as Peron's hands as it robbed the dead former president of his charismatic control.

Perón in death had to suffer even more humiliation, this time at the hands of his heirs. Unable to restore his hands and his political authority, public interest in the value of his body waned as private feuds between the Duarte family (Eva's relatives) and Isabelita Martínez de Perón, Peron's last wife, measured and valued his estate. Shortly after his body was found mutilated, stories emerged from Montevideo that Perón had sent suitcases full of money there after his overthrow in 1955.[23] The ransoming of his hands perpetuated rumors of Swiss bank accounts, and the need for Perón's fingerprints to access them. This rumor was so entrenched that Argentine journalists even went to Switzerland to find out if fingerprint identification was necessary to gain access to secret accounts (they are not). To add insult to injury, a court case forced officials to exhume Perón's body in 1996 to have a DNA test at the request of Marta Holgado, who claimed to be Perón's illegitimate daughter.[24] And heirs from the Perón side of the family feuded with heirs from the Duarte family over the rights to royalties, as well as property.

Recently, after the fiftieth anniversary of the death of Eva Perón, new plans emerged to move her body once again, this time to the crypts of the Franciscan Convent in downtown Buenos Aires. Now there is sentiment building to restore Perón's cadaver and replace his hands, like the arm of Obregón, with reconstructed ones of wax. To further commodify his body, plans are also being made to reunite the bodies of Juan and Evita in San Vicente, a suburb of Buenos Aires. In that way Juan's body could benefit from the religious veneration of Evita's corpse.[25]

The Catholic Church also wants to benefit from the rehabilitation of the Peróns. It is not insignificant that the Franciscans, in whose robes Eva Perón was originally buried and whose order was supported both religiously and financially by both Peróns, should want to claim the final resting place of Eva's body. In that way, the former First Lady would be removed symbolically from the realm of popular religious practice in Recoleta where on the dates of her birth and death new flowers and visitors flood the cemetery and new plaques are installed, and returned to the formal church where her role was more submissive. In other words, the church could control any activities related to the tomb that would be considered unacceptable. The fact that Perón's family wants his body restored and placed alongside that of Eva shows the desires to enhance the memory of Juan through the charisma of her cult.

To understand this tug of war between Menemist and church efforts to end the hero worship of the Peróns, and the ways that popular religious practices keep the memory of Eva alive, we need to know more about Argentine popular religion and its glorification and commodification of dead bodies.

What is the cultural significance of death in Argentina? In addition to the traditional grieving and religious services, death sets in motion a whole series of activities designed to prepare the body and perpetuate the memory of the individual. In most cases, this means burial in a family crypt or plot, cared for by relatives. Death is commodified when relatives have to pay for services, maintain the crypt, and place flowers and remembrances. In Argentina many vendors set up shop outside cemeteries to cater to the ongoing demand for flowers to decorate tombs; flowers as well as visitors to the tomb serve as a visible index of the decedent's popularity after death has ended earthly life.

In some cases, however, death initiates a more intricate and complicated process. It marks the end of a real life and the formation of a new identity based on a combination of religious ideas and popular myths. Sometimes an entire body is venerated. In others, the presence, or absence, of body parts affects the nature of worship. In death, some attain a power and presence never achieved in life, and this process is accentuated by the intervention of the market place. Such is the case of Eva and Juan Perón. Their stories demonstrate the conflict, always present in Argentine history, between the official process of hero worship of dead people, and the popular and more personal adoration of the dead embodied in religion.

The cult of dead bodies has always played a factor in Argentine political and religious life. Politicians placed their own values on political funerals, but the public's right to place a value on, promote, or demote the cult of its dead is less well studied. Popular religion has always had its own pantheon of saints. In addition to the cult of the religious body relics and formal saints, there have been cults tied to individuals ignored and even deplored by the formal Catholic Church but cherished by the public. According to Félix Coluccio, canonization is not an act restricted to the Vatican. "Popular religiosity, not always respectful of Roman orthodoxy, often de facto canonizes both real and imaginary people to whom oral tradition has attributed the accomplishment of real miracles."[26] In Argentina these figures include politicians such as Eva Perón; singers (Carlos Gardel, Rodrigo "el Potro" Bueno, Gilda); spiritists (Madre María); cowboys (el Gaucho Bazán Frías, el Gaucho Juan Bautista Bairoletto, el Gaucho Cubillos, el Gaucho Gil, el Gaucho Mariano Córdoba, el Gaucho Altamirano, el Gaucho José Dolores); and young people who died tragically (María Soledad Morales, Rodrigo and Gilda). Significantly, there is also a cult of death itself in the form of San La Muerte (Saint Death). Most of these cults are regional in nature, and their popularity waxes and wanes over time, an index of the fragility of fame and the changing spiritual preoccupations of Argentines.

Daniel Santamaría defines popular religion as "the group of experiences, attitudes and symbolic behaviors that demonstrate the existence of a social imaginary that includes the supernatural in daily reality."[27] Various types of behavior can lead to popular sainthood including a tragically young death by natural means, death as the result of violence that empowers the victim, a sacrificial death, and the glorification of an individual who has defied the powers of authority, typically people who have died at the hands of the law. There are also popular saints who emanate from millennial movements, such as the Canudos Rebellion in Brazil that immortalized Antonio Conselheiro (the Counselor). The important aspect of these designations is that they *come from the masses,* rather than from higher authority.[28]

In a country like Argentina with a long tradition of liberalism and anticlericalism, the presence of popular saints has always been difficult to explain. Traditionally there have been pejorative explanations that relate such phenomena to a lack of knowledge of Catholicism or to the charismatic power of superstition and popular leaders for the poor and uneducated people of the Argentine interior.

The popular support of Juan Manuel de Rosas (discussed elsewhere in this volume), the nineteenth-century caudillo whose body was returned to Argentina in the 1980s, was criticized by José Ramos Mejía, a nineteenth-century physician and early psychologist, as part of this type of cult of the masses.[29] Ramos Mejía labeled it a form of madness that affected the national psyche, and the typical person associated with this was "the humble individual, with an equivocal conscience, vague intelligence, not very analytical, and a relatively rudimentary and uneducated nervous system."[30] Although Ramos Mejía was not referring specifically to popular religion, he was describing elite urban attitudes toward lower-class rural people who empowered themselves through their heroes.

To the dismay of Argentine intelligentsia, the perpetuation of popular cults, often with religious overtones and spurred on by commodification rather than class relations, continued throughout the twentieth century, emanating both from the Argentine interior as well as from urban areas, continued to flourish in the twenty-first century. Its effervescence is no longer related to a simple rurality (and it is unclear if that categorization was merely a class-based view), but rather it is rooted in the crisis-filled nature of modern Argentine society and a popular desire of the masses to empower themselves so that they can translate and control the meanings of public and mythical figures. Inherent in this process is a rejection of official hero making (represented recently in Menem's repatriation of the body of Rosas) and politics as usual, and a profound questioning of the official meanings attributed to crime, sacrifice, gender, and heroics. To understand the deaths of Juan and Eva Perón, the kidnapping of Evita's body, and the later disappearance of Juan's hands, these events must be placed in this larger cultural context.

The battle between formal religious and popular authority is not new in Argentina. In the province of San Juan, Argentina, there is a huge shrine dedicated to the worship of the Difunta Correa (the Dead Woman Correa). There, thousands of people arrive each week to pay their respects to a woman who supposedly lived and died by the side of the road during the wars of the caudillos in the early nineteenth century. According to religious lore, sometime between 1820 and 1860 María Dalinda (or Deolinda) Antonia Correa died of thirst with her infant at her side. María Dalinda had been in search of her husband, and when she and her infant son ran out of water, she supposedly prayed that her son might live. Miraculously, her son was found later still suckling milk from his dead mother's breast. She has become the patron saint of truck drivers because it was mule drivers who found her body and her son. Small shrines have been set up along country roads of the Argentine interior, where people leave offerings of water bottles and miniature shelters (see Illustrations 8.2 and 8.3).[31] At her main shrine in the town of Vallecito, San Juan, several acres of land have been dedicated to her cult, and all types of symbolic houses, miniatures and large enough to be shrines, have been constructed to celebrate her ability to help everyone from truck drivers to soccer players, brides to military men. A simple church across the street tries to lure the Difunta's devotees. The majority of people both rich and poor consume religion by purchasing all types of souvenirs of the Difunta from ribbons to hang in every brand of auto and truck to pro-tect the traveler, to prepared food and plastic water-filled snowglobes with the Difunta and her suckling child (not only kitsch but also ironic in the middle of the desert!).

There are very strong connections between the cult of the Difunta and the cult of Eva Perón. Both women died at an early age, and both were known to be very faithful to their husbands. V. S. Naipaul, who compared Eva to Difunta, noted that the water left for the Difunta at the shrines always evaporated, meaning to the faithful that the Difunta had sated her thirst: "The simple miracle is ceaselessly renewed." Born in poverty and illegitimacy, Eva reappeared from the depths of anonymity to end up in the most aristocratic cemetery to ensure the people that there would always be a source of future miracles.[32]

Popular religiosity in Argentina has a special fondness for men who challenged the law. This, too, has its roots in popular culture since the time when Argentine writers began to romanticize the Argentine gaucho. According to Josefina Ludmer, gauchesco literature has always involved a tension among various voices. While the intellec-tual elites associated the demise of the independent gaucho as neces-sary for national consolidation, the voices of the gauchos, and their defiance of legal and political discourse, became appropriated and manipulated by Argentine writers to form the gauchesco tradition.[33]

Gauchos also form an integral part of the discourse of popular heroes and popular religion. Their associations with criminal life, par-ticularly those "Robin Hood" figures who robbed from the rich and gave to the poor, resonate in a positive way for people seeking to name their own heroes. According to Félix Conoccio, there are at least six popular saints identified as being part of this gauchesco tradition.

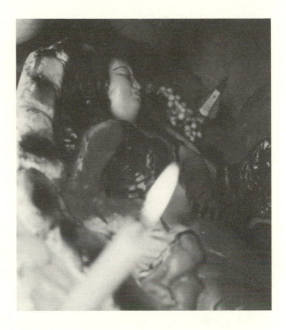

8.2   *Difunta Correa sanctuary in Tafí del Valle, Tucumán, Argentina (Photo: Donna Guy).*

8.3   *Difunta Correa sanctuary along the highway, Catamarca Province, Argentina (Photo: Donna Guy).*

The Gaucho Bazán Frías is one of them. It is curious that he would be considered a gaucho, because he was really an urban bandit, but he still fit the concept of the gaucho as a man on the edge of society, willing to challenge the dominant order. The man who had identified himself in police records as a hotel waiter, Andrés Bazán Frías, son of a policeman, ended up being killed in a shootout with the police in 1926. Prior to his death he had been imprisoned several times and each time had tried to escape, and he evidently complained about prison conditions. This anger over the callousness of public authorities has always resonated with the public in northwestern Argentina. To this day in the city of San Miguel de Tucumán, each Monday devotees head to the Cementerio del Norte to light candles at his grave (see Illustration 8.4). Soon after he was buried, people began to attribute miracles to him, including curing arthritis, and his tomb was moved to accommodate the crowds that lit candles for their hero.[34]

What led people to worship a criminal? In 1926 Dr. Emilio Catalán, a psychologist and public health physician, analyzed Bazán Frías's popular sainthood and attributed it to the phenomenon earlier described by Ramos Mejía, "psicología colectiva," or mass psychology. He argued that the popular religion typically led to the "adoration of the dead to whom tradition attributes virtues that are more or less supernatural."[35] He noted derisively that the cult had replaced an earlier devotion to Catalina González, a prostitute and alcoholic to whom the public in Tucumán had prayed before Bazán Frías's death. According to the medico-legal examination of the man considered by the police to be a common bandit, Bazán Frías "was the product of the heady brew instilled by the criminal life of the underworld with their tenebrous associates," definitely not a saint.[36] Catalán cautioned his educated readers that it would be difficult to wipe out such cults, particularly during times of great stress. While that may be true, it does not explain the persistence of this particular cult and of other expressions of popular religion in Argentina.

What relationship does Bazán Frías have to the cults of Juan and Eva Perón? Certainly both were accused of robbing the rich to give to the poor, and Perón himself was imprisoned both before he became president in 1946 and after he was overthrown in 1955. One of the factors impeding his return to Argentina was arrest warrants for having sex with a minor girl, Nelly Rivas. In the end, these charges were dropped to allow Perón to return and run again for president. For opponents of the Peróns, Juan had shared much in common with

8.4 *Tomb of Bazán Frías in the Cementerio del Norte, Tucumán, Argentina (Photo: Donna Guy).*

nineteenth-century gauchos and caudillos, and he was often compared with Juan Manuel de Rosas (just as Eva was compared to Rosas's wife). Even more important than the direct comparisons are the links between the value placed on masculine behavior that took action to protect the poor and the weak, a sentiment that was a hallmark of Peronist social policy and is still seen in the biographies of popular male saints.

Yet Perón could not maintain his connectivity to the rural folk, the people called the "cabecitas negras," who, in the 1940s, supported his government, nor could his buried corpse deepen the suggested symbolic link between himself and the gauchos. One of the factors militating against this relationship was the fact that Perón died in bed, an old man, after going to Paraguay to watch a military parade with his old friend, the dictator Alfredo Stroessner. The vigor and charisma that had associated him with gauchos, as well as his physical appearance that resembled the famous tango singer Carlos Gardel, dissipated over time as age robbed the Argentine political leader of his youth. And, in the last year of his life, Perón turned against the young rebels within his party as he opposed the guerrilla movements that assaulted the military. After he became president again in 1974 he proposed a social pact that would rob the workers of their special authority within Peronism. They were supposed to refrain from striking just as merchants were supposed to prevent hoarding and increased prices. In life, both age and politics had stripped Perón of much of his gauchesco authority. In death, the theft of his hands removed the remnants of what had become the symbol of youthful virility of the man who never sired a child. People investigating the theft of his hands disrobed him to see if he had been robbed of his masculinity. In fact, the robbery of the hands partly emasculated him.

The rest was accomplished by his successor, Carlos Saúl Menem. The politician from La Rioja campaigned for the presidency in 1989 often dressed as a cross between a rock star and a gaucho, dyeing his hair and altering the length of his sideburns, and even appearing in tight-fitting leather pants. Later he posed for a magazine spread dressed only in his undershorts. Once in power, however, he broke his ties with traditional Peronism by allying himself domestically with economic conservatives, and internationally with Great Britain and with the United States. By supporting conservative policies he also had no more need to court the youth who would not accept him. Subsequently his public dispute with and later divorce of his wife, Zulema, was partly due to her desire to replace Eva as the populist savior of the masses. Years later, he subsequently married a young Chilean beauty queen who attempted, again unsuccessfully, to replace Evita. Whether Menem can catapult himself into a lasting personal cult remains to be seen, but he quite effectively limited Perón's popularity.

Recently, three new popular saints have been added to the Argentine pantheon, ones who resonate more strongly with Eva than with Juan. Furthermore, their history casts an unpleasant light on the new Peronism, and points to the new commodification of death in Argentina. An examination of these cases provides some additional perspective from which to view the future sanctity and commodification of the Peróns.

María Soledad Morales died tragically at the age of seventeen in 1990. She had been drugged, raped, scalped, and left naked on the side of Highway 37 in Catamarca, in September of that year, a shocking event in the small and very traditional province. In Argentina, such crimes have often eluded the scrutiny of the courts, and this case languished for seven years because of the political connections of the young men accused of the terrible crime who were sons of powerful Peronist politicians loyal to Menem. One, Guillermo Luque, was the son of a legislator allied with Governor Ramón Saadi, and a second,

Luis Tula, was María Soledad's boyfriend. There were others involved, all linked politically to the Saadi family, but only Tula and Luque were finally convicted of the crime.[37]

For years, all efforts to try the individuals involved were fruitless. Soon after the tragedy, students at María Soledad's Catholic secondary school began to march around the main plaza in the capital city of Catamarca. The Carmelite nun who headed the school, Sister Martha Pelloni, joined them. Usually after the demonstration a priest offered a closing prayer. In this way, the official Catholic Church initially supported the protests. Gradually, however, confronted by political pressures, church officials told Sister Martha to stop presiding over the weekly protest walks, and after about one year, the priests stopped participating as well. Nevertheless, Sister Martha remained among the marchers.[38]

These marches soon made their way to the spot where María Soledad was found. There, poorer people erected wooden crosses and left flower offerings, and eventually a larger obelisk was placed there to commemorate the crime. As Norma Morandini put it, "Like the Difunta Correa, . . . María Soledad has been converted by her resting on the road," a place "that predicted her future as saint."[39]

The battle between the official and the popular church took place in Catamarca in 1991 when the province hosted an Episcopal conference that coincided with the one hundredth anniversary of the canonization of La Virgen del Valle, the local virgin with a dark face. The bishops tried to ignore the María Soledad case, although claims of miraculous appearances involving demands for water—like the Difunta Correa—encouraged a popular following. Ultimately the cult of María Soledad won out because the political scandals associated with the cover-up of the crime forced President Menem to remove Ramón Saadi from office just before the bishops' meeting, and throughout the event Saadi supporters held violent protests.[40]

Poor María Soledad had to have three autopsies before the truth of her death was made public. She died from a cocaine overdose, and the rape and mutilation of her body occurred after death to cover up the connection with drugs, just as the father of one of her classmates had learned through rumors months earlier. Most of the forensic evidence, however, by then was too deteriorated to serve as evidence.[41] The trial was assigned successively to four judges, most of who were compromised by ties to the Saadi political group. Testimony placed Guillermo Luque in Buenos Aires, instead of Catamarca, and false affidavits claimed he had attended classes in the national capital, but more honest witnesses came forward to contradict the evidence. By February 1991 Luque was imprisoned but not sentenced. Tula was still free. It was not until 1998 that the two were sentenced for their crimes. By that time María Soledad had joined the pantheon of popular saints.[42]

This case not only became a cause celèbre in Argentina and the place of death a shrine for the murdered girl, it has also taken the fancy of astrologers who find meaning in the location of Catamarca, as well as the significant dates associated with the murder. There are astrological Internet pages associated with the phenomenon and tours of Catamarca include the spot where she was found, which now has flowers constantly placed to mark the spot. Significantly, the Web site is called *comprecatamarca*, or "buy Catamarca."[43] It also points to the Internet as a new form of dissemination of saintliness, something that certainly has catapulted the last person to popular sainthood.

The saga of the second saint began on Saturday, June 24, 2000, when a young musician died in a tragic automobile accident on the road from Buenos Aires to the city of La Plata. Rodrigo "el Potro" ("the Colt") Bueno was one of Argentina's most successful popular singers with eight albums. That Saturday he lost control of his SUV, crashed, and died. While the death of a celebrity often becomes a media event, Rodrigo's was transformed into something else. More than twenty thousand people attended his funeral, and floral wreaths were sent by the president of Argentina, the governor of the province of Buenos Aires, as well as other famous people. Despite the rain, attendees sang songs and purchased artificial flowers.[44]

Since that time, miracles have been attributed to the fallen singer, including the appearance of grass in the asphalt where he died. People go there to ask for work and claim that he has become an angel. On the anniversary of his death, hoards of well wishers head to the marker at kilometer 26 to leave their offerings. In these ways, Rodrigo lives on in the memories of those who loved his songs and who seek consolation at his grave site. He has also become a commodity on the Internet. (See Illustrations 8.5 and 8.6.) There one can buy his pictures, CDs, and all kinds of memorabilia. People write to him and ask to be protected while they sleep, to bring them happiness, to cure leukemia, and he has been identified as the source of cures for eye ailments and, through his CDs, a source of energy.[45] He has become a virtual saint. At the Rodrigo Web site *http://www.elmitorodrigo.com.ar/*,

8.5   *Statue of Rodrigo in the Province of Buenos Aires (Photo: Luis Blacha).*

8.6   *Shrine to Rodrigo in the Province of Buenos Aires (Photo: Luis Blacha).*

significantly called the "Myth of Rodrigo," screen savers, virtual music, and all kinds of Rodrigomania are for sale.

In this way Rodrigo Bueno is similar to Eva Perón, who, thanks to the Madonna movie, the Eva Perón Historical Foundation, and a host of Web sites formed by devotees of Evitamania, photos and aspects of the biography and works of Eva Perón are now available on the Internet. In fact, the two are linked by a monument at the Rodrigo site that says, "Volvimos y somos miles" (We returned and we are thousands), referring to Rodrigo's devotees, and the famous saying about Perón's faithful attributed to Eva: "Volveré y sere mil-liones" (I will return and will be millions) (see Illustration 8.7). In obvious contrast, there is little popular reference to Juan Perón, except through the Instituto Nacional Juan Perón (*http://www.jdperon. gov.ar*; a government-organized Web site). Most Web sites come from outside Argentina, and there is little to indicate that San Perón is still remembered. The masses have not been interested in perpetuating his virtual sainthood.

The final popular saint that needs to be examined is Santa Gilda, or Gilda Myriam Alejandra Bianchi (see Illustration 8.8). This young woman became a singer after a failed marriage and failed careers. Of modest means and named after the famous movie character immortalized by Rita Hayworth, Gilda suddenly had achieved fame and a degree of fortune in her late twenties. Then Gilda died in 1996 when her van was hit by a truck in the province of Entre Rios, not only killing her but also her mother, her daughter, and three members of her musical entourage. She was immediately placed on the Internet by her musical director and companion, Toti Giménez, and soon the cult became more important than his desire to sell her records. Many who placed flowers on her grave and at the site where she died commemorated her death, like the others.[46] People believe that she will keep them company as they sleep and care for them when they are sick, once again demonstrating the psychic need felt by young Argentines to connect with and be protected by a tragic figure. Their mothers might have had Eva, but they have Santa Gilda.

The growth of popular saints has had an inverse relationship to the perpetuation of Juan Perón as a popular hero, while the dedication of the people to his wife has continued unabated. Perhaps the final explanation for the limited commodification and veneration of Juan Perón in death has to do with the links between popular

8.7   *Rodrigo slogan mirrors Evita's plaque in the Province of Buenos Aires (Photo: Luis Blacha).*

8.8   *Santa Gilda (Photo: Luis Blacha).*

relation and economic crises, ones that have led to a fervent cult of San Cayetano, the patron saint of work.

San Cayetano founded numerous organizations in sixteenth-century Italy, mostly devoted to helping the poor and impoverished. Canonized in the seventeenth century, in the midst of extreme political and extreme economic crisis, San Cayetano's devotion to the poor has become a magnet for the official Catholic Church to attract the faithful and criticize the Peronist government of Eduardo Duhalde. From July 26 (the date Eva Perón died) until August 7, 2002, thousands made pilgrimages to the church dedicated to San Cayetano in a neighborhood of Buenos Aires to hear the archbishop of Buenos Aires celebrate mass in celebration of the saint. It seems that the festival of San Cayetano grows as faith in the ability of political leaders to solve the economic crisis deteriorates. And for what do people pray to San Cayetano? Precisely the things Eva Perón had promised people: the redistribution of wealth, succor for the poor, food on the table, and a dignified life. Evidently the nonconsecrated saints are insufficient to overcome the general poverty and lack of work in Argentina. So once again the formal church has an opportunity to define its own popular hero—one selected by its own methods rather than that of the people. And, bolstered by the faithful, local commerce devoted to selling traditional offerings to San Cayetano benefited from what little the faithful have to spend.[47]

The relationship of Juan and Eva Perón to popular religion and to the popular memory is a complicated matter. It clearly does not correspond directly to events during their lives, and one might argue that it is linked instead to subsequent political and economic crises afflicting the Southern Cone nation. Their experiences show that official manipulation of their memories can afford them a place in history books, but not always in the popular religious practices of Argentines. Since the nineteenth century the use of the popular Argentine imagination to create heroes has troubled those who would have preferred that people extol officially acceptable saints, both inside and outside the official Catholic Church. The increased presence of capitalism and the commodification of death in Argentina, along with a strong popular preference for those who give to, rather than those who take from the people, enables popular saints to continue to capture the imagination as well as the pesos of the people.

Notes

The research for this paper was funded by an American Council of Learned Societies Fellowship and research funds from the Ohio State University. I would also like to thank Laura Michelle Diener and Luis Blacha, for research assistance, and Dora Barrancos and Lyman Johnson, for their comments on earlier drafts.

1. Hugo Ezequiel Lezama, "Juego de villanos," *La Prensa*, 5 July 1987, 7.
2. During this time the orphanages controlled by the Sociedad were under federal intervention, although the elite women still met with the government official who controlled them. Archivo Consejo Nacional del Menor y de la Familia, Legao 58167. In accordance with the wishes of the Consejo, no names have been revealed.
3. Eva did not close down the Sociedad de Beneficencia. See Donna J. Guy, "La 'verdadera' historia de la Sociedad de Beneficencia," in *La política social antes de la política social (Caridad, beneficencia y política social en Buenos Aires, siglos XVII aXX)*, ed. José Luis Moreno (Buenos Aires: Promoteo Libros, 2000), 321–41; reprinted in Barbara Potthast and Eugenia Scarzanella, eds., *Mujeres y naciones en América Latina: Problemas de inclusión y exclusion* (Madrid and Frankfurt am Main: Vervuert, 2001), 253–70.
4. Archivo General de la Nación Argentina (AGN), Archivo Intermedio, Fondo Ministerio del Interior, Numeración Especial, Letra P., foja 20.800, letter dated 3 July 1949.
5. *Chicago Tribune*, 27 July 1952, 4 F. See also Barron H. Lerner, "The Illness and Death of Eva Perón: Cancer, Politics, and Secrecy, *The Lancet* 355 (2000): 1988–91.
6. For opposing viewpoints, see J. M. Taylor, *Eva Perón: Myths of a Woman* (Chicago: University of Chicago Press, 1979); Tomás Eloy Martínez, *Santa Evita: Novela* (Buenos Aires: Planeta, 1995).
7. Quoted in Nicolas Fraser and Maryssa Navarro, *Eva Perón* (London: André Deutsch Ltd., 1980), 170.
8. See Pedro Ara, *El caso Eva Perón (Apuntes para la historia)* (Buenos Aires: CVS Editores, 1974); Sergio Rubin, "Otra vez hablan de trasladar el cuerpo de Eva Perón, *Clarín*, 31 July 2002, found at *http://old.clarin.com/diario/2002/07/31/p–01701.htm*.
9. A facsimile of the letter signed by Eva's mother can be found in the unpaginated appendix of documents in Sergio Rubín, *Eva Perón: Secreto de onfesión. Cómo y por qué la Iglesia ocultó su cuerpo durante 14*

años (Buenos Aires: Lohlé Lumen, 2002). See also his account of the removal of her body to Italy.

10. *La Prensa*, 3 July 1987, 4. Eva's family members were allowed to build a mausoleum in Recoleta cemetery because Eva had been given a high award by Juan, one that gave her the right to be buried there.

11. Sergio Rubin, "Un cadáver secuestrado, ultrajado y desterrado," *Clarín*, 7 October 2002, found in *http://old.clarin.com/suplementos/especiales2/2002/07/26/1-420677.htm*.

12. Eva Perón, *Eva Perón: Discursos completos, 1946–48* (Buenos Aires: Editorial Edigraf, 1986), 52.

13. Fraser and Navarro, *Eva Perón*, 112.

14. Raúl Damonte Taborda, *Ayer fue San Perón: 12 años de humillación argentina* (Buenos Aires: Ediciones GURE, 1955).

15. Damian Nabot y David Cox, *Perón, la otra muerte: El robo de las manos del general* (Buenos Aires: Grupo Editorial Agora, 1997), 11.

16. "Cuando plantaba el jazmón/ y otrora su flor me entregaba,/ llega tu mano de amor/ como mariposas blancas," quoted in *La Prensa*, 7 July 1987, 4.

17. "La policía se equivocó" manifestó Vicente Saadi, *La Prensa*, 3 July 1987, 4.

18. Ibid., 15–16. See also Juan Carlos Iglesias and Claudio Negrete, *La profanación: El robo de las manos de Perón. La historia de uno de los secretos mejor guardados de la Argentina* (Buenos Aires: Editorial Sudamericana, 2002), 49–52.

19. Iglesias and Negrete have done the most research in *La profanación*. Nevertheless, no one has come to trial, and many questions remain unanswered.

20. Lezama, "Juego de villanos," 7–8.

21. "Case of the Severed Hands, *Time*, 20 July 1987, 51.

22. Rosana Guber, "Las manos de la memoria," *Desarrollo Económico* 36, no. 141 (April–June 1996): 423–41.

23. "Escandalosa revelación," *La Prensa*, 24 July 1987, 6.

24. "Court Orders Exhumation of Juan Peron's Corpse," *NandoTimes*, 30 August 1996 at *http://archive.nandotimes.com/newsroom/n . . . /world18_11588.htm*.

25. A thorough treatment of this issue can be found in Iglesias and Negrete, *La profanación*. For efforts to restore Perón's hands, see "Proyectan restaurar el cadáver de Perón y ponerle manos," *la Tercera.el*, 31 August 2002, found at *http://www.latercera.com/diario/2002/08/31.1258.MUN.PERON.htm*.

26. Félix Coluccio, *Cultos y canonizaciones populares de Argentina* (Buenos Aires: Ediciones del Sol, 1986), 7.

27. Daniel J. Santamaría, "La cuestión de la religiosidad popular en la Argentina," in *Religiosidad popular en la Argentina*, ed. M. E. Chapp, M. Iglesias, M. Pascual, V. Roldán, and D. J. Santamaría (Buenos Aires: Centro Editor de América Latina, 1991), 13.

28. See the various articles in ibid. Antonio the Counselor led a millennial movement in the drought-stricken area of northern Brazil that was wiped out by government troops in the late nineteenth century.

29. José María Ramos Mejía, *Las multitudes argentinas: estudio de psicología colectiva para servir de introducción al libro "Rosas y su tiempo"* (Madrid: V. Suárez, 1912). See the paper by Jeffrey M. Shumway in this volume for details on the return of Rosas's body.

30. Quoted in Hugo Vezetti, *La locura en la Argentina* (Buenos Aires: Paidós, 1985), 113.

31. See Donna J. Guy, "Mothers Alive and Dead; Multiple Concepts of Mothering in Buenos Aires," in *Sex and Sexuality in Latin America*, ed. Donna J. Guy and Daniel Balderston (New York: New York University Press, 1997), 155–73.

32. V. S. Naipaul, *The Return of Eva Perón*. (New York: Alfred A. Knopf, 1980), 168–69.

33. See Josefina Ludmer, *Género gauchesco: The Gaucho Genre: A Treatise on the Motherland* (Chapel Hill, NC: Duke University Press, 2002).

34. Alberto Rojas Paz, "Superstición y milagrerías tucumanas por 'el' Bazán," Archivo de *La Gaceta*, 1979.

35. Dr. Emilio Catalán, "Un delincuente convertido en 'Santo Milagroso' por la superstición popular," reprint of article published in the *Revista de Criminología, Psiquiatría y Medicina Legal* 13, no.73 (January–February 1926): 9. José Ingenieros, one of the first psychologists in Argentina, wrote a series of books about mass psychology. See Hugo Vezetti, *La locura en la Argentina* (Buenos Aires: Folios Ediciones, 1983).

36. Ibid., 21.

37. See Norma Morandini, *Catamarca: Cuando el tirano cae su poder termina. Cuando la víctima muere su poder empieza* (Buenos Aires: Planeta, 1991).

38. Ibid., 85–90, 98.

39. Ibid., 73.

40. Ibid., 98–99.

41. Ibid., 117; see also the father's account on 87–88.

42. See the special issue on María Soledad on-line at *http://www.clarin.com/diario/especiales/soledad/*.

43. See *http://www.viviam.com/siderum/catamarca.htm*, *http://www.comprecatamarca.com.ar/turismo/circuitosturisticos.htm*

44. See *http://www.fortunecity.ed/losqueamamos/canario/64/rodrigo_el_potro. htm*.

45. See *http://personales.com/argentina/rosariio/rd128/milagros.htm*.

46. See *http://apysandu.com/atinafm/biografias/gilda.htm*; *http://www.isurf.com.ar/00–06-junio/nota11_12.htm*.

47. See *Página 12* at *http://pagina12.feedback.net.ar/secciones/sociedad/index.php?id_nota=8647&seccion=3*.

Chapter Nine

Vargas Morto: The Death and Life of a Brazilian Statesman

Daryle Williams and Barbara Weinstein

In the early morning hours of Tuesday, August 24, 1954, Brazilian president, Getúlio Dornelles Vargas, lumbered to the third floor of the Palácio do Catete, the ornate Rio de Janeiro mansion that had served as the official presidential residence since 1897. Vargas was seeking relief from a maelstrom that threatened to topple his presidency and, in all likelihood, would end a storied political career that began three decades earlier, when as an ambitious party hack from Rio Grande do Sul, Vargas arrived in Rio to assume the post of minister of finance. Weighing heavily on Vargas's mind was a deep economic crisis that cut into the gains of the democratic, populist state that he had tried to fashion after 1950. Equally worrisome was the collapse of support from well-placed civilian and military interests that had historically tolerated the president's well-known political and ideological shiftiness. Most troubling was the knowledge that members of Vargas's inner circle had conspired to murder a political foe, only to see the assassination attempt result in the accidental death of an air force officer. During the three weeks preceding August 24, Vargas had defiantly declared his intention to complete his elected term, stated that he might resign quietly, and then contradicted himself by asserting that he was prepared to leave the presidential palace as a "cadaver." By the time Vargas reached his bedroom around 4:45 A.M. on the 24th, the weary president took note that his security staff was busily arranging sandbags in the palace gardens in preparation for a possible attack. A small group of protesters chanted "Down with Vargas! Death to Vargas!" outside the palace gates.[1]

Vargas changed into his pajamas, though it remains doubtful that he actually managed to rest. Twice, he was interrupted with discouraging news about his hopes to quell yet another political crisis. When word arrived that a plan for a temporary suspension of presidential powers would not appease rebellious officers, Vargas walked into the hallway and informed his butler that he intended to lie down. The butler later reported seeing an unidentified heavy object in the pocket of the president's robe. Sometime between 8:30 and 8:45, alone in his bedroom, the beleaguered president removed what turned out to be a 32-calibre Colt revolver, placed the barrel at close range to the left side of his upper chest, and pulled the trigger. Rushing to the bedroom at the sound of the gunshot, Joint Chief of Staff General Aguinaldo Caiado de Castro found Vargas lying immobile on the bed. Alzira Vargas do Amaral Peixoto, the president's daughter and close advisor, entered the room to find her father's striped pajamas, bed sheets, and mattress covered in blood. Death came quickly, without any recorded last words.

Stunned by the bloody scene, Vargas's family and advisors informed the household staff of the president's suicide and searched the room for reasons why Vargas might have taken his own life thus abruptly ending a career characterized by a will for political survival. On the dresser, the president's son-in-law found a note declaring the intention to shed blood in the defense of the Brazilian *povo* (people). As they tried to make sense of the real and symbolic meanings of this pact signed in blood, the family began the difficult task of preparing the bloodied body for a speedy removal. Once news of Vargas's death hit the radio waves, the hostile crowds outside Catete were overwhelmed by bereaved mourners, made up of men and women who tearfully gazed past the now-useless sandbags and imagined what Vargas might look like in death.

As the various articles in this collection attest, the Latin America bodies that end up being the bones of political contention, so to speak, are most often the bodies of figures who were exemplary in life as well as in death; they are the bodies of heroes as well as martyrs. Che Guevara, Emiliano Zapata, and Eva Perón were claimed and acclaimed by a wide variety of groups well before their storied deaths. For many, the charismatic (or despised) qualities of these figures' lives became even more explicit and unambiguous after death. Che becomes the pure revolutionary, Zapata the stoic peasant rebel, Evita *una santa*, a saint.

Brazil's Getúlio Vargas presents an alternative narrative of death and life, one that deals with a self-confessed master of ambiguity. In life, Vargas once described an encounter with a would-be biographer whose attempts to gain an interview had been firmly rebuffed. "I prefer to be interpreted than to explain myself," Vargas confided to his journal.[2] In death, Vargas offered an equally enigmatic story. His death-by-suicide simultaneously traded on the image of a valiant warrior, selflessly fighting for the protection of national interests, alongside the image of a crafty and calculating statesman, whose political machinations reeked of demagoguery and self-interest. If death itself was a finality for Vargas on the morning of August 24, 1954, the interpretation of his death and life remains uncertain and unstable to this very day.

Prelude to a Tale of Two Corpses

Vargas, who headed the Brazilian state variously as chief of the provisional government, dictator, and popularly elected president for all but five years between 1930 and 1954, did not cut an especially commanding figure.[3] Relatively trim in his youth, the lawyer-turned-politician already showed signs of stoutness when he burst onto the national political scene in the so-called Revolution of 1930. Political cartoonists of Vargas's first tenure in office (1930–45) often poked fun at the wily president-dictator, depicting him as a short, portly man, dressed in a double-breasted suit, smoking a cigar, and smiling about some inside joke. Fans and opponents knew that Vargas's speaking voice and rhetorical style could be lackluster and that his political positions could be blatantly opportunistic. By the time Vargas stormed across the country in the 1950 presidential campaign, the public received Vargas with mixed emotions, seeing the short and compact politician as both friend and trickster.

This does not mean to say that Vargas was not successful at cultivating a genuine popular following during his lifetime. Among the earliest Latin American populists, Vargas successfully styled himself the *pai do povo*, or the father of the people/the poor, even before he took "the populist gamble" in 1944–45, openly seeking working-class political support during the final months of the Second World War.[4] And, even after Vargas staked his future on a *trabalhista* (laborite) vision of national politics, this scion of a wealthy landowning family from Rio Grande do Sul still managed to maintain the support of the *classes conservadoras* (literally, "the conservative classes," but closer to elites). Although an understudied feature of the Vargas mystique, it is clear that Vargas was also able to count on the support of the growing middle class, who benefited from the expansion of the central state, the pleasures of urban industrial life, and a strengthened sense of *brasilidade*, or Brazilianness.[5]

Even at the height of the Estado Novo dictatorship (1937–45), when Vargas often ruled by intimidation and decree, he found it prudent to negotiate among seemingly antagonistic interests, cultivating artists and intellectuals of both fascist and communist convictions, and maintaining support within organized labor, even as he suppressed independent trade unions. Vargas was the sort of politician who could imprison the general secretary of the Brazilian Communist Party, ship his Jewish communist wife off to a terrible fate in Nazi Germany, and later form an alliance with that very same communist leader.[6] Thus, not only was the former dictator able to ascend to the presidency in 1950 through popular election, but he did so with the support of both working-class organizations and industrialist associations, with the latter explicitly valuing Vargas as a leader who "always sought to establish cooperation among the different social classes and never sought to incite class conflict."[7] Somehow, Vargas was capable of embodying a range of political aspirations and ideological positions, synthesizing them into an apparently singular Brazilian national calling.

The high-wire act became more difficult in the final years of Vargas's second period in power (1951–54), when labor relations, especially wages levels for urban workers, set the tone for a broad range of conflicts over state priorities. The centrist Democratic Social Party (Partido Social Democrático, or PSD) and center-left Brazilian Labor Party (Partido Trabalhista Brasileiro, or PTB) continued to throw their legislative support behind Vargas's purified vision of trabalhismo, but growing segments of the elite and middle class who once tolerated the populist rhetoric as a means of assuring class collaboration began to see Vargas as out of touch and corrupt. Some even complained that he was a closet socialist. As Vargas intensified his appeals to organized labor, important factions of the military, influenced by a creeping cold-war antileftism, withdrew their support from their former ally. Civilian opponents, particularly those affiliated with the center-right National Democratic Union (União Democrática Nacional, or UDN), denounced Vargas as a rank opportunist and cheap demagogue. Even groups that had consistently positioned themselves on the Left, such as the Communist Party, expressed serious reservations about Vargas's heightened populism.[8]

Broad segments of the Brazilian population still managed to find the familiar Vargas preferable to the UDN's "liberal democrats." Other potential rivals, including the oligarchic clans who dominated the interior, urban populists like São Paulo mayor Adhemar de Barros, and charismatic military leaders, lacked Vargas's national projection. Vargas tried to change with the times, recasting himself as a friend of democratic institutions despite a long history of dispensing with constitutional protections when they proved inconvenient. Vargas, however, was never wholly successful in making himself out to be a true man of the people. His most devout followers regarded him with affection, noting his avuncular bearing and affable public persona. They tended to overlook his past use of censorship and repression against political enemies. (Vargas certainly did not remind them of his past authoritarian streak.) His political allies offered a calculated respect for his ability to mobilize "the masses" in the delicate negotiations among labor leaders, domestic and international capital, and regional interests over the means and ends of national development. To his supporters, Vargas was ultimately an imperfect but beloved populist.[9]

Those who opposed Vargas saw much more than a lack of perfection. As the opposition party, the UDN was especially vocal and well organized in working to contain or undermine the kind of nationalistic labor policies pursued after 1951. Enjoying easy access to the mainstream press, udenistas mounted a spirited campaign to reveal favoritism and corruption in the administration. Most vocal among the udenista critics was Carlos Lacerda, a young and ambitious journalist-politician from Rio de Janeiro who bombarded Vargas day and night with vitriolic accusations and criticisms. Cultivating his own political aspirations as the moralizing, middle-class antidote to Vargas's corrupt trabalhismo, Lacerda used the printed word and radio to crusade against a president portrayed as the root of all that was wrong in postwar Brazil.[10] By mid-1954, Lacerda's newspaper, Rio's Tribuna da Imprensa, was agitating for impeachment proceedings on the charge that Vargas had maintained improper dealings with Argentine populist Juan Perón (a figure about to suffer his own fall from grace).[11] Although the impeachment attempt failed in congress, it set the tone for Lacerda's verbal guerrilla war on Vargas and varguismo.

Fearful that Lacerda might succeed in his campaign to bring down Vargas, close associates of the president contemplated ways of silencing the opposition. Chief among Vargas's protectors was Gregório Fortunato (1900–62), an Afro-Brazilian who began life as a humble ranch hand on the Vargas family estate and would later accompany the up-and-coming Getúlio to Catete Palace, winning the plum position as chief of the president's forty-eight-man security detail.[12] Fingering Lacerda as the most serious threat, Fortunato enlisted a small group of men to shadow the journalist during his numerous public appearances. Lacerda quickly realized that he was under surveillance and petitioned the police to carry a firearm. Motivated equally by well-founded paranoia and rising anti-Vargas hysteria, the journalist began to travel with armed military escorts. The increased security around Lacerda, who reveled in the political theater, did not deter Fortunato from finalizing a secret plot to have the president's foe murdered. The unfolding of the plan, which felled Lacerda's military escort rather than Lacerda, set off a duel of dead bodies that climaxed with Vargas's own death on August 24, 1954.

Three Weeks and Two Corpses

Just after midnight on August 5, 1954, Lacerda, his teenage son Sérgio, and the military officer assigned to protect the bombastic journalist pulled up to 180 Toneleros Street, a fashionable address in the upscale neighborhood of Copacabana. The street was relatively quiet as Lacerda bid goodbye to his escort, thirty-two-year-old air force major Rubens Florentino Vaz, and walked toward the building. As Lacerda neared the garage entrance, a man rushed across the street, firing a pistol. Struck by a bullet, Lacerda drew his sidearm and returned fire. Major Vaz, in the meantime, stepped in to intervene. The gunman shot the major at close range and then shot and wounded a municipal police officer before speeding away in a car driven by an accomplice. Newspaper reporters were on the scene within minutes, finding a distraught Lacerda, who had suffered a minor injury to his left foot, bent over Vaz's dying body.[13]

In the months leading up to the botched assassination attempt, Lacerda had carped about the rising disorder of public life. His very public decision to carry a firearm and travel with armed escort was part of the campaign to demonstrate how insecure Brazilian streets had become. Within hours of the attack, Lacerda made a direct connection between disorder and the president, asserting, "I accuse one man as responsible for the crime. He is the protector of thieves whose freedom from punishment gives them the audacity to commit such crimes. That man is named Getúlio Vargas."[14] The UDN seized on Lacerda's accusation, making Vargas out to be in cahoots with cold-blooded murderers. The attack on Lacerda and the unintended death of Vaz, according to one of Vargas's prominent political supporters, "gave the opposition exactly what they needed: the cadaver of an innocent man who just happened to be an esteemed and well-placed military officer."[15] The wounded Lacerda lambasted the Vargas administration, demanding a formal inquiry. Air force officials quickly responded, forming a commission to investigate Vaz's murder.

Taking their cue from Lacerda, the president's opponents intensified their denunciations. Support for Vargas rapidly eroded in the empirically nebulous, but politically important realm of "public opinion." Indeed, Vaz's dead body probably served the purposes of the opposition even more effectively than Lacerda's might have had the assassin's bullet found its intended target. Lacerda's vitriolic and often hysterical attacks on the president had made him many enemies, and even alienated some who were hardly defenders of the president. Vaz's lifeless body, imbued with the military's aura of being above politics, was a more transparent affront to public decency and social order. If Vargas played any role in the major's death, he had committed a crime against the same public decency and social order that the military symbolically upheld.

Vaz's funeral proved to be a veritable field day for opinion-makers in the press. The major dailies published a multitude of photographs of the funeral procession that wended its way from the Aeronautical Club, past the Senate, to São João Batista cemetery. The images were marked by poignancy, as representatives of all branches of the military joined the Vaz family in burying the slain airman in a municipal cemetery that also served as the final resting place for other fallen military heroes, including the government soldiers killed during an unsuccessful left-wing mutiny that broke out in military garrisons in November 1935. On August 12, the archbishop of Rio led a Seventh Day Mass (a requiem mass that is central to Brazilian Catholic funerary rituals) in Rio's imposing Candelaria Church. The major's bereaved widow and four children figured prominently in the countless press reports issued in the week leading up to the mass for Vaz's departed soul.[16] The spectacle of Vaz's respectable, white, middle-class family grieving for its departed paterfamilias provided a perfect foil for representations of corruption and unsavory dealings in the Vargas government. The press sympathetically chronicled the expression of public and legislative outrage among Vargas's well-known opponents as well as a newly politicized officer corps.

Not surprisingly, the same dailies that made a bourgeois martyr of Vaz filled their columns with incriminations and revelations about those suspected of orchestrating the assassination attempt. Gregório Fortunato, chief of the president's security detail, was luridly profiled as the prime suspect. Against the propriety of a prematurely dead, middle-class military officer who selflessly gave up his life in defending the life of Carlos Lacerda, the press could not resist describing Fortunato, a freed slave's son who rose from rural poverty to circulate throughout the presidential palace, as a "sinister" figure whose dark visage sullied the nation's highest office.[17] To Fortunato's detractors, any sign of middle-class male respectability—his finely tailored suits, his honorable wife and children, and his important position— were to be attributed not to individual merit, intelligence, or ambition but rather to overly dependent relations with the corrupt Vargas and his nefarious brother, Benjamin.[18] (See Illustration 9.1.) Carlos Lacerda went so far as to make the outrageous accusation that Fortunato, a childhood playmate to a young Getúlio, was the president's lover.[19]

As the "crisis of 1954" unfolded, anti-Vargas factions painted a racially coded portrait of a criminal Fortunato, whose physical characteristics, in combination with his suspiciously intimate relations with the president, categorically denied him any claim to the laurels of respectability and personal honor. Dubbed the "Black Angel" in the press, Fortunato's life as the president's bodyguard was rendered irrecoverably suspect and dirty. During the murder trial that followed Vargas's suicide, Fortunato responded to the charge that he was a "negro sujo" (dirty black) by detailing a record of service to Vargas and the nation, summing up the defense of his personal honor by declaring "Sou negro de bem"(I am a good black).[20] Long after Vargas was dead and buried, the image of filth would endure, with Vargas's son-in-law, Ernani do Amaral Peixoto, describing Fortunato as a "coarse man, bordering on savage" and as a dimwitted gangster.[21]

Even as Vargas felt compelled to disband his security detail out of the fear that it could only bring more dishonor to the presidency, other, more ostensibly "respectable" figures among Vargas's associates

9.1   *Gregório Fortunato appears alongside Vargas, 1951. As chief of the presidential security detail, Fortunato (left) often appeared in close proximity to Vargas (center left) and high political figures, including Minas Gerais state governor and future president Juscelino Kubitschek (center right) (Photo: CPDOC/FGV, Arquivo Getúlio Vargas).*

were implicated in the moral miasma that enveloped the president. Euvaldo Lodi, a prominent industrialist and longtime president of the Confederação Nacional da Indústria, had to answer to the charge of complicity in Vaz's death.[22] Accusations of collusion in the plot even extended to members of Vargas's immediate family; protesters defaced posters from his son Lutero's congressional campaign, and first lady Darcy found herself obliged to give testimony to the police. As for Vargas himself, the press was circumspect in making the accusation of direct presidential involvement, but implied that he was indirectly responsible for the incident as the guiding figure in a government that had spawned the corruption and dirty dealing that made such ignominious acts possible.[23]

Pro-Vargas forces had a difficult time responding to the respectful coverage of Vaz's funeral and the sordid charges of corruption, demagoguery, and murderous conspiracies. During the earlier campaigns to compel Vargas to resign, the president's defenders responded by impugning their opponents' commitment to democracy and to the welfare of the people/nation. *Getulistas* had argued that what motivated Lacerda, the udenistas, and their allies in the military was a thirst for political power, which had been repeatedly frustrated by their inability to rally the voters to their side in recent democratic contests. As Tancredo Neves, one of Vargas's most prominent and ardent supporters, recalled, "Not once did Getúlio face a democratic opposition. From the outset, what Getúlio faced was a subversive opposition. The men of the UDN, and especially UDN elements in the military, could never accept the defeat that they had suffered [in the 1950 presidential campaign]."[24]

The brazen way in which Vaz had been killed, and the very public way in which the body had been lain to rest, undermined this well-rehearsed defense. With their freshly murdered martyr in tow, Vargas's opponents seized on the moral, rather than merely "political," rationale for outrage. Demonstrations against Vargas could take the form of funeral processions or solemn ceremonies, rather than public disturbances. Vaz's martyrdom allowed Vargas's adversaries to sacralize their opposition to his presidency, and by serendipity it created a "legitimate" basis for a degree of turbulence that, together with the assassination attempt, provided grounds for the military to claim that the Vargas presidency threatened the very stability and security of the nation. Perhaps the low-point in Vargas's fortunes was the moment when Lacerda publicly demanded that the Avenida Presidente Vargas, the centerpiece of urban reforms in Rio during the first Vargas regime and staging ground for some of the largest civic ceremonies of the Estado Novo dictatorship, be renamed for Major Vaz.[25]

The political environment continued to deteriorate for Vargas after Vaz's requiem mass. The investigative commission organized at the Galeão air base aggressively looked towards the presidential palace for evidence related to the "Attempt on Toneleros Street." On August 13, Alcino João de Nascimento, the hapless triggerman, was brought in for questioning; Fortunato fell into the snare two days later. The latter's arrest included the seizure of a large cache of documents linking the president's security forces to the assassination

attempt on Lacerda, influence peddling, and the *jogo do bicho*, a num-
bers-running game popular in Rio.[26] By August 19, several major
dailies in Rio and São Paulo, including Lacerda's *Tribuna da Imprensa*
and the staunchly anti-Vargas *O Estado de São Paulo*, contemplated
Vargas's forcible removal from office.[27] Revelations that Fortunato,
who was undergoing an intensive regime of interrogation that likely
included torture, had coordinated the attack on Lacerda fueled the
ardor with which the paper editors and opposition politicians railed
against Vargas. Even more moderate papers, such as Rio's *O Globo* and
São Paulo's *O Correio da Manhã*, called on Vargas to resolve the crisis
"honorably" by resigning his office. An editorial in the São Paulo daily
appealed, "There is only one solution: Mr. Getúlio Vargas's resignation from the office of the president of the Republic. This would put
him in high standing and assure the survival of his administration."[28]
Striking the tone of the *gente decente* (the respectable class), who
afforded themselves the duty to rise above the missteps of wayward
elites and impressionable popular sectors, these editorials offered the
president the opportunity to take the high ground (*coloca em nível alto*)
without further scandal and social unrest.

Vargas himself was undoubtedly aware that his honor was at stake.
Gustavo Capanema, PSD leader in the Congress, reported that on
the day before his suicide, Vargas confided to him that the question
of political survival was secondary to the question of maintaining the
honor of the presidency and especially personal honor. "My most
important task is to defend my honor," Vargas told his longtime ally.
"I cannot leave [the presidential palace] tarnished. I cannot leave with
the suspicion of impropriety or murder. I cannot leave here in dishonor [*Não posso sair daqui em desonra*]. I must remain for however
long it takes to be able to defend my name." In a eulogy delivered on
the floor of the Congress, Capanema argued that Vargas had
remained true to this pact with honor.[29]

Capanema's quote may have been apocryphal. It does, however,
alert us to the dilemma of honor faced by Vargas: Could a resignation under duress trump the morally unassailable martyrdom of the
fallen air force major? How could Vargas compete with the claim to
restoring national honor that had been seized by the wounded
Lacerda? Where was Vargas to go, honorably, if he were ousted by a
military coup? If the democratizing spirit of the immediate postwar
period protected Vargas from the loss of political rights following the
first military coup to remove him from office in 1945, the prospects

for another wave of political forgiveness seemed remote. Indeed, Vargas's voluntary resignation was unlikely to bring him personal or political honor. Twenty days after Lacerda first contrasted an honorable Vaz to a dishonored Vargas, the president responded to a situation that he memorably described as a "sea of mud" by taking his own life. This was, of course, a high-risk move for Vargas for he thus deprived himself of his one indisputable virtue—his political wits—in his ultimate attempt to reestablish the honor and integrity of his office and person.

Within the limited circle of relatives and advisors who had immediate access to Vargas's body, the death by suicide provoked what must have been a knee-jerk reaction to make the fallen leader into the most respectable of statesmen. Almost immediately after finding Vargas dying in his bedroom, these associates set about preparing the wounded body for a public presentation befitting a president, even if he was a dead president felled by his own hand amidst a crisis of his own making. The scramble for respectability was instantly obvious to the two detectives from Rio's Fourth Police District who arrived at Catete for a forensic investigation within an hour of the president's death. The scene they encountered was quite different from the one found by Caiado de Castro and Alzira Vargas an hour earlier: Upon entering the room, the detectives found Vargas lying in bed, on his back, head facing the ceiling and eyes closed. The hands were calmly clasped together at the stomach. He wore a dark wool suit, dark cashmere vest, and black socks and shoes. A bouquet of white roses lay at the foot of the bed. The tableau was exceedingly orderly, almost as if it had been painted.

As the forensic inspection progressed, the police discovered that the scene was a macabre stagecraft of sorts. The president's body, which had not yet reached rigor mortis, had been carefully prepped for the police and the subsequent appearance in public: the head was held high by a long white cloth placed under the chin. The pallid hands were carefully bound together by a white handkerchief. The suit had been slipped over the pajamas that Vargas had been wearing when he bid goodnight to his butler.

Upon removing the suit, vest, and blood-stained pajama top, the detectives discovered that the gunshot wound had been cleaned and bandaged. Except for a small entry wound near the left nipple, Vargas's chest was free of signs of trauma.[30] The forensic field tests quickly proved that Vargas had taken his own life, committing the ultimate act of self-destruction. Yet the scene staged for the police (and the one which was printed in the few forensic photos released to the press) suggested that Vargas had died peacefully, perhaps due to a sudden hemorrhage. (See Illustrations 9.2, 9.3, and 9.4.)

Outside the presidential palace, things were far less nuanced. News of the suicide spread quickly throughout Rio and the nation, provoking shock and dismay even among Vargas's opponents. Bereaved political allies rushed to the presidential palace, where they confronted a multitude of weeping mourners drawn from all walks of Carioca society. José Américo de Almeida, minister of transportation, recalled the scene after leaving his Copacabana apartment: "I ran to Catete. In every direction, I saw a stupefied populace, greatly concerned, lamenting their idol, a simple man who liked simple things and had the proverbial secret of making friends. Reaching the palace, I broke through the wave, seeing convulsed faces and hearing cries of desperation."[31] Elsewhere in the capital, and in other cities, angry mobs set upon the offices of newspapers and political interests who had denounced Vargas in the scandal-ridden weeks leading up to the suicide.[32] The offices of several multinational corporations as well as the U.S. embassy were vandalized. Carlos Lacerda sought refuge, out of fear that he be caught by the pro-Vargas bands who shouted "Death to Lacerda" in the streets of downtown Rio.

The insults, sacking, and arson visited upon Vargas's foes—real and imagined—were fueled by the suicide letter found at Vargas's bedside. The text of the *Carta Testamento* was read and reread ad nauseum over the airwaves, in the special editions rushed to press, and on the lips of Brazilians from all walks of life. The famous letter narrated Vargas's political career, from the Revolution of 1930 to the populist second administration, stressing the gains of nationalist consolidation, while eliding the authoritarianism, corporatism, and scandal that shaped all of Vargas's career.[33]

Events moved rapidly in the twenty-four hours that followed the release of the *Carta Testamento*. Vice President João Café Filho, Vargas's constitutional successor, worked to assemble a cabinet, while trying to test the political waters among the former president's allies. The waters turned out to be exceedingly cold around Vargas's family, who informed the incoming president that the new government should discard any hopes of organizing an official burial. Well aware of the popular ire directed at interests perceived to have been disloyal to Vargas, Café Filho responded as best he could, maintaining a low

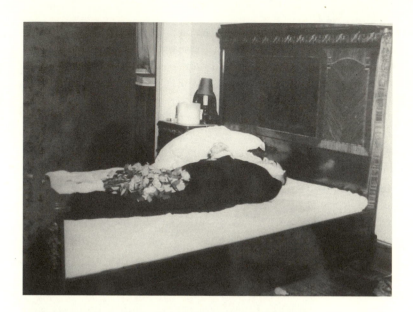

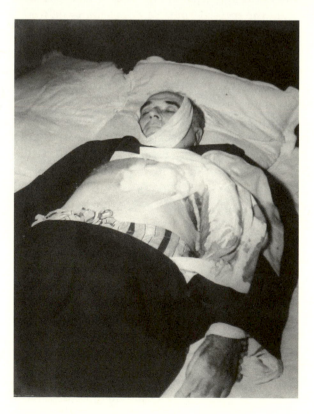

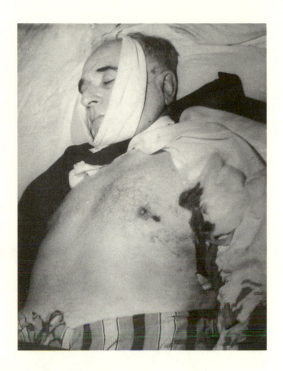

9.2–9.4 *Vargas deceased, Catete Palace, August 24, 1954. Police detectives found Vargas's body laid out in the presidential bedroom, fully dressed and without any outward signs of trauma. Curiously, detective Carlos de Mello Éboli had participated in investigation surrounding the shooting of Carlos Lacerda and Major Rubens Vaz, whose bodies "dueled" with Vargas in August 1954 (Photo: Museu da República-Arquivo Histórico, Arquivo Getúlio Vargas).*

public profile and declaring a period of national mourning.[34] In the meantime, the president's embalmed cadaver was prepared for an impromptu public viewing, arranged downstairs in the presidential palace. The viewing began in the late afternoon and lasted through the early morning of August 25. The somber mood surrounding the president's coffin was punctuated by countless outbursts of grief, as political leaders and ordinary people of various physical and social types fell weak and wept (and were photographed falling weak and weeping, especially with handkerchief pressed to forehead) at the glass-topped coffin containing the former president's body, which had been re-dressed in a dark suit and adorned with a large rosary. The newsweekly *Manchete*, which joined its competitors in publishing richly illustrated special editions on the events of August 24–25, reported that there had been an estimated two thousand cases of fainting during the public viewing.[35] (See Illustrations 9.5 and 9.6.)

After leaving Catete, Vargas's body was led through the streets of Rio to Santos Dumont airport (see Illustration 9.7). From there a civil aeronautics plane (Vargas's family having refused the air force's offer of an official military escort) took the fallen president to Porto Alegre and then on to São Borja, Vargas's hometown, where the body was to be displayed in the town hall. As the plane departed the national capital, the earlier scenes of somber faces and white handkerchiefs raised in the air were replaced by episodes of civil unrest that lasted through

9.5 *Medics aid bereaved mourners, Catete Palace, August 24–25, 1954. More than 2,000 mourners reportedly required medical attention during the impromptu wake held at Catete Palace. Extensive photojournalistic coverage was especially attentive to female mourners, like those depicted here, who were overcome with sorrow. The image of the bereaved women, pitched forward with handkerchief to the face, would be an icon of death and memory for Vargas (Photo: CPDOC/FGV, Arquivo André Carrazzoni).*

9.6 *Wake for Getúlio Vargas, Catete Palace, August 24, 1954. The impromptu wake for Getúlio Vargas, whose embalmed body wore a serene facial expression, dark suit, and rosary, drew thousands of mourners to the presidential palace. This extraordinary opportunity to see the fallen president in death would be possible once again, after a fashion, in November 1960, when the Museum of the Republic opened, allowing visitors to see the room in which Vargas shot himself (Photo: CPDOC/FGV, Arquivo André Carrazzoni).*

the night. The burial, held under a light rain the morning of August 26, was a relatively private affair for such a public figure. Close associates of Vargas in his final days, including former labor minister João Goulart, were present, but longtime associates like Gustavo Capanema remained in Rio to reclaim the moral high ground lost in the previous month's scandals.[36] Members of the incoming Café Filho administration were conspicuously absent. The highlight of the afternoon was an impassioned eulogy delivered by longtime friend and occasional rival Oswaldo Aranha, who drew on Vargas's blood imagery, proclaiming "when they want to write the History of Brazil, whether they like it or not, they will have to wet their pens in the blood of Rio Grande [do Sul], and from this day forward, he who writes and tells the future of Brazil will have to wet his pen in the blood of your heart."[37] (See Illustration 9.8.) Once the flag-draped

9.7   *Cortege for Getúlio Vargas's body, Avenida Beira-Mar, Rio de Janeiro,*
August 25, 1954. Tens of thousands of mourners accompanied the
cortege that carried Vargas's body from the presidential palace to Santos
Dumont Airport, retracing a route that Vargas himself made many
times during the grand civic ceremonies of the dictatorial Estado Novo,
as well as his daily comings and goings as president (Photo:
CPDOC/FGV, Arquivo André Carrazzoni).

coffin was laid to rest in the modest family vault, the crowd of locals, friends, and reporters departed for home. Brazilians were now left with the strange task of making sense of a Brazil without Vargas.

By nightfall on August 26—three weeks after the assassination attempt on Carlos Lacerda—several hundred thousand Brazilians had participated in the funeral corteges, memorial services, and street protests that followed the deaths of Major Vaz and President Vargas. Millions more mourned, prayed, and cried in their homes, schools, and churches. These numbers indicate the truly massive

9.8   *Burial of Getúlio Vargas, São Borja, August 26, 1954. Refusing the
honors of a state burial or monument, Vargas's family and close associates arranged a semipublic burial and memorial service in Vargas's
hometown, São Borja, Rio Grande do Sul. This photo captures the
tumult that surrounded the flag-draped coffin that carried Vargas's
corpse to the family mausoleum, and also presents a "family portrait" of
the Vargas state, including former foreign minister and long-time
friend Oswaldo Aranha (left of coffin, with white hair), former labor
minister and future president João Goulart (to the right of the coffin
with left armed raised), wife Darcy Vargas (in profile, lower right), and
the ubiquitous press (Photo: CPDOC/FGV Arquivo, Oswaldo Aranha).*

nature of funerary culture in August 1954, eclipsing the intense
ardor of funerary rites that surrounded public figures of the Old
Republic.[38] In the three-week duel of dead bodies, Vargas had certainly emerged the winner, as his suicide would play a major role in
determining the course of Brazilian politics during the next decade,
but even Vargas, the consummate politician, could not control his
political afterlife or the ritualized politics of memory that surrounded his largely absent corpse.[39]

The Chronicle of a Death by Suicide

Vargas's dead body—real and staged—turned out to be a complicated site upon which to enact the politics of remembrance for the man and his fabled career. Once the immediate outbursts of grief and indignation had subsided, those who would mourn and memorialize Vargas quickly faced two complications. One was the remoteness of the chosen grave site, which removed Vargas's physical remains from the realm of popular observance. The other complication was the ritual and metaphorical ramifications of a death by suicide. Vargas had never been a particularly religious man, so the denial of a Catholic funeral was not especially insulting. Nevertheless, custom would have deemed it appropriate for a Seventh Day Mass to be celebrated on August 31. Rio's Metropolitan Curia initially announced that, due to the exceptional circumstances, it might allow a mass to be performed for Vargas's soul in the Candelaria Church, even though his suicide clearly violated church doctrine. Thus, Vargas's soul would have been celebrated in the same space from which Major Vaz's soul had departed for heaven. But at the last minute, the curate reversed course and denied use of Rio's most prominent temple. Ignoring ecclesiastical prohibitions, mourners by the tens of thousands descended on La Candelaria, which ironically was located at the terminus of Avenida Presidente Vargas, to hold a popular religious ceremony in the spacious plaza that fronted the church. Men and women sank to their knees on the hard, rough ground of the plaza, burned candles by the thousands, and publicly displayed their devotion. Conducted without the benefit of priests or church approval, the prayers for Vargas's soul were led by lay preachers and simultaneously broadcast over the radio. As had so often happened in the history of religious ritual in Brazil, the official position of the church had been subverted by the popular will.

In many ways, this renegade mass in a very public space was the climax of popular mourning for the departed president. The worshipful throngs that had succeeded in defying the church's prohibition on the celebration of a Seventh Day Mass had not necessarily won the right to control Vargas's embodied memory. To be sure, Vargas had seemingly "willed" his body to the masses in the text of the *Carta Testamento*, promising that, in death, he would belong to the people/nation with whom he had forged an irrevocable compact of mutual need. Whatever his intentions, the choices made by the members of his inner circle in the solitude of the presidential bedroom left nagging questions about whether that promise could be fulfilled. Was Vargas really the Father of the Poor when the humble had to scrape for a brief, if emotional, farewell that did not even win church sanction? What was to become of the populist pact forged by Vargas without Vargas himself? For all its bravado, the suicide note painted a somber and surprisingly accurate portrait of the structural tensions between the drive for industrial development and the yearning for social justice. Given the opposition's control of the mainstream press and much of the incoming government, and the ensuing machinations among anti-getulista factions within the military, we could ask whether popular claims to Vargas's legacy were a means of political empowerment or, at best, artifacts of sentiment.

Furthermore, both Vargas's intimates and his grieving public had to conjure with the implications of a death by suicide. The rather bizarre scene staged by Vargas's aides and family members in the minutes following his death indicates the confusion displayed by even his closest associates over whether this was an honorable or dishonorable way to die.[40] Was Vargas's death that of a martyr whose suffering should be made as palpable as possible? Or was it the result of a desperate, unbalanced, even cowardly gesture whose physical manifestations had to be concealed at all costs? Historian Brian Hall has argued that "for a national hero, suicide is a bad career move."[41] Leaving aside the question of whether Vargas could be considered a hero, his decision to take his own life does not seem, at first, to have been such a bad move. Given the ambiguities of his particular political career—his reputation for opportunism and for sudden reversals in direction—ending his life in such a sincere fashion could be seen as a pointed rejoinder to his relentless critics. And his suicide certainly allowed Vargas to "turn the tables" on his foes and to release momentarily the popular sympathy that had been dammed up by the "sea of mud."[42] Yet both the reaction of Vargas's intimates and the eventual attenuation of popular efforts to memorialize him, indicate a degree of uneasiness with his decision to take his own life.

Indeed, the hours immediately following the suicide were marked by competing demands for political decorum, public access, personal revenge, and instant memorialization of a traumatized corpse. Vargas's family acted with remarkable dispatch to present the dead body in the most dignified light. (One can only imagine the dark comedy of manipulating Vargas's lifeless body in order to pull a wool suit over bloodied pajamas before the police arrived.) Although Darcy Vargas had never been entirely comfortable with the more populist aspects of her husband's political career, she nonetheless understood that it was incumbent on the family to allow the (sanitized) body to be viewed publicly.[43] The impromptu public wake and cortege of August 24–25 fit the bill well. In the same act of allowing a public mourning, the Vargas family rejected the propriety and honors of a state funeral, which proved to be an especially peculiar move since Vargas, after all, had died in office. Vargas's intimates thus deprived the interim president, João Café Filho (who had publicly broken with Vargas just two days earlier by proposing their joint resignation), of the opportunity to assume the mantle of the fallen president. And by denying military officials and other "disloyal" government figures the right to mourn publicly, Vargas's widow and the getulista stalwarts weakened the opposition's attempt to disassociate itself from the implication that Vargas's blood was on their hands. In response to the claims by Lacerda and others that Vargas's death was actually the result of his betrayal by his closest associates, Getúlio's inner circle left no doubt about whom they regarded as bearing the guilt for Vargas's desperate final act.

Victorious in the initial skirmish over assigning meaning to Vargas's cadaver, Vargas's family recognized the narrow limits of the populist ploy. Although the body underwent a highly atypical embalming during the forensic analysis, Darcy Vargas was eager to have her husband's body removed from Rio, where it might incite uncontrollable popular outpourings of grief. Clearly unwelcome within the inner circle of familial mourners, the mainstream press channeled some of the first lady's apprehensions, chronicling with alarm the various "excesses" that disturbed public and private life in the last week of August 1954 (see Illustration 9.9). The press warned of communist agitators who sought to take advantage of the people's grief, urging all Brazilians, no matter what their political affiliations, to resist the temptation to use the brief public appearance of Vargas's body as an opportunity to betray their essentially "peaceful and orderly" nature.[44] In this vein, a photo published in *O Mundo Ilustrado* portrayed an "agitator" trying to "incite *os populares* to assume attitudes incompatible with the nature of the Brazilian people."[45]

If Vargas's body remained somewhat unstable territory upon which to build a lasting image of his long career, the suicide letter found on

9.9   *Riots following Vargas's suicide, Rio de Janeiro, August 24, 1954. The cities of Rio de Janeiro and Porto Alegre were especially hard hit by public unrest in the hours following the broadcast of Vargas's* Carta Testamento. *Popular outrage, which proved especially violent among a diverse cross-section of urban men, was directed at press outlets hostile to Vargas, including the daily O Globo, multinational corporations, and the U. S. embassy. (Photo: CPDOC/FGV, Arquivo André Carrazzoni).*

his dresser provided an unparalleled opportunity to fix the meaning of his life in politics. The *Carta Testamento* is a masterpiece of populist rhetoric.[46] In a classic discursive operation of inclusion and exclusion, Vargas describes his suicide as a sacrifice for the people/nation and portrays the forces that have driven him to this act as alien to the interests of the people/nation. He depicts his (soon-to-be) dead body as an offering to the nation, to the weak and the humble. In contrast, his adversaries are represented as the rich and powerful, willing to betray the nation and collaborate with foreign agents. To be sure, even in this final (conscious) discursive act Vargas is still ambiguous (and ambivalent?) about his ideological inclinations, but he leaves no doubt that he wants the suicide to be seen as an act of sacrifice for the Brazilian "people," who he represents as coterminous with the Brazilian nation.

In his last moments, Vargas appears to be conclusively casting his lot with the poor and unprotected.

But as always, matters were more complicated than that. Despite the compelling circumstances of its authorship, Vargas could not manage the reception of his final appeal to the nation. Now that literary theorists have declared all authors dead (metaphorically speaking), we know that a writer—even one about to take his or her own life—has little control over the meanings that readers give to his or her text. Hence, the *Carta Testamento*, drafted several days in advance of the suicide and probably doctored by Vargas's inner circle, could easily be read as pure artifice. The "unconquerable revolution" described in the first paragraph in fact began as a run-of-the-mill *golpe de estado*. The extraconstitutional machinations that made the first Vargas regime revolutionary (after a fashion) were not even mentioned. The alleged "subterranean campaign of international groups joined with national interests, revolting against the regime of worker's guarantees" obscured a serious lack of fiscal discipline among Vargas's economic planners during the second regime. The entire notion that Vargas was a tireless defender of workers' rights elided his deep commitment to a corpus of labor laws and a labor judicial system that heavily favored state-sanctioned union leaders, while muffling rank-and-file concerns.[47]

The body described in the letter bleeds for the Brazilian people, without mention of the blood spilled by the Brazilian political prisoners tortured in secret cells on the Ilha das Cobras and in the abysmal penal colonies of Ilha Grande and Fernando de Noronha.[48] The Christlike forgiveness that envelops Vargas in the letter's final paragraph hardly corresponded to his actual persona. Vargas was rarely outright capricious, but he was even more rarely beatific. The suicide letter, much like the body left by suicide, could never condense the multiple meanings of Vargas's remarkable political career into a single heroic image. Instead, Brazilians were left with a disquieting, if heartfelt, sense of loss for a vital organ abruptly removed from the national body politic.

Getúlio as a Museum Piece

In the months that followed the president's death, the Brazilian polity experienced mixed success in charting a path without Vargas. On August 25, the PTB adopted a resolution declaring the *Carta Testamento* as the party's guiding ideological statement, seeking to take advantage of the continuing popular sympathy generated by the suicide, but the party soon found it increasingly difficult to manage getulismo without Getúlio.[49] Unionized labor and industrialists won some added maneuverability, but the structural crises of 1954–55 limited their ability to broker a new political pact of development.[50] The fallen president's close advisors, as was the custom among politicians from elite or middle-class families, made their peace with the new Café Filho administration, sought legislative office, or temporarily retired to private life, waiting for an opportunity to return to the national stage. Vargas's popular minister of labor, João Goulart, was particularly eager to reenter the fray.

Intimates of Vargas who hailed from more humble backgrounds faced more uncertain and precarious futures. Gregório Fortunato, Vargas's all-too-loyal bodyguard, was tried and sentenced to twenty-five years in prison. (The term would subsequently be reduced by presidents Juscelino Kubitschek and Goulart, but to no avail, as Fortunato was killed by a prison inmate in 1962.) Vargas's povo, meanwhile, got their first, bitter taste of runaway inflation.

The opposition did not necessarily fare any better. Major Vaz continued to climb through the ranks after death, being posthumously promoted to lieutenant colonel and then again to colonel in 1965 by a military regime looking to invent a heroic past. Carlos Lacerda, after briefly seeking refuge on the Galeão military base, returned to the national political scene first to beat out Lutero Vargas for a congressional seat, and then to become the leader of the UDN in congress and governor of the state of Guanabara. Fixated on dishonoring Vargas even in death, Lacerda's 1954 successful congressional campaign was rhetorically organized around the defeat of the "gregórios."[51] As a party, the UDN did not fare as well as Lacerda. In spite of its hopes of finally seizing the presidential palace emptied of Vargas and his cronies, the UDN suffered losses in the congressional elections of 1954 and the presidential elections of 1955. In 1960, the party opted to support the independent Jânio Quadros, fearing that a straight UDN candidacy would again lead to defeat. Quadros won the presidency, only to resign in an act of political suicide that, ironically, tried to echo Vargas's exit from office. To the intense frustration of its leadership, the UDN remained the minority party for the entire democratic interregnum that lasted from the end of the Second World War until the coup d'etat of April 1, 1964.

As the PTB, unions, industrialists, and the UDN thrashed about, trying to make or break getulismo without Getúlio, another pillar of Vargas's political edifice—the state apparatus—slowly moved to find its place in a world without Vargas. No federal organ had a clear claim to guiding Vargas into the History that the former president charted for himself in his suicide note. Moreover, the rapid timeline that took Vargas from his deathbed to the family grave in São Borja in just over forty-eight hours made it almost impossible for state planners to craft a public space that might effectively embody Vargas in death and life. Monumental public venues closely associated with Vargas's first administration—the modernist Ministry of Education headquarters, Vasco da Gama Stadium, the Avenida Presidente Vargas—had lost much of their allure well before the crises of August 1954. Other recognizable sites closely attached to Vargas's vision of national cultural renewal, such as the historic town of Ouro Preto, had become increasingly delinked from the office and body of the president. Plans to use the death mask molded from Vargas's cadaver on the day of the suicide as a model for a public monument went nowhere.[52] In theory, the cultural "landmarks" most successfully consecrated by the second Vargas regime, including the "national sport" capoeira, commercialized Carnaval music, and the ideology of racial democracy, might have proved useful to memory makers, but these figures would confront the fact that these monuments were less extensions of Vargas's political corpus and more artifacts of a complex interplay of popular, commercial, and international actors vying to articulate a modern Brazilian culture that did not necessarily turn about Vargas and the state.

Thus, the official memory makers loyal to Vargas in the late 1950s, a time when Juscelino Kubitschek's "Fifty Years of Progress in Five" used the recent past mainly as a foil for an ever-brighter future, were faced with a dilemma. The president's dead body was safely buried in a family grave located in a remote border city. The actual instruments of Vargas's death (His Passion, if you will) were in the possession of the Rio police or family members. The death scene was off-limits to public visitation. The difficulties in locating a space to sacralize Vargas's body was somewhat ironic in that Vargas himself had learned that there was much political capital to be gained from attending public rituals enacted at the official tombs of national heroes such as the Duke of Caxias, Dom Pedro II, and the participants of the Inconfidência Mineira.[53]

The institution best prepared to venerate Vargas in death—with or without the support of Vargas's family and political allies and even without direct access to his mortal remains—was the Museu Histórico Nacional (MHN). As early as 1930, the museum had been a beneficiary of Vargas's material and symbolic support to the point that the museum's permanent exhibition included a special gallery honoring Vargas.[54] So, within eight months of Vargas's suicide, the museum director Gustavo Barroso gladly relieved the Café Filho administration of the indelicate burden of what to do with the objects associated with Vargas's death, taking possession of most of the furniture found in Vargas's bedroom.[55] Taking advantage of a reorganization of gallery space already underway in 1954–55, the museum made room in its permanent exhibition for a new gallery, named the Sala 24 de Agosto. The room re-created the mise-en-scène of Vargas's final hours. Barroso later informed the president's daughter Alzira that the museum would guarantee that "everything that evoked Vargas's historic personage as a man of state and a man of sentiment [*sua figura histórica do homem de estado e de homem de coração*] would be religiously preserved."[56] Thus was born the precursor to one of the few sacred spaces in the otherwise secular national museum network.

Unfortunately, there is no photographic record of the MHN's Sala 24 de Agosto. There is, however, evidence that the new gallery and the older Sala Getúlio Vargas became sites where a bereaved public paid homage to their slain hero, even if the central state was unable to create a formal mausoleum. In mid-December 1954, *Última Hora*, the Rio daily that remained ardently loyal to Vargas and trabalhismo throughout the second regime, reported:

> The Sala Getúlio Vargas is one of the most visited at the Museum, for the beauty and rarity of the objects on display, and, most importantly, because the gallery is a true reliquary of memories for the great popular leader who sacrificed himself to the wrath of his enemies. The people will never forget him. He is in the streets and the humble homes, suffering at their side. He is also in the silence of that gallery, which does so well to protect his everlasting presence.[57]

The report then described an unnamed woman bowed before one of the gallery's display cases, crying at the sight of a golden plaque containing a particularly melodramatic statement of Vargas's selfless commitment to Brazil's *humildes* (humble).

The episode reported by *Última Hora* may not be entirely accurate—the MHN's records indicate that the museum was closed to public visitation from June 1954 through March 1955—but this does not discount the fact that interests sympathetic to Vargas worked, in the absence of an official place of mourning, to make monuments out of sites already invested with Vargas's physical and spiritual presence.[58] Even as a fiction, the *Última Hora* article tells us that the Vargas galleries at the National Historical Museum had become sites where the faithful might continue to pitch themselves forward in emotional outbursts, reinscribing a ritual of grief (one that the mainstream press consistently gendered as female) that marked the national body politic in August 1954.

Women and men faithful to Vargas's memory earned a more authentic place to see a reembodied Vargas as a result of Kubitschek's drive to craft a plan of national development that would satisfy the interests that Vargas failed to reconcile in 1954. On March 3, 1960, Kubitschek, wagering heavily on a go-for-broke scheme to complete Brasília before the end of his term, authorized the transformation of the Palácio do Catete into a new federal museum to serve as the official repository for objects related to the history of the republic. In short order, the scene of Vargas's suicide would be a permanent, public part of the new Museu da República (MR).

Months before the museum actually opened, MHN director Josué Montello stated to the press that the transfer of the Sala 24 de Agosto to the MR would be of special interest to the visitor, who now could see the objects in their historical setting. And, once the museum was open to the public, Montello's observations about popular interest in the Vargas bedroom suite proved correct, as the bedroom and its blood-stained mattress became crowd-pleasers. Public visitation to the museum for the last six weeks of 1960 topped 15,000, climbing to a very impressive 156,751 visits during the first full year of operation.[59]

The archival records say relatively little about the ways in which visitors actually experienced the Vargas suite during their visits. The bedroom was certainly a site of curiosity, and for some it may have been a site of ritual pilgrimage. The scene described in *Última Hora* would suggest that the forces most loyal to getulismo looked to museums as sacred spaces to remember Vargas. It seems plausible, then, to think that some visitors to the Museum of the Republic would have been overcome with emotion once they saw the bed where Vargas fell dead, still in his pajamas. (Never mind the fact that few would know that the dead body had been staged for its first public viewing just as the museumified bedroom suite was a stage for remembrance.)

Their need to grieve, however, could not compete with the political polarization that plagued the presidency of João Goulart. The coup of 1964, which ousted Goulart and suspended the political rights of politicians and activists associated with the Left, made it all the more awkward for a state institution such as the MR to give aid to a cult of veneration for a populist such as Vargas. The possibilities for a legitimate public memorial to Vargas's death grew slimmer as the military regime matured into a full-fledged bureaucratic-authoritarian state.[60]

At the Museu da República, the signs of a narrowing politics of memory were subtle, but the astute observer could see that the progressive deterioration of the palace gardens formed a poignant reminder that Catete's role as the seat of the nation's republican memory was unraveling. Throughout the 1960s, museum director Jenny Dreyfus was frustrated in her attempts to secure the funds necessary to recuperate the once-lush museum grounds, which had degenerated into a mass of rat-infested foliage and stagnant, mosquito-filled pools. These unpleasant conditions surely contributed to the steady decline in annual visitation figures, which dropped by half between 1961 and 1967.

More troubling for Dreyfus were rumors that briefly circulated in the press in the first half of 1967 that the Serviço Nacional de Informações (SNI), the military government's internal intelligence unit, and the political police were secretly using the garages behind the Palácio do Catete as interrogation cells. Dreyfus's superiors denied knowledge of any such interrogations, while conceding that the annex to the former presidential palace was under the control of the Ministry of Justice and other state agencies.[61]

The rumors of clandestine interrogations vanished almost as quickly as they surfaced, no doubt influenced by the appointment of a naval officer, Leo Fonseca e Silva, to oversee the Museum of the Republic staff. With the support of Fonseca e Silva, the MR cultivated closer relationships with the military state, inaugurating a gallery to honor General Humberto Castelo Branco, author of the April 1964 coup. More ominously, the rising tide of press censorship, intimidation, and direct repression of dissent that culminated in the imposition of Institutional Act 5 (December 1968) made it highly unlikely that the mainstream press would report on possible human rights violations on the museum premises. The psychic and cultural damage was, nonetheless, done. By 1969, the public would find it difficult to count on the Museu da República as a site for patriotic pilgrimage or diversion, even if they were able to see the curious bloodstains on Vargas's mattress (which, magically, resisted all purported attempts at cleaning). The combination of new admission fees to the museum, a small arson attempt resulting in the temporary closure of the Sala Getúlio Vargas, and labor disputes that closed the entire museum for a time pushed Vargas's death scene near the edge of oblivion.

In short, the museum galleries dedicated to Getúlio Vargas at the Museu Histórico Nacional and the Museu da República gained multiple, contradictory meanings. Run out of the presidential palace in 1954, Getúlio remained a resident of the Casa do Brasil, as the Museu Histórico fancied itself, into the late 1950s. The conversion of the Palácio do Catete into a public museum stoked, for a time, public interest in another of Getúlio's reconstituted state homes. The interest in the Vargas suite at the MR was just as much driven by respect and duty to the fallen leader as by puerile voyeurism. But, in time, the visit to Catete grew bittersweet, as the visitor saw a decaying edifice that symbolized the shifts in Brazil's political and cultural capital. Even with the attraction of Vargas's deathbed, the museum offered diminished opportunities for emotional connection. To this melancholic mood we must add the psychological discomfort caused by the nagging rumors, never factually substantiated, yet eminently plausible, that Catete had become a node in a growing network of state offices used for the systematic violation of political and human rights. On dates such as April 19 (Vargas's birthday), May 1, and August 24 (Vargas's death date), Getúlio's life and death could continue to frame a certain politics of public commemoration, albeit quietly. The surrogate tomb erected in the Museu da República, however, grew increasingly uninviting, and for some, symbolic of the nation's descent into a kind of politics of terror that was widely regarded as originating, ironically, in the first Vargas regime.

Bodies of Evidence

The declining popularity of the Vargas exhibit in the Museu da República mirrored both the sorry state of republican ideals under the military and the disavowal of getulismo by both the Right and the Left. In the eyes of the military and its supporters Vargas's politics exemplified the demagoguery and corruption that the National Security State had been designed and imposed to combat, especially with the hardening of the dictatorship after 1968. The Vargas who inhabited this right-wing imaginary was the elected populist president of the early 1950s whose nationalist appeals to the povo and whose alliances with the labor Left had supposedly set Brazil on a course the Right regarded as leading ineluctably to a disastrous revolutionary conflagration (had the armed forces not intervened). Ironically, the rebuff by the Right did nothing to endear Vargas to the Left. On the contrary, by the late 1960s scholars and intellectuals on the Left in Brazil identified Vargas as responsible for the authoritarian/corporatist policies that had led (also ineluctably) to the military regime; more specifically, prominent intellectuals such as Francisco Weffort claimed that Vargas's authoritarian-populist politics had produced a labor movement whose leadership was beholden to the state and thus limited workers' capacity for militant action.[62] In this left-wing imaginary, Vargas was forever the dictator of the Estado Novo, the authoritarian figure with vaguely fascist leanings who manipulated the labor movement to his own political advantage. Furthermore, this view of Vargas did not remain confined to academic circles; among the founding principles of the Workers' Party was a rejection of the formal ties between labor and the state that had originated under the first Vargas regime.[63]

Thus, Vargas remained a figure of multiple meanings but none of them had significant political appeal during the era of the military dictatorship. Indeed, Vargas's family may have been the only group actively interested in amplifying the memory of the clan's political patriarch. In this regard, Vargas's devoted daughter, Alzira Vargas do Amaral Peixoto, played a prominent role in making an honorable political figure out of Vargas. Daughter to a man who styled himself to be the "father" of the Brazilian people and to a matrician first lady, the possibilities for Alzira to assert political agency would appear to have been limited to acts associated with conventional feminine gender roles. Alzira herself tells us that her father's vision of appropriate womanly knowledge could be reduced to mastery of typing, driving, and speaking English, semaphores for a modern, but domesticated femininity.[64] The manly roguery of the political sphere was, apparently, beyond the pale for a female member of a respectable political clan. Unlike many of her male relatives, Alzira neither joined a party nor sought elected office, and when she was publicly associated with established political parties, her name was attached to feminized labels like "nanny of the PTB" and "mother of the PSD."[65] Thus, her "public" political performance during the dramatic events of August 24, supervising the cleansing of Vargas's wounds and stoically standing by her father's coffin, could be read as honorable and indispensable feminized forays into the otherwise dangerous world of male body politics.

Truth be told, Alzira was a hard-nosed political actor who served as a close confidant to her father throughout his two presidencies.[66] Although she was quite capable of playing the "appropriate" role as loyal daughter and faithful and demure wife to politician-diplomat Ernani Amaral Peixoto, Alzira was intimate with the innermost workings of the Vargas state. Her physical presence within the state body began in the early days of the Revolution of 1930 and lasted until the fateful ministerial meeting, held at 3:00 A.M. on August 24, 1954, during which Alzira advised her father on how to respond to the collapse of military support. Alzira was, then, well positioned to negotiate the proper insertion of the late president into the Brazilian public's fickle appetites for a memory of Vargas.

In the preface to her memoirs of the first Vargas regime, *Getúlio Vargas, Meu Pai* (*Getúlio Vargas, My Father*), "Alzirinha" positioned herself as the family gatekeeper to Vargas's memory.[67] By the 1970s, Alzira had decided to take her memorial work to a more public forum, organizing her father's voluminous papers and preparing them for transfer to a public archive. The fortunate recipient was the Centro de Pesquisa de Documentação da História Contemporânea do Brasil (CPDOC), a semiprivate research center established in 1973 within Rio's Fundação Getúlio Vargas. The Getúlio Vargas archive organized at CPDOC opened up entirely new ways of knowing Vargas, knowledge based upon the ever-growing body of archival materials once handled, in some way, by Vargas and his intimates. Alzira, the Vargas family's "guardian of memory," remained generous to CPDOC and public institutions dedicated to preserving and promoting Vargas studies until her death in 1992. A reinvigorated Museu da República even won the bloodied pajamas worn by Vargas on the night of his suicide. Alzira's daughter, Celina Vargas do Amaral Peixoto, continued the family tradition of rememorializing Vargas through a series of donations made to CPDOC, the Museu da República, and the city of Volta Redonda in the 1990s.[68]

The philanthropic interest exhibited by Vargas's family in institutions dedicated to memory proved to be the perfect counterbalance to the physical atrophy of the Vargas state (and, of course, his long-dead body). As a political body, Vargas was reborn in the CPDOC archives, gaining vitality in direct relationship to the temporal distance from the fateful events of August 1954. Following the example set by Alzira (and brokered by Celina, who served as director of CPDOC and the National Archives), the families of many of Vargas's most important interlocutors—Gustavo Capanema, Oswaldo Aranha, and Alexandre Marcondes Filho, just to name a few—made large donations of documents, photographs, and print publications, many of them official papers that made their way into the "personal" archives. The archival collections assembled after the initial donation of Vargas's archive have turned CPDOC into the single-most important research center for post-1930 Brazilian historical studies. The scholarship produced by the CPDOC research staff pioneered new standards in Brazilian political and intellectual (and later social, cultural, and business) history as well as archive management. Given the dearth of solid documentation in official archival repositories, many topics in the history of the Vargas era can *only* be researched at CPDOC.

The Vargas family, who denied Café Filho the privilege of staging a state funeral, proved to be quite generous to researchers, both academic and amateur, as well as to educators and documentary filmmakers who sought out Vargas in death. CPDOC became, in a sense, a kind of surrogate memory site for Vargas. The fact that the site has precious few images of Vargas on permanent display; that the mechanisms to enforce a "standard" interpretation of Vargas are very weak; and, that the majority of the visitors are historians and social scientists toting pen-and-paper or laptop computers rather than white handkerchiefs readied for the unexpected emotional outburst, cannot discount the fact that the floors occupied by CPDOC in Oscar Niemeyer's edifice on Rio's Praia de Botafogo are a site for seeing, touching, and scrutinizing the *restos mortais* of Vargas and his era.

The reembodied access to Vargas's enigmatic mind and contradictory legacy proves to be all the more significant at a time when, according to former president Fernando Henrique Cardoso, "the Vargas era is over."[69] The Brazilian and international scholarly community continue to reinvest their interests in Vargas as a symbol if not a person. An enduring, if sardonic, popular interest in Vargas also suggests that Vargas will remain with Brazilians. The popularity of Rubem Fonseca's novel *Agosto* (1990) and the TV Globo miniseries of the same name brought the events of August 1954 into the libraries and living rooms of millions of Brazilians.[70] The theatrical reenactment of the final weeks of Vargas's life, staged within the Museu da República in the last quarter of 1992 (amid the popular and legislative battle to have president Fernando Collor de Mello removed from office for corruption), brought the public into the very spaces through which Vargas passed during the victories of his first administration and the crises of his last days.

Finally, the 1997 reinstallation of the permanent exhibition of the Museu da República, named *A Ventura Republicana* (the Republican [Ad]Venture), brought Vargas's bedroom back into the museumgoers' gaze. Spartanly decorated with the same furniture used by the president-populist-dictator during his second administration, the bedroom is the closest that the iconoclastic reinstallation comes to an emotional climax.[71] Together, *A Ventura Republicana* and *Eu Getúlio*, a museographic valentine organized in 1999 by the Museu da República in response to a large donation from Celina Vargas do Amaral Peixoto, de- and reconstructs Vargas for generations of Brazilians who were not alive when he dominated the national political scene. For these Brazilians, Vargas's inimitable contradictions and ambiguities are not necessarily so hard to reconcile.[72] They are, after all, part of the Brazilian body politic to which these museum visits belong.

Conclusion

Sometimes presented as Shakespearean in drama, Vargas's final moments play out more like a Greek tragedy: a well-known, yet aging, patriarch, mired in a moral quagmire brought on by arrogance, willful ignorance, and deceitful associates returns to the stage one last time to make an impassioned appeal to declare his convictions before the audience. Covered in blood drawn from a self-inflicted wound, the protagonist recounts the trials and tribulations of duty and sacrifice, honor and nation.[73] He declares his intention to leave life and enter History. The audience recognizes the leader for his demagogic sleights of hand, yet is compelled to look on in horror as the final death scene plays itself out. The death is, indeed, tragic, full of chest-beating, accusations, and self-recrimination. For a select few, the loss of status, material possessions, and even life are at stake. Eulogies are hastily thrown together and cathartic rituals enacted. But the perverse twist to this Brazilian tragedy is that Vargas's death did not end in a burial service on sacred ground in which the collective was able to regather to mourn the dead and bid him fortune in the afterlife. No deus ex machina restored order on or after August 24. Instead, political and moral instability dogged those who tried to assume, or reject, the personal and institutional mantles of the fallen president.

In the epilogue to our tragedy, an unscripted plot of mourning and memorial, in which closure and catharsis would remain incomplete, rules the day. This unconventional script of postdeath was not unlike Vargas's unconventional political career—full of contradictions, oscillating between affection and cruelty, unbounded hope and cynical calculation, and fused together by a deep emotional commitment to an organic Brazilian body politic that Vargas himself knew to be more dream than reality.

In closing, we return, one last time, to the mise-en-scène of Vargas's death suite, now found in the permanent exhibition of the Museu da República (see Illustration 9.10). Vargas's bedroom furniture, the blood-stained pajamas, and the infamous 32-calibre bullet can be seen as we would want them to be—isolated and untouchable, but tantalizingly close. One can almost imagine seeing Vargas lying on the bed, dressed in the same suit and vest that he "wore" for the police detectives who arrived around 9:30 on the morning of August 24, 1954. As we take one last glimpse into the room, viewed through flowing curtains added during the 1996 reinstallation, we come to a small room next to Vargas's bedroom; it is the last gallery of the exhibition. An old man, cinematographically projected onto a single narrow bed, restlessly dreams of a national history seen in the hundreds of photographs and film clips projected onto a large white sheet behind the bed. The images are constantly being consumed by flames, only to regenerate for the next audience. *Vargas morto*, Vargas in death, is part of this national history, constantly consumed by destructive flames, yet immune to actual destruction. As the museum visitors descend the stairs and exit into the now-vibrant museum gardens, they are left to ponder how and why this history endures as a museum exhibit and as a point of reference in the hurly-burly of everyday Brazilian political life.

9.10 *Vargas's bedroom suite, Museu da República. The scene of Vargas's death has been a museum exhibit since 1958. The installation attracted widespread visitor interest in the early 1960s before fading into obscurity for much of the military dictatorship. Today, the president's austere bedroom suite remains largely the same as it did in 1966, with the exception of the two display cases, one containing the blood-stained pajama top worn on August 24, 1954, and the other containing the fatal bullet recovered from Vargas's chest, now completing the mise-en-scène (Photo: Visitor Guide to the Museu da República, 1966).*

Notes

1. Getúlio's final hours have been discussed in minute detail. Journalist Araken Távora offers a minute-by-minute account of August 24–25 in his *O dia em que Vargas morreu* (Rio de Janeiro: Repórter, 1966). For other chronicles of the "Crisis of 1954," see Hélio Silva, *1954: Um Tiro no Coração* (Rio de Janeiro: Editora Três, 1978); Carlos Heitor Cony, *Quem Matou Vargas* (Rio de Janeiro: Edições Bloch,

1974); and Claudio Lacerda, *Uma crise de agosto: O atentado da rua Toneleros* (Rio de Janeiro: Nova Fronteira, 1994).

2. Getúlio Vargas, *Diário* (Rio de Janeiro: Siciliano/Editora da FGV, 1995), 209.

3. A still-valuable narrative of Vargas's political career in the context of changing Brazilian political structures can be found in Thomas E. Skidmore, *Politics in Brazil: An Experiment in Democracy, 1930–1964* (Oxford: Oxford University Press, 1967). A more recent synthesis of Vargas's political life and legacy is found in Robert Levine, *Father of the Poor? Vargas and his Era* (New York: Cambridge University Press, 1998).

4. John D. French, "The Populist Gamble of Getúlio Vargas in 1945: Political and Ideological Transitions in Brazil," in *Latin America in the 1940s: War and Postwar Transitions*, ed. David Rock (Berkeley: University of California Press, 1994), 141–65.

5. The development of the Brazilian middle class is treated in Brian Owensby, *Intimate Ironies: Modernity and the Making of Middle-Class Lives in Brazil* (Stanford, Calif.: Stanford University Press, 1999).

6. On the different intellectuals and artists who participated in the first Vargas regime, see Daryle Williams, *Culture Wars in Brazil: The First Vargas Regime, 1930–1945* (Durham, NC: Duke University Press, 2001); on the incident involving Olga Benario Prestes, the wife of communist leader Luíz Carlos Prestes, see Fernando Morais, *Olga* (São Paulo: Alfa-Omega, 1985).

7. Barbara Weinstein, *For Social Peace in Brazil: Industrialists and the Remaking of the Working Class in São Paulo, 1920–1964* (Chapel Hill: University of North Carolina Press, 1996), 280.

8. On the crises of the era, see Maria Celina Soares d'Araújo, *O Segundo Governo Vargas* (Rio de Janeiro: Zahar, 1982); and Maria Victória de Mesquita Benevides, *O PTB e o Trabalhismo* (São Paulo: Brasiliense, 1989). On the Brazilian Communist Party and the second Vargas government, see Flávia Millena Biroli, "A nação diante do suicídio de Vargas: Uma análise do discurso do PCB," MA thesis, Unicamp, 1999.

9. For a comparison between Juan Perón, a full-fledged populist, and Vargas's more limited populist appeal, see Ernesto Laclau, "Toward a Theory of Populism," in his *Politics and Ideology of Marxist Theory* (London: Verso, 1977), 143–98; and Maria Helena R. Capelato, *Multidões em Cena: Propaganda Política no Varguismo e no Peronismo* (Campinas: Papirus, 1998).

10. On Lacerda as a middle-class crusader-cum-populist, see Bryan McCann, "Carlos Lacerda: The Rise and Fall of a Middle-Class

Populist in 1950s Brazil," *Hispanic American Historical Review* 83, no. 4 (November 2003): 661–96.

11. For a brief but fascinating discussion of the press' attempt to conflate its campaign with "public opinion," see Flávia M. Biroli, "Verdade, opinião e política: Um ensaio sobre imprensa e democracia no Brasil dos anos 50" (unpublished ms.).

12. For a highly sympathetic biography of Fortunato, see José Louzeiro, *O anjo de fidelidade (a história sincera de Gregório Fortunato na Era Vargas)* (Rio de Janeiro: Francisco Alves, 2000).

13. John W. F. Dulles, *Carlos Lacerda, Brazilian Crusader*, vol. 1 (Austin: University of Texas Press, 1991), 157–58.

14. Ibid., 159.

15. *Getúlio, Uma História Oral*, Valentina da Rocha Lima, ed. (Rio de Janeiro: Editora Record, 1986), 190. Similarly, Amaral Peixoto recalled "It [the UDN] now had a cadaver at its disposal, and we know perfectly well how this shocks public opinion" (191).

16. See, for example, *O Mundo Ilustrado* (Rio de Janeiro), 18 August 1954, 81. Though the photographs mainly portrayed peaceful demonstrators and mourners, or family photos of Vaz in happier days, the magazine did include one shot of protesters setting fire to a PTB car near La Candelaria.

17. The blackness of Fortunato and other principals of the botched assassination attempt is an unmistakable leitmotif in contemporaneous and retrospective accounts of August 1954. This close association between blackness, criminality, and corruption strongly suggests how highly racist language could enter national political discourse even in the heyday of the ideology of racial democracy.

18. José Loureiro strongly suggests that it was Benjamin Vargas who masterminded most of the corrupt dealings in the presidential palace.

19. McCann, "Carlos Lacerda," 690.

20. Louzeiro, *O anjo de fidelidade*, 420–21; The *negro sujo* episode might be more accurately translated as a Fortunato's claim to being a "Good Negro" against the insult of being called a "Dirty Nigger."

21. Aspásia Camargo, Lucia Hippolito, et al. *Artes da Política: Diálogo com Amaral Peixoto* (Rio de Janeiro: Nova Fronteira, 1986), 368–72.

22. On Lodi's role as a mediator between the Vargas regime and industrialist interests, see Weinstein, *For Social Peace in Brazil*, 99–100.

23. See, for example, "Indignação, Lágrimas e Revolta durante o Sepultamento do Major Assassinado no Covarde Atentado contra Carlos Lacerda," *Folha da Noite* (São Paulo), 6 August 1954, 7.

24. *Getúlio, Uma História Oral*, 178. Tancredo Neves was himself a future distinguished dead body: indirectly elected to be the first civilian president following the twenty-one-year military dictatorship (1964–85), he died of stomach cancer before he was able to take office. His death set off an eruption of national grief and mourning.

25. *Folha da Tarde* (Porto Alegre), (24 August 1954), 10.

26. Gustavo Borges, one of the principals of the República do Galeão, chronicled the tribunal's inner workings in *Getúlio e o mar de lama: A verdade sobre 1954* (Rio de Janeiro: Editora Lacerda, 2001).

27. Alzira Alves de Abreu and Fernando Lattman-Weltman, "Fechando o cerco: a imprensa e a crise de agosto de 1954," in *Vargas e a crise dos anos 50*, org. Angela Maria de Castro Gomes (Rio de Janeiro: Relume Dumará, 1994), 31–35.

28. Cited in Biroli, "Verdade, opinião e política," 6.

29. Centro de Pesquisa e Documentação da História Contemporânea do Brasil/Fundação Getúlio Vargas (Rio), Arquivo Gustavo Capanema [hereafter CPDOC-GC] k 1954.04.05 Doc. III-41. Hand-corrected manuscript version of Capanema's eulogy, delivered on the floor of the Chamber of Deputies, 25 August 1954.

30. Museu da República-Arquivo Histórico, Arquivo Getúlio Vargas, Documentos Complementares GV 954.08.24 "Guia para o Necrotério" Departamento Federal de Segurança Pública do Instituto Médico Legal, 24 August 1954.

31. José Americo de Almeida, *Ocasos de sangue* (Rio de Janeiro: José Olympio, 1954), 36.

32. Jorge Luis Ferreira, "O carnaval da tristeza: os motins urbanos do 24 de agosto," in *Vargas e a crise dos anos 50*, org. Angela Maria de Castro Gomes (Rio de Janeiro: Relume Dumará, 1994), 61–96.

33. The original text of the *Carta Testamento*, first read on Radio Nacional before 10:00 A.M. on 24 August 1954, has been reproduced in the on-line version of the *Dicionário Histórico-Biográfico Brasileiro*, available at: <http://www.cpdoc.fgv.br/>. English translations appear in a number of sources, including *The Brazil Reader: History, Culture, Politics*, ed. Robert M. Levine and John J. Crocitti (Durham, NC: Duke University Press, 1999), 222–24.

34. Café Filho later described the tricky situation: "No other man in Brazil, besides me, had assumed the presidency of the Republic under such painful and aggressive circumstances. Within Catete, the president was dead by his own hand. Outside, the choral wail of thousands of people. . . . The manifestation of the hostility of the

Vargas family, who refused all government role in Getúlio's funeral
. . . the fires and tumults . . . all left me feeling without guarantees."
See *Do Sindicato ao Catete: memórias políticas e confissões humanas*, vol.
1 (Rio de Janeiro: José Olympio, 1966), 354–56.

35. Arlindo Silva text in *Manchete* no. 25 (August 1954).

36. CPDOC-GCk 1954.04.05 Doc. III-41.

37. Aranha's speech, spoken with the tenderness of a longtime friend and
the rhetorical flourish of a would-be populist, is reprinted in Távora,
O dia em que Vargas morreu, 113–19.

38. On funerals of "national heroes" as a centerpiece of Brazilian civic
culture during the First Republic (1889–1930), see Geraldo Mártires
Coelho, *O Brilho da Supernova: A Morte Bela de Carlos Gomes* (Rio de
Janeiro: Agir, 1995); and João Felipe Gonçalves, "Enterrando Rui
Barbosa: Um Estudo de Caso da Construção Fúnebre de Heróis
Nacionais na Primeira República," *Estudos Históricos* 25 (2000–2001):
135–61.

39. On the (successful) use of Vargas's memory by subsequent presiden-
tial candidates, see *Getúlio, Uma História Oral*, 262. According to
Tancredo Neves, "Getúlio's suicide really made the career of
Juscelino [Kubitschek]. Jango's [Goulart] as well. Even Jânio's
[Quadros]. Jânio exploited Getúlio more than anybody."

40. For retrospective comments by political allies and family members
on Vargas's decision to commit suicide, see *Getúlio, Uma História
Oral*, 261–68. His daughter Alzira disputes the claim that her father
was a "born suicide" (*um suicida nato*) and insists that he regarded suicide under most circumstances to be "uma verdadeira covardia," a
true act of cowardice (263).

41. Brian Hall, "Undaunted Craziness," *New York Times*, 21 January
2003, 27.

42. Several of the commentators cited above used the specific phrase
"virou a mesa." See, for example, Antonio Balbino's testimony, *Getúlio,
Uma História Oral*, 263.

43. For a discussion of Darcy as a sort of "anti-Evita," see Barbara
Weinstein, "Getúlio Vargas, *Diário*, 1937/1942," *Luso-Brazilian Review*
34, no. 2 (winter 1997): 137–41.

44. Ferreira, "O carnaval da tristeza," 62.

45. *O Mundo Ilustrado*, 1 September 1954, 9.

46. The authenticity of Vargas's suicide note is one of the great who-
dunits in Brazilian history. Oral histories, corroborated by archival
evidence, indicate that Vargas crafted several good-bye messages, of

various levels of drama and blood, in his last weeks in office. Vargas's speechwriter, José Soares Macedo Filho, likely played a role in crafting the final, hyperdramatic, suicide note. Vargas's family and close associates have consistently maintained that the *Carta Testamento* was entirely authored by Vargas. Vargas detractors have claimed that the letter was seriously altered, or outright fabricated, for political gain. If the letter was indeed altered or invented on August 24, the work was done exceedingly quickly and well, as the text was widely circulating on the radio shortly after Vargas was found dead. For the transcription of two of Vargas's *Carta Testamentos*, see *As Instituições Brasileiras da Era Vargas*, ed. Maria Celina D'Araújo (Rio de Janeiro: EdUERJ/Editora da FGV, 1999), 161.

47. This is *not* to endorse the widely discredited view that the labor legislation embodied in the *Consolidação das Leis do Trabalho* (CLT) was little more than an instrument of social control. For an excellent discussion of this question, see John D. French, "Drowning in Laws but Starving (for Justice?): Brazilian Labor Law and the Workers' Quest to Realize the Imaginary," *Political Power and Social Theory* 12 (1998): 181–218.

48. For the darker side of the Vargas regime, see novelist Graciliano Ramos's posthumously published memoir of his incarceration on Ilha Grande, *Memórias do Cárcere* (Rio de Janeiro: José Olympio, 1953); see also Elizabeth Cancelli, *O Mundo da Violência: A Polícia da Era Vargas* (Brasília: Editora Universidade de Brasília, 1993).

49. Ângela Maria de Castro Gomes, "Trabalhismo e democracia: o PTB sem Vargas," in *Vargas e a crise dos anos 50*, org. Angela Maria de Castro Gomes (Rio de Janeiro: Relume Dumará, 1994), 133–60.

50. Maria Antonieta P. Leopoldi, "O difícil caminho do meio: Estado, burgesia, e industrialização no segundo governo Vargas (1951–1954); see also Weinstein, *For Social Peace in Brazil*, 294–97.

51. Dulles, *Carlos Lacerda*, 171.

52. A full-page photo of the death mask, molded by Museu Nacional de Belas Artes sculptor Flori Gama, appeared in the inside cover of *O Mundo Ilustrado*, 1 September 1954, 2.

53. Vargas was a regular at the annual Dia do Soldado ceremonies, held at the equestrian statue to the Duke of Caxias (Rio's Largo do Machado, before being moved to the front of the Ministry of War building on Avenida Presidente Vargas). During the Estado Novo, Vargas was also a regular attendee at the graveside ceremonies to honor the loyalist troops killed in the 1935 uprising known as the

Intentona Comunista. The tomb for Emperor Pedro II and wife Christina, inaugurated at the Catedral Imperial in Petrópolis in 1939, and the ultramodernist Panteão dos Inconfidentes, installed in the Museu da Inconfidência in 1942, were also funerary monuments well known to Vargas.

54. On the long, intimate ties between the Museu Histórico Nacional and Vargas, see Daryle Williams, "Sobre patronos, heróis, e visitantes: O Museu Histórico Nacional, 1930–1960," *Anais do Museu Histórico Nacional* 29 (1997): 141–86.

55. Museu Histórico Nacional, Rio de Janeiro-Setor do Controle do Patrimônio [hereafter MHN-SCP] 3/55 Dec. 1 Letter from Cincinato Galvão Ferreira to Gustavo Barroso that accompanied transfer of Vargas's bedroom suite, 15 June 1955.

56. MHN-SCP 5/59 Doc. 2 Letter from Gustavo Barroso to Alzira Vargas, 21 July 1959.

57. Museu Histórico Nacional, Rio de Janeiro-Arquivo Histórico, Arquivo Gustavo Barroso GB avl 15 Série V, *Última Hora*, 13 December 1954.

58. Museu Histórico Nacional, Rio de Janeiro-Arquivo Permanente [hereafter MHN-AP] *Relatório do Museu Histórico Nacional*, 1955.

59. *Anuário Estatístico do Brasil*, 1936–1995.

60. To quote Tancredo Neves one more time, he claimed that "Vargas has still not been adequately studied because the Revolution of '64 had an anti-varguista, anti-Getúlio spirit. Perhaps here the explanation is Freudian, a sort of repression, a resentment, a frustration over Vargas. [The revolution sought] a total rupture with Varguismo. . . . As if the history of nations didn't occur through sedimentation, as if it didn't occur through a process of continuity" (*Getúlio, Uma História Oral*, 263).

61. MHN-AP/Recortes *Jornal do Brasil* (Rio), 5 May 1967.

62. Francisco Weffort, "Participação e Conflito Industrial: Contagem e Osasco, 1968," *Caderno do CEBRAP* 3 (1972).

63. On the Partido dos Trabalhadores's break with the corporatist politics of Vargas and the PTB, see Margaret Keck, *The Workers' Party and Democratization in Brazil* (New Haven, CT: Yale University Press, 1992). For a study that emphasizes continuities between getulismo and the PT, see Isabel Ribeiro de Oliveira, *Trabalho e Política: As Origens do Partido dos Trabalhadores* (Petrópolis: Vozes, 1988).

64. Ângela de Castro Gomes, "A guardiã da memória," *Acervo: Revista do Arquivo Nacional* 9, nos. 1–2 (1996): 22.

65. Castro Gomes, "A guardiã da memória," 26–27.

66. On Alzira's role in the first Vargas regime, see Weinstein, "Getúlio Vargas, *Diário*," 137–41.

67. Alzira Vargas do Amaral Peixoto, *Getúlio Vargas, Meu Pai* (Rio de Janeiro: Globo, 1960).

68. On Celina Vargas do Amaral Peixoto's relationship to the memory of Vargas, see her introduction to Vargas's, *Diário*, 1:vii–xiii. On the Memorial in Volta Redonda (the steel town that was the apotheosis of Vargas's developmental nationalism), inaugurated in 1992 and later augmented by Celina's donations, visit: <*http://www.portalvr.com/portal/cultura/memorial/index.php*>.

69. The repeated statements by then-president Cardoso that the Vargas era had ended provoked a significant popular and academic response. The public discussion included a great deal of vocalized wondering about the possible meanings of Cardoso's statement, given the omnipresence of the Vargas state within the interstices of national and everyday life in Brazil, as well as the widespread indifference to Vargas as a palpable national legacy. For a discussion of the persistence of the Vargas state, see Helena Bomeny, "Três Decretos e um Ministério: A Propósito da Educação no Estado Novo," in *Repensando o Estado Novo*, org. Dulce Pandolfi (Rio de Janeiro: Editora da FGV, 1999), 137–66.

70. On comparisons between the novel, the Globo miniseries, and the actual events of August 1954, see Mônica Almeida Kornis, "Agosto e agostos: a história na mídia," in *Vargas e a crise dos anos 50*, org. Angela Maria de Castro Gomes (Rio de Janeiro: Relume Dumará, 1994), 97–112.

71. Curated by the well-known designer Gisela Magalhães, *A Ventura Republicana* is a misguided gesture toward a re/de-sacralizaton of the national historical memory. The installation is, nonetheless, well worth the visit. Visit: <*http://www.museudarepublica.org.br/Indice/ndx-exposicoes.html*>.

72. *Eu, Getúlio* (Rio de Janeiro: Museu da República, 1999).

73. The idea that he was the only individual capable of keeping the Brazilian nation together, and the burden this imposed on him, was a long-standing theme in Vargas's private writings. See Weinstein, "Getúlio Vargas, *Diário*," 137–41.

Chapter Ten

San Ernesto de la Higuera:

The Resurrection of Che Guevara

Paul J. Dosal

I n every one of the thirty-five houses in La Higuera, Bolivia, there is some sort of shrine dedicated to Che Guevara. An old photograph surrounded by candles or an aging newspaper reminds the residents of the legendary *comandante* who died in their town. Every October 8 the people pay homage to San Ernesto de la Higuera, one of two patron saints of the town. The other one, the Virgin of Guadalupe, is honored too, but there are few shrines dedicated to her. Her festival lacks the energy and enthusiasm that erupts on the day of San Ernesto, when the people pull out their Che memorabilia and regale foreign pilgrims with their stories of the day they met Che, who was about to give his life for them. With ¡Che vive! graffiti splashed on adobe walls throughout the village, there is little doubt that residents of La Higuera revere San Ernesto more than the Indian virgin who appeared in Mexico nearly five hundred years ago.[1]

On October 8, 1997, the thirtieth anniversary of Che's capture, pilgrims from around the world flocked to the town to pay their respects to San Ernesto. One group of disciples organized the Vallegrande Che Festival, promoted as a "World Encounter for Solidarity, Freedom, and Justice," October 5 through 11, 1997. "While such values still subsist, we can envision a better future for persons, people, and nations toward the third millennium." In a series of artistic and cultural events the pilgrims intended "to leave testimony of our worries, think about the destiny of human kind and proclaim our hopes." The events included a concert by Silvio Rodríguez, movies about "El Che," books about "El Che," art exhibits, and a theatrical performance. Visitors

317

could hike along "El Che Route," retracing the steps that led Che to his capture and execution. In the minds of this particular millenarian group, Che had died leading "a little group of dreamers that died searching for liberation and change." To them, Vallegrande symbolized the place where Che "signed with his blood the utopia of the New Man."[2]

Only two thousand pilgrims, including Danielle Mitterand, widow of former French president Francois Mitterand, attended the Vallegrande festival. Silvio Rodríguez, revolutionary Cuba's acclaimed musician, apparently did not attend, though he gave a concert for El Che in Buenos Aires. Perhaps it takes generations for a saint to attract a multitude. Yet the faith of his followers is evident, even in the ranks of the nonreligious Communist Party of Cuba. Fidel Castro, opening the Fifth Party Congress in October 1997, called on Che to bless the proceedings: "The memory, the spirit, and the unforgettable presence of Che are presiding over this Fifth Party Congress." Castro's invocation drew a standing ovation from the faithful.[3]

Many people still revere Che for what he was in life, a militant anti-imperialist and an atheist. He had no cause other than the armed struggle, no faith apart from revolution. In his farewell letter to Fidel Castro, written before he launched a new guerrilla front in the Congo, he wrote, "I will carry the faith that you instilled in me, the revolutionary spirit of my people, the sensation of fulfilling the most sacred of duties—to struggle against imperialism wherever it may be."[4] Che Guevara died in an unsuccessful effort to launch an anti-imperialist war on three continents simultaneously, convinced that only an unrelenting war to the death around the world would bring down Yankee imperialism. Many guerrillas remain committed to his brand of revolutionary warfare. However, the popular image sold in Cuba and elsewhere is the image of San Ernesto, a harmless but ever handsome guerrilla. The cause for which he died in Bolivia—global revolution—has been displaced by a meaningless commodity, an image that sells as well in the capitalist West as in communist Cuba. The real Che died in La Higuera. The mythical Che, the secular saint of revolutionary causes, was born in La Higuera in 1967.

The mythical Che was one of only two Latin Americans honored on *Time* magazine's list of the one hundred most important figures of the twentieth Century. He is undoubtedly a popular icon, a symbol of rebellion throughout the world. For middle-aged North Americans he is a convenient link to their own versions of a politically vibrant, socially active, and sexually liberated past, an era when they like to think that they too would have died for an important cause. Nostalgia fuels the consumption of Che in the heart of the country he fought against, the United States. According to Jorge Castañeda, a Che biographer, Guevara the icon represents a "nostalgia for values, for people who sacrificed themselves for ideals. It is also nostalgia for the '60s, both by people who were in their early 20s at the time and their sons and daughters who want the experience even if it is only a vicarious revisiting of fashion, music, events, and people."[5]

Thus, the American bourgeoisie and their Generation X children have adopted as a symbol of their allegedly rebellious past a dead guerrilla who despised their materialism and self-absorption. Their consumption of Che products does not represent a reaffirmation of Che's ideals, but simply a means of making a predictably safe statement of rebellion today. They are obviously not rededicating themselves to the destruction of themselves as a class or to the society that abundantly indulges their fashionable rebelliousness. Che now represents something other than what he advocated in life. According to novelist Ariel Dorfman, "The humanity that worships Che has by and large turned away from just about everything he believed in." Che, with his wavy long hair and thin beard, makes the perfect image for today's nostalgic yuppies. Dorfman raises the possibility that Che's popularity, including his ascent to *Time's* list, was made possible because Che, having been stripped of all his revolutionary ideals, is no longer dangerous.[6]

Legendary figures are fated, perhaps, to lose their complexity in their postmortem careers. With the passage of time their lives are reduced to a single message or an exemplary moment. The result of such inevitable reductionism in the capitalist world is the commodification of Che's legendary image and its consumption by mass popular culture in Europe and North America. In addition to the ubiquitous Che T-shirts and posters that are still fashionably chic, there are Che watches, key rings, socks, and even underwear. Che's image has also been used by private enterprises to market coffee, skis, and grunge rock music.[7] When Che served revolutionary Cuba as the minister of industry he used moral incentives to eliminate the decadent material values spawned by Cuba's sixty-year association with American capitalism. The Che mania sweeping the capitalist world thirty-five years after his death is clear testimony to the failure and naivete of his campaign, but the greater paradox is that revolutionary

Cuba participated in and currently profits from the Che marketing moment as well. The commercialization of Che today is the popular manifestation of complex historical processes that reduced the real Che to a simple and therefore marketable figure, in Cuba and abroad.

Revolutionary Cuba has certainly not turned away from everything Che advocated in life, but few elements of Che's revolutionary principles survive on the island. Che dreamed of a communist utopia in which "man as a commodity ceases to exist." To build this new society, Che intended to develop a revolutionary consciousness among the mobilized masses, creating new categories and values as the vestiges of the old society disappeared. The instrument by which this new man would be created had to be of a "fundamentally moral nature," Che argued.[8] In the luxurious hotels of Varadero beach, foreigners can sip on a *mojito* and wonder what happened to Che's theory of moral incentives as they pay waiters, taxi drivers, and prostitutes in dollars. The "new man" in Cuba now works for American cash, not the utopian revolution of which Che dreamed. Cubans can visit the Che mausoleum, chant "we will be like Che," and gawk at life-size statues of Che and Camilo Cienfuegos, another heroic figure from the Cuban insurrection, storming into battle in the Museum of the Revolution. But Cubans, like Americans, consume a version of Che created by the revolutionary government Guevara once served. Although part of this myth is based on reality, San Ernesto still had to be created. The Bolivians and Americans did their part by giving him a martyr's death, displaying him like a savior, and then burying him in an unmarked grave. Fidel Castro delivered the eulogy in Havana a week after Che's death, turning the *faithless* Che Guevara into a symbol for the revolutionary *faithful*. Orlando Borrego, a former associate of Che's in Cuba, observes, "Che, a Christian? My ass. Che wasn't defeated in La Higuera. He was reborn there."[9]

Che himself contributed to this postmortem deification by insisting on the need for revolutionaries to sacrifice their lives for the cause. In March 1965, Che wrote "Socialism and Man in Cuba," knowing that he was about to leave Cuba to open a guerrilla front in the eastern Congo. In this elegant and romantic farewell of a man headed into battle, a soldier justifying a death that he welcomes, Che expressed no regrets about the choices he had made, happily embracing the destiny that awaited him. "It must be said with all sincerity that in a true revolution, to which one gives oneself completely, from which one expects no material compensation, the task of the vanguard revolutionary is both magnificent and anguishing."[10] Then, Che justified the sacrifices he had made in language characteristic of religious martyrs: "Let me say, with the risk of appearing ridiculous, that the true revolutionary is guided by strong feelings of love." That statement gained saintly significance after Che's death, when Che confirmed that he so loved the people that he gave his life. Love, the militant Che Guevara admitted, was the fundamental characteristic of the "new man" that he had always hoped to be: "It is impossible to think of an authentic revolutionary without this quality."[11]

In life, however, Che also used hatred to motivate himself and others. When he wrote "Socialism and Man in Cuba," he was trying to launch wars of national liberation on three continents simultaneously, each guerrilla front supported by either the Soviet Union or China. The objective of his global strategy, summarized in his "Message to the Tricontinental," was "to create a second or a third Vietnam," dragging the United States into wars of national liberation that would drain the Americans of their resources and morale. Love motivated Che to fight on behalf of the people, but hate compelled him to fight the Americans and their alleged puppets. He called on revolutionaries to wage a merciless war against imperialists in every part of the world. "We must attack him wherever he may be, make him feel like a cornered beast wherever he may move." Che argued that "relentless hatred of the enemy" would transform people into "effective, violent, selective, and cold killing machines."[12]

Che Guevara had himself killed men in cold blood when he wrote the "Message to the Tricontinental," and he intended to kill more in Bolivia; these were sacrifices offered on the road to his revolutionary utopia. He did not fear his own death, for if he died fighting for his convictions at some "small point of the world map," he would find eternal solace. "Whenever death may surprise us it will be welcome, provided that this, our battle cry, reach some receptive ear, that another hand be extended to take up our weapons, and that other men come forward to intone our funeral dirge with the staccato of machine guns and new cries of battle and victory."[13]

Death surprised Ernesto "Che" Guevara in La Higuera, Bolivia, on October 9, 1967. He had established a guerrilla front in southeastern Bolivia in November 1966 with a group of seasoned and loyal Cuban combatants. Che expected the Bolivians to rally to the banner of continental revolution, but few people joined Che's guerrilla army, leaving Che's guerrilla band weak and isolated. Bolivian soldiers, advised and trained by Americans, harassed and hounded Che until they surrounded Che's weary band of guerrillas and captured him as he tried to climb out of a ravine. A Bolivian sergeant executed Che the next day. His body was then displayed in a laundry room (see Illustration 10.1). The photographs of Che's corpse, printed in every major newspaper around the world, conveyed the image of Che as a fallen martyr, hero, or saint, a perfect, noble ending to a legendary and remarkable career.

If Che Guevara had been surprised by death in some other fashion, the meaning of his life might have been altered. One can only imagine the consequences of Che dying in another way. What if his body had been blown to bits by a direct shot from a mortar? There would have been no Christlike figure to display. The manner, timing,

10.1 *Che Guevara on display in Vallegrande, October 9, 1967 (Photo: Freddy Alborta).*

and place of his death, as well as the manner, timing, and place of his wake, all of it arranged by his enemies, affirmed his life's message. Che could not have died like any other soldier in combat, an anonymous figure dropped by an invisible bullet, a death unnoticed (see Illustrations 10.2 and 10.3). He had to destroy imperialism or die fighting it. Che would not be San Ernesto today if he had not died the way he did.

Che, then approaching his thirty-ninth year, intended to triumph in Bolivia or die in the effort, finding death on the battlefield preferable to an agonizing death as a functionary in the Cuban bureaucracy. Soon after he arrived in southeastern Bolivia, he explained his intentions to Mario Monje, leader of the Bolivian Communist Party: "I am here now, and the only way I will leave is dead."[14]

His aggressive character in combat, combined with his own ominous prophecies, suggests suicidal tendencies in Che Guevara's personality. However, Che did not simply want to kill himself; he wanted to die in an exemplary fashion. Suffering from chronic asthma since the age of two, his severe attacks usually produced an intense sensation of suffocating. As a result he never felt far from death. But he

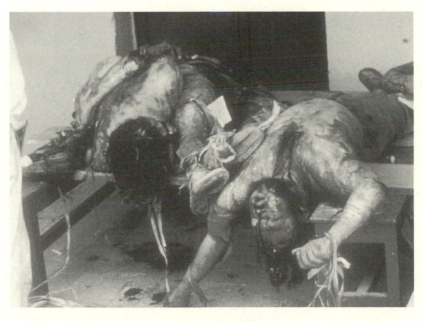

10.2 *Bodies of the guerrillas killed in the Vado del Yeso ambush, August 31, 1967 (author's collection).*

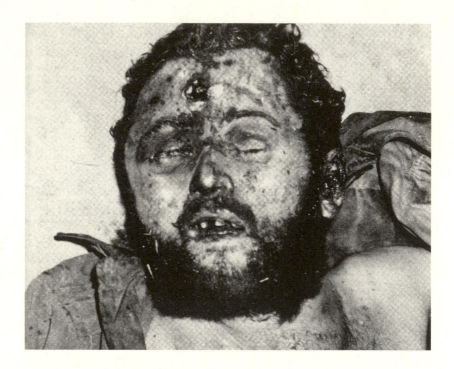

10.3 *Juan Carlos (Chino) Chang, Peruvian guerrilla captured and summarily executed in La Higuera, October 8, 1967 (Photo: Luis J. González and Gustavo A. Sánchez Salazar,* The Great Rebel: Che Guevara in Bolivia, *New York: Grove Press, 1967).*

refused to accept this as the *way* he was apparently destined to die. A poem he wrote on January 17, 1947, reflected a troubled young mind eager to determine his own fate: "The bullets, what can the bullets do to me if my destiny is to die by drowning. But I am going to overcome destiny. Destiny can be achieved by willpower. Die, yes, but riddled with bullets, destroyed by the bayonets, if not, no. Drowned, no . . . a memory more lasting than my name is to fight, to die fighting."[15]

He wanted to die in a heroic and dramatic gesture on behalf of a cause. A long life did not attract Che as much as a meaningful death. He accepted this as his destiny and lived his life to fulfill his own prophecy. The twenty-four-year-old Guevara wrote in 1952, "I see it imprinted on the night that I, the eclectic dissector of doctrines and psychoanalyst of dogmas, howling like a man possessed, will assail the

barricades and trenches, will stain my weapon with blood and, consumed with rage, will slaughter any enemy I lay hands on. And then,
as if an immense weariness were consuming my recent exhilaration,
I see myself being sacrificed to the authentic revolution."[16]

The end approached Che on October 8, 1967. The events
appeared unlikely to lead to the heroic death he anticipated. On the
heights overlooking Yuro Ravine in southeastern Bolivia, Che saw
Bolivian rangers moving along the crest of a ridge above him, block-
ing his exit in every direction. His guerrilla column, battered and
beaten, hounded by the Bolivian army for six months, had been
reduced to sixteen men. Che had failed to inspire a general revolt
among the peasants, nor had he registered any major military victory.
The guerrilla column was short of supplies and had lost contact with
Havana. Che had no asthma medicine. He did not even have shoes.
He had wrapped strands of leather around his feet after giving his
boots to one of his soldiers. Still, Che plotted a way out of disaster.
He divided his men into three squads and hoped that they could delay
battle until nightfall, when they could break out of the trap under the
cover of darkness. Che, accompanied only by Simón Cubas, a Bolivian
recruit, took cover behind a large rock in a potato patch. At 1:10 P.M.
a Bolivian squad fired on his position with a machine gun. Che
returned fire with his M-2 carbine, but it was knocked out of commission when struck by a bullet. Another bullet then hit Che in the
left calf; a third one hit his black beret, knocking it off his head. Death
had missed Che by only a few inches. Che, now wounded and carrying only a 9-mm pistol with one clip, attempted to scale the side of
the ravine while leaning on Cubas, who was dragging a submachine
gun behind him. Suddenly, they walked into the barrels of two rifles
pointed directly at their chests.

"HALT! SURRENDER!" the Bolivian soldiers demanded. Che
raised his hands. "Don't shoot! I am Che Guevara, and I'm worth
more to you alive than dead." Cubas dropped his weapon.[17]

In that instant, Che denied himself the battlefield death he had
anticipated. Wounded and exhausted, he had had no chance to resist
his adversaries; an inglorious surrender seemed to be his only option.
The Bolivians took Che and Cubas to Captain Gary Prado, commander of the Ranger Company that had executed a textbook-like
entrapment. Che, a prisoner for the first time, looked like a man who
had been chased through woods and ravines for seven months (see
Illustration 10.4). Wild and unwashed hair fell below his shoulders,

ragged fatigues barely concealed his emaciated body, leather straps covered his aching feet, and his lower legs were colored red from his calf wound. He looked so unlike the handsome and heroic coman-dante that Captain Prado had to ask Che to identify himself. Che con-fessed again, but Prado still had to confirm his identity by comparing the wounded animal in front of him with a drawing of Che he carried in his pocket. Prado noted a pronounced brow ridge and a scar on the neck of his prisoner and concluded that he had indeed captured Che Guevara. He had the hands and feet of the prisoners tied and ordered the guards to shoot them if they attempted to escape. "Don't worry Captain, it's all over," Che assured him.[18]

The struggle was over for Che, but the campaign to control his body had just begun. During the next forty-eight hours, Che's ene-mies decided that he must die and decided how his body would be displayed and disposed of. Their decisions would affect how, where, and even why people would come to visualize and commemorate Che's death. The Bolivian rangers could have killed Che on the spot and dumped his corpse on the side of a road. Instead, they impris-oned, interrogated, and then executed him. After his execution, they washed his hair, cleaned his body, and displayed his corpse in a manner that left an indelible impression on all those who saw him then and those who see the photos today, a Christlike figure martyred for a rev-olutionary cause.

In an ironic twist of fate, Che's opponents displayed a profound respect for him in life and his body after death. Félix Rodríguez, a Cuban-born CIA agent who advised the Bolivian troops, found Che on a barren floor in a mud-brick schoolhouse in La Higuera. Che, dirtied and bloodied, hands tied behind his back, did not look so dan-gerous anymore. Rodríguez initially thought of executing Che by a firing squad, as Che had done to counterrevolutionaries at La Cabaña fortress in Havana, but he was under orders from Washington to keep Che alive. Rodríguez apparently tried to convince the Bolivians to spare Guevara's life. He admired his famous prisoner and did his best to accord him what little respect could be offered to a condemned man. "Our ideals are different," Rodríguez said. "But I admire you. You used to be a minister of state in Cuba. Now look at you, you are like this because you believe in your ideals."[19]

Rodríguez also recognized the historic value of the drama in which he played a leading role. He took Che outside, gave his camera to a Bolivian soldier, and posed for a picture with him, partly to prove to

10.4 *Che Guevara in captivity, October 8, 1967 (Photo: Che Guevara and the Bolivian Guerrillas Collection, Latin American Library, Tulane University).*

his CIA handlers that he had Guevara, but also to place himself in posterity. The Bolivian soldier asked Rodríguez to return the favor by snapping a photo of him with Che, but Rodríguez deliberately exposed the film so that he would have the last photograph of Che alive. He also claimed Che's Rolex watch as his own trophy, a relic of the secular saint about to be martyred.[20]

Just before 1 P.M. on October 9, Rodríguez told Che that the Bolivians had ordered his execution. They did not want to put Che on trial and endure the global scrutiny that would come with it. For a moment Che regretted the fate that had befallen him. He admitted to Rodríguez that he should not have allowed himself to be captured alive. He composed himself, embraced the Cuban agent, and faced his end with courage and honor, earning the respect of Rodríguez at the end. Rodriguez not only admired the way Che handled himself, he also made sure that the Bolivians did not leave Che a bloody and mangled mess on the floor. Some of the Bolivian soldiers would have liked to take out their revenge on Che by giving him a painful death, but Rodríguez insisted on a clean and quick execution. When he passed the execution orders from the Bolivian president to Sergeant Mario Terán, who drew the assignment by picking the shortest straw, he ordered him to aim below the neck. Since radio broadcasts had already reported that Che had fallen in combat, he did not want to display a body with an obvious exit wound in the forehead. Not only would that show that Che had been executed, it would have made a mess of a body that had to be displayed to and recognized by an incredulous world.[21]

Che was seated in a wooden chair propped up against the wall of the schoolhouse when Sergeant Terán walked in. Sensing that his time had finally come, Che asked Terán for a moment so that he could stand. Terán, more nervous than Che, turned and walked out of the room. The Bolivian officers ordered him to go back in and complete his mission. Guevara, still standing when Terán returned, gave Terán the command to fire: "Shoot, coward, you are only going to kill a man."[22]

Che certainly did not consider himself a saint, but in his last statement he essentially forgave Terán, who knew not what he was about to do. Terán pulled the trigger of his semiautomatic rifle and hit Che in the arms and legs. Che fell to the ground in agony, biting his wrist to muffle his cries. Terán fired another burst and completed the act. One bullet entered two inches below the left nipple and sliced through Che's heart, killing him instantly. There were eight bullet wounds in his body, including the one in his right calf.[23]

Che's executioners cared for his body with such tenderness that one wonders why they killed him. Immediately after the execution, Félix Rodríguez stopped a Bolivian soldier from beating Che's corpse with a stick. Rodríguez saw no reason to desecrate his body. He took a pail of water, washed the blood from Che's face, closed his eyes, then tried to close Che's jaw, letting his honorable antagonist rest in peace (see Illustration 10.5).[24]

Che's enemies, beginning with Felix Rodríguez, collaborated in the beatification of Che Guevara by creating the image the world wanted to consume. Che went through a dramatic makeover from his first appearance as a wild animal in La Higuera to the poster boy of revolutionary causes, all because Che's Bolivian and North American

10.5 *Che's body as it was being prepared for display; note that the eyes are still closed (Photo: Che Guevara and the Bolivian Guerrillas Collection, Latin American Library, Tulane University).*

enemies arranged the perfect, ethereal appearance for San Ernesto. They could not have buried him in an unmarked grave without first displaying his body, because nobody would have believed that they had killed Che. They could not have shot him in the back of the head and thrown him in a heap of mangled bodies, as they had done with other guerrillas. If they had displayed Che's body like that, they would have infuriated some and left others incredulous. The Bolivian and American authorities had to prove that they had killed Guevara, and nobody would have believed that the wounded animal that they captured on October 8 was the revolutionary saint that they expected to see. If they did not prove his identity, Che's sympathizers would not learn the lesson that his enemies intended to teach that afternoon: · that all guerrillas would meet this same violent end. The world expected to see the self-sacrificing guerrilla, and the Bolivians and Americans had to put him on stage. His body did not just have to approximate reality; it had to coincide with the world's anticipated end for an idealized hero. In other words, the legendary Che had to make his final appearance.

Thus Bolivian doctors and American CIA agents created Che's postmortem image. The world was waiting for Che's arrival in Vallegrande, and on Che's enemies fell the honor of arranging the final scene in this revolutionary act. They decided to display his body in the laundry room located behind Malta Hospital, an adobe shed located on a barren plain. The bodies of two other guerrillas, Coco and Tania, had lain there a few days earlier. There, in this makeshift guerrilla morgue, the Bolivians and Americans prepared Che for his final appearance. The canvas stretcher bearing Che's body was placed lengthwise across a high concrete washbasin in the center of the room. Two doctors, two nuns, and two male nurses went to work. The doctors made an incision in Che's neck and injected formaldahyde to retard decomposition. With the back of Che's head propped up on a wooden slab, Che's beard covered the incision in his neck. The nuns and nurses proceeded to wash Che's body, feet, and hair. Che's naturally wavy hair came back to life, and, with his emaciated body washed of blood and dirt, he looked much less like the killing machine captured a day earlier by Captain Prado.[25]

After the body was washed, the CIA agents and identification experts from the Bolivian ministry of the interior began the job of establishing a positive identification by fingerprinting and photographing the body. Gustavo Villoldo, another Cuban-born CIA agent known as Eduardo González in Bolivia, supervised the proceedings. To confirm the identity of Che, he wanted to photograph the corpse with its eyes open. So he kept propping the eyelids open while he snapped the shots. When he was done, rigor mortis had set in and Che's eyes remained open, negating Felix Rodríguez's earlier attempts to let him rest with his eyes closed. As a result, with Che's head propped up and his eyes open, the legendary *guerrillero* seemed to be looking back at the Bolivian officers who poked at him.[26]

Once the body had been prepared, General Alfredo Ovando, chief of the Bolivian army, displayed it to reporters, photographers, and townspeople, all of whom had been waiting for hours to see if Che Guevara was really dead. The Bolivian officers wanted to prove their claims and send a warning to those who would emulate Che in Bolivia or elsewhere. The message that they intended to send was quite unlike the message that people received. The famous photograph taken by Freddy Alborta confirmed the value of Che's life, giving Che the glorious death that he had anticipated in his writings. Alborta stood over the half-naked corpse and captured the lasting image of the dead Che. Eyes wide open, right fist nearly clenched, and lips slightly parted, Che looked content, at peace even with the generals who gloated above him. To the enemy he hated, Che had given the most valuable trophy a Latin American general could receive, his lifeless body. From them in turn, he had received the authenticity he had craved, the fulfillment of his own mythic prognostication. There he lay, staring coldly into eternity, the sacrificial icon of a cause and a generation.

Art historian John Berger compared the Alborta photograph of the dead Che to Mantegna's classical painting of the dead Jesus Christ. "The drapery over the lower part of the body is creased and formed in the same manner as the blood-sodden, unbuttoned, olive-green trousers on Guevara. The head is raised at the same angle. The mouth is slack of expression in the same way," Berger explains.[27] Other observers have compared the final display of Che to the depiction of the dead Christ by Holbein the younger. In both images, the corpse is emaciated, wounded, and covered from the waist down; the eyes are wide open and staring into eternity. The long hair and scraggly beard are strikingly similar. (See Alborta photo, Illustration 10.1, p. 322.)

The image of Che in death, captured by Alborta in 1967, gave life to an image captured by a Cuban photographer in 1960. Alborta immortalized Che at the moment he became a twentieth-century savior who died trying to save the world, but that depiction of death did not convey the message that his followers wanted to propagate. They wanted the living Che, and they found the perfect image of revolutionary purity in an unknown photo tacked on an unseen wall in the Havana home of Alberto Korda, who snapped the picture when he was a staff photographer for the Cuban newspaper *Revolución*.

In the summer of 1967, Italian publisher Giangiacomo Feltrinelli came to Korda's house bearing a letter of introduction from Haydee Santamaría, president of la Casa de las Américas. Feltrinelli, who had already gained international notoriety by smuggling the novel *Dr. Zhivago* out of the Soviet Union, wanted a photograph of Che. Korda showed him what he considered his best shot, an unpublished photo taken on March 5, 1960. That day, Che walked arm in arm with the revolutionary leadership in a funeral procession along the Malecón in Havana, commemorating the victims of *La Coubre*, a French freighter carrying Belgian arms that had exploded in Havana harbor the previous day.[28] Fidel had held the United States responsible for the explosion, which killed more than one hundred people. At Colón cemetery, Che stood on a podium beneath a large Cuban flag, listening to Castro dare the Yankees to land their own troops in Cuba. Korda stood less than ten yards away from the podium, panning the entire stage, when Che stepped forward. Wearing an olive green jacket and a black beret, Che gazed defiantly into eternity, the perfect symbol of the self-sacrificing revolutionary that Castro had in mind when he called on the Cubans to fight or die for their country. Korda snapped two pictures in less than thirty seconds, then Che went back to his position behind Fidel. Korda developed the two photos but the editors of *Revolución* selected a photograph of Fidel to accompany its article on the event.[29]

Feltrinelli, however, loved the photograph and wanted it. Not knowing of Feltrinelli's background, Korda gave Feltrinelli two prints for free, thinking Feltrinelli was a friend of the revolution. After Che's death, Feltrinelli produced a poster-size reprint of the original and sold them to leftist demonstrators in Milan. They would be the first to carry the image of the heroic guerrilla in protests on October 15, 1967. Feltrinelli sold millions of posters over the years and made a fortune, while Korda received nothing for the most reproduced image in the history of photography (see Illustration 10.6).[30]

Thus, the Korda image became popular only after Freddy Alborta captured the perfect image of Che's ideal death. Alborta recognized the historical importance of the moment and even the Christian imagery that had overwhelmed a room that smelled of rotting flesh. "I had the impression that I was photographing a Christ," Alborta explained. "I had in fact entered that dimension. It was not a cadaver that I was photographing but something extraordinary."[31] Alborta did not know of the classical Christian iconography to which his photographs have been compared, yet his photographs, by evoking those images, validated the meaning of Che's life. Che had frequently expressed his willingness to give his life for the oppressed, anytime and anywhere. He fulfilled his prophecies by dying for oppressed Bolivians, just as Jesus confirmed his life by dying on the cross. Thus,

10.6 *Che Guevara, the "Heroic Guerrilla" (Photo: Alberto Korda).*

the myth of the self-sacrificing revolutionary captured by Korda in Havana in 1960 became reality in the lens of Freddy Alborta in Bolivia in 1967, giving Che, an atheist, eternal life as a secular saint.

However, the Bolivians who filed past the body in the laundry room did not need an art historian to see the comparison with Jesus. The nuns who worked at the hospital, the nurse who cleaned his body, and the men and women of Vallegrande immediately noted the supernatural resemblance to Jesus Christ. They had not understood his message, and they certainly had not rallied to his cause, but when they saw him like that, he looked like the heroic liberator that he had always claimed to be. Although he never claimed to be a savior, his promise of an earthly liberation paralleled the Christian concept of heaven on earth. Knowing that Che had died for them, the Bolivians, just like the Roman soldiers who guarded Christ, saved mementos for themselves. One woman cut a lock of Che's hair. She later donated it to the Museum of the Revolution in Havana. Bolivian officers posed for photographs next to the martyr. Lieutenant Colonel Andrés Selich claimed Che's leather portfolio and one of his Rolex watches. Colonel Zenteno Anaya made off with Che's rifle.[32]

The apparition of San Ernesto in Vallegrande convinced most of the world that Che was indeed dead. To eliminate any doubt, the Bolivians decided to retain incontrovertible evidence of his identity. Some Bolivian officers urged General Alfredo Ovando to decapitate the body and send the head to Fidel Castro. Others suggested that they simply cut off a finger and send it to Havana so that the Cubans could make a positive identification from their own print. Gustavo Villoldo urged Ovando not to mutilate the body because it would stain the reputation of the Bolivian army, which had just scored its most impressive victory. Ovando settled on a compromise. In the end, he authorized the amputation of Guevara's hands, which were placed in a jar of formaldahyde and sent to Havana a year later. Fidel keeps them in the palace of the revolution and shows them only to a few privileged visitors.[33]

At the time of the decision, foreign journalists, Cuban revolutionaries, and the Guevara family wanted Che's body. The Bolivians did not want to bury him in a grave that would immediately become a revolutionary shrine. Some officers recommended that Ovando cremate the body to eliminate all traces of it and thereby prevent his followers from using his tomb for political purposes. Gustavo Villoldo pointed out, however, that the Bolivians did not have the appropriate facilities for cremation, so the result would have been a "horrible barbecue." Thus, General Ovando ordered Villoldo to bury Guevara and his comrades in an unmarked grave. Villoldo picked up the handless corpse at 2 A.M. on October 11 and buried it along with two others near a runway at the Vallegrande airport.[34]

By denying the body to Che's followers, the Bolivians and Americans hoped to prevent them from constructing pseudoreligious shrines on Bolivian soil. It did not matter. In the absence of a grave site the faithful flocked to the site where San Ernesto appeared: the *lavandería* of the Vallegrande hospital. Worshippers still place photographs and flowers on the wash basin where Che lay on October 9 and 10, 1967. They inscribe their names and revolutionary slogans on the walls. Some people actually pray to Che. According to biographer Paco Ignacio Taibo, the Bolivian peasants have developed a strange litany, a prayer like: "Little soul of Che, by your leave please work the miracle that will make my cow well again. Grant me that wish, little soul of Che."[35]

Even Fidel Castro prays, in a secular way, to San Ernesto. In fact, Fidel delivered the eulogy that defined the life and meaning of San Ernesto on October 18, 1967. Speaking to several hundred thousand people in the Plaza de la Revolución, Fidel borrowed the Christian concept of an afterlife to create the saint of Cuba's nonreligious revolution. Che had not died, Fidel asserted, because the ideas for which he died were immortal. "After his heroic and glorious death," Fidel asserted, "some people attempt to deny the truth or value of his concepts, his guerrilla theories. The artist may die, especially when he is an artist in a field as dangerous as revolutionary struggle, but what will surely never die is the art to which he dedicated his life, the art to which he dedicated his intelligence."[36]

Although Fidel claimed that Cuba would remain faithful to Che's guerrilla concepts, he immediately began to articulate a new meaning of Che's life, one quite removed from his tricontinental strategy of unrelenting war. Castro attributed the most saintly characteristics to his former comrade, describing him as "so altruistic, so selfless, so willing to always do the most difficult things, to constantly risk his life." He added, Che was the "fullest expression of the virtues of a revolutionary: a person of total integrity, a person of supreme sense of honor, of absolute sincerity, a person of stoic and Spartan living habits, a person in whose conduct not one stain can be found. He constituted, through his virtues, what can be called a truly model revolutionary." From that moment on, Che was stripped of his militant vices and clothed solely in revolutionary virtues. Che was "a pure example of revolutionary virtues."[37]

Fidel outlined the characteristics that the Cuban revolutionaries have used ever since to educate and indoctrinate Cuba's youth. Che was extraordinarily sensitive to the needs of people; he had an insatiable lust for learning and he studied constantly; he devoted his off days to voluntary work. Fidel wanted all Cubans to emulate Che. "If we wish to express what we expect our revolutionary combatants, our militants, our people to be, we must say, without hesitation: let them be like Che! If we wish to express what we want the people of future generations to be, we must say: let them be like Che!"[38]

That popular slogan has been propagated in Cuban schools for the last thirty-five years. Che is the model human to which all true revolutionaries aspire, for there is no better example than Che. Che only looked like a saint or a savior in Freddy Alborta's photographs. Fidel gave Christian substance to the images of the dead Che, transforming him into a secular saint by referring to him in superlative terms that no mortal could possibly attain. "Che died defending no other interest, no other cause than the cause of the exploited and the oppressed of this continent," Fidel claimed. "Che died defending no other cause than the cause of the poor and the humble of this earth. And the exemplary manner and the selflessness with which he defended that cause cannot be disputed even by his most bitter enemies."[39]

Che's enemies had allowed him the opportunity to die in an exemplary manner, but Fidel made no allusion to their collaboration. Castro criticized them for not returning the body to Cuba, but it would not matter, he said, for while they had eliminated him physically, they could not destroy his ideas or his example. "It will not be long before it will be proved that his death will, in the long run, be like a seed that will give rise to many people determined to imitate him, many people determined to follow his example," Castro predicted.[40]

When Guevara's remains were returned to Cuba in 1997, however, Castro used the body to reiterate the same political message he had delivered in 1967. Coming during revolutionary Cuba's most difficult political and economic crisis, Fidel received Che's body as a badly needed reinforcement, an invincible combatant who had returned to Cuba to fight alongside his comrades. The Cuban government officially declared 1997 as "the Year of the 30th Anniversary of the Death in Combat of the Heroic Guerrilla and his Comrades in Bolivia." Throughout the year, the state media broadcast documentaries about his life, former comrades met to discuss his life and legacy, and the government organized a series of formal ceremonies. His daughter, Aleida Guevara March, was given the honor of receiving Che's remains first. In a ceremony in mid-July, she touched on the theme of eternal life, which would echo throughout all subsequent ceremonies. "Che and the remains of six men who died with him do not return to us as defeated men. They come back as heroes, eternally young," Aleida asserted. "They will always be alive, together with their children, in the people."[41]

Fidel reaffirmed what he had said thirty years earlier, that the spirit of the "true revolutionary" could not be killed. "The memory, the spirit, and the unforgettable presence of Che are presiding over this Fifth Party Congress," Castro asserted in his opening address on October 8, 1997. Che was no longer in Higuera, "but he is everywhere, wherever there is a just cause to defend," Castro asserted.[42]

Two days later the remains of Che and his six comrades lay in state at the José Martí Monument in the Plaza de la Revolución in Havana. Fidel and his brother Raúl took the first shift in an honor guard that included all the highest-ranking officials from the Political Bureau and the Central Committee of the Communist Party. Finally given the opportunity to pay their last respects to the remains of a man who had been their holy ghost for thirty years, thousands of Cubans filed through the monument. But the Cuban government decided that Che would finally rest in a specially constructed mausoleum in Santa Clara, located two hundred miles east of Havana. Che had directed a brilliant campaign against this city in late 1958. His guerrilla column, after a stunning march across the island, laid siege to Santa Clara, divided the island in two, and forced Batista to resign. Castro evidently concluded that Santa Clara, where the Cuban government had already established a museum dedicated to Che, was the most appropriate place for Che to rest. On October 15, the government sent the remains of Che and six other comrades in an official caravan to Santa Clara, escorted by soldiers in parade dress.[43]

Fidel spoke one more time at the interment ceremonies at the Che Guevara museum in Santa Clara on October 17, 1999. He referred again to Che as a "pure man," a "pure revolutionary," and a "true communist." Perhaps this deity, known officially as the "Heroic Guerrilla" could pull Cuba out of its worst crisis. Fidel essentially prayed to Che in nonreligious terms: "Thank you for coming to reinforce us in the difficult struggle that we are undergoing today, to preserve the ideas that you fought so hard for, to save the Revolution, the country, and the conquests of socialism," Castro said.[44]

Like many Cubans, Castro claims that Che speaks to him from the grave. Che Guevara remains a living presence in the life of Fidel Castro and, by extension, the Cuban Revolution. "I dreamed I spoke with him [Che], that he was alive," Castro admitted in 1987.[45] Men who fought with him or worked with him feel a unique honor in having served him, but they are also haunted by the knowledge they did not die with Che. Some, like Joel Iglesias, Victor Dreke, and Rogelio Acevedo, who fought with Che in Cuba or the Congo, have been tormented by the simple fact that Che had not asked them to go with him to Bolivia. They wonder if they might have been able to change the outcome of the Bolivian campaign if they had fought at Che's side.[46] Che Guevara's spirit remains a powerful force in the lives of Cuban revolutionaries, though the meaning of his life is often lost in the religious symbolism and commercialism that surrounds him. Paco Ignacio Taibo, a Che biographer and a disciple, still sees the pure revolutionary behind the commodified Che in all the photographs, T-shirts, tapes, postcards, and paraphernalia. "Che is watching over us. He is our secular saint," Taibo concludes. "Thirty years after his death, his image cuts across generations, his myth hovers over neoliberalism's delusions of grandeur."[47]

Che is even watching over his enemies, haunting them perhaps. Félix Rodríguez, for example, claims that he developed asthma only after Che's execution. "Che may have been dead, but somehow his asthma, a condition that I had never had in my life, had attached itself to me. To this day my chronic shortness of breath is a constant reminder of Che and his last hours alive in the tiny town of La Higuera."[48]

Although Che's enemies do not worship San Ernesto, they certainly have good reason to fear the powers he commands from the grave. The men associated with Che's execution have died violently, beginning with the then president of Bolivia, General René Barrientos, who died in a helicopter crash in April 1969. Army goons operating under orders from right-wing president General Hugo Banzer Suárez in 1973 beat to death Lieutenant Colonel Andrés Selich, who had given the order to execute Che. Captain Gary Prado held the rank of colonel when he was shot during an uprising in Santa Cruz in 1981; the gunshot left him paralyzed from the waist down. Sergeant Mario Terán, Che's executioner, has lived in fear for thirty-five years. Occasionally wearing wigs and other disguises to throw off the assassins that either Che or Cuban agents have sent after him, he reportedly drinks heavily and wanders around the streets of Cochabamba. Haunted by the ghost of Che, he has allegedly sought psychiatric counseling, like other soldiers involved in the capture and execution of Che.[49]

Che Guevara would have been the first person to object to his deification. He saw evidence of this symbolic construction while he lived. He once visited a peasant's home in eastern Cuba and saw his own portrait on an altar lit by appropriate candles. He did not know what to make of it, but he was not comfortable about being worshipped as a saint. Friends, family, and sympathizers know that Che would not have appreciated his official beatification by Cuba, but he is nevertheless revolutionary Cuba's official saint, if not a god. Cuban parents might name a child Ernesto in honor of the fallen hero, but "to be called Che [in Cuba] is equivalent to being named Jesus

Christ," according to Jon Lee Anderson, Che's biographer. "The unspoken consensus is that only one person has the right to bear the name: Che Guevara himself."[50]

Notes

1. Fiona Adams, "Searching for Che's Ghost," *Bolivian Times*, 14 August 1997, 4; "Riding the Che-chic Route (Bolivia commemorates the 30th Anniversary of the Death of Che Guevara by Initiating Che Guevara Week)," *The Economist*, 11 October 1997.
2. "Vallegrande Che Festival Page," *www.geocities.com/CapitolHill/9051/index.html*.
3. "Honored, Despised or Exploited, Che Lives On," Reuters, 8 October 1997, *www.geocities.com/Hollywood/8702/honored.html*.
4. Che Guevara to Fidel Castro, 1 April 1965, in Ernesto Guevara, *Che: Selected Works of Ernesto Guevara*, ed. Rolando E. Bonachea and Nelson P. Valdés (Cambridge, MA: MIT Press, 1969), 423.
5. Ira J. Hadnot, "Che Becomes Chic," *The Dallas Morning News*, 13 July 1997, J11.
6. Ariel Dorfman, "The Guerrilla: Che Guevara," *Time*, 14 June 1999.
7. Alejandro Reuss, "The Che Marketing Moment," *Dollars & Sense* 212 (July–August 1997); Brook Larmer, "Che Chic," *Newsweek*, 21 July 1997.
8. Che Guevara, "Socialism and Man in Cuba" [published in *Marcha* (Uruguay), 12 March 1965], in *Che: Selected Works*, 159–60.
9. García, Fernando D., and Oscar Sola, eds. *Che: Images of a Revolutionary* (London: Pluto Press, 1997), 195.
10. Ibid., 167.
11. Ibid.
12. Guevara, "Message to the Tricontinental," in Guevara, *Che: Selected Works*, 180.
13. Ibid., 182.
14. Inti Peredo, "My Campaign with Che," in Ernesto Guevara, *The Bolivian Diary*, ed. Mary-Alice Waters (New York: Pathfinder, 1994), 339–41. All accounts of the argument agree that the fundamental disagreement between the two men was over the leadership of the movement.
15. Cited in Anderson, *Che Guevara*, 44.
16. Ernesto Guevara, *Motorcycle Diaries; A Journey around South America*, trans. Ann Wright (London: Verso, 1995), 152.

17. Gary Prado Salmón, *The Defeat of Che Guevara: Military Response to Guerrilla Challenge* (New York: Praeger, 1990), 177; Richard Harris, *Death of a Revolutionary: Che Guevara's Last Mission*, rev. ed. (New York: W. W. Norton, 2000), 157–58; González and Sánchez, *Great Rebel*, 189.

18. Anderson, *Che Guevara*, 733; Prado, *Defeat of Che Guevara*, 177–78; Luis J. González and Gustavo A. Sánchez Salazar, *The Great Rebel: Che Guevara in Bolivia* (New York: Grove Press, 1969), 189–90.

19. Felix Rodríguez and John Weisman, *Shadow Warrior: The CIA Hero of a Hundred Unknown Battles* (New York: Simon and Schuster, 1989), 166.

20. Ibid., 167–70.

21. Ibid., 168–69.

22. Adys Cupull and Froilán González, *La CIA contra el Che* (Havana: Editora Política, 1993), 100–102; Harris, *Death of a Revolutionary*, 160–61.

23. González and Sánchez Salazar, *Great Rebel*, 250–51.

24. Rodríguez, *Shadow Warrior*, 170.

25. González and Sánchez Salazar, *Great Rebel*, 198–200; Anderson, *Che Guevara*, 741–42.

26. González and Sánchez Salazar, *Great Rebel*, 198–200; Harris, *Death of a Revolutionary*, 130–31.

27. John Berger, "Out of the Way: Che Guevara Dead," *New Society* 10, no. 265 (26 October 1967): 597.

28. Tad Szulc, "Shadowy Power Behind Castro," *New York Times Magazine*, 19 June 1960, 5; Robert Quirk, *Fidel Castro* (New York: W. W. Norton, 1993), 300–301; Carlos Franqui, *Family Portrait with Fidel: A Memoir* (New York: Vintage Books, 1984), 69–70; Paco Ignacio Taibo II, *Guevara: Also Known as Che*, trans. Martin Michael Roberts (New York: St. Martin's Press, 1997), 384; Anderson, *Che Guevara*, 464.

29. Anderson, *Che Guevara*, 464–65; "La más famosa foto del Che," *Granma Internacional* (1997), *www.granma.cu/che/korda.html*.

30. Ibid. And see "Guevara's Image Saved from Drink," BBC News, 15 September 2000.

31. Jeffrey Skoller, "The Future's Past: Re-Imaging the Cuban Revolution," *Afterimage* 26, no. 5 (March–April 1999): 13.

32. García and Sola, eds., *Che: Images*, 195; Anderson, *Che Guevara*, 742.

33. "Yo enterré al Che," *Caretas*, 2 October 1997; Jorge Castañeda, *Compañero: The Life and Death of Che Guevara*, trans. Marina Castañeda (New York: Alfred A. Knopf, 1997), 401–2.

34. "Yo enterré al Che," *Caretas*, 2 October 1997.

35. Taibo, *Guevara*, 584.

36. Speech by Fidel Castro on 18 October 1967, in David Deutschmann, ed., *Che: A Memoir by Fidel Castro* (Melbourne, Australia: Ocean Press, 1994), 71.

37. Ibid., 70, 74, 75.

38. Ibid., 78.

39. Ibid., 77.

40. Ibid., 78.

41. "Palabras de Aleida Guevara March, hija del Che, en el recibimiento de los restos del Guerrillero Heroico," *Granma Nacional*, 15 July 1997, *www.granma.cubaweb.cu/temas/articulo3.html*.

42. "Castro Opens Party Congress with Tribute to Che," CNN, 8 October 1997, *www.cnn.com/WORLD/9710/08/cuba.party.congress/index.html#1*.

43. "Encabezan Fidel y Raúl honras fúnebres al Che y sus compañeros de armas," *Granma*, 10 October 1997; "Recorrido hasta Santa Clara de la caravana integrada por siete armones," *Granma*, 15 October 1997.

44. "Discurso de Fidel en la ceremonia de inhumación de los restos del Che," *Granma*, 18 October 1997, *www.granma.cubaweb.cu/temas/articulo7.html*; "Cuba Salutes Che Guevara," CNN, 17 October 1997.

45. Deutschmann, *Che*, 112.

46. Taibo, *Guevara*, 586.

47. Ibid., 587.

48. Rodríguez, *Shadow Warrior*, 171.

49. Anderson, *Che Guevara*, 749–50; Taibo, *Guevara*, 580–82.

50. Jon Lee Anderson, "Cult of the Guerrilla," *Geographical Magazine* 69, no. 10 (October 1997): 21.

Contributors

Christon I. Archer is Professor of History at the University of Calgary. He has written extensively on the army of New Spain and on the Mexican Wars of Independence. His recent edited books are *The Wars of Independence in Spanish America* (Scholarly Resources, 2000); and *The Birth of Modern Mexico, 1780–1824* (Scholarly Resources, 2003), and an interpretive work in military history with John Ferris, Holger Herwig, and Tim Travers, *World History of Warfare* (University of Nebraska Press, 2002). Archer has a forthcoming book, *La mordida de la hidra: El ejército de Nueva España en la guerra de independencia* (El Colegio de Michoacán, 2004). His second major research field concerns Spanish maritime history and Pacific Ocean exploration in the eighteenth century.

Samuel Brunk is an Associate Professor of History at the University of Texas at El Paso, where he teaches graduate and undergraduate courses on twentieth-century Mexico, Latin America, and World History. He has published a biography of Mexican revolutionary Emiliano Zapata, *Emiliano Zapata: Revolution and Betrayal in Mexico* (University of New Mexico Press, 1995), as well as articles in such journals as the *Hispanic American Historical Review* and the *American Historical Review*. He is currently finishing a book on memories of Zapata, tentatively entitled "The Myth of Emiliano Zapata and Mexico's Twentieth Century." His next project is an environmental history of the Chihuahuan desert.

Jürgen Buchenau is Associate Professor of History and Director of Latin American Studies at UNC Charlotte. He has a PhD in Latin American history from the University of North Carolina at Chapel Hill. He is the author of *In the Shadow of the Giant: The Making of Mexico's Central America Policy, 1876–1930* (University of Alabama Press, 1996) and *Tools of Progress: A German Merchant Family in Mexico City, 1865–Present* (University of New Mexico Press, 2004), which was also published in a German edition. His current work examines the life and times of Mexican revolutionary leader Plutarco Elías Calles.

Paul J. Dosal is Professor of History at the University of South Florida in Tampa. He has a PhD in history from Tulane University. He has published *Doing Business with the Dictators: A Political History of United Fruit in Guatemala, 1899–1944* (Scholarly Resources, 1993), and *Power in Transition: The Rise of Guatemala's Industrial Oligarchy, 1871–1944* (Praeger, 1995). His most recent book, *Comandante Che: Guerrilla Soldier, Commander, and Strategist, 1956–1967* (Penn State University Press, 2003), examines the military career and strategies of Ernesto "Che" Guevara in Cuba, the Congo, and Bolivia.

Donna J. Guy is Professor of History and Distinguished Professor of Humanities at Ohio State University. As a specialist in Argentine history, her research has focused on a variety of topics including the political economy of sugar, the history of legalized prostitution in Argentina, the history of sexuality, and women's history. Currently she is finishing a book on the history of street children and their relationship to the rise of the welfare state in Argentina. Although she has always been fascinated by the history of Juan and Evita Perón, this is her first article devoted principally to their biographies.

Lyman L. Johnson is Professor of History at UNC Charlotte. He is interested in the history of eighteenth- and nineteenth-century Argentina. His most recent book, *Faces of Honor* (University of New Mexico Press, 2002), edited with Sonya Lipsett-Rivera, examines the relationship between the culture of honor and the construction of gender. Professor Johnson is also coauthor of *Colonial Latin America* (5th ed., Oxford University Press, 2004), with Mark Burkholder, and *The Earth and Its Peoples* (3rd ed., Houghton Mifflin Company, 2004). He is currently working on a study of Buenos Aires in the era of the Atlantic revolutions. He is the senior advisory editor of the Diálogos series for the University of New Mexico Press.

Jeffrey M. Shumway is Assistant Professor of History at Brigham Young University. He received his PhD from the University of Arizona in 1999. He has published in *The Americas*, and his book, *The Case of the Ugly Suitor and Other Histories of Love, Gender, and Nation in Buenos Aires, 1776–1870*, is forthcoming from the University of Nebraska Press. His current research delves further into politics, culture, and gender in nineteenth-century Buenos Aires, including the various worlds—mortal and postmortem—of Juan Manuel de Rosas.

Ward Stavig's research focuses on colonial indigenous and social history in the Peruvian and Bolivian Andes. His work, such as *The World of Túpac Amaru: Conflict, Community and Identity in the Andes*, stresses the historical agency and humanity of the people whose lives are revealed in the archives. Stavig is working on a study of ethnic identity and conflict in the indigenous communities in the immediate orbit of Potosí. He currently teaches at the University of South Florida in Tampa, Florida, which unfortunately is about as far away from the Andes as one can get mentally and environmentally.

Barbara Weinstein is Professor of History at the University of Maryland and coeditor of the *Hispanic American Historical Review*. Her research focuses on the social and political history of postcolonial Brazil. Her most recent book is *For Social Peace in Brazil: Industrialists and the Remaking of the Working Class in São Paulo* (University of North Carolina Press, 1996). She is currently completing a study of the racialization and gendering of regional identities in twentieth-century Brazil, entitled *Region vs. Nation*, forthcoming from Duke University Press.

Daryle Williams is Associate Professor of History at the University of Maryland and author of *Culture Wars in Brazil: The First Vargas Regime, 1930–1945* (Duke University Press, 2001), the 2001 winner of the American Historical Association's John Edwin Fagg prize. He received a PhD from Stanford University in 1995. Recently, Williams has completed research on the politics of World Heritage in the Southern Cone and started a new project on the fine arts in Brazilian slave society. Through 2007, Williams will serve as associate editor of the *Hispanic American Historical Review*.

Index

Lopez de Sosa, Antonio, 46
López Portillo, José, 165
Luna, Felix, 82, 88
Luna, Francisco, 246–47
Luque, Guillermo, 262,
    263–64

Madero, Francisco, 163, 181,
    192, 219, 222, 226
Madre María (spiritist), 256
Manco Inca, 29, 31, 32, 33–34,
    35, 40
Mármol, José, 111, 114, 123,
    125
Marmolejo, Emigdio, 141, 156
Martínez, Tomás Eloy, 171
Masons, 230–31
Matos Montezuma, Eduardo,
    225
Maximilian of Habsburg, 95,
    212
mazorca, 110, 127
Médiz Bolio, Antonio, 197
Menem, Carlos Saúl, 12, 21,
    106, 118–20, 125–26, 126,
    127, 128, 253–54, 262; and
    pardoning of convicted
    military personnel, 124,
    131; with Pro-Repatriation
    Committee, 120; and
    reconciliation, 107, 118,
    132–33; repatriation of
    body of Rosas, 257
Menem, Zulema, 262
Mexican Revolution, 144, 199,
    218
Mier, Servando Teresa de, 92
Mitre, Bartolomé (of 19th
    century), 106, 107, 111,
    112, 119, 122

Mitre, Bartolomé (of 20th
    century), 122
Monje, Mario, 323
Montaño, Otilio, 143
Montello, Josué, 300
Montoneros, 248, 249
Monument of Independence
    (Mexico City), 14
Monument to the Revolution,
    162, 163, 164, 165, 166,
    167, 169, 192, 193
Monumento Obregón, 181,
    182, 194, 196–97, 200
Moori Koenig, Carlos, 248
Morales, María Soledad, 256,
    262–63
Morelos, José María, 13, 21,
    65, 72–82, 91, 92, 93, 95,
    96, 145, 180, 212, 213,
    219, 226, 236; capture of,
    77; displayed remains of,
    14; portrait of, 73
Moreno Toscano, Alejandra, xv
Morones, Luis N., 189, 191
Moscoso y Peralta, Juan
    Manuel, 45–46
Mothers of Plaza de Mayo,
    124, 131
Motolinía. *See* Benavente,
    Toribio de
Movimiento Revolucionario
    Túpac Amaru, 57
Museu da República, 300, 301,
    302, 304; exhibit of
    Vargas's bedroom,
    306–307, 308
Museu Histórico Nacional,
    299–300, 302
Museum of the Revolution, 320